THE TREASURY OF JUDAISM

A New Collection and Translation of Essential Texts

VOLUME TWO: THE LIFE CYCLE

Jacob Neusner

Studies in Judaism

University Press of America,® Inc.
Lanham · Boulder · New York · Toronto · Plymouth, UK

Library of Congress Control Number: 2008922658
ISBN-13: 978-0-7618-4048-0 (paperback : alk. paper)
ISBN-10: 0-7618-4048-6 (paperback : alk. paper)

Studies in Judaism

CONTENTS

Preface

Focusing upon the formative period, this anthology sets forth teachings of Rabbinic Judaism in its classical, formative age in late antiquity, the first six centuries of the Common Era. The topical abstracts, which deal with the sacred calendar (volume one), events in the life cycle (volume two), and theological expositions (volume three), are presented in documentary sequence, from the Mishnah, ca. 200, through the Bavli or Talmud of Babylonia, ca. 600.

The literary evidence, in the form of well-crafted, systematic and coherent documents, presents us with a Judaism called "Rabbinic," by reason of the title of honor accorded many of its principal authorities, or "classical" or "normative," by reason of its later standing, or "Talmudic," because of its final and definitive statement, in the Talmud of Babylonia. Its governing myth, the story of how at Sinai God revealed the Torah to Moses in two media, written and oral, with the oral part finally given written articulation in the Mishnah and associated writings of rabbis themselves, contributes the title, "Judaism of the dual Torah."

The formative history of that particular Judaism as it took over and defined the life of the Jews in the first six centuries of the Common Era cannot be recovered. We have no evidence about the state of affairs for the Jews in general, such as would tell us how that Judaic system came to dictate the character of the Jews' social world and culture. One may argue that the evidence driving from the archaeology of synagogues, not that reaching us from the limited circles of learned sages, tells us about the common practices of the time. But, what sort of religious system emerges out of the material evidence remains to be determined.

How the Judaic system set forth in the Rabbinic writings related to the religious life of Jews beyond the circles of sages, the ways in which the particular way of life and world view set forth by that system came to define the actual character of the "Israel" to which that Judaism spoke — these are historical questions we cannot answer. The Rabbinic books tell us what their writers and compilers thought, but not about the world beyond their circle and its view of matters. And what we learn about "Judaism" from other than Judaic sources, for instance, pagan and Christian and Zoroastrian writers about Judaism, tells us no more than we know about Judaism from the written Torah. Christian writers about Judaism, for example, utilize the Hebrew Scriptures for their picture of the Judaism that they criticize.

But a different sort of history of Judaism in late antiquity emerges from the Rabbinic documents. It is the documentary history of the ideas that inform the religious system of Rabbinic Judaism. For if we follow the unfolding of the documents of that Judaism, Stated in documentary terms, the formative history of Judaism tells a story in these sentences.

[1] It shows, first, how the Judaic system emerged in the Mishnah, ca. 200 C.E., and its associated Midrash-compilations, ca. 200-300 C.E., as [1] a philosophical structure comprising a politics, philosophy, economics. These categories were defined as philosophers in general understood them: a theory of legitimate violence, an account of knowledge gained through the methods of natural history, and a theory of the rational disposition (and increase) of scarce resources.

[2] This philosophical system then was turned by the Talmud of the Land of Israel and related Midrash-compilations, ca. 400-500 C.E., into [2] a religious system. The system was effected through the formation of counterpart categories: an anti-politics of weakness, an anti-economics of the rational utilization of an infinitely renewable resource, a philosophy of truth revealed rather than rules discovered.

[3] The religious system was thoroughly analyzed with philosophical rigor and recast as theology in the medium of criticized law in the Talmud of Babylonia, ca. 600 C.E. That Talmud's union of the religious narrative with philosophical modes of thought set forth Rabbinic Judaism's normative statement. In this anthology we see how the Talmud of Babylonia took over the received traditions and vastly extended them.

The first stage in the documentary history takes up the urgent questions precipitated by the political calamities of the first and second centuries, the destruction of the Temple, the paganization of Jerusalem, and the chaos following the Bar Kokhba disaster. The second stage responds to the issues made urgent by the political triumph of Christianity and the consequent challenge to the situation of Israel as Jews read Scripture's account of their particular Israel. The third stage marks the recapitulation of the philosophical system in the religious idiom and its subjection to a process of dialectical criticism. Time and again in these pages we see how the Bavli took over the topical program of the prior documents and amplified it.

To the extent that the documentary history corresponds to the major turnings in political history, we may reconstruct not only the unfolding of ideas, but the relationship between ideas and the social world of the people that held those ideas, that the history of a religion proposes to narrate. The Mishnah emerges out of the century of reconstruction following the Bar Kokhba debacle, 132-135 C.E.. The Talmud of the Land of Israel responds to the establishment of Christianity as the state religion of the Roman Empire in the fourth century C.E. The Talmud of Babylonia formed a chapter in the reconsideration of the received traditions of the Middle East in response to the advent of Islam in the seventh century C.E. Its earliest manuscript evidence derives from the ninth century C.E. In the challenge of the waning years of the Zoroastrian religion of Sasanian Iran and the advent of nascent Islam, the process of review and revision got under way among the Rabbis.

THE CRISIS OF 70 AND THE MISHNAIC STAGE IN THE FORMATION OF RABBINIC JUDAISM: The temple in Jerusalem, where sacrifices were offered to God, constituted the focus of Pentateuchal Judaism. Indeed, the cycle of holy time was marked by sacrifice. Thus the lives of the patriarchs repeatedly drew them into relationship with the sacrificial cult in various holy places, but especially in Jerusalem, and the laws of the Torah dealt in detail with the sacrifices, the priests, the maintenance of the priestly caste, and other cultic matters. So the power of the Torah composed in this time lay in its focus on the Temple. This central Temple cult, with its total exclusion of the non-Israelite raised high those walls of separation we have talked about between Jew and "other." They underlined such distinctiveness as already existed. What made Israel Israel was the center, the altar; the life of Israel flowed from the altar. But in 70 C. E., in the course of a war fought by Jews against Roman rule in the Land of Israel, Jerusalem fell and the Temple, except for the Western wall of the platform on which it stood, was destroyed.

How then, are we to define the urgent question and self-evident answer of the Judaic System of the Dual Torah, Oral and Written that emerged in the Mishnah? The principal question formulated by the sages who produced writings beyond 70 — writings that ultimately were portrayed as the oral part of the one whole Torah of Moses, "our lord" our rabbi ot *rabbenu* — centered upon the sanctification of Israel now that the Temple, the locus of holiness, lay in ruins and the cult was no more. The Judaism of the dual Torah set forth a twin-ideal: [1] sanctification of the everyday life in the here and now, which when fully realized would lead to [2] salvation of all Israel in the age to come. But what remained to be sanctified, as the Temple had been sanctified through its cult, now that the Temple was gone? One locus of sanctification endured beyond 70: the holy people itself. That people's life would be made holy — in the holy land at first, but later, as this Judaism spread across the world through exile in the diaspora, everywhere the people lived. Holy of course meant separate and distinct from the ordinary, and the chronic question of who is a Jew and what is Israel would find its self-evident response in the same categories as the Pentateuchal system had defined for itself.

The stress of the Judaism of the dual Torah, of the post-Temple sages or rabbis who constructed it, on the sanctification of the home and the paradigmatic power of the Temple for the home points to a more extreme position within the priestly paradigm than that of the priests who wrote parts of Exodus, Leviticus and Numbers. What the priests wanted for the Temple, the dual Torah's sages wanted for the community, Israel, at large. The premise of the written Torah, we recall, rested on a simple allegation: if Israel observes the terms of the covenant, leading a sanctified life, Israel will enjoy prosperity in a serene land, a national life outside of history. The traumatic event of annihilation and rebirth, of death and resurrection of the nation (as manifested in the reworking of ancient Israelite writings into the Pentateuch) brought about yearning for one thing above all: no more. The picture of what had happened presented solace — that is why people wanted to accept the portrait of their world. The restoration gave Israel a second chance at life, but Israel also could rely on its knowledge of the rules that governed its national life, those of the Torah and its repeated allegations of an agreement, or covenant, between Israel and God, to make certain there would be no more experiences of exile and alienation (whether or not followed by reconciliation and restoration). This same paradigm governed in the framing of the Judaism of the dual Torah. What shifted was the redefinition of salvation from the here and now to the end of time. And that change, of course, was not only plausible, it also was necessary in light of the destruction of the Temple in 70.

The reason for the transfer of the hope for salvation from now to the end of time derives from a political event in some ways bearing greater weight than the destruction of the Temple in 70. This event is the failure to recover the city and rebuild the Temple through war three generations later. Had the war been successful, it could have replicated the events that began in 586 and ended in 450. That is, it could have restored the people to the land and the government and temple to Jerusalem. Indeed, when the war broke out in 132, the Jews evidently expected that after three generations, God would call an end to the punishment as God had done by restoring the Temple some "seventy years" after its first destruction (586). But that did not happen. Israel again suffered defeat — a defeat worse than before. The Temple now lay in permanent ruins; Jerusalem became a forbidden city for Jews. So Israel, the Jewish people, necessarily set out to assimilate enduring defeat.

THE MISHNAH'S JUDAISM OF SANCTIFICATION WITHOUT THE TEMPLE: The Mishnah manifests the Judaism that took shape in the aftermath of the Jews' defeat in this Second War against Rome, fought from 132 through 135. Although later considered the written manifestation of the oral tradition that formed part of the Torah received by Moses at Sinai, and accorded proportionate status, the Mishnah was in fact a philosophical system in the form of a law code that responded to problems arising from the destruction of the Temple and Bar Kokhba's subsequent defeat. When in the aftermath of the destruction in C.E.70 and the still more disheartening defeat of 135 the Mishnah's sages worked out a Judaism without a Temple and a cult, they produced in the Mishnah a system of sanctification focused on the holiness of the priesthood, the cultic festivals, the Temple and its sacrifices, and on the rules for protecting that holiness from Levitical uncleanness. Four of the six divisions of the Mishnah expound on this single theme.

In an act of supererogatory imagination, defying the facts of the circumstance of a defeated nation, the Mishnah's system-builders composed a world at rest, perfect and complete, made holy because it is complete and perfect. In mythic terms, the Mishnah reaches back to creation to interpret the world of destruction round about. The system of the Mishnah confronts the fall from Eden with Eden, the world in time beyond the closure of Jerusalem to Israel with the timeless world on the eve of the Sabbath of Creation: "Thus the heavens and the earth were finished and all the host of them. And on the seventh day God finished his work which he had done, and he rested on the seventh day from all his work which he had done. So God blessed the seventh day and hallowed it, because on it God rested from all his work which he had done in creation" (Gen. 2:1-3).

The Mishnah's framers posited an economy embedded in a social system awaiting the seventh day, and that day's divine act of sanctification which, as at the creation of the world, would set the seal of holy rest upon an again-complete creation. That would be a creation that was well ordered, with all things called by their rightful names, in their proper classification, from the least to the greatest, and from the many to the One. There is no place for action and actors when what is besought is no action whatsoever, but only unchanging perfection. There is room only for a description of how things are, for the present tense, for a sequence of completed statements and static problems. All the action lies within, in how these statements are made. Once they stand fully expressed, when nothing remains to be said, nothing remains to be done. There is no need for actors, whether political entities such as king, scribes, priests, or economic entities, householders.

That is why the Mishnah's framers invented a utopia, one that exists nowhere in particular, a fantasy related to whom it may concern. The politics of Judaism began in the imagination of a generation of intellectuals who, in the aftermath of the Jerusalem government's and Temple's destruction (70) and the military defeat Jews suffered three generations later (132-135), had witnessed the end of the political system and structure that the Jews had known for the preceding millennium. The political theory of Judaism laid out political institutions and described how they should work. In that way these intellectuals, who enjoyed no documented access to power of any kind and who certainly were unable to coerce many people to do very much, sorted out issues of power. They took account, in mind at least, of the issues of legitimate coercion within Israel, the holy people, which they considered more than a voluntary association, more than a community formed around a cult.

The Mishnah's principal message, which makes the Judaism of this document and of its social components distinctive and cogent, is that man is at the center of creation, the head of all creatures upon earth, corresponding to God in heaven, in whose image man is made. The way in which the Mishnah makes this simple and fundamental statement is to impute power to man to inaugurate and initiate those corresponding processes, sanctification and uncleanness, which play so critical a role in the Mishnah's account of reality. The will of man, expressed through the deed of man, is the active power in the world. Will and deed constitute those actors of creation which work upon neutral realms, subject to either sanctification or uncleanness: the Temple and table, the field and family, the altar and hearth, woman, time, space, transactions in the material world and in the world above as well. An object, a substance, a transaction, even a phrase or a sentence is inert but may be made holy, when the interplay of the will and deed of man arouses or generates its potential to be sanctified. Each may be treated as ordinary or (where relevant) made unclean by the neglect of the will and inattentive act of man. Just as the entire system of uncleanness and holiness awaits the intervention of man, which imparts the capacity to become unclean upon what was formerly inert, or which removes the capacity to impart cleanness from what was formerly in its natural and puissant condition, so in the other ranges of reality, man is at the center on earth, just as is God in heaven. Man is counterpart and partner and creation, in that, like God he has power over the status and condition of creation, through his intentionality putting everything in its proper place, through the exercise of his will calling everything by its rightful name. The goal then was the restoration of creation to its original perfection. Then it was that God ceased from labor, blessed creation, and sanctified it.

THE TALMUD'S JUDAISM OF SANCTIFICATION AND SALVATION: The Mishnah enjoyed two centuries of study and amplification. Indeed, a massive system deriving from and connecting with the Mishnah's but essentially distinct from it emerged in the Talmud of the Land of Israel (closed ca. 400). The urgent question that predominates in that enormous document, and that takes the form of an extended elaboration of the Mishnah, is salvation: when and why will it come, and, above all, how long must it be postponed? The urgency of the issue derived from two events that we have already touched upon. First of all, in 312 Constantine legalized Christianity, and in the course of the next three generations, the state became officially Christian. In the course of suppressing paganism, the Christian state adopted rules that for the first time since the Maccabees, in the second century B. C., denied the licit practice of Judaism. That trauma was intensified by a brief moment of relief, when one of the heirs of Constantine, Julian, left Christianity, reaffirmed paganism and, in 361 proposed to discredit Christianity by permitting the Jews to rebuild the Temple in Jerusalem. Unfortunately, he died soon afterward and nothing came of the project.

The urgency with which the Jews pursued the question of salvation is hardly a surprising. Consider that from their own political triumph and the Jews' deep disappointment by Julian's failed scheme, the Christians claimed that the political shifts in the standing of Christianity and Judaism confirmed the truth of Christianity and underlined the falsity of Judaism. In particular, Christianity stressed the falsity of the Jews' hope for a coming messiah. It argued that the Jews had been saved in the time of the return to Zion (450 B.C.E.). That return, Christians claimed, fulfilled the Old Testament prophecies of Israel's salvation. But from that moment, by rejecting the messiahship of Jesus, Jews had lost all further standing in the divine scheme for saving humanity. So the question of salvation turned from a chronic concern to an acute crisis for the Jews — in positive and negative ways. And predictably, it was addressed by the sages who revised the Mishnah by setting forth the Talmud of the Land of Israel.

Two hundred years after that Talmud took shape, (ca. 400), a second one, the Talmud of Babylonia, recast matters in a permanent and authoritative form (ca. 600). From then to the present, "the Talmud," meaning the Talmud of Babylonia, together with its commentaries, codes of laws deriving from it, and institutions of autonomous administration resting on it, has defined the life of most Jews and the Judaic system that prevailed as normative. Its successful definition of the essentials of Judaism for Jews living in Christian and the Muslim worlds depends on the compelling power of its account of who is a Jew, what it means to be Israel, and how the holy people must work out its life in the here and now so as to attain salvation at the end of time. This was, then, a Judaism intersecting with the Mishnah's but essentially asymmetrical with. It was a system for salvation focused on the salvific power of the sanctification of the holy people.

What the Judaism of the dual Torah as portrayed in the two Talmuds did was shift the focus from the Temple and its supernatural history to the people Israel and its natural, this-worldly history. Once Israel, holy Israel, had come to form the counterpart to the Temple and its supernatural life, that other history — Israel's — would stand at the center of things. Accordingly, a new sort of memorable event came to the fore in the Talmud of the Land of Israel. It was the story of Israel's suffering — remembrance of that suffering on the one side, and an effort to explain events of such tragedy on the other. And that story enjoyed the standing of self-evident, indeed self-validating truth because Jews found that it corresponded to and satisfactorily explained the powerless political situation in which they found themselves.

THE MISHNAH: JUDAISM AS A PHILOSOPHY IN THE FIRST AND SECOND CENTURIES: From this brief account of the unfolding, in response to historical crises, of the Judaism of the dual Torah, let us turn to the intellectual characterization of each of its stages, with stress on the shift from philosophy to religion. The Mishnah presents a philosophical theory of the social order, a system of thought that, in the context of the same time and place, people generally deemed philosophers will have recognized as philosophical. The Mishnah's method of hierarchical classification in important ways is like that of the natural history of Aristotle, and the central component of its message proves congruent to that of neo-Platonism.

Specifically, the Mishnah's Judaic system sets forth in stupefying detail a version of one critical proposition of neo-Platonism, demonstrated through a standard Aristotelian method. The repeated proof through the Aristotelian method of hierarchical classification demonstrates in detail that many things really form a single thing, many species, a single genus, many genera, an encompassing and well-crafted, cogent whole. Every time we speciate, — and the Mishnah is a mass of speciated lists — we affirm that position; each successful labor of forming relationships among species, e.g., making them into a genus, or identifying the hierarchy of the species, proves it again. Not only so, but when we can show that many things are really one, or that one thing yields many (the reverse and confirmation of the former), we say in a fresh way a single immutable truth, the one of this philosophy concerning the unity of all being in an orderly composition of all things within a single taxon. Accordingly, this Judaism's initial system, the Mishnah's, finds its natural place within philosophy because it appeals to the Aristotelian methods and medium of natural philosophy — classification, comparison and contrast, expressed in the forms of *Listenwissenschaft* — to register its position, which is an important one in Middle Platonism and later (close to a century after the closure of the Mishnah) would come to profound expression in Plotinus.

The philosophical Judaism moreover utilized economics — the rational disposition of scarce resources — in order to set forth a systemic statement of fundamental importance. Entirely congruent with the philosophical economics of Aristotle, the Mishnah's economics answered the same questions concerning the definition of wealth, property, production and the means of production, ownership and control of the means of production, the determination of price and value and the like. And that fact signifies that the Judaic system to which the Mishnah attests is philosophical not only in method and message but in its very systemic composition. The principal components of its theory of the social order, its account of the way of life of its Israel and its picture of the conduct of the public policy of its social entity, — all of these in detail correspond in their basic definitions and indicative traits with the economics and the politics of Greco-Roman philosophy in the Aristotelian tradition. Specifically, the Mishnah's economics, in general in the theory of the rational disposition of scarce resources and of the management and increase thereof, and specifically in its definitions of wealth and ownership, production and consumption, point by point, corresponds to that of Aristotle.

The power of economics as framed by Aristotle, the only economic theorist of antiquity worthy of the name, was to develop the relationship between the economy to society as a whole. And the framers of the Mishnah did the same when they incorporated issues of economics at a profound theoretical level into the system of society as a whole that they proposed to construct . That is why the authorship of the Mishnah will be seen as attacking the problem of man's livelihood within a system of sanctification of a holy people with a radicalism of which no later religious thinkers about utopias were capable. None has ever penetrated deeper into the material organization of man's life under the aspect of God's rule. In effect, they posed, in all its breadth, the question of the critical, indeed definitive place occupied by the economy in society under God's rule. The points in common between Aristotle's and the Mishnah's economics in detail prove no less indicative. Both Aristotle and the Mishnah presented an anachronistic system of economics. The theory of both falls into the same classification of economic theory, that of distributive economics, familiar in the Near and Middle East from Sumerian times down to, but not including, the age of Aristotle (let alone that of the Mishnah five centuries later). But market-economics had been well-established prior to Aristotle's time. Aristotle's economics is distributive for systemic reasons, the Mishnah's replicates the received principles of the economics planned by the Temple priests and set forth in the Priestly Code of the Pentateuch, Leviticus in particular. The result — fabricated or replicated principles — was the same. Both systems — the Mishnah's and Aristotle's — in vast detail expressed the ancient distributive economics, in their theories of fixed value and conception of the distribution of scarce resources by appeal to other than the rationality of the market. The theory of money characteristic of Aristotle (but not of Plato) and of the Mishnah for instance conforms to that required by distributive economics; exchange takes place through barter, not through the abstract price-setting mechanism represented by money. Consequently, the representation of the Mishnah as a philosophical Judaism derives from not only general characteristics but very specific and indicative traits held in common with the principal figure of the Greco-Roman philosophical tradition in economics.

There was a common social foundation for the economic theory of both systems. Both Aristotle and the Mishnah's framers deemed the fundamental unit of production to be the household, and the larger social unit, the village, composed of households, marked the limits of the social entity. The Mishnah's economic tractates, such as the tractates on civil law, invariably refer to the householder, making him the subject of most predicates; where issues other than economics are in play, e.g., in the political tractates such as Sanhedrin, the householder scarcely appears as a social actor. Not only so, but both Aristotle and the authorship of the Mishnah formed the conception of "true value," which maintained that something — an object, a piece of land — possessed a value extrinsic to the market and intrinsic to itself, such that, if a transaction varied from that imputed true value by (in the case of the Mishnah) 18%, the exchange was null. Not only so, but the sole definition of wealth for both Aristotle's and the Mishnah's economics was real estate, only land however small. Since land does not contract or expand, of course, the conception of an increase in value through other than a steady-state exchange of real value, "true value," between parties to a transaction lay outside of the theory of economics. Therefore all profit, classified as usury, was illegitimate and must be prevented.

The Mishnah's politics — its theory of the legitimate use of violence and the disposition of power in society, — describes matters in a manner that is fundamentally philosophical in the Aristotelian context. Israel forms a political entity, fully empowered in an entirely secular sense, just as Scripture had described matters. To political institutions of the social order, king, priest, and court or civil administration, each in its jurisdiction, is assigned the right legitimately to exercise violence here on earth, corresponding to, and shared with, the same empowerment accorded to institutions of Heaven. These institutions moreover are conceived permanently to ration and rationalize the uses of that power. The picture, of course, is this-worldly, but, not distinguishing crime from sin, it is not secular, since the same system that legitimates king, high priest, and court posits in Heaven a corresponding politics, with God and the court on high exercising jurisdiction for some crimes or sins, the king, priesthood, or court down below for others. Three specific traits, direct our attention toward the philosophical classification for the Mishnah's politics in framing a systemic composition, even though, to be sure, the parallels prove structural and general, rather than detailed and doctrinal as was the case with economics.

First, like the politics of Plato and Aristotle, the Mishnah's politics describes only a utopian politics, a structure and system of a fictive and a fabricated kind: intellectuals' conception of a politics. Serving the larger purpose of system-construction, politics of necessity emerges as invention, e.g., by Heaven or in the model of Heaven, not as a secular revision and reform of an existing system. While in the middle second-century Rome incorporated their country, which they called the Land of Israel and the Romans called Palestine, into its imperial system, denying Jews access to their capital, Jerusalem, permanently closing their cult-center, its Temple, the authorship of the Mishnah described a government of a king and a high priest and an administration fully empowered to carry out the law through legitimate violence. So the two politics — the Mishnah's, the Greco-Roman tradition represented by Plato's and Aristotle's — share in common their origins in intellectuals' theoretical and imaginative life and form an instance, within that life, of the concrete realization of a larger theory of matters. In strange and odd forms, the Mishnah's politics falls into the class of the *Staatsroman,* the classification that encompasses, also, Plato's *Republic* and Aristotle's *Politics.* But, admittedly, the same may be said for the strange politics of the Pentateuch.

Second and more to the point, the Mishnah's sages stand well within the philosophical mode of political thought that begins with Aristotle, who sees politics as a fundamental component of his system when he says, "political science...legislates as to what we are to do and what we are to abstain from;" and, as to the institutionalization of power, one cannot imagine a more ample definition of the Mishnah's system's utilization of politics than that. While that statement, also, applies to the Pentateuchal politics, the systemic message borne by politics within the Pentateuchal system and that carried by politics in the Mishnah's system do not correspond in any important ways. Aristotle and the philosophers of the Mishnah utilize politics to make systemic statements that correspond to one another, in that both comparison and contrast prove apt and pointed. Both spoke of an empowered social entity; both took for granted that on-going institutions legitimately exercise governance in accord with a rationality discerned by distinguishing among those empowered to inflict sanctions. Both see politics as a medium for accomplishing systemic goals, and the goals derive from the larger purpose of the social order, to which politics is subordinated and merely instrumental.

But, third, the comparison also yields a contrast of importance. Specifically, since political analysis comes only after economic analysis and depends upon the results of that prior inquiry into a social system's disposition of scarce resources and theory of control of means of production, we have no choice but to follow up the results of the preceding chapter and compare the politics of Aristotle and the politics of the Mishnah, just as we did the economics of each system. For when we know who commands the means of production, we turn to inquire about who tells whom what to do and why: who legitimately coerces others even through violence. And here the Mishnah's system decisively parts company with that of the Pentateuch and also with that of Aristotle. As to the former, the distributive economics of the Pentateuch, in the Priestly stratum at the foundations, assigns both economic and political privilege to the same class of persons, the priesthood, effecting distributive economics and distributive politics. But that is not the way things are in the Mishnah's politics, which distinguishes the one in control of the means of production from the one control of the right legitimately to commit violence. The former, the householder, is not a political entity at all, and, dominant as the subject of most sentences in the economic tractates, he never appears in the political ones at all.

The point of difference from Aristotle is to be seen only within the context of the similarity that permits comparison and contrast. While the economics of Aristotle and the economics of Judaism commence with the consideration of the place and power of the person ("class," "caste," economic interest) in control of the means of production, the social metaphors that animate the politics of the two systems part company. Aristotle in his *Politics* is consistent in starting with that very same person ("class") when he considers issues of power, producing a distributive politics to match his distributive economics. But the Mishnah's philosophers build their politics on with an altogether different set of building blocks. The simple fact is that the householder, fundamental to their economics, does not form a subject of political discourse at all and in no way constitutes a political class or caste. When the Mishnah's writers speak of economics, the subject of most active verbs is the householder; when they speak of politics, the householder never takes an active role or even appears as a differentiated political class. In this sense, the economics of the Mishnah is disembedded from its politics, and the politics from its economics. By contrast the economics and politics of Aristotle's system are deeply embedded within a larger and nurturing, wholly cogent theory of political economy.

THE YERUSHALMI'S TRANSFORMATION OF PHILOSOPHY INTO RELIGION: The successor-system, represented by the Talmud of the Land of Israel and related writings, ca. 400-450, presented a theory of the social order lacking any theory politics, philosophy, and economics of a conventional order. Now that we have seen the philosophical character of the initial system's world-view, way of life, and theory of the social entity, that is, its philosophy, economics, and politics, we ask how these same categories fared in the successor-system's documentary evidence. As a matter of simple fact, while sharing the goal of presenting a theory of the social order, as to their categorical formations and structures, the initial, philosophical Judaic system and the successor system differ in a fundamental way. Stated very simply, what happened is that the successor-system held up a mirror to the received categories and so redefined matters that everything was reversed. Left became right, down, up, and, as we shall see, in a very explicit transvaluation of values, power is turned into weakness, things of real value is transformed into intangibles. This transvaluation, yielding the transformation of the prior system altogether, is articulated and not left implicit; it is a specific judgment made concrete through mythic and symbolic revision by the later authorships themselves. A free-standing document, received with reverence, served to precipitate the transvaluation of all of the values of that document's initial statement.

What the philosophical Judaism kept apart, the religious Judaism portrayed by the Talmud of the Land of Israel and related writings now joined together, and it is just there, at that critical joining, that we identify the key to the system: its reversal of a received point of differentiation, its introduction of new points of differentiation altogether. The source of generative problems for the Mishnah's politics is simply not the same as the source that served the successor-system's politics, and, systemic analysis being what it is, it is the union of what was formerly asunder that identifies for us in quite objective terms the critical point of tension, the sources of problems, the centerpiece of systemic concern throughout. Let me show how this process of reintegration was worked out in the categorical reformation underway in the Yerushalmi and related writings.

We begin with the shift from philosophy to Torah-study, that is from abstract reflection to concrete text-exegesis and digression out of sacred scripture; philosophy yields accurate and rational understanding of things; knowledge of the Torah, by contrast, yields power over this world and the next, capacity to coerce to the sage's will the natural and supernatural worlds alike, on that account. The Torah is thus transformed from a philosophical enterprise of the sifting and classification of the facts of this world into a gnostic process of changing persons through knowledge. It is on that basis that in the Yerushalmi and related writings we find in the Torah the counterpart-category to philosophy in the Mishnah. Now we deal with a new intellectual category: Torah, meaning, religious learning *in place of* philosophical learning. What is the difference between the one and the other? First comes appeal to revealed truth as against perceived facts of nature and their regularities, second, the conception of an other-worldly source of explanation and the development of a propositional program focused upon not nature but Scripture, not the nations in general but Israel in particular, and third, the Gnosticization of knowledge in the conception that knowing works salvation.

What was to change, therefore, was not the mode of thought. What was new, rather, was the propositions to be demonstrated philosophically, and what made these propositions new was the focus of interest, on the one side, and data assembled by way of demonstrating them, on the other. From a philosophical proposition within the framework of free-standing philosophy of religion and metaphysics that the Mishnah's system aimed to establish, we move to religious and even theological propositions within the setting of contingent exegesis of Scripture. Then how do we know that what was changing was not merely topical and propositional but *categorical* in character? The answer lies in the symbolic vocabulary that would be commonly used in the late fourth and fifth century writings but not at all, or not in the same way, in the late second century ones. When people select data not formerly taken into account and represent the data by appeal to symbols not formerly found evocative or expressive, or not utilized in the way in which they later on were used, then we are justified in raising questions about category-formation and the development of new categories alongside, or instead, of the received ones. In the case at hand, the character of the transformation we witness is shown by the formation of a symbol serving to represent a category.

To signal what is to come, we find the quite bald statement that, in the weighing of the comparative value of capital, which in this time and place meant land or real property, and Torah, Torah was worthwhile, and land was not — a symbolic syllogism that is explicit, concrete, repeated, and utterly fresh for the documents we consider. On the basis of that quite explicit symbolic comparison we speak of transformation — symbolic and therefore *categorical* transformation, not merely thematic shifts in emphasis or even propositional change. Here we witness in the successor-writings the formation of a system connected with, but asymmetrical to, the initial, philosophical one. Then for the world-view of the transformed Judaism, the counterpart-category to philosophy is formulated by appeal to the symbolic medium for the theological message, and it is the category, the Torah, expressed, as a matter of fact, by the symbol of *Torah.*

Philosophy sought the generalizations that cases might yield. So too did religion (and, in due course, theology would too). But the range of generalization vastly differed. Philosophy spoke of the nature of things, while theology represented the special nature of Israel in particular. Philosophy then appealed to the traits of things, while theology to the special indicative qualities of Israel. What of the propositional program that the document sets forth? The philosophical proposition of the Mishnah demonstrated from the facts and traits of things the hierarchical order of all being, with the obvious if merely implicit proposition that God stands at the head of the social order. The religious propositions of the successor-documents speak in other words of other things, having simply nothing in common with the propositional program of the Mishnah's philosophy.

The shift in economics is no less striking. Consideration of the transvaluation of value brings us to the successor-system's counterpart category, that is, the one that in context forms the counterpart to the Mishnah's concrete, this-worldly, material and tangible definition of value in conformity with the familiar, philosophical economics. We have now to ask, what, in place of the received definition of value and the economics thereof, did the new system set forth? The transformation of economics involved the redefinition of scarce and valued resources in so radical a manner that the concept of value, while remaining material in consequence and character, nonetheless took on a quite different sense altogether. The counterpart category of the successor-system concerned themselves with the same questions as did the conventional economics, presenting an economics in function and structure, but one that concerned things of value other than those identified by the initial system. So indeed we deal with an economics, an economics of something other than real estate.

But it was an economics just as profoundly embedded in the social order, just as deeply a political economics, just as pervasively a systemic economics, as the economics of the Mishnah and of Aristotle. Why so? Because issues such as the definition of wealth, the means of production and the meaning of control thereof, the disposition of wealth through distributive or other media, theory of money, reward for labor, and the like — all these issues found their answers in the counterpart-category of economics, as much as in the received and conventional philosophical economics. The new "scarce resource" accomplished what the old did, but it was a different resource, a new currency. At stake in the category meant to address the issues of the way of life of the social entity, therefore, were precisely the same considerations as confront economics in its (to us) conventional and commonplace, philosophical sense. But since the definition of wealth changes, as we have already seen, from land to Torah, much else would be transformed on that account.

Land produced a living; so did Torah. Land formed the foundation of the social entity, so did Torah. The transvaluation of value was such that an economics concerning the rational management and increase of scarce resources worked itself out in such a way as to answer, for quite different things of value from real property or from capital such as we know as value, precisely the same questions that the received economics addressed in connection with wealth of a real character: land and its produce. Systemic transformation comes to the surface in articulated symbolic change. The utter transvaluation of value finds expression in a jarring juxtaposition, an utter shift of rationality, specifically, the substitution of Torah for real estate. We recall how in a successor-document (but in none prior to the fifth century compilations) Tarfon thought wealth took the form of land, while Aqiba explained to him that wealth takes the form of Torah-learning. That the sense is material and concrete is explicit: land for Torah, Torah for land. Thus, to repeat the matter of how Torah serves as an explicit symbol to convey the systemic worldview, let us note the main point of this passage:

LEVITICUS RABBAH XXXIV:XVI

1. B.   R. Tarfon gave to R. Aqiba six silver centenarii, saying to him, "Go, buy us a piece of land, so we can get a living from it and labor in the study of Torah together."

C. He took the money and handed it over to scribes, Mishnah-teachers, and those who study Torah.

D. After some time R. Tarfon met him and said to him, "Did you buy the land that I mentioned to you?"

E. He said to him, "Yes."

F. He said to him, "Is it any good?"

G. He said to him, "Yes."

H. He said to him, "And do you not want to show it to me?"

I. He took him and showed him the scribes, Mishnah teachers, and people who were studying Torah, and the Torah that they had acquired.

J. He said to him, "Is there anyone who works for nothing? Where is the deed covering the field?"

K. He said to him, "It is with King David, concerning whom it is written, 'He has scattered, he has given to the poor, his righteousness endures forever' (Ps. 112:9)."

The successor-system has its own definitions not only for learning, symbolized by the word Torah but also for wealth, expressed in the same symbol. Accordingly, the category-formation for worldview, Torah in place of philosophy, dictates, as a matter of fact, a still more striking category-reformation, in which the entire matter of scarce resources is reconsidered, and a counterpart-category set forth.

Philosophical politics tells who may legitimately do what to whom. When a politics wants to know who ought *not* to be doing what to whom, we find in hand the counterpart-category to the received politics — anti-politics, a theory of the illegitimacy of power, the legitimacy of being victim. The received category set forth politics as the theory of legitimate violence, the counterpart-category, politics as the theory of *illegitimate* violence. The received politics had been one of isolation and interiority, portraying Israel as *sui generis* and autocephalic in all ways. The portrait in the successor-documents is a politics of integration among the nations; a perspective of exteriority replaces the inner-facing one of the Mishnah, which recognized no government of Israel but God's — and then essentially ab initio. The issues of power had found definition in questions concerning who legitimately inflicts sanctions upon whom within Israel. They now shift to give an account of who illegitimately inflicts sanctions upon ("persecutes") Israel. So the points of systemic differentiation are radically revised, and the politics of the successor-system becomes not a revision of the received category but a formation that in many ways mirrors the received one: once more a counterpart-category. Just as, in the definition of scarce resources, Torah-study has replaced land, so now weakness forms the focus in place of strength, illegitimacy in place of legitimacy. Once more the mirror-image of the received category presents the perspective of the counterpart-category.

Now we find the answers to these questions: to whom is violence illegitimately done, and also, who may not legitimately inflict violence? With the move from the politics of legitimate to that of illegitimate power, the systemic interest now lies in defining not the who legitimately does what, but rather, the to whom, against whom, is power illegitimately exercised. And this movement represents not the revision of the received category, but its inversion. For thought on legitimate violence is turned on its head. A new category of empowerment is worked out alongside the old. The entity that is victim of power is at the center, rather than the entity that legitimately exercises power. That entity is now Israel *en masse,* rather than the institutions and agencies of Israel on earth, Heaven above — a very considerable shift in thought on the systemic social entity. Israel as disempowered, rather than king, high priest, and sage as Israel's media of empowerment, defines the new system's politics. The upshot is that the successor-system has reconsidered not merely the contents of the received structure, but the composition of the structure itself. In place of its philosophy, we have now a new medium for the formulation of a world-view; in place of a way of life formulated as an economics, a new valuation of value, in place of an account of the social entity framed as a politics, a new conception of legitimate violence. So much for the formation of counterpart categories.

FROM PHILOSOPHY TO RELIGION. SYSTEMIC INTEGRATION: What holds the system together identifies the critical question that the system as a whole means to answer, its aspect of self-evidence. Seeing the whole all at once, we may then undertake that work of comparison and contrast that produces connections from system to system. How then may we characterize the shift from a philosophical to a religious system? The answer derives from our choice of the systemic center, e.g., a symbol that captures the whole, that holds the whole together. Certainly, the integration of the philosophical system is readily stated in a phrase: the philosophical Judaism set forth a system of hierarchical classification. Having emphasized the succession — philosophy out, Torah in — one may ask whether for the religious system of Judaism, the systemic center is captured by the symbol of the Torah — focused on the holy man sanctified through mastery of revelation. The answer is negative, because, as a matter of fact, knowledge of the Torah forms a way-station on a path to a more distant, more central goal, it is a dependent variable, contingent and stipulative. Then wherein lies the systemic center? It is the quest for *zekhut,* properly translated as "the heritage of virtue and its consequent entitlements." It is the simple fact that Torah-study is one means of attaining access to that heritage, of gaining *zekhut* — and there are other equally suitable means. The *zekhut* gained by Torah-study is no different from the merit gained by acts of supererogatory grace. So we must take seriously the contingent status, the standing of a dependent variable, accorded to Torah-study in such stories as the following:

Y. TAANIT 3:11.IV.1

C. There was a house that was about to collapse over there [in Babylonia], and Rab set one of his disciples in the house, until they had cleared out everything from the house. When the disciple left the house, the house collapsed.

D. And there are those who say that it was R. Adda bar Ahwah.

E. Sages sent and said to him, "What sort of good deeds are to your credit [that you have that much merit]?"

F. He said to them, "In my whole life no man ever got to the synagogue in the morning before I did. I never left anybody there when I went out. I never walked four cubits without speaking words of Torah. Nor did I ever mention teachings of Torah in an inappropriate setting. I never laid out a bed and slept for a regular period of time. I never took great strides among the associates. I never called my fellow by a nickname. I never rejoiced in the embarrassment of my fellow. I never cursed my fellow when I was lying by myself in bed. I never walked over in the marketplace to someone who owed me money.

G. "In my entire life I never lost my temper in my household."

H. This was meant to carry out that which is stated as follows: "I will give heed to the way that is blameless. Oh when wilt thou come to me? I will walk with integrity of heart within my house" (Ps. 101:2).

What is striking in this story is that mastery of the Torah is only one means of attaining the *zekhut* that had enabled the sage to keep the house from collapsing. And Torah-study is not the primary means of attaining *zekhut*. The question at E provides the key, together with its answer at F. For what the sage did to gain such remarkable *zekhut* is not to master such-and-so many tractates of the Mishnah. It was rather acts of courtesy, consideration, gentility, restraint. These produced *zekhut* , all of them acts of self-abnegation or the avoidance of power over others and the submission to the will and the requirement of self-esteem of others. Torah-study is simply an item on a list of actions or attitudes that generate *zekhut*.

Here, in a moral setting, we find the politics replicated: the form of power that the system promises derives from the rejection of power that the world recognizes — legitimate violence replaced by legitimation of the absence of the power to commit violence or of the failure to commit violence. And, when we ask, whence that sort of power? the answer lies in the gaining of *zekhut* in a variety of ways, not in the acquisition of *zekhut* through the study of the Torah solely or even primarily. But, we note, the story at hand speaks of a sage in particular. He has gained *zekhut* by not acting the way sages are commonly assumed to behave but in a humble way.

Ordinary folk, not disciples of sages, have access to *zekhut* entirely outside of study of the Torah. In stories not told about rabbis, a single remarkable deed, exemplary for its deep humanity, sufficed to win for an ordinary person the *zekhut*

— "the heritage of virtue and its consequent entitlements" — that elicits the same marks of supernatural favor enjoyed by some rabbis on account of their Torah-study. Accordingly, the systemic centrality of *zekhut* in the structure, the critical importance of the heritage of virtue together with its supernatural entitlements — these emerge in a striking claim. It is framed in extreme form — another mark of the unique place of *zekhut* within the system. Even though a man was degraded, one action sufficed to win for him that heavenly glory to which rabbis in lives of Torah-study aspired.

The mark of the system's integration around *zekhut* lies in its insistence that all Israelites, not only sages, could gain *zekhut* for themselves (and their descendants). A single remarkable deed, exemplary for its deep humanity, sufficed to win for an ordinary person the *zekhut* that elicits supernatural favor enjoyed by some rabbis on account of their Torah-study. The centrality of *zekhut* in the systemic structure, the critical importance of the heritage of virtue together with its supernatural entitlements therefore emerge in a striking claim. Even though a man was degraded, one action sufficed to win for him that heavenly glory to which rabbis in general aspired. The rabbinical storyteller whose writing we shall consider assuredly identifies with this lesson, since it is the point of his story and its climax.

Zekhut serves, in particular, that counterpart category that speaks of not legitimate but illegitimate violence, not power but weakness. In context, time and again, we observe that *zekhut* is the power of the weak. People who through their own merit and capacity can accomplish nothing, can accomplish miracles through what others do for them in leaving a heritage of *zekhut*.. And, not to miss the stunning message of the triplet of stories cited above, *zekhut* also is what the weak and excluded and despised can do that outweighs in power what the great masters of the Torah have accomplished. In the context of a system that represents Torah as supernatural, that claim of priority for *zekhut* represents a considerable transvaluation of power, as much as of value. And, by the way, *zekhut* also forms the inheritance of the disinherited: what you receive as a heritage when you have nothing in the present and have gotten nothing in the past, that scarce resource that is free and unearned but much valued. So let us dwell upon the definitive character of the transferability of *zekhut* in its formulation, *zekhut* avot, the *zekhut* handed on by the ancestors, the transitive character of the concept and its standing as a heritage of entitlements.

So *zekhut* forms the political economy of the religious system of the social order put forward by the Talmud of the Land of Israel and related writings. Here we find the power that brought about the transvaluation of value, the reversal of the meaning of power and its legitimacy. *Zekhut* expresses and accounts for the economic valuation of the scarce resource of what we should call moral authority. *Zekhut* stands for the political valorization of weakness, that which endows the weak with a power that is not only their own but their ancestors'. It enables the weak to accomplish goals through not their own power, but their very incapacity to accomplish acts of violence — a transvaluation as radical as that effected in economics. And *zekhut* holds together both the economics and the politics of this Judaism: it makes the same statement twice. *Zekhut* as the power of the powerless, the riches of the disinherited, the valuation and valorization of the will of those who have no right to will. In that conception the politics, social order, and theology of Rabbinic Judaism came together. For the millennium and a half that would follow, this is the Judaism that governed.

  This anthology sets forth the statements of the formative canon of Rabbinic Judaism on three large topics: the calendar, the life cycle, and theology. The translations are my own, and so is the reference-system. In the Talmuds, which are multi-lingual documents, I use regular type to signal the use of biblical or Mishnaic (Middle) Hebrew, italics to signal that the original language of the text is Aramaic, and bold face type to indicate the origin of a passage in a prior document, the Mishnah or the Tosefta. The order of presentation of the selections follows the order of closure of the canonical documents from the Mishnah, ca. 200 C.E., through the Bavli, ca. 600 C.E. The dates all are estimates, and for some documents we do not possess even grounds for a guess.

The Mishnah: a philosophical law code, organized by topics into six divisions, covering [1] agriculture, [2] appointed times,[3] family life ("women"), [4] civil law ("damages"), [5] Holy Things, and [6] Purities, ca. 200

Tractate Abot: a collection of Rabbinic aphorisms, ca. 250 C.E.

The Tosefta: a collection of laws that complement the Mishnah and survey the same topical program as the Mishnah, ca. 250

Mekhilta Attributed to R. Ishmael: a commentary to parts of the book of Exodus

Sifra: a commentary to Leviticus, ca. 300

Sifré to Numbers: a commentary to Numbers, ca. 300

Sifré to Deuteronomy; a commentary to Deuteronomy, ca. 300

The Talmud of the Land of Israel: an analytical commentary to the Mishnah's first four divisions, ca. 400

Genesis Rabbah: a commentary to Genesis, ca. 450

Leviticus Rabbah: a commentary to Leviticus, ca. 450

Pesiqta deRab Kahana; a propositional exposition of the topics of the synagogue's special Sabbaths, ca. 500

Lamentations Rabbah: a commentary to Lamentations

Song of Songs Rabbah: a commentary to Song of Songs

Esther Rabbah I: a commentary to parts of Esther

Ruth Rabbah; a commentary to Ruth

The Fathers according to Rabbi Nathan: a commentary and amplification of tractate
    Abot

The Talmud of Babylonia: an analytical commentary to the Mishnah's second,
    third, fourth, and fifth divisions

My thanks go to Rabbi Seymour Rossel and Dr. David Altshuler for
suggesting this project to me. It is part of a life-long effort to make available in
English the classical documents of Judaism.

JACOB NEUSNER

DISTINGUISHED SERVICE PROFESSOR
OF THE HISTORY AND THEOLOGY OF JUDAISM
SENIOR FELLOW, INSTITUTE OF ADVANCED THEOLOGY
BARD COLLEGE
ANNANDALE-ON-HUDSON, NEW YORK 12504

jneusner@frontiernet.net

1

The Mishnah

NEDARIM

3:11 A.   [If a man said,] "Qonam if I have benefit from the children of Noah"' he is permitted [to enjoy benefit] from Israelites and prohibited [to enjoy benefit] from the nations of the world.

B.   ". . . if I have benefit from the seed of Abraham," he is prohibited [to enjoy benefit] from Israelites, and permitted [to enjoy benefit] from the nations of the world.

C.   [If he said, "Qonam] if I have benefit from Israelites," he buys for more and sells for less.

D.   ". . . if Israelites enjoy benefit from me," he buys for less and sells for more —

E.   (if anyone will pay attention to him!)

F.   ". . . if I derive benefit from them and they from me" — he derives benefit from strangers.

G.   [If he said,] "Qonam if I derive benefit from the uncircumcised," he is permitted [to derive benefit] from uncircumcised Israelites but prohibited [from deriving benefit] from circumcised gentiles.

H.   "Qonam if I derive benefit from the circumcised" — he is prohibited [to derive benefit] from uncircumcised Israelites and permitted [to derive benefit] from circumcised gentiles.

I.   For the word "uncircumcised" is used only as a name for gentiles, as it is written, "For all the nations are uncircumcised, and the whole house of Israel is uncircumcised at heart" (Jer. 9:26).

J.   And it says, "This uncircumcised Philistine" (1 Sam. 17:36).

K.   And it says, "Lest the daughters of the Philistines rejoice, lest the daughters of the uncircumcised triumph" (1 Sam. 1:20).

1

L.   R. Eleazar b. Azariah says, "The foreskin is disgusting, for evil men are shamed by reference to it, as it is written, For all the nations are uncircumcised."

M.   R. Ishmael says, "Great is circumcision, for thirteen covenants are made thereby."

N.   R. Yose says, "Great is circumcision, since it overrides the prohibitions of the Sabbath, which is subject to strict rules."

O.   R. Joshua b. Qorha says, "Great is circumcision, for it was not suspended even for a moment for the sake of Moses, the righteous."

P.   R. Nehemiah says, "Great is circumcision, for it overrides the prohibition [against removing the marks of] Negaim."

Q.   Rabbi says, "Great is circumcision, for, despite all the commandments which Abraham our father carried out, he was called complete and whole only when he had circumcised himself as it is said, 'Walk before me and be perfect' (Gen. 17:1).

R.   "Another matter: Great is circumcision, for if it were not for that, the Holy One, blessed be he, would not have created his world, since it says, 'Thus says the Lord: But for my covenant day and night, I should not have set forth the ordinances of heaven and earth' (Jer. 33:25)."

CIRCUMCISION ON THE SABBATH

MISHNAH SHABBAT

18:3 A.   They do not deliver the young of cattle on the festival, but they help out.

B.   And they do deliver the young of a woman on the Sabbath.

C.   They call a midwife for her from a distant place,

D.   and they violate the Sabbath on her [the woman in childbirth's] account.

E.   And they tie the umbilical cord.

F.   R. Yose says, "Also: They cut it."

G.   And all things required for circumcision do they perform on the Sabbath."

19:1 A.   R. Eliezer says, "If one did not bring a utensil [used for circumcision] on the eve of the Sabbath, he brings it openly on the Sabbath."

B.   And in the time of the danger, one covers it up in the presence of witnesses.

C.   And further did R. Eliezer state, "They cut wood to make coals W prepare an iron utensil [for circumcision]."

D.   An operative principle did R. Aqiba state, "Any sort of labor [in connection with circumcision] that it is possible to do on the eve of the Sabbath does not override [the restrictions of] the Sabbath, and that which it is not possible to do on the eve of the Sabbath does override [the prohibitions of] the Sabbath."

19:2 A. They do prepare all that is needed for circumcision on the Sabbath:
    B. they (1) cut [the mark of circumcision], (2) tear, (3) suck [out the wound].
    C. And they put on it a poultice and cummin.
    D. If one did not pound it on the eve of the Sabbath, he chews it in his teeth and puts it on.
    E. If one did not mix wine and oil on the eve of the Sabbath, let this be put on by itself and that by itself.
    F. And they do not make a bandage in the first instance.
    G. But they wrap a rag around [the wound of the circumcision].
    H. If one did not prepare [the necessary rag] on the eve of the Sabbath, he wraps [the rag] around his finger and brings it, and even from a different courtyard.

19:3 A. They wash off the infant,
    B. both before the circumcision and after the circumcision,
    C. and they sprinkle him,
    D. by hand but not with a utensil.
    E. R. Eleazar b. Azariah says, "They wash the infant on the third day after circumcision [even if it] coincides with the Sabbath,
    F. "since it says, 'And it came to pass on the third day when they were sore' (Gen, 34:25)."
    G. [If the sexual traits of the infant are a matter of] doubt, of [if the infant] bears the sexual traits of both sexes, they do not violate the Sabbath on his account.
    H. And R. Judah permits in the case of an infant bearing the traits of both sexes.

19:4 A. He who had two infants, one to circumcise after the Sabbath and one to circumcise on the Sabbath,
    B. and who forgot [which was which] and circumcised the one to be circumcised after the Sabbath on the Sabbath,
    C. is liable.
    D. [If he had] one to circumcise on the eve of the Sabbath and one to circumcise on the Sabbath,
    E. and he forgot and on the Sabbath, circumcised the one to be circumcised on the eve of the Sabbath,
    F. R. Eliezer declares him liable to a sin offering.
    G. And R. Joshua exempts him.

19:5 A. An infant is circumcised on the eighth, ninth, tenth, eleventh or twelfth days [after birth],
    B. never sooner, never later.
    C. How so?
    D. Under normal circumstances, it is on the eighth day.
    E. [If] he was born at twilight, he is circumcised on the ninth day.

F.   [If he was born] at twilight on the eve of the Sabbath, he is circumcised on the tenth day [the following Sunday].

G.   In the case of a festival that falls after the Sabbath, he will be circumcised on the eleventh day [Monday].

H.   In the case of two festival days of the New Year, he will be circumcised on the twelfth day [Tuesday].

I.   An infant who is sick — they do not circumcise him until he gets well.

19:6 A.   These are the shreds [of the foreskin, if they remain] that render the circumcision invalid:

B.   flesh that covers the greater part of the corona —

C.   and such a one does not eat heave offering.

D.   And if he was fat [so the corona appears to be covered up], one has to fix it up for appearance's sake.

E.   [If] one circumcised but did not tear the inner lining [the cut did not uncover the corona, since the membrane was not split and pulled down], it is as if he did not perform the act of circumcision.

COMING OF AGE

MISHNAH NIDDAH

5:6 A.   A girl eleven years and one day old — her vows are examined.

B.   A girl twelve years and one day old — her vows are confirmed.

C.   And they examine throughout the twelfth year

D.   A boy eleven years and one day old — his vows are examined.

E.   A boy thirteen years and one day old — his vows are confirmed.

F.   And they examine through the thirteenth year

G.   Before this time, even though they have said, "We know before Whom we have vowed," " for Whose [sanctity] we have sanctified" — their vows are not vows, and that which they have sanctified is deemed not sanctified.

H.   After this time, even though they said, " We do not know before Whom we have vowed," " for Whose [sanctity] we have sanctified" — their vow is a vow, and that which they have sanctified is deemed sanctified.

FROM FATHER TO SON

MISHNAH TRACTATE EDUYYOT

2:9 A.   R. Aqiba would say, "The father endows the son with (1) beauty, (2) power, (3) wealth, (4) wisdom, (5) years, and (6) [the merits of] the number of generations which come before him,

B.   "which is the end [of the earlier generations], as it is said, 'Calling the generations from the beginning' (Is. 41:4).

C.   "Even though it is written, 'And they shall serve them and they shan afflict them for four hundred years' (Gen . 15 :16) ,

D. "it also is written, 'And in the fourth generation they shall come here again' (Gen . 15:16)."

OBLIGATIONS OF MEN AND WOMEN TO THE COMMANDMENTS

MISHNAH QIDDUSHIN

1:7 I A. For every commandment concerning the son to which the father is subject — men are liable, and women are exempt.

B. And for every commandment concerning the father to which the son is subject, men and women are equally liable.

C. For every positive commandment dependent upon the time [of year], men are liable, and women are exempt.

D. And for every positive commandment not dependent upon the time, men and women are equally liable.

E. For every negative commandment, whether dependent upon the time or not dependent upon the time, men and women are equally liable,

F. except for not marring the comers of the beard, not rounding the comers of the head (Lev. 19:27), and not becoming unclean because of the dead (Lev. 21:1).

1:8 A. [The cultic rites of] laying on of hands, waving, drawing near, taking the handful, burning the incense, breaking the neck of a bird, sprinkling, and receiving [the blood]

B. apply to men and not to women,

C. except in the case of a meal offering of an accused wife and of a Nazirite girl, which they wave.

1:9 A. Every commandment which is dependent upon the Land applies only in the Land,

B. and which does not depend upon the Land applies both in the Land and outside the Land,

C. except for orlah and mixed seeds [Lev. 19:23, 19:19].

D. R. Eliezer says, "Also: Except for [the prohibition against eating] new [produce before the omer is waved on the sixteenth of Nisan] [Lev. 23:14]."

1:10 A. Whoever does a single commandment — they do well for him and lengthen his days.

B. And he inherits the Land.

C. And whoever does not do a single commandment — they do not do well for him and do not lengthen his days.

D. And he does not inherit the Land.

E. Whoever has learning in Scripture, Mishnah, and right conduct will not quickly sin,

F. since it is said, "And a threefold cord is not quickly broken" (Qoh. 4:12).

G. And whoever does not have learning in Scripture, Mishnah, and right conduct has no share in society.

OBLIGATIONS OF HUSBANDS AND WIVES TO ONE ANOTHER

MISHNAH KETUBOT

7:1 A. He who prohibits his wife by vow from deriving benefit from him

B. for a period of thirty days, appoints an agent to provide for her.

C. [If the effects of the vow are not nullified] for a longer period, he puts her away and pays off her marriage contract.

D. R. Judah says, "In the case of an Israelite, for [a vow lasting] one month he may continue in the marriage, but for two [or more], he must put her away and pay off her marriage contract.

E. "But in the case of a priest, for two months he may continue in the marriage, and after three he must put her away and pay off her marriage contract."

7:2 I A. He who prohibits his wife by vow from tasting any single kind of produce whatsoever

B. must put her away and pay off her marriage contract.

C. R. Judah says, "In the case of an Israelite, [if the vow is] for one day he may persist in the marriage, but [if it is] for two he must put her away and pay off her marriage contract.

D. "And in the case of a priest, [if it is] for two days he may persist in the marriage, but [if it is] for three he must put her away and pay off her marriage contract."

7:3 A. He who prohibits his wife by a vow from adorning herself with any single sort of jewelry must put her away and pay off her marriage contract.

B. R. Yose says, "In the case of poor girls, [if] he has not assigned a time limit [he must divorce them].

C. "But in the case of rich girls, [he may persist in the marriage if he set a time limit] of thirty days."

7:4 A. He who prohibits his wife by a vow from going home to her father's house —

B. when he [father] is with her in [the same] town,

C. [if it is] for a month, he may persist in the marriage,

D. [If it is] for two, he must put her away and pay off her marriage contract.

E. And when he is in another town, [if the vow is in effect] for one festival season he may persist in the marriage. [But if the vow remains in force] for three, he must put her away and pay off her marriage contract.

7:5 A. He who prohibits his wife by a vow from going to a house of mourning or to a house of celebration must put her away and pay off her marriage contract,

B. because he locks the door before her.

C. But if he claimed that he took such a vow because of some other thing, he is permitted to impose such a vow.

D. [If he took a vow,] saying to her, (i) "On condition that you say to soand-so what you said to me," or (2) "What I said to you," or (3) "that you draw water and pour it out onto the ash heap,"

E. he must put her away and pay off her marriage contract.

7:6 A. And those women go forth without the payment of the marriage contract at all:

B. She who transgresses against the law of Moses and Jewish law.

C. And what is the law of Moses [which she has transgressed]? [If] (1) she feeds him food which has not been tithed, or (2) has sexual relations with him while she is menstruating, or [if] (3) she does not cut off her dough offering, or (4) [if] she vows and does not carry out her vow.

D. And what is the Jewish law? If (1) she goes out with her hair flowing loose, or (2) she spins in the marketplace, or (3) she talks with just anybody,

E. Abba Saul says, "Also: if she curses his parents in his presence."

F. R. Tarfon says, "Also: if she is a loudmouth."

G. What is a loudmouth? When she talks in her own house, her neighbors can hear her voice.

2

The Tosefta

SUKKOT: BLESSINGS

TOSEFTA BERAKHOT

6:9 A. One who performs any of the commandments must recite a benediction over them.

B. One who makes a *Sukkah* for himself says, "Praised [be Thou, O Lord. . .] who has brought us to this occasion."

C. [One who] enters to dwell in it says, "Praised [be Thou, O Lord...] who has sanctified us through his commandments and commanded us to dwell in the *Sukkah.*"

D. Once he recites a benediction over it on the first day, he need not recite the benediction again [on the remaining days of the festival].

6:10 A. One who makes a *lulab* for himself says, "Praised [be Thou, O Lord . . .] who gave us life and preserved us and brought us to this occasion."

B. When he takes it [in hand] he says, "Praised [be Thou, O Lord . . .]who has sanctified us through his commandments and commanded us concerning the taking of the *lulab.*"

C. And he must recite the benediction over it [the *lulab*] all seven [days of the festival].

D. One who makes fringes for himself [on his garment] says, "Praised [be Thou, O Lord . . .] who has given us life . . ."

E. When he wraps himself [in the garment] he says, "Praised [be Thou, O Lord. . .] who has sanctified us through his commandments and commanded us to wrap ourselves in fringes."

F. And he must recite a benediction over them [the fringes] every day when he puts on the garment].

9

G. One who makes phylacteries [*Tefillin*] for himself says, "Praised [be Thou, O Lord. . .] who has given us life. . ."

H. When he puts them on [he says], "Praised [be Thou, O Lord. . .] who has sanctified us through his commandments and commanded us to put on phylacteries."

I. When does he put them on? In the morning.

J. [If] he did not put them on in the morning, he may put them on [any time] throughout the entire day.

BLESSINGS FOR VARIOUS OCCASIONS

TOSEFTA BERAKHOT

6:2 A. One who beholds idolatry says, "Praised [be Thou, O Lord. . .] who is slow to anger."

B. One who beholds a place from which idolatry was uprooted says, "Praised be Thou, O Lord . . .— who uprooted idolatry from our land [M. Ber. 9: 1].

C. "May it be thy will, Lord our God, that idolatry be uprooted from every place in Israel, and turn the hearts of thy servants to serve thee." [ed. princ. adds: And outside the Land one need not recite this, for the majority of the inhabitants are gentile.

D. R. Simeon (says), "Even outside the Land one must recite this, for they are destined to convert, as it says, 'at that time I will change the speech of the people to a pure speech, that all of them may call on the name of the Lord and serve him with one accord' (Zeph. 3:9)."]

E. He who sees a crowd says, "Praised [be Thou, O Lord...] sage knower of secrets, for their faces do not resemble one another and their opinions do not resemble one another."

F. When Ben Zoma saw a crowd on the Temple Mount, he said, "Praised be He who created [all] these [people] to serve me. How hard did Adam toil before he could taste a morsel [of food]: he seeded, plowed, reaped, sheaved, threshed, winnowed, separated, ground, sifted, kneaded, and baked, and only then could he eat. But I arise in the morning and find all these [foods ready] before me.

G. "How hard did Adam toil before he could put on a garment: he sheared, bleached, separated, dyed, spun, and wove, and only then could he put it on. But I arise in the morning and find all these [garments ready] before me.

H. "How many skilled craftsmen are industrious and rise early [to their work]. And I arise in the morning and find all these [ready] before me."

I. And so Ben Zoma would say, "What does a good guest say? 'May my host be remembered [by God] for good. How many kinds of wine did he bring before us! How many kinds of cuts [of meat] did he bring before us! How many kinds of cakes did he bring before us! And he prepared all this just for me!'

J. "But what does a bad guest say? 'And what have I eaten of his? I ate only a loaf of his bread. I drank only a cup of his wine. He prepared all of this only to provide for his wife and children.'

K. "As Scripture states, 'Remember to extol his work, of which men have sung' (Job 36:24) [i.e., one should behave like a good guest]."

6:3 A. One who sees a Negro, or an albino, or [a man] red-spotted in the face, or [a man] white-spotted in the face [a man afflicted with psoriasis, or elephantiasis], or a hunchback, or a dwarf [E, ed. princ. omit: or a deaf man, or an imbecile, or a drunk] says, "Praised [be Thou, O Lord...] who creates such varied creatures."

B. [One who sees] an amputee, or a lame man, or a blind man, or a man afflicted with boils, says, "Praised be the true judge" [cf. M. Ber. 9:2].

6:4 A. One who sees attractive people or attractive trees says, "Praised be He who has [made] such attractive creations."

6:5 A. One who sees a rainbow in the clouds says, "Praised [be Thou, O Lord . . .] who is faithful to his covenant, who remembers the covenant."

6:6 A. One who was walking between graves [in a cemetery] says, "Praised [be Thou, O Lord . . .] . . . who knows your number. He will judge you and he will resurrect you to judgment. Praised [be Thou, O Lord . . .] whose word is trustworthy, who resurrects the dead."

B. One who sees the sun, or the moon, or the stars, or the constellations says, "Praised [be Thou, O Lord . . .] who made creation."

C. R. Judah says, "One who recites a benediction for the sun, behold this is heresy [drk 'hrt]" [cf. T. Ber. 6:20, T. Ter. 7].

D. And so R. Judah would say, "If one sees the sea regularly, and something about it has changed, he must recite [a benediction]" [cf. M. Ber. 9:2].

6 :7 A. R. Meir says, "Behold Scripture states, 'And you shall love the Lord your God with all your heart' — that means with both of your impulses: with the good impulse and with the evil impulse [M. Ber. 9:5].

B. "And with all your soul — even if he takes your soul" [M. Ber. 9:5].

C. "And thus Scripture states, 'For thy sake we are slain all day long' (Ps. 44:23 [= RSV 44:22])."

D. Another interpretation: And with all your soul — with each and every soul that was created in you,

E. as it is written, "Let my soul live That I may praise thee" (Ps. 119:175). And Scripture states, "All my bones shall say, 'O Lord who is like thee?'" (Ps. 35: 10).

F. Ben Azzai says, " With all your soul — give your soul for the [observance of the] commandments."

G.   There are [kinds of] prayers which are considered frivolous [uttered in vain].

H.   How so? [If] one gathered in one hundred measures [of produce], [and said [as a prayer], "May it be [thy] will that there be [here] two hundred,"

I.   [or if] he gathered in one hundred barrels, [and] said, "May it be [thy] will that there be [here] two hundred," lo, this is an idle prayer [uttered in vain].

J.   But he [may rather] pray that what he brings in may be for a blessing and not for a curse [viz., that it should not spoil] [cf. M. Ber. 9:3].

Tosefta Berakhot

6:9 [I:2   A]   [One recites a blessing over the performance of all the commandments.]

[B]   One who makes for himself a sukkah recites, "Blessed [art Thou, O Lord, our God, King of the Universe,] who sanctified us with his commandments and commanded us to make a sukkah" [T. 6:9].

[C]   [One who makes a sukkah] for others [recites, "Blessed art Thou, O Lord, our God, King of the Universe,] to make for Him a sukkah for his sake."

[D]   When he enters to dwell in it he recites, "Blessed [art Thou, O Lord, our God, King of the Universe,] who sanctified us with his commandments and commanded us to dwell in a sukkah."

[E]   Once he recites the blessing for [the commandment to dwell in] it on the first night of the festival he need not recite it again [for the remainder of the festival].

[F]   Likewise, one who makes for himself a lulab recites, "Blessed [art Thou, O Lord, our God, King of the Universe,] who sanctified us with his commandments and commanded us to make a lulab."

[G]   [One who makes a lulab] for another [recites, "Blessed art Thou, O Lord, our God, King of the Universe] to make lulab for his sake."

[H]   When he takes hold of it [to fulfill the commandment] he recites, Blessed [art Thou, O Lord, our God, King of the Universe, who commanded us to take hold of the lulab," and "Blessed [art Thou, O Lord, our God, King of the Universe,] who has kept us alive, [and sustained us, and brought us to] this occasion." And he must recite the blessings each time he takes hold of it.

[I]   One who makes for himself a mezuzah recites, "Blessed [art Thou, O Lord, our God, King of the Universe, who sanctified us with his commandments and commanded us] to make a mezuzah."

[J]   [One who makes a mezuzah] for another [recites, "Blessed art Thou, O Lord, our God, King of the Universe, who sanctified us with his commandments and commanded us] to make a mezuzah for his sake."

[K]   When he sets it [in the door post] he recites, "Blessed [art Thou, O Lord, our God, King of the Universe,] who sanctified us with his commandments and commanded us regarding the commandments of the mezuzah.

[L] One who makes for himself tefillin [recites, "Blessed art Thou, O Lord, our God, King of the Universe, who sanctified us with his commandments and commanded us to make tefillin."]

[M] One who makes for others tefillin [recites, "Blessed art Thou, O Lord, our God, King of the Universe, who sanctified us with his commandments and commanded us to make tefillin for his sake."]

[N] When he puts them on he recites, "Blessed [art Thou, O Lord, our God, King of the Universe,] concerning the commandment of the tefillin.

[O] One who makes fringes [in a garment] for himself [recites, "Blessed art Thou, O Lord, our God, King of the Universe, who sanctified us with his commandments and commanded us to make fringes."]

[P] [One who makes fringes] for others [recites, "Blessed art Thou, O Lord, our God, King of the Universe, who sanctified us with his commandments and commanded us to make fringes for his sake."]

[Q] When he puts them on, [he recites, "Blessed art Thou, O Lord, our God, King of the Universe, who sanctified us with his commandments and commanded us concerning the commandment of fringes."]

[R] One who separates heave-offerings and tithes recites, "Blessed [art Thou, O Lord, our God, King of the Universe] who sanctified us with his commandments and commanded us to separate heave-offering and tithes."

[S] [One who separates these] for others recites, "Blessed [art Thou, O Lord, our God, King of the Universe,] to separate heave-offering and tithes for his sake."

[T] He who slaughters must recite, "Blessed [art Thou, O Lord, our God, King of the Universe, who sanctified us with his commandments and] commanded us regarding slaughtering."

[U] He who covers the blood recites, "Blessed [art Thou, O Lord, our God, King of the Universe, who sanctified us with his commandments and commanded us] concerning the covering of the blood."

[V] He who circumcises must recite, "Blessed [art Thou, O Lord, our God, King of the Universe, who sanctified us with his commandments] and commanded us regarding circumcision."

[W] The child's father recites, "Blessed [art Thou, O Lord, our God, King of the Universe, who sanctified us with his commandments] and commanded us to bring him into the covenant of Abraham our forefather."

[X] Those [guests] who are standing [at the ceremony] must recite, "Just as you have brought him into the covenant, so shall you bring him to Torah, and marriage [and good deeds]."

[Y] The one who recites the blessing [which follows the ceremony] must recite this blessing, "Blessed [art Thou, O Lord, our God,

King of the Universe] who sanctified [Isaac] the beloved in the womb and placed the mark of His statute in his flesh, and [placed it] on his offspring as a seal the sign of the sacred covenant. So on the merits of this, living God, our support, our rock, you commanded us [to circumcise our sons] so we may save our beloved kindred from destruction. Blessed art Thou O Lord, who establishes the covenant." [The version of this passage in T. 6:9 has several additions and omissions and a slightly different order. Some identify Abraham as the "beloved."]

CIRCUMCISION

TOSEFTA NEDARIM

2:5 A.   Rabbi says, "Great is circumcision, for, despite all the commandments which Abraham our father carried out, he was called complete and whole only when he had circumcised himself, as il is said, 'Walk before me and be perfect' (Gen. 17:1)."

2:6 A.   Another matter: Great is circumcision, for it is deemed equivalent to all the other commandments in the Torah put together,

    B.   since it says, "Lo, the blood of the covenant which the Lord made (Ex. 24:8)."

2:7 A.   Another matter: Great is circumcision, for if it were not for that, the heaven and the earth could not endure, since it says, "Thus says the Lord. Bul for my covenant day and night, I should not have set forth the ordinances of heaven and earth" (Jer. 33:25).

CIRCUMCISION BLESSING

TOSEFTA BERAKHOT

6:13 A.   What does the one who recites a benediction [after the circumcision is performed] say?

    B.   [He says], ["Praised be Thou, O Lord . . .] who sanctified the beloved [i.e., Isaac] from the womb and placed [the mark of] a statute in his flesh, and sealed his offspring with the sign of the holy covenant. As [our] reward for [having observed] this [commandment], O living God, our Portion and our Rock, now save the beloved of our flesh from destruction [i.e., let the wound heal and preserve the child's life]. Praised [be Thou, O Lord,] who establishes the covenant." [*ed. princ.* adds: He who circumcises proselytes says, "(Praised be Thou, O Lord . . . who has sanctified us) through his commandments and commanded us to circumcise proselytes, to cause the blood of the covenant to flow from them, for were it not for the blood of the covenant, the heavens and earth would not exist, as it is written, '*If I have not established my covenant with day and night and the ordinances of heaven and earth*' (Jer. 33:25). Praised (be Thou, O Lord,) who establishes the covenant." He who circumcises slaves says, "Praised (be Thou, O Lord . . .) who has sanctified us through his commandments and commanded us concerning circumcision." The one who recites a benediction (after the circumcision is performed) says, "Praised (be Thou, O Lord. ..) who has sanctified us through his commandments and commanded us to circumcise slaves and to cause the blood of the covenant to flow from them, etc."

COMMANDMENTS FOR WOMEN

TOSEFTA QIDDUSHIN

1:10 A. What is a positive commandment dependent upon the time [of year, for which men are liable and women are exempt (M. Qid. 1:7C)]?

B. For example, building the Sukkah, taking the lulab, putting Tefillin.

C. What is a positive commandment not dependent upon the time of year (M. Qid. 1:7D)?

D. For example, restoring lost property to its rightful owner, sending forth the bird, building a parapet, and putting on Sisit.

E. R. Simeon declares women exempt from the requirement of wearing Sisit, because it is a positive commandment dependent upon time.

CREATION OF MAN ALONE

TOSEFTA SANHEDRIN

8:4 A. Man was created one and alone.

B. And why was he created one and alone in the world?

C. So that the righteous should not say, "We are the sons of the righteous one," and so that the evil ones should not say, "We are the sons of the evil one."

D. Another matter: Why was he created one and alone? So that families should not quarrel with one another. For if now, that man was created one and alone, they quarrel with another, had there been two created at the outset, how much the more so! [Cf. M. San. 4:5L].

E. Another matter: Why was he created one and alone? Because of the thieves and robbers. And if now, that he was created one and alone, people steal and rob, had there been two, how much the more so!

8:5 A. Another matter: Why was he created one and alone?

B. To show the grandeur of the King of the kings of kings, blessed be He.

C. For with a single seal he created the entire world, and from a single seal all those many seals have come forth,

D. as it is said, "It is changed as clay under the seal, and all these things stand forth as in a garment" (Job 38:14) [cf. M. San 4:5N].

8:6 A. And on what account are faces not like one another?

B.   On account of imposters,

C.   so no one should jump into his neighbor's field or jump in bed with his neighbor's wife,

D.   as it is said, "And from the wicked their light is withheld and the strong arm is broken" (Job 38:15).

E.   R. Meir says, "The omnipresent has varied the appearance, intelligence, and voice —

F.   "appearance and intelligence, because of robbers and thieves, and voice, because of the possibilities of licentiousness "

8:7 A.   Man was created last [in the order of creation].

B.   And why was man created last?

C.   So that the minim should not be able to say, "There was a partner with him in his work [of creation]" [cf. M. San. 4:5M].

8:8 A.   Another matter: Why was he created last?

B.   So that he should not grow proud.

C.   For they can say to him, "The mosquito came before you in the works of creation."

D.   Another matter: So that he might immediately take up the doing of a religious duty.

8:9 A.   Another matter: So that he might enter the banquet at once [with everything ready for him].

B.   They have made a parable: To what is the matter comparable?

C.   To a king who built a palace and dedicated it and prepared a meal and [only] afterward invited the guests.

D.   And so Scripture says, The wisest of women has built her house (Prov. 9:1).

E.   This refers to the King of the kings of kings, blessed be He, who built his world In seven days by wisdom.

F.   She has hewn out her seven pillars (Prov. 9:1 these are the seven days of creation.

G.   "She has killed her beasts and mixed her wine" (Prov. 9:2) — These are the oceans, rivers, wastes, and all the other things which the world needs.

H.   And afterward: "She has sent forth her maidens, she cries on the high places of the city, Who is simple — let him turn in hither, and he who is void of understanding" (Prov. 3:4) — these refer to mankind and the wild beasts.

THE FATHER'S OBLIGATIONS TO THE SON

TOSEFTA QIDDUSHIN

1:11 A.   What is a commandment pertaining to the son concerning the father to which men and women are equally liable (M. Qid. 1:7B)]?

B.   Giving him food to eat and something to drink and clothing him and covering him and taking him out and bringing him in and washing his face, his hands, and his feet.

C. All the same are men and women. But the husband has sufficient means to do these things for the child, and the wife does not have sufficient means to do them,

D. for others have power over her.

E. What is a commandment pertaining to the father concerning the son [M . Qid. 1:7A]?

F. To circumcise him, to redeem him [if he is kidnapped], and to teach him Torah, and to teach him a trade, and to marry him off to a girl.

G. And there are those who say, "Also: to row him across the river."

H. R. Judah says, "Whoever does not teach his son a trade teaches him to be a mugger."

I. Rabban Gamaliel says, "Whoever has a trade, to what is he compared? To a vineyard surrounded by a fence, to a furrow surrounded by a border.

J. "And whoever does not have a trade — to what is he compared? To a vineyard not surrounded by a fence, to a furrow not surrounded by a border."

K. R. Yosé says in the name of Rabban Gamaliel, "Whoever has a trade — to what is he compared? To a woman who has a husband. Whether she pretties herself or does not pretty herself, people don't stare at her. And if she doesn't pretty herself, he curses her.

L. "And whoever does not have a trade — to what is he compared? To a woman who does not have a husband. Whether she pretties herself or does not pretty herself, everybody stares at her. And if she doesn't pretty herself, he doesn't curse her."

M. R. Yosé b. R. Eleazar said in the name of Rabban Gamaliel, "Whoever has a trade — to what is he compared? To a fenced-in vineyard into which cattle and beasts cannot enter. And people who go back and forth don't trample in it. And people don't see what's in it.

N. "And whoever does not have a trade — to what is he compared? To a vineyard with a broken-down fence, into which cattle and beasts can enter and people who go back and forth trample through it. And everybody sees what's in it."

HABUROT [ASSOCIATIONS] FOR VARIOUS PURPOSES

TOSEFTA MEGILLAH

3:15 D. Said R. Eleazar b. R. Sadoq, "Thus was the practice of the association's (haburot) which were in Jerusalem: "Some were for celebration, some for mourning, some for a meal in celebration of a betrothal, some for a meal in celebration of a marriage, some for the celebration of the week of a son's birth, and some for the gathering of bones [of parents, for secondary burial]."

E. [If one has to celebrate] the week of a son's birth and the occasion of gathering the bones of parents, the celebration of the week of a

son's birth takes precedence over the gathering of the bones of
parents.

F.   [If one has the occasion to join in] a house of celebration or a
      house of mourning, the house of celebration takes precedence over
      the house of mourning.

G.   R. Ishmael would give precedence to the house of mourning over
      all other occasions,

H.   "since it is said,' It is better to go to the house of mourning lthan to
      go to the house of feasting, for this is the end of all men, and the
      living will lay it to heart' (Qoh. 7:2)."

3:16 A.   R. Meir said in the name of R. 'Aqiba, "What is the meaning of the
           verse,' And the living will lay it to heart' (Qoh. 7:2)?

B.   "[In Aramaic:] Do [for others], so they will do for you, accompany
      [others] to the grave, so they will accompany you, make a
      lamentation [for others], so they will make a lamentation for you,
      bury [others], so they will bury you" [= T. Ket. 7:6].

MARKS OF MATURITY

TOSEFTA HAGIGAH

1:2 A.   A minor goes forth in reliance upon the *'erub* put out by his mother
          [not by his father].

B.   And he is liable to observe the commandment of dwelling in a
      Sukkah.

C.   And they prepare for him an *'erub* consisting of food sufficient for
      two meals, in connection with the commingling of Sabbath-
      boundaries.

D.   [If] he knows how to shake [an object], he is liable to observe the
      commandment of the *lulab.*

E.   [If] he knows how to cloak himself, he is liable for the
      commandment of fringes.

F.   [If] he knows how to speak, his father teaches him the *Shema',*
      Torah, and the Holy Language [Hebrew].

G.   And if not, it would have been better had he not come into the
      world.

H.   [If] he knows how to take care of his phylacteries, his father
      purchases phylacteries for him.

I.   [If] he knows how to take care of his person, they eat food preserved
      in a state of cultic cleanness depending upon the cleanness of his
      person.

J.   [If he knows how to take care of his] hands, they eat food preserved
      in a state of cultic cleanness depending upon the cleanness of his
      hands.

K.   How do they examine him [to see whether he is able to take care of
      himself]?

L.   They immerse him and give him unconsecrated food as if it were
      heave-offering.

M. [If] he knows how to fold over the corner of his garment [to receive heave-offering therein], they give him a share [of the heave-offering and tithes] at the threshing floor.

N. [If] he has sufficient intelligence to answer a question, then a doubt involving him in private domain is resolved as unclean, [and] one involving him in public domain is resolved as clean.

O. [If] he knows how to effect proper slaughter of an animal, then an act of slaughter on his part is valid.

P. [If] he can eat an olive's bulk of grain, they dispose of his excrement and urine at a distance of four cubits [from a settlement].

Q. [If he can eat] an olive's bulk of roast meat, they slaughter a Passover-sacrifice on his account.

R. R. Judah says, "Under no circumstances do they slaughter a Passover-sacrifice on his account unless he knows how to distinguish good food from bad.'

S. Who knows how to distinguish good food from bad?

T. Any one to whom they give an egg, which he takes, and a stone, which he throws away.

1:3 A. A girl who has produced two pubic hairs is liable to observe all of the commandments which are stated in the Torah.

B. She either carries out the rite of *halisah* or enters into levirate marriage.

C. And so a boy who produced two pubic hairs is liable to observe all of the commandments which are stated in the Torah.

D. He is able to enter into the status of a willful and rebellious son (Deut. 31:18).

E. Once his [pubic] beard has filled out, he is able to be appointed the messenger of the community to pass before the ark and to raise his hands [in the priestly benediction].

F. And he does not take a share in the Holy Things of the sanctuary until he produces two pubic hairs.

G. Rabbi says, "I say, 'Until he is twenty years old,' since it says, *They appointed the Levites, from twenty years old and upward, to have the oversight of the work of the house of the Lord* (Ezra 3:8)."

MATCHES FOR MARRIAGE

TOSEFTA SOTAH

5:9 A. R. Meir would say, "Just as there are diverse tastes in regard to food, so there are diverse tastes in regard to women['s behavior].

B. "You can find a man on whose cup a fly flits by, and he will put it aside and won't even taste what's in that cup. This one is a bad lot for women, for he is [always] contemplating divorcing his wife.

C. "You can find a man in whose cup a fly takes up residence. So he tosses it out and does not drink what is in it. Such a one is like Pappos b. Judah, who used to lock his door to keep his wife inside when he went out.

D. "And you can find a man into whose cup a fly falls, and he tosses it away and drinks what is in the cup.

E. "This is the trait of the ordinary man, who sees his wife talking with her neighbors or with her relatives and leaves her be [M. Sot. 4:4C].

F. "And you have a man into whose meal a fly falls, and he picks it up and sucks it [for the soup it absorbed] and tosses it away, and then eats what is on his plate.

G. "This is the trait of a bad man, who sees his wife going around with her hair in a mess, with her shoulders uncovered, shameless before her boy servants, shameless before her girl servants, going out and doing her spinning in the marketplace, bathing, talking with anybody at all.

H. "It is a commandment to divorce such a woman, as it is said, 'When a man takes a wife and marries her, if then she finds no favor in his eyes because he has found some indecency in her, and he writes ,her a bill of divorce and puts it in her hand and sends her out of his house and she departs out of his house'" (Deut. 24:1).

I. "And if she goes and becomes another man's wife" (Deut. 24:2) — and Scripture calls him, "A different man," because he is not his match.

J. The first man put her away because of transgression, and this other one comes along and stumbles through her.

L. The second husband, if he has merit in Heaven, puts her away. And if not, in the end, she will bury him,

M. since it is said, Or if the latter husband dies, who took her to be his wife (Deut. 24:3) —

N. this man is deserving of death, for he received such a woman into his house.

5:10 A. He who hopes that his wife will die so that he will inherit her property, or that she will die so that he may marry her sister — in the end she will bury him.

B. And so in the case of a woman who hopes that her husband will die so that she marry someone else — in the end he will bury her.

5:11 A. He who betrothed a girl because he is shamed by her father or her brother or her relatives into doing so — in the end she will bury him.

B. And so she who is betrothed to a man because she is shamed into doing so by his father, brothers, or relatives — in the end he will bury her.

C. R. Meir did say, "He who marries a woman who is unworthy of him transgresses five negative rules.

D. "On the count of not taking retribution, and not having vengeance, and not hating one's brother in his heart, and loving one's neighbor as himself, and the count that 'your brother should be able to live with you' (Lev. 19:18, 19:17, 19:18, 25:36).

E. "And not only so, but he stops procreation from happening in this world."

OLD AGE

TOSEFTA MEGILLAH

3:24 A. What is the sort of "rising" about which the Torah spoke, in saying, "You shall rise up before the hoary head land honor the face of an old man, and you shall fear your God" (Lev. 19:32)?

B. One rises before him and asks after his welfare and answers while within four cubits [of the old man].

C. What is the sort of "honor" about which the Torah spoke in saying "And honor the face of an old man"?

D. One does not stand in the place in which he usually stands, nor does one speak in his place, nor does one contradict what he says.

E. One behaves toward him with fear and reverence, deals with him when he comes and goes in like manner,

F. and [the elders] take precedence over everyone else, since it says, "And place such men over the people" (Ex. 18:21).

PRAYERS: BRIEF AND OCCASIONAL

TOSEFTA BERAKHOT

3:5 A. Said R. Judah, "When R. Aqiba would pray with the congregation [in public], he would shorten [his prayer] more than all of them.

B. "And when he would pray by himself, one could leave him in one corner [of the room] and find him [later] in another corner,

C. "on account of his [repeated] bowing and prostration [during his lengthy prayer]" [cf. M. Ber. 4:3].

3:6 A. Lest one think that he may pray continuously all day long, Scripture specifies [to the contrary] in the case of Daniel, "And he got down upon his knees three times a day land prayed and gave thanks before his God . . ." (Dan. 6:11 [= RSV 6:10]). [ed. princ. adds: "Lest one think that he may pray facing any direction he wishes, Scripture states [to the contrary], "He had windows in his upper chamber open towards Jerusalem" (ibid.).]

B. Lest one think [that Daniel prayed only] when he came to the [lands of the] dispersion, Scripture states [to the contrary], "As he had done previously (ibid.).

C. Lest one think that he must pray out loud, Scripture specifies [to the contrary] in the case of Hannah, as it says, Hannah was speaking in her heart (I Sam . 1:13).

D. Lest one think that he may recite all of them [the three daily Prayers] at one time, Scripture specifies [to the contrary] in the case of David, as it says, "Evening and morning and noon I utter my complaint and moan" (Ps. 55:18):

E.   evening — this is the evening Prayer; morning — this is the morning Prayer; noon — this is the afternoon Prayer.

F.   Lest one think that he may present his petition and [then immediately] depart [from God's presence], Scripture specifies [to the contrary] in the case of Solomon, as it says, "yet have regard to the prayer of thy servant and to his supplication, O Lord my God/ hearkening to the cry and to the prayer which thy servant prays before thee this day" (I Kings 8:28):

G   the cry — this is the cry [of praise and rejoicing which must accompany petitionary prayer], as it says, "Rejoice in the Lord O ye righteous! Praise befits the upright" (Ps. 33:1);

H.   prayer — this is petition.

I.   One does not utter words [of private petition and supplication] after "True and firm" [the benediction recited after the shema', immediately before reciting the Prayer], but he may utter words [of petition] after [reciting] the Prayer [cf. M. Ber. 2:2, T. Ber. 1:2C],

J.   even [if the petition is] as [long as] the order of the confession on the Day of Atonement.

TOSEFTA BERAKHOT

3:7 A.   One who was walking in a place of danger and of bandits recites a brief prayer [M. Ber. 4:4B].

B.   What is this brief prayer?

C.   R. Eliezer says, "May thy will be done in the heavens above, and grant ease to those who fear you, and do what is good in thine own eyes. Praised [be Thou, O Lord,] who hearkens to prayer."

D.   R. Yosé says, "Hearken to the prayer of thy people Israel and quickly fulfill their requests. Praised [be Thou, O Lord], who hearkens to prayer."

E.   R. Eleazar b. R. Sadok says, "Hearken to the sound of the cries of your people Israel and quickly fulfill their requests. Praised (be Thou, O Lord,) who hearkens to prayer."]

F.   Others say, "The needs of thy people are many and they are impatient. May it be thy will, Lord our God, to give to each and every one according to his needs, and to each and every creature that which he lacks. Praised [be Thou, O Lord,] who hearkens to prayer."

G   Said R. Eleazar b. R. Sadok, "My father used to recite a short prayer on the eve of the Sabbath: 'And on account of the love, Lord our God, with which Thou hast loved thy people Israel, and on account of the compassion, our King, which Thou hast bestowed on the members of thy covenant, Thou hast given us, Lord our God, this great and holy seventh day with love.'

H.   "Over the cup [of wine] he would say, 'who sanctified the Sabbath day,' and he would not conclude [the benediction with a closing benedictory formula]."

ALL MOURN THE SAGE WHO DIES

TOSEFTA MOED

2:17 A. A sage who died —

B. all are deemed his relations [cf. M. M.Q. 3:7A].

C. All tear their garments.

D. And all bare [their shoulders].

E. And all lament.

F. And all receive a mourner's meal on his account,

G. even in the street of the town.

TEACHING A TRADE TO ONE'S CHILDREN

TOSEFTA QIDDUSHIN

5:14 A. Whoever has business with women should not be alone with women [M. Qid. 4:14D]—

B. for example, goldsmiths, carders, [handmill] cleaners, peddlers, wooldressers, barbers, launderers, and mill-stone chiselers.

C. R. Meir says, "You have no trade which has ever disappeared from the world.

D. "Yet woe is the man who sees his parents in a mean calling"

5:15 A. Rabbi says, "A man should always endeavor to teach his son a trade which is clean of thievery and easy.

B. "And he should pray to him lo whom belongs all wealth.

C'. "For you have no trade in which is not found poverty

D. "to inform you that wealth and poverty are not derived from a particular trade" [M. Qid. 4:14F-I].

E R. Simeon b. Eleazar says, "In your whole life, did you ever see a lion working as a porter, a deer working as a fruit picker, a fox working as a storekeeper? a wolf selling pots, a domestic beast or a wild beast or a bird who had a trade?

F. "Now these are created only to work for me, and I was made only to work. for my Master.

G. "Now is there not an argument a fortiori: Now if these, who were created only to work for me, lo, they make a living without anguish, I who have been created to work for my Master, is it not reasonable that I too should make a living without anguish!

H. "But my deeds have ruined things, and I have spoiled my living" [cf.: M. Qid. 4:14J].

STUDY OF THE TORAH VERSUS LEARNING A TRADE

TOSEFTA QIDDUSHIN

5:16 A. R. Nehorai says, "I should leave every trade there is in the world and teach my son only Torah.

B. "For they eat the fruit of labor in Torah in this world, but the principal lasts for the world to come.

C. "For every sort of trade which there is in the world serves a man only when he is young, when he yet has his strength.

D. "But when he falls ill or grows old or has pains, and does not work any more, in the end he dies of hunger.

E. "But Torah keeps a man from all evil when he is young and gives him a future and a hope when he is old. When he is young, what does it say? "They who Walt upon the Lord shall renew their strength" (Is. 40:31). And concerning his old age, what does it say? "They shall still bring forth fruit in old age" (Ps 92:14) [M. Qid. 4:14N-T].

5:17 A. And so you find with regard to the patriarch, Abraham, that the Omnipresent blessed him in his old age more than in his youth, as it is said "And Abraham was old and well along in years and the Lord blessed Abraham in all things" (Gen. 24:1) [M. Qid. 4:14U].

B. R. Meir says, "That he had no daughter."

C. R. Simeon says, in the name of R. Judah, "That he did have a daughter."

D. R. Eleazar the Modite says, "Abraham possessed an astrological instrument, on account of which everybody came to him."

E. R. Simeon b. Yohai says, "This was a fine gem, which was hung around the neck of the patriarch, Abraham.

F. "And whoever stared at it was cured forthwith.

G. "When Abraham the patriarch died, the Omnipresent took it and hung it around the orb of the sun."

5:18 A. Another point: That Esau did not rebel during his lifetime.

5:19 A. A third measure: That Ishmael repented during his lifetime.

5:20 A. Others say, "Abraham did have a daughter, and her name was, In all things."

5:21 A. And the Omnipresent blessed when in his old age more than in his youth.

B. And why all this?

C. Because he kept the entire Torah even before it had come, since it says, "Since Abraham obeyed my voice and kept my charge, my commandments, my statutes and my Torahs" (Gen. 26:5)—

D. My Torah is not said, but rather, my Torahs—

E. this teaches that to him were revealed the mysteries of the Torah in all their details.

WHY NO SEX BETWEEN FREE AGENTS

TOSEFTA QIDDUSHIN

1:3 A. "Do not profane your daughter by making her a harlot lest the land fall into harlotry and the land become full of wickedness" (Lev. 9:29).

B. R. Eleazar says, "This is an unmarried man who has sexual relations with an unmarried woman not for the sake of effecting a marriage."

C. R. Eleazar says, "How do we know that he is punished before the Omnipresent as is he who has sexual relations with a woman and her mother?

D. "Here it is said wickedness, and elsewhere it is said, 'If a man takes a wife and her mother also, it is wickedness' (Lev. 20:14)."

E. R. Eliezer b. Jacob says, "Since he has sexual relations with many girls and does not know with which one he has had sexual relations, and she has received sexual relations from many men and does not know from which ones she has received sexual relations, this man turns out to marry his daughter, and that one marries his sister, and the whole world is turned into mamzerim.

F. "On that account it is said, 'And the land became full of wickedness' (Lev. 19:29)."

G. R. Judah b. Betera says, "Lo, it says, Lest the land fall into harlotry (Lev. 19:29) — The produce turns into weeds: What is this child? Neither a priest, nor a Levite, nor an Israelite [since no one knows]."

H. Sages voted to support the opinion of R. Judah,

I. since it is said, "Lift up your eyes to the bare heights and see! Where have you not been lain with? You have polluted the land with your vile harlotry. Therefore the showers have been withheld, and the spring rain has not come" (Jer. 3:22).

WHY NO SEX WITH A MARRIED WOMAN

TOSEFTA HAGIGAH

1:7 A. If the festival passed and one did not make a festal-offering, he is not liable to make it good.

B. Of such a person it is said, "That which is crooked cannot be made straight, and that which is wanting cannot be reckoned (Qoh. 1:16)" [M . Hag. I :6B-C].

C. And it says, "The wicked borrows and cannot pay back, but the righteous is generous and gives" (Ps. 37:21).

D. R. Simeon b. Menassia says, "[If] a man steals, he can restore what he stole. [If] he robbed, he can restore that which he robbed.

E. "[But] if he had sexual relations with a married woman and invalidated her from continuing marriage with her husband, he is tormented and driven from the world,

F. "and concerning such a person it is written, 'That which is crooked cannot be made straight' (Qoh. 1:15)" [cf. M. Hag. 1:7A-C].

3

Mekhilta Attributed to R. Ishmael

HONORING PARENTS

MEKHILTA BAHODESH 8 LIV:I.

1. A. "Honor your father and your mother [that your days may be long in the land which the Lord your God gives you]:"
   B. Might I infer that this is with words?
   C. Scripture says, "Honor the Lord with your substance" (Prov. 3:9).
   C. That means, with food, drink, and fresh garments.
2. A. Another interpretation of the verse, "Honor your father and your mother [that your days may be long in the land which the Lord your God gives you]:"
   B. "Why is this stated?
   C. "Since it is said, 'For whatever man curses his mother or his father...' (Lev. 20:9), I know only that subject to the law is only a man.
   D. "How do I know that a woman, one of undefined gender-traits, one who exhibits gender traits for both genders [are subject to the law]?
   E. "Scripture says, 'Honor your father and your mother' — under all circumstances.
   F. "Just as in the case of honor, there is no distinction between a man and a woman, so as to fearing parents, there should be no distinction between man and woman," the words of R. Ishmael.
   G. R. Judah b. Batera says, "Scripture says, 'You shall fear every man his mother and his father, and you shall keep my Sabbaths' (Lev. 19:3):
   H. "Just as in the case of the Sabbath, the law does not distinguish between a man, a woman, one of undefined gender-traits, and one who exhibits gender traits for both genders, so in the case of fear

of parents, there should be no distinction between man and woman, one of undefined gender-traits, and one who exhibits gender traits for both genders."

3. A.   Rabbi says, "Precious before the One who spoke and brought the world into being is the honor owing to father and mother,

   B.   "for he has declared equal the honor owing to them and the honor owing to him, the fear owing to them and the fear owing to him, curing them and cursing him.

   C.   "It is written: Honor your father and your mother," and as a counterpart: 'Honor the Lord with your substance' (Prov. 3:9).

   D.   "Scripture thus has declared equal the honor owing to them and the honor owing to him.

   E.   "'You shall fear every man his mother and his father' (Lev. 19:3), and, as a counterpart: 'You shall fear the Lord your God' (Dt. 6:13).

   F.   "Scripture thus has declared equal the fear owing to them and the fear owing to him.

   G.   "'And he who curses his father or his mother shall surely be put to death' (Ex. 21:17), and correspondingly: 'Whoever curses his God' (Lev. 24:15).

   H.   "Scripture thus has declared equal the cursing them and cursing him."

4. A.   [Rabbi continues,] "Come and note that the reward [for obeying the two commandments is the same].

   B.   "'Honor the Lord with your substance...so shall your barns be filled with plenty' (Prov. 3:9-10, and 'Honor your father and your mother that your days may be long in the land which the Lord your God gives you.'

   C.   "'You shall fear the Lord your God' (Dt. 6:13), as a reward: 'But to you that fear my name shall the sun of righteousness arise with healing in its wings' (Mal. 3:20).

   D.   "'You shall fear every man his mother and his father and you shall keep my Sabbaths' (Lev. 19:3).

"And as a reward? 'If you turn away your foot because of the Sabbath, then you shall delight yourself in the Lord' (Is. 58:13-14)."

5. A.   Rabbi says, "It is perfectly self-evident before the One who spoke and brought the world into being that a person honors the mother more than the father, because she brings him along with words. Therefore Scripture gave precedence to the father over the mother as to honor.

   B.   "And it is perfectly self-evident before the One who spoke and brought the world into being that a person fears his father more than the mother, because the father teaches him Torah. Therefore Scripture gave precedence to the mother over the father as to fear.

   C.   "In a case in which something is lacking, [Scripture] thereby made it whole.

   D.   "But might one suppose that whoever takes precedence in Scripture takes precedence in deed?

    E.   "Scripture says, 'You shall fear every man his mother and his father' (Lev. 19:3),

    F.   "indicating that both of them are equal to one another."

6. A.   "Honor your father and your mother that your days may be long in the land which the Lord your God gives you:"

    B.   If you have honored them, "that your days may be long in the land which the Lord your God gives you."

    C.   And if not, "that your days may be cut short."

    D.   For the words of the Torah are *notarikon.*

    E.   For thus words of the Torah are so interpreted that from an affirmative statement one derives the negative, and from the negative, the affirmative.

7. A.   "in the land which the Lord your God gives you:"

    B.   In this connection sages have said, "In the case of every religious duty in which Scripture specifies the reward along side, the earthly court is not admonished to enforce the rule."

4

Sifra

Israel Keeps Itself Pure

Sifra CXCIV:III

4. A. "Do not defile yourselves in any of those ways":
   B. whether in all of them or in only some of them.
5. A. "...for it is by such that the nations":
   B. this refers to the Egyptians
   C. "...that I am casting out before you":
   D. this refers to the Canaanites.
6. A. "Thus the land became defiled":
   B. this teaches that the land contracts uncleanness on account of these things.
7. A. "...and I called it to account for its iniquity":
   B. "Once I open the ledger, I immediately collect all that is coming."
8. A. "...and the land spewed out its inhabitants":
   B. "like a person who vomits up his meal."
9. A. "But you must keep":
   B. "You are worthy of keeping them, for you opened them."
   C. And so Scripture says, "A garden locked is my own, my bride, a fountain locked, a sealed up spring" (Song 4:12).
10. A. "...and you must not do any of those abhorrent things":
    B. whether all of them or some of them.
11. A. ["neither the citizen nor the stranger who resides among you":]
    B. "citizen": lo, that covers a citizen.
    C. "...the citizen": this encompasses wives of citizens.
    D. "...stranger": this refers to a proselyte.
    E. "...the stranger": this encompasses wives of proselytes.
    F. "...among you": this encompasses women and slaves.

12. A.   "...for all those abhorrent things were done by the people who were in the land before you; and the land became defiled":

     B.   this teaches that the land contracted uncleanness on account of these things.

13. A.   "So let not the land spew you out for defiling it, as it spewed out the nation that came before you":

     B.   This teaches that the land is subject to the penalty of exile on account of these things.

14. A.   "All who do any of those abhorrent things":

     B.   whether all of them or only some of them.

15. A.   "...such persons shall be cut off:

     B.   What is the sense of Scripture here?

     C.   Since reference is made to "a man," I might suppose that only a man is subject to extirpation on account of a woman. How do I know that a woman is subject to extirpation on account of a man?

     D.   Scripture says, "persons,"

     E.   covering both [participants in an incestuous relationship].

16. A.   "...who do...":

     B.   What is the sense of Scripture here?

     C.   Since Scripture says, "you will not draw near," might one suppose that people might be liable to extirpation because of merely drawing near?

     D.   Scripture says, "...who do...," and not merely who draw near.

17. A.   "...from their people":

     B.   but their people will remain untouched.

18. A.   "You shall keep my charge":

     B.   "Keep a charge for me."

19. A.   "You shall keep my charge":

     B.   this serves to admonish the court [to enforce the law].

20. A.   "...not to engage in any of the abhorrent practices that were carried on before you, and you shall not defile yourselves through them":

     B.   this teaches that all incestuous relationships are called "uncleanness."

21. A.   "...and you shall not defile yourselves through them":

     B.   [God says,] "if you become unclean through them, you will be made invalid from following after me, so what pleasure shall I have in you, when you come liable before me for destruction?"

     C.   That is why it is said, "I the Lord am your God."

     D.   So Ezra says, "Shall we once again violate your commandments by intermarrying with these peoples who follow such abhorrent practices? Will you not rage against us till we are destroyed without remnant or survivor? O Lord, God of Israel, you are benevolent, [for we have survived as a remnant, as is now the case. We stand before you in all our guilt for we cannot face you on this account]" (Ezra 9:14-15).

SEXUAL PROHIBITIONS

SIFRA CsXCIV:II

1. A.   "The Lord spoke to Moses saying, Speak to the Israelite people and say to them, I am the Lord your God":

     B.   R. Simeon b. Yohai says, "That is in line with what is said elsewhere: 'I am the Lord your God [who brought you out of the land of Egypt, out of the house of bondage]' (Ex. 20:2).

     C.   "'Am I the Lord, whose sovereignty you took upon yourself in Egypt?'

     D.   "They said to him, 'Indeed.'

     E.   "'Indeed you have accepted my dominion.'

     F.   "'They accepted my decrees: "You will have no other gods before me."'

     G.   "That is what is said here: 'I am the Lord your God,' meaning, 'Am I the one whose dominion you accepted at Sinai?'

     H.   "They said to him, 'Indeed.'

     I.   "'Indeed you have accepted my dominion.'

     J.   "'They accepted my decrees: "You shall not copy the practices of the land of Egypt where you dwelt, or of the land of Canaan to which I am taking you; nor shall you follow their laws."'"

2. A.   R. Ishmael says, "The weighty character of the laws against incest is shown by the fact that Scripture begins and ends its presentation of them by invoking the name of the Lord.

     B.   "At the beginning: 'None of you shall come near anyone of his own flesh to uncover nakedness; I am the Lord.'

     C.   "And at the end: 'You shall keep my charge not to engage in any of the abhorrent practices that were carried on before you, and you shall not defile yourselves through them; I the Lord am your God.'

     D.   "Lo, the weighty character of the laws against incest is shown by the fact that Scripture begins and ends its presentation of them by invoking the name of the Lord.."

3. A.   Rabbi says, "It was self-evident to the One who spoke and brought the world into being that in the end they would [Jastrow, p. 945:] bear unwillingly the restrictive laws concerning sexual relations.

     B.   "That is why he set the matter forth for them through a decree: 'I am the Lord, your God.'

     C.   "'Know who it is who makes this decree over you.'

     D.   "And so we find that they actually did unwillingly bear the restrictive laws concerning sexual relations.

     E.   "For it is said, 'Moses heard the people weeping, every clan apart, each person at the entrance of his tent' (Num. 11:10).

     F.   "So too Malachi says to them, 'And this you do as well: you cover the altar of the Lord with tears, weeping and moaning, [so that he refuses to regard the oblation any more and to accept what you offer. But you ask, Because of what? Because the Lord is a witness between you and the wife of your youth with whom you have broken faith, though she is your partner and covenanted spouse]' (Mal. 2:13-14).

G.   "He said to them, 'Now this is not your first time! You cried in the time of Moses.'

H.   "They said to him, 'Did not One make all, so that all remaining life-breath is his?' (Mal. 2:15).

I.   "'Is not the one who created Israel the same one who created the nations?'

J.   "He said to them, 'And what does that One seek but godly folk?' (Mal. 2:15).

K.   "They responded all together, saying, 'May the Lord leave to him who does this no descendants dwelling in the tents of Jacob and presenting offerings to the Lord of Hosts' (Mal. 2:12).

L.   "'May such a person leave no descendant among the sages and no one responding among the disciples, and, if he was a present, then no one 'presenting offerings to the Lord of Hosts.'

M. "And so Scripture states, 'One of the sons of Joiada son of the high priest Eliashib was a son-in-law of Sanballat the Horonite; I [drove him away from me]' (Neh. 13:28)."

4. A. Rabbi says, "'[The Lord spoke to Moses saying,] Speak to the Israelite people and say to them, I am the Lord your God':

B.   "Say to them, 'I too am admonished just as I have spoken to you [Moses], and you have accepted [my rule]. So speak to them so that they will accept it.'"

5. A. "...and say to them":

B.   lo, this is an admonition to the court.

6. A. "I am the Lord your God":

B.   "I am Judge to exact punishment and reliable to pay a reward."

7. A. "You shall not copy the practices of the land of Egypt where you dwelt":

B.   Scripture makes the point that the practices of the Egyptians were the most corrupt of those of all peoples,

C.   and that place in which Israel dwelt was the most corrupt in the land of Egypt.

8. A. "...or of the land of Canaan to which I am taking you":

B.   Now was it not perfectly well-known that they were coming to the land of Canaan?

C.   Why does Scripture make this point, saying "or of the land of Canaan to which I am taking you"?

D.   But Scripture so makes the point that the practices of the Canaanites were the most corrupt of those of all peoples,

E.   and that place to which the Israelites were planning to go was the most corrupt of all.

9. A. "You shall not copy the practices of the land of Egypt where you dwelt, or of the land of Canaan to which I am taking you":

B.   Scripture thereby treats as analogous the practices of the Egyptians and the practices of the Canaanites.

C. What were the practices of the Canaanites?

D. They were flooded with idolatry, fornication, murder, pederasty, and bestiality.

E. So the practices of the Egyptians were the same.

F. Then why did the Egyptians receive their punishment forty years ahead of the Canaanites?

G. It was as a reward for their paying honor to that righteous man, as it is said, 'Hear us, my lord, you are the elect of God among us' (Gen. 23:6).

H. and further: "[The name of Hebron was formerly Kiriath-arba;] he was the great man among the Anakites. And the land had rest from war" (Josh. 14:15).

10. A. "...nor shall you follow their laws":

B. Now [in making this inclusive statement,] what is it that Scripture has neglected to say?

C. Has it not already been said, "Let no one be found among you who consigns his son or daughter to the fire, or who is an augur, a soothsayer, a diviner, a sorcerer, one who casts spells, or one who consults ghosts or familiar spirits, or one who inquires of the dead" (Dt. 18:10)?

D. Why then does Scripture say, "nor shall you follow their laws"?

E. It is that you should not follow their customs in matters that are established by law for them, for example, going to their theaters, circuses, and playing fields.

F. R. Meir says, "These are forbidden under the rubric of 'the ways of the Amorites,' which sages have specified."

G. R. Judah b. Betera says, "The meaning is that you should not grow your hair as they do, you should not make your show-fringes long, you should not get a haircut in the manner of their priests."

H. And should you argue, "For them they are laws, for us they are not laws?"

I. Scripture says, "My rules alone shall you observe and faithfully follow my laws: I the Lord am your God."

J. Still, the impulse to do evil can still quibble and say, "Theirs are nicer than ours"!

K. Scripture says, "You shall keep and do it, for it is your wisdom and your understanding" (Dt. 4:6).

11. A. "You shall keep my laws":

B. This refers to matters that are written in the Torah.

C. But if they had not been written in the Torah, it would have been entirely logical to write them,

D. for example, rules governing thievery, fornication, idolatry, blasphemy, murder,

E. examples of rules that, had they not been written in the Torah, would have been logical to include them.

F. Then there are those concerning which the impulse to do evil raises doubt, the nations of the world, idolators, raise doubt,

G.   for instance, the prohibition against eating pork, wearing mixed species, the rite of removing the shoe in the case of the deceased childless brother's widow, the purification-rite for the person afflicted with the skin ailment, the goat that is sent forth –

H.   cases in which the impulse to do evil raises doubt, the nations of the world, idolators, raise doubt.

I.   In this regard Scripture says, "I the Lord have made these ordinances, and you have no right to raise doubts concerning them."

12. A.   "[My rules alone shall you observe] and faithfully follow [my laws]":

B.   Treat them as principal and do not treat them as peripheral.

13. A.   "…and faithfully follow":

B.   your give and took should be only in them.

C.   You should never mix up with them other matters,

D.   for instance, you should not say, "I have learned the wisdom of Israel, not I shall learn the wisdom of the nations."

E.   Scripture says, "…and faithfully follow,"

F.   You do not have the right to take your leave of them.

G.   And so Scripture says, "Tie them over your heart always, bind them around your throat. When you walk it will lead you; when you lie down it will watch over you; and when you are awake it will talk with you" (Prov. 6:21-22).

H.   "When you walk it will lead you": in this world.

I.   "…when you lie down it will watch over you": in the hour of death.

J.   "…and when you are awake it will talk with you": in the age to come.

K.   And so Scripture says, "Awake and shout for joy, you who dwell in the dust, for your dew is like the dew on fresh growth, you make the land of the shades to come to life" (Is. 26:19).

L.   And might you say, "My hope is lost, my prospects are lost"?

M.   Scripture says, "I am the Lord":

N.   "I am your hope, I am your prospects, in my is your trust."

O.   And so Scripture says, "Till you grow old, I will be the same; when you turn gray, it is I who will carry; I was the Maker and I will be the Bearer; and I will carry and rescue you" (Is. 46:4).

P.   And so Scripture says, "Thus said the Lord, the King of Israel, their redeemer, the Lord of hosts: I am the first and I am the last, and there is no god but me" (Is. 44:6).

Q.   And further: ""Who has wrought and achieved this? He who announced the generations from the start – I the Lord who was first and will be with the last as well" (Is. 41:4).

14. A.   "You shall keep my laws and my rules":

B.   I know only what Scripture has spelled out.

C.   How do we know about the other details of the passage?

D.   Scripture says, "You shall keep my laws and my rules."

15. A.   "…by the pursuit of which man shall live":

B. R. Jeremiah says, "How do I know that even a gentile who keeps the Torah, lo, he is like the high priest?

C. "Scripture says, 'by the pursuit of which man shall live.'"

D. And so he says, "'And this is the Torah of the priests, Levites, and Israelites,' is not what is said here, but rather, 'This is the Torah of the man, O Lord God' (2 Sam. 7:19)."

E. And so he says, "'open the gates and let priests, Levites, and Israelites will enter it' is not what is said, but rather, 'Open the gates and let the righteous nation, who keeps faith, enter it' (Is. 26:2)."

F. And so he says, "'This is the gate of the Lord. Priests, Levites, and Israelites...' is not what is said, but rather, 'the righteous shall enter into it' (Ps. 118:20).

G. And so he says, "'What is said is not, 'Rejoice, priests, Levites, and Israelites,' but rather, 'Rejoice, O righteous, in the Lord' (Ps. 33:1)."

H. And so he says, "It is not, 'Do good, O Lord, to the priests, Levites, and Israelites,' but rather, 'Do good, O Lord, to the good, to the upright in heart' (Ps. 125:4)."

I. "Thus, even a gentile who keeps the Torah, lo, he is like the high priest."

16. A. "...by the pursuit of which man shall live":

B. not that he should die by them.

C. R. Ishmael would say, "How do you know that if people should say to someone when entirely alone, 'Worship an idol and do not be put to death,' the person should worship the idol and not be put to death?

D. "Scripture says, 'by the pursuit of which man shall live,' not that he should die by them."

E. "But even if it is in public should he obey them?

F. "Scripture says, '[You shall faithfully observe my commandments; I am the Lord.] You shall not profane my holy name, that I may be sanctified in the midst of the Israelite people – I the Lord who sanctify you, I who brought you out of the land of Egypt to be your God, I the Lord' (Lev. 22:31-32).

G. "If you sanctify my name, then I shall sanctify my name through you.

H. "For that is just as Hananiah, Mishael, and Azariah did.

I. "When all of the nations of the world at that time were prostrate before the idol, while they stood up like palm trees.

J. "And concerning them it is stated explicitly in tradition: 'Your stately form is like the palm' (Song 7:8).

K. "'I say, let me climb the palm, let me take hold of its branches; [let your breasts be like clusters of grapes, your breath like the fragrance of apples, and your mouth like choicest wine]' (Ps. 7:9).

L. "'This day I shall be exalted through the in the sight of the nations of the world, who deny the Torah.

M.   "'This day I shall exact vengeance for them from those who hate them.

N.   "'This day I shall resurrect the dead among them.'

O.   "I am the Lord":

P.   "I am Judge to exact punishment and faithful to pay a reward."

5

Sifré to Numbers

SIFRE TO NUMBERS CV:VI

1. A. "And Moses cried to the Lord, 'Heal her, O God, I beseech you:"

B. On what account did Moses not draw out his prayer? It was so that the Israelites should not say, "It is because she is his sister that he is standing and laying forth abundant prayers."

C. Another reason: It is so that the Israelites should not say, "His sister is in trouble and he is standing and saying a lot of prayers."

D. "Is this not Moses who is saying a prayer and the Omnipresent is listening to his prayer, as it is said, 'In all your designs you will succeed and light will shine on your path' (Job 22:28)."

E. And further: "Then if you call the Lord will answer, if you cry to him, he will say, 'Here I am'" (Is. 58:9).

2. A. His disciples asked R. Eliezer, "How long should a person draw out his prayer?"

B. He said to them, "Someone should not draw out his prayer more than did Moses, as it is said, 'And I prostrated myself before the Lord as at the first for forty days and for forty nights' (Deut. 9:18)."

C. "And how much should one cut his short prayer short?"

D. He said to them, "A person should not cut his prayer shorter than did Moses, as it is said, "Heal her, O God, I beseech you.'

E. "There is a time to cut prayer short, and there is a time to draw it out."

6

Genesis Rabbah

How to Die

2. A.   "Strength and dignity are her clothing, and she laughs at the time to come" (Prov. 31:25):

B.   The whole of the reward of the righteous is readied for them in the age to come, but the Holy One, blessed be he, shows it to them while they are yet in this world. Since he shows them their full recompense in the world to come while they are yet in this world, their soul is satisfied and they go to sleep peacefully.

C.   Said R. Eleazar, "The matter may be compared to the case of a king who called a banquet and invited guests and showed them in advance what they were going to eat and drink, so their souls were satisfied and they fell asleep. So the Holy One, blessed be he, shows the righteous while they are yet in this world the coming recompense that he is going to give to them in the age to some, and their souls are satisfied and they fall asleep.

D.   "What scriptural verse indicates it? 'For now I should have lain still and been quiet, I should have slept, then I had been at rest' (Job 3:13). Thus when the righteous leave, the Holy One, blessed be he, shows them the recompense that is coming."

3. A.   When R. Abbahu was dying, they showed him thirteen rivers of balsam. He said to them, "To whom do these belong?"

B.   They said to him, "To you."

C.   He said to them, "These belong to Abbahu? And I had thought, 'I have labored in vain, I have spent my strength for nought and vanity, yet surely my right is worth the Lord, and my recompense with my God' (Is. 44:4). [But I was wrong.]"

41

4. A. Zabedi b. Levi, R. Joshua b. Levi and R. Yosé b. Petros: each of them recited a verse as he lay dying.

B. One of them said, "For this let every one who is godly pray to you in a time when you may be found" (Ps. 32:6). "For in him does our heart rejoice, because we have trusted in his holy name" (Ps. 33:21).

C. One of them said, "You prepare a table before me in the presence of my enemies" (Ps. 23:5). "So shall all those who take refuge in you rejoice" (Ps. 5:12).

D. The third said, "For a day in your courts is better than a thousand" (Ps. 84:11).

E. Rabbis said, "Oh how abundant is your goodness, which you have laid up for those who fear you" (Ps. 31:20).

F. This indicates that when the righteous leave, the Holy One, blessed be he, shows them the recompense that is coming.

5. A. Ben Azzai says, "'Precious in the sight of the Lord is the death of his saints' (Ps. 116:15). When does the Holy One, blessed be he, show them the recompense that is coming? Right near their death.

B. "That is in line with this verse: '... is the death of his saints.' Therefore: 'She laughs at the time to come' (Prov. 31:25)."

6. A. What is the difference between the death of the young and the death of the old?

B. R. Judah and R. Abbahu:

C. R. Judah said, "When a lamp goes out on its own, it is good for the lamp and good for the wick, but when it goes out not on its own, it is bad for it and bad for the wick."

D.   R. Abbahu said, "When figs are picked in season, it is good for them and good for the fig-tree, and when not picked in season, it is bad for them and bad for the fig-tree."

7. A. There is this story. R. Hiyya and his disciples, and some say, R. Aqiba and his disciples, were accustomed to get up early and to go into session under a fig tree. And the owner of the fig tree would get up early and pick off the figs. They said, "Is it possible that he suspects us [of stealing his figs]? We should change our place."

B. What did they do? They changed their place. He went to them and said to them, "My lords, the merit of one religious duty that you would study under my fig tree has accrued to me, and now you have taken it away."

C. They said to him, "We wondered, Is it possible that you suspect us [of stealing his figs]? [We therefore changed our place.]"

D. He assured them [that that was not the case], and they went back to their original place.

E. What did he then do? He ceased to gather his figs at dawn. The figs then began to rot [on the tree].

F. They said, "The owner of the fig-tree knows when the season of each fig has come, and that is when he picks it. [That is why he picked the figs early in the morning.] So too, the Holy One, blessed be he, knows the season of the righteous, and he then gathers them. What is the scriptural basis for this view? 'My beloved has gone down to his garden' (Song 6:2)."

8. A.   Another version of the same story: R. Hiyya the Elder and and his disciples, and some say, R. Hoshaia and his disciples, were accustomed to get up early and to study under a fig tree. And the owner of the fig tree day by day would get up early and pick off the figs. They said, "Is it possible that he suspects us [of stealing his figs? We should change our place."

   B.   [What did they do?] They changed their place. The owner of the fig tree got up early to pick off his figs and did not find them there. He went looking for them. He said to them, "My lords, the merit of one religious duty that you would carry out [to my benefit] you now withhold from me."

   C.   They said to him, "God forbid!"

   D.   He said to them, "On what account did you abandon your place and go into session somewhere else?"

   E.   They said to him, "We said, we should change our place, for it may be that you suspect us [of stealing his figs]. [We therefore changed our place.]"

   F.   He said to them, "God forbid. Let me tell you why I would get up early in the morning and go to my fig tree to collect the ripe figs. Once the sun has shown on them, they start rotting."

   G.   [He relieved their doubts, and] they went back to their original meeting place.

   H.   On that day he left them alone and did not gather his figs, and the sun shown on the figs, and they split some of them and found that they had rotted.

   I.   They said, "The owner of the fig-tree knows when the season of each fig has come, and that is when he picks it. So too, the Holy One, blessed be he, knows the season of the righteous, and he then gathers them. What is the scriptural basis for this view? 'My beloved has gone down to his garden' (Song 6:2)."

9. A.   "In a good old age" (Gen. 25:8):

   B.   Said R. Simeon b. Laqish, "There are three concerning whom 'good old age' is stated, Abraham , and he had it coming, David, and he had it coming, [and Gideon,] but Gideon did not have it coming.

   C.   "Why not? Because 'Gideon made an ephod thereof' (Judges. 8:27) for idolatry."

Genesis Rabbah C:II.

2. A.   Our master [Judah the Patriarch] gave three commandments before he died. He said to them, "Do not carry out a lamentation for me in the villages, and do not move my widow from my house, and whoever took care of me when I was alive should take care of me when I die."

B.   "Do not carry out a lamentation for me in the villages:" on account of dissension.

C.   "...and do not move my widow from my house:" But is this not an explicit statement of the Mishnah-code: **A widow who said, "I do not wish to move from the house of my husband" — the heirs have not got the power to say to her, "Go to the house of your father, and we shall provide food for you there. But they must provide food for her and give her a home appropriate to the honor owing to her [M. Ket. 12:3]**? [Why did Rabbi have to make the matter explicit?]

D.   It was because all of the property of the patriarch ordinarily is deemed to belong to the community. But this one, since he had not derived benefit from the community at all, had the right to say, "Let my widow not move from out of my house."

E.   Said R. Dosetai, "It was so that people should not say to her, 'The house of the patriarch is subject to the possession of the patriarchate.'"

F.   "...and whoever took care of me when I was alive should take care of me when I die:"

G.   Said R. Haninah of Sepphoris, "For example, Yosé Hefyanos and Yosé of Ephrath."

H.   R. Hezekiah added two more: "Do not make a great many shrouds for me, and let my coffin be open to the ground."

I.   "Do not make a great many shrouds for me:" on account of worms.

J.   "...and let my coffin be open to the ground:" on account of secretions.

K.   For Rabbi [Judah the Patriarch] said, "It is not the way in which a mortal goes that he comes back [but at the resurrection he comes back in new garments, hence there is no need to worry about the condition of the garments in which he is buried]."

L.   The view of rabbis [differs,] for they say, "As a mortal goes, so he comes back."

3. A.   R. Yohanan gave orders, saying, "Do not shroud me in white or black shrouds, but only in colored ones. If I am called with the righteous, the wicked will not know about me, and if I am called with the wicked, the righteous will not know about me."

B.   R. Josiah gave orders, saying, "Shroud me in white hemmed shrouds."

C.   They said to him, "Your master said this, and you say that?"

D.   He said to them, "Why should I be fearful on account of the things I have done?"

4. A.   R. Jeremiah gave orders, saying, "Shroud me in white hemmed garments, and put my slippers on me and place my staff in my hand, and put my sandals on my feet, and place me beside a road. So if I am summoned, I shall stand up ready to proceed."

B. That is in line with what R. Jonah said in the name of R. Hama, "A person's feet are pledges, bringing him anywhere he is called."

MARRYING OFF ONE'S DAUGHTERS

GENESIS RABBAH

XXVI:IV.

2. A. "To multiply upon the face of the ground" (Gen. 6:1):

B. This teaches that they spilled their seed on the trees and stones [having intercourse in unseemly places], for they were stuffed with lust, so the Holy One, blessed be he, gave them many daughters.

C. That is in line with this verse: "When men began to multiply on the face of the ground, then daughters were born to them" (Gen. 6:1).

3. A. The wife of R. Simeon b. Rabbi produced a daughter. R. Hiyya the elder met him and said to him, "The Holy One, blessed be he, has begun to bless you."

B. He said to him, "In what sense?"

C. He said to him, "It is written, 'And it came to pass, when man began to multiply, and daughters were born to them.'"

D. He went to his father, who said to him, "Has the Babylonian [Hiyya] pleased you?"

E. He said to him, "Indeed so, and this is what he said to me."

F. He said to him, "Nonetheless there is need for wine and there is need for vinegar, and greater is the need for wine than for vinegar. There is need for wheat and there is need for barley, and greater is the need for wheat than for barley. When a man marries off his daughter and pays off the expense of the wedding, he says to her, 'May you never come back here [but remain happily married to your husband].'"

4. A. Rabban Gamaliel married off his daughter, She said to him, "Father, pray for me."

B. He said to her, "May you never come back here."

C. She produced a son. She said to him, "Father, pray for me."

D. He said to her, "May the cry of 'woe' never leave your lips."

E. She said to him, "Father, on two occasions for rejoicing which have come to me, you curse me!"

F. He said to her, "Both of them were blessings. Because there will be peace in your home, may you never come back here, and because your son will live, may you never stop saying, 'Woe.' [That is,] 'Woe, my son has not yet eaten!' 'Woe, he has not yet drunk!' 'Woe, he has not yet gone to the school!'"

7

Leviticus Rabbah

CIRCUMCISION

LEVITICUS RABBAH XXV:VI

1. A.   R. Huna in the name of Bar Qappara said, "Abraham, our father, sat and constructed an argument a fortiori [as follows]:

   B.   "The matter of uncircumcision is stated with regard to a tree [Lev. 19:23] and the matter of uncircumcision is stated with regard to a man.

   C.   "Just as the matter of uncircumcision stated with regard to a tree applies to the place at which it produces fruit,

   D.   "so the uncircumcision stated with regard to a man applies to the place in which he produces progeny."

   E.   Said R. Hanan b. R. Pazzi, "And did Abraham, our father, actually know anything about constructing arguments a fortiori or arguments based on analogy?

   F.   "But he found an intimation of the matter in the following verse of Scripture: 'And I will set my covenant between me and you, [and I will make you multiply very much]' [Gen. 17:2].

   G.   "[The mark of the covenant is to be] in the place at which a man is fruitful and multiplies."

2. A.   R. Ishmael taught, "The Holy One, blessed be he, wanted to take the priesthood away from Shem [as its progenitor], as it is said, 'And Melchizedek, king of Salem, brought out bread and wine; he was priest of God Most High. [And he blessed (Abraham) and said, "Blessed be Abram by God Most High, maker of heaven and earth, and blessed be God Most high who has delivered your enemies into your hand"]' [Gen. 14:18-19].

47

B. "Since he placed the blessing of Abraham before the blessing of the Omnipresent, Abraham said to him, 'Now does one place the blessing of the servant before the blessing of his master?'

C. "The Omnipresent removed [the priesthood] from Shem and handed it over to Abraham, as it is said, 'The Lord says to my lord, [Sit at my right hand.]' [Ps. 110:1]. And after that statement it is written, 'The Lord has sworn and will not change his mind, You are a priest forever after the matter of Melchizedek' [Ps. 110:4]. It is on account of the matter of Melchizedek.

D. "That is in line with the following verse of Scripture: 'He was priest of God Most High'" (Gen. 14:18).

3. A. R. Ishmael and R. Aqiba:

B. R. Ishmael said, "Abraham was high priest, as it is said, 'The Lord has sworn and will not change his mind. [You are a priest forever]' [Ps. 110:4].

C. "And it is written, 'And you will circumcise the flesh of your foreskin' [Gen. 17:11].

D. "Now where was he to make the mark of circumcision [since as we now see, it could apply to the ear, mouth, heart, and body equally, so far as biblical usage is concerned]?

E. "If he were to circumcise his ear, he would then not be fit to make an offering.

F. "If he were to circumcise his mouth, he would not be fit to make an offering.

G. "If he were to circumcise his heart, he would not be fit to make an offering.

H. "At what point, then, could he make the mark of circumcision and yet be [unblemished and thus] fit to make an offering? It could only be circumcision of the body [at the penis]."

I. R. Aqiba says, "There are four sorts of uncircumcision.

J. "'Uncircumcision' is stated with regard to the ear: 'And lo, their ears are uncircumcised' [Jer. 6:10].

K. "'Uncircumcision' is stated with regard to the mouth: 'And I am of uncircumcised lips' [Ex. 6:30].

L. "'Uncircumcision' is stated with regard to the heart: 'And all of the house of Israel are of uncircumcised heart' [Jer. 9:25].

M. "Yet it is written, 'Walk before me and be perfect [and unblemished]' [Gen. 17:1].

N. "Whence then could he be circumcised? If he should be circumcised at the ear, he would not be perfect.

O. "If he should be circumcised at the mouth, he should not be perfect.

P. "If he should be circumcised at the heart, he should not be perfect.

Q. "Where then could he be circumcised and be perfect?

R. "One must say, 'This refers to the circumcision of the body.'"

S. Nagra said, "It is written, '[Circumcise] at eight days of age' [Gen. 17:12].

T. "Where then should one place the mark of circumcision?

U. "If one circumcises at the ear, he will be unable to hear.

V. "If he did so at the mouth, he will be unable to speak.

W. "If he did so at the heart, he will be unable to think.

X. "Where should he be circumcised and remain able to hear, speak, and think?

Y. "It must follow that this refers to circumcision of the body."

Z. Said R. Tanhuma, What Nagra says is most reasonable.

4. A. "And the uncircumcised male who is not circumcised" (Gen. 17:14).

B. R. Yudan in the name of R. Isaac and, R. Berekhiah in the name of R. Isaac, and there is one who teaches it in the name of R. Yosé b. Halapta, "'And the uncircumcised male . . . ' [Gen. 17:14].

C. "Now is there such a thing as an uncircumcised female?

D. "But the point is that at the place which people examine to know whether one is male or female, there they make the mark of circumcision [on the male]."

XXV:VII

1. A. R. Levi bar Sisi gave the following exposition: "'And you were a whore with the sons of Egypt, your neighbors, large of flesh' [Ez. 16:26]. What does 'large of flesh' mean?

B. "Now did one have one leg and another three?"

C. "Rabbi said, 'They had large penises.'"

2. A. R. Berekhiah and R. Simon in the name of R. Samuel bar Nehemiah, "It is written, 'And [Joshua] circumcised the children of Israel at the Hill of Foreskins' [Josh. 5:3].

B. "What is the meaning of 'Hill of Foreskins?' That it was in the shape of a mountain made of foreskins."

XXV:VIII

1. A. "His legs are alabaster columns, [set upon bases of fine gold]" (Song of Songs 5:15).

B. "His legs" refer to the world.

C. "Alabaster columns (SS):" For [the world] rests on the six (SST) days of creation, for it is written, "For in six days did God create the world" (Ex. 20:11).

D. "Set upon bases of fine gold:" This refers to words of Torah, "which are more to be desired than fine gold" (Ps. 19:11).

2. A. Another interpretation: "Set upon bases of fine gold" refers to the sections of the Torah which are interpreted both in light of what precedes them and also in light of what follows them.

B. To what may they be compared?

C. R. Huna in the name of Bar Qappara said, "To a column that has a base on the bottom and a capitol on the top.

D. "So too are the sections of the Torah to be interpreted both in light of what precedes them and also in light of what follows them." [This proposition is now illustrated.]

3. A. "When you come into the land and plant all kinds of trees for food" (Lev. 19:23).

B.   And it is written [in the immediately preceding verses], "If a man
lies carnally with a woman [who is a slave] . . . " (Lev. 19:20-22).
C.   Now what has one matter got to do with the other?
D.   But [it is to teach] that one who weeds [and farms] with his fellow
gradually becomes part of the household. Since he comes and goes
in his house, he becomes suspect [of having sexual relations] with
his slave girl.
E.   He says, "Is it not a sin offering that I now owe, is it not a guilt
offering? I'll bring a sin offering, I'll bring a guilt offering."
F.   For R. Yudan in the name of R. Levi said, "Those who in this
world treat slave girls as though they are [sexually] permitted are
destined to hang by the scalp of their head in the world to come.
G.   "That is in line with the following verse of Scripture: 'But God
will shatter the heads of his enemies, the hair crown of him who
walks in his guilty ways'" (Ps. 68:21).
H.   What is the meaning of "walks in his guilty ways"?
I.   Everybody says, "Let that man go in his guilt, let that man go in
his guilt."
4. A.   Passages of the Torah also may be interpreted in light of what
follows them.
B.   For it is said, "For three years it shall be [as though] uncircumcised
for you" (Lev. 19:23).
C.   And it is written, "You shall not eat any flesh with the blood in it"
(Lev. 19:26).
D.   What has one thing got to do with the other?
E.   Said the Holy One, blessed be he, to Israel, "You are prepared to
wait for the uncircumcised fruit tree for three years; and for your
wife do you not wait, while she observes the period of her
menstruation?
F.   "For your uncircumcised tree you are prepared to wait for three
years; and for [meat of] your beast are you not prepared to wait
until the blood is fully drained from it?"
5. A.   And who observed the religious duty governing the blood?
B.   It was Saul, for it is said, "Then they told Saul, Behold the people
are sinning against the Lord [by eating with the blood. And he
said, You have dealt treacherously; roll a great stone to me here.]
And Saul said, Disperse yourselves among the people [and say to
them, Let every man bring his ox or his sheep] and slay them here;
[and eat, but do not sin against the Lord by eating with the blood]"
(1 Sam. 14:33-34).
C.   What is the meaning of "here (BZH)"? Rabbis say, "A knife fourteen
fingers long did he show them, B stands for two, Z for seven, H
for five, so he said to them, 'In this manner will you slaughter and
eat meat [with a knife of proper length].'"
D.   How did the Holy One, blessed be he, reward him?
E.   One has to say, it was on the day of battle.

F. That is in line with the following verse of Scripture: "So on the day of the battle there was neither [sword nor spear] found [in the hand of any of the people with Saul and Jonathan; but with Saul and Jonathan his son (weaponry) was found. And the garrison of the Philistines went out to the pass of Mickmash]" (1 Sam. 13:22).

G. First it says, "was not found," and then it says, "But . . . was found!" Who provided it to him?

H. R. Haggai in the name of R. Isaac said, "An angel provided him [with the needed weapons]."

I. And rabbis say, "The Holy One, blessed be he, provided him with the needed weapons."

6. A. It is written, "And Saul built an altar to the Lord; it was the first altar built to the Lord" (1 Sam. 14:35).

B. How many altars had the earlier ancients already built — Noah, Abraham, Isaac, Jacob, Moses, Joshua — and yet you say, "It was the first [altar]!"

C. Rabbis say, "That one was the first built by kings."

D. Said R. Yudan, "Because he was ready to give his life for this matter, Scripture treated it in his behalf as if he were the first one who built an altar to the Lord."

7. A. Said R. Simeon b. Yosé b. Laqoniah, "Now in this world, a person builds a building, and someone else uses it.

B. "A person may plant a tree, and someone else eats its fruit.

C. "But in the age to come: 'They shall not build and another inhabit, [they shall not plant and another eat] . . . They shall not work in vain' (Is 65:22-23).

D. "'And their seed shall be known among the nations'" (Is. 61:9).

DIETARY LAWS AND THEIR MEANING

LEVITICUS RABBAH XIII:III

1. A. "Every word of God is refined; he is a shield to those who take refuge in him" (Prov. 30:5).

B. Rab said, "The religious duties were handed over only to refine human beings through them."

C. Why so much [engagement]?

D. "He is a shield to those who take refuge in him" (Prov. 30:5) [and through the practice of religious duties gives people the opportunity to gain merit].

2. A. Said R. Yudan b. R. Simeon, "Behemoth and Leviathan will serve as the beasts of chase for the righteous in the world to come.

B. "And any person who has not come as a spectator to the wild-beast contests of the nations of the world in this age will enjoy the merit of witnessing them in the world to come.

C. "How will they be properly slaughtered [for Israelite consumption]? The Behemoth will hit the Leviathan with its horns and tear him,

and the Leviathan will hit the Behemoth with its fins and pierce
him.

D. "Then the righteous will say, 'Now is this a valid mode of
slaughter?' [Obviously not!]"

E. For have we not learned in the following passage of the Mishnah:
**"All persons are suitable to carry out an act of slaughter, and
with any sort of sharp instrument do they carry out the act of
slaughter, and at all times do they slaughter [a beast] — except
[when] a scythe, saw, or teeth [cut out of a dead animal are
used for slaughter], because they [cause pain through] choking"**
(M. Hul. 1:2).

F. Said R. Abba bar Kahana, "Said the Holy One, blessed be he,
'Torah comes forth from me' [Is. 51:4]. It is an innovation in the
law of the Torah that has come forth from me [that on an ad hoc
basis such a mode of slaughter will be valid, even though, in the
law overall, it is not]."

3. A. R. Berekhiah in the name of R. Isaac: "A great banquet will the
Holy One, blessed be he, prepare for his righteous servants in the
world to come, and everybody who did not eat carrion and meat
from torn beasts in this world will enjoy the merit of joining in the
banqueting in the world to come.

B. "That is in line with the following verse of Scripture: 'The fat of
an animal that dies of itself [carrion] and the fat of one that is torn
by beasts may be put to any other use, but on no account shall you
eat it' [Lev. 7:24], so that you may indeed eat of it in the world to
come.

C. "Accordingly, Moses admonished Israel, saying to them, 'These
are the living things which you may eat among all the beasts that
are on the earth'" (Lev. 11:2).

4. A. ["These are the living things which you may eat among all the
beasts that are on the earth" (Lev. 11:2)]. R. Hiyya taught, "[The
cited verse] teaches that Moses took a wild beast and showed it to
Israel and said to them, 'This beast you may eat, and that beast you
may not eat.'

B. "'These you may eat of all that are in the waters' [Lev. 11:9].

C. "'This you may eat and this you may not eat.'

D. "'And these you shall have in abomination among the birds, [they
shall not be eaten, they are an abomination]' [Lev. 11:13].

E. "These you shall treat as an abomination, and these you shall not
treat as an abomination.'

F. "'And these are unclean to you [among the swarming things that
swarm upon the earth]' [Lev. 11:29].

G. "'This one is unclean, and this one is not unclean.'

H. "'These are the living things which you may eat'" (Lev. 11:2).

XIII:IV

1. A. [Returning to] the body [of the matter: "This . . . you may eat"],
said R. Abbahu, "It was a kind of fiery skull that the Holy One,

blessed be he, showed to Moses. He said to him, 'If [during a slaughter] the membrane of the brain is perforated, in any measure at all, [the beast is] invalid[ly slaughtered and may not be eaten].'"

B. And Rabbis say, "'This is the living thing [which you may eat]' [Lev. 11:2].

C. "That beast which would survive even after being torn you may eat, and that beast which would not survive after being torn you may not eat."

2. A. Said R. Simeon b. Laqish, "If you have merit, you shall eat. If you do not have merit, you shall be eaten — by the kingdoms."

B. Said R. Aha, "It is written, 'If you are willing and obedient, you shall eat the good of the land; but if you refuse and rebel, you shall be devoured by the sword (HRB); [for the mouth of the Lord has spoken]' [Is. 1:19-20].

C. "You shall eat carobs (HRWB)."

D. For R. Aha said, "When a Jew has [to resort to eating] carobs, he carries out repentance.

E. "And as becoming is poverty for the Jews as a red ribbon on the chest of a white horse."

EXPOSITION OF THE MEANING OF THE TABOO-ANIMALS IN THE CONTEXT OF ISRAEL'S PARADIGM

XIII:V

1. A. Said R. Ishmael b. R. Nehemiah, "All the prophets foresaw what the pagan kingdoms would do [to Israel].

B. "The first man foresaw what the pagan kingdoms would do [to Israel].

C. "That is in line with the following verse of Scripture: 'A river flowed out of Eden [to water the garden, and there it divided and became four rivers]' [Gen. 2:10]. [The four rivers stand for the four kingdoms, Babylonia, Media, Greece, and Rome]."

2. A. R. Tanhuma said it, [and so did] R. Menahema [in the name of] R. Joshua b. Levi: "The Holy One, blessed be he, will give the cup of reeling to the nations of the world to drink in the world to come.

B. "That is in line with the following verse of Scripture: 'A river flowed out of Eden (YDN)' [Gen 2:10], the place from which justice [DYN] goes forth."

3. A. "[There it divided] and became four rivers" (Gen 2:10) — this refers to the four kingdoms.

B. "The name of the first is Pishon (PSWN); [it is the one which flows around the whole land of Havilah, where there is gold; and the gold of that land is good; Bdellium and onyx stone are there]" (Gen. 2:11-12).

C. This refers to Babylonia, on account [of the reference to Babylonia in the following verse:] "And their [the Babylonians'] horsemen spread themselves (PSW)" (Hab. 1:8).

D. [It is further] on account of [Nebuchadnezzar's being] a dwarf, shorter than ordinary men by a handbreadth.

E. "[It is the one which flows around the whole land of Havilah" (Gen. 2:11).

F. This [reference to the river's flowing around the whole land] speaks of Nebuchadnezzar, the wicked man, who came up and surrounded the entire Land of Israel, which places its hope in the Holy One, blessed be he.

G. That is in line with the following verse of Scripture: "Hope in God, for I shall again praise him" (Ps. 42:5).

H. "Where there is gold" (Gen. 2:11) — this refers to the words of Torah, "which are more to be desired than gold, more than much fine gold" (Ps. 19:11).

I. "And the gold of that land is good" (Gen. 2:12).

J. This teaches that there is no Torah like the Torah that is taught in the Land of Israel, and there is no wisdom like the wisdom that is taught in the Land of Israel.

K. "Bdellium and onyx stone are there" (Gen. 2:12) — Scripture, Mishnah, Talmud, and lore.

4. A. "The name of the second river is Gihon; [it is the one which flows around the whole land of Cush]" (Gen. 2:13).

B. This refers to Media, which produced Haman, that wicked man, who spit out venom like a serpent.

C. It is on account of the verse: "On your belly will you go" (Gen. 3:14).

D. "It is the one which flows around the whole land of Cush" (Gen. 2:13).

E. [We know that this refers to Media, because it is said:] "Who rules from India to Cush" (Est. 1:1).

5. A. "And the name of the third river is Tigris (HDQL), [which flows east of Assyria]" (Gen. 2:14).

B. This refers to Greece [Syria], which was sharp (HD) and frivolous (QL) in making its decrees, saying to Israel, "Write on the horn of an ox [= announce publicly] that you have no portion in the God of Israel."

C. "Which flows east (QDMT) of Assyria" (Gen. 2:14).

D. Said R. Huna, "In three aspects the kingdom of Greece was in advance (QDMH) of the present evil kingdom [Rome]: in respect to shipbuilding, the arrangement of camp vigils, and language."

E. Said R. Huna, "Any and every kingdom may be called 'Assyria' ('SR = powerful), on account of all of their making themselves powerful (MTSRYM) at Israel's expense."

F. Said R. Yosé b. R. Hanina, "Any and every kingdom may be called Nineveh (NNWH), on account of their adorning (NWY) themselves at Israel's expense."

G. Said R. Yosé b. R. Hanina, "Any and every kingdom may be called Egypt (MSRYM), on account of their oppressing (MSYRYM) Israel."

6. A. "And the fourth river is the Euphrates (PRT)" (Gen. 2:14).

B. This refers to Edom [Rome], since it was fruitful (PRT), and multiplied through the prayer of the elder [Isaac at Gen. 27:39].

C. Another interpretation: "It was because it was fruitful and multiplied, and so cramped his world."

D. Another explanation: Because it was fruitful and multiplied and cramped his son.

E. Another explanation: Because it was fruitful and multiplied and cramped his house.

F. Another explanation: "Parat" — because in the end, "I am going to exact a penalty (PR) from it."

G. That is in line with the following verse of Scripture: "I have trodden (PWRH) the winepress alone" (Is. 63:3).

7. A. (Gen. R. 42:2:) Abraham foresaw what the evil kingdoms would do [to Israel].

B. "[As the sun was going down,] a deep sleep fell on Abraham; [and lo, a dread and great darkness fell upon him]" (Gen. 15:12).

C. "Dread" (YMH) refers to Babylonia, on account of the statement, "Then Nebuchadnezzar was full of fury (HMH)" (Dan. 3:19).

D. "Darkness" refers to Media, which brought darkness to Israel through its decrees: "to destroy, to slay, and to wipe out all the Jews" (Est. 7:4).

E. "Great" refers to Greece.

F. Said R. Judah b. R. Simon, "The verse teaches that the kingdom of Greece set up one hundred twenty-seven governors, one hundred and twenty-seven hyparchs, and one hundred twenty-seven commanders."

G. And rabbis say, "They were sixty in each category."

H. R. Berekhiah and R. Hanan in support of this position taken by rabbis: "'Who led you through the great terrible wilderness, with its fiery serpents and scorpions [and thirsty ground where there was no water]' [Deut. 8:15].

I. "Just as the scorpion produces eggs by sixties, so the kingdom of Greece would set up its administration in groups of sixty."

J. "Fell on him" (Gen. 15:12).

K. This refers to Edom, on account of the following verse: "The earth quakes at the noise of their [Edom's] fall" (Jer. 49:21).

L. There are those who reverse matters.

M. "Fear" refers to Edom, on account of the following verse: "And this I saw, a fourth beast, fearful, and terrible" (Dan. 7:7).

N. "Darkness" refers to Greece, which brought gloom through its decrees. For they said to Israel, "Write on the horn of an ox that you have no portion in the God of Israel."

O. "Great" refers to Media, on account of the verse: "King Ahasuerus made Haman [the Median] great" (Est. 3:1).

P. "Fell on him" refers to Babylonia, on account of the following verse: "Fallen, fallen is Babylonia" (Is. 21:9).

8. A. Daniel foresaw what the evil kingdoms would do [to Israel].

B. "[Daniel said], I saw in my vision by night, and behold, the four winds of heaven were stirring up the great sea. And four great beasts came up out of the sea, [different from one another. The first was like a lion and had eagles' wings. Then as I looked, its wings were plucked off . . . And behold, another beast, a second one, like a bear . . . After this I looked, and lo, another, like a leopard . . . After this I saw in the night visions, and behold, a fourth beast, terrible and dreadful and exceedingly strong; and it had great iron teeth]" (Dan. 7:3-7).

C. If you enjoy sufficient merit, it will emerge from the sea, but if not, it will come out of the forest.

D. The animal that comes up from the sea is not violent, but the one that comes up out of the forest is violent.

E. Along these same lines: "The boar out of the wood ravages it" (Ps. 80:14).

F. If you enjoy sufficient merit, it will come from the river, and if not, from the forest.

G. The animal that comes up from the river is not violent, but the one that comes up out of the forest is violent.

H. "Different (SNYN) from one another" (Dan. 7:3).

I. Hating (SNN) one another.

J. This teaches that every nation that rules in the world hates Israel and reduces them to slavery.

K. "The first was like a lion [and had eagles' wings]" (Dan. 7:4).

L. This refers to Babylonia.

M. Jeremiah saw [Babylonia] as a lion. Then he went and saw it as an eagle.

N. He saw it as a lion: "A lion has come up from his thicket" (Jer. 4:7).

O. And [as an eagle:] "Behold, he shall come up and swoop down as the eagle" (Jer. 49:22).

P. [People] said to Daniel, "What do you see?"

Q. He said to them, "I see the face like that of a lion and wings like those of an eagle: 'The first was like a lion and had eagles' wings. Then, as I looked, its wings were plucked off, and it was lifted up from the ground [and made to stand upon two feet like a man and the heart of a man was given to it]'" (Dan. 7:4).

R. R. Eleazar and R. Ishmael b. R. Nehemiah:

S. R. Eleazar said, "While the entire lion was smitten, its heart was not smitten.

T. "That is in line with the following statement: 'And the heart of a man was given to it'" (Dan. 7:4).

U. And R. Ishmael b. R. Nehemiah said, "Even its heart was smitten, for it is written, 'Let his heart be changed from a man's'" (Dan. 4:17).

V. "And behold, another beast, a second one, like a bear. [It was raised up one side; it had three ribs in its mouth between its teeth, and it was told, Arise, devour much flesh]" (Dan. 7:5).

W. This refers to Media.

X. Said R. Yohanan, "It is like a bear."

Y. It is written, "Similar to a wolf" (DB); thus, "And a wolf was there."

Z. That is in accord with the view of R. Yohanan, for R. Yohanan said, "'Therefore a lion out of the forest [slays them]' [Jer. 5:6] — this refers to Babylonia.

AA. "'A wolf of the deserts spoils them' [Jer. 5:6] refers to Media.

BB. "'A leopard watches over their cities' [Jer. 5:6] refers to Greece.

CC. "'Whoever goes out from them will be savaged' [Jer. 5:6] refers to Edom.

DD. "Why so? 'Because their transgressions are many, and their backslidings still more'" (Jer. 5:6).

EE. "After this, I looked, and lo, another, like a leopard [with four wings of a bird on its back; and the beast had four heads; and dominion was given to it]" (Dan. 7:6).

FF. This [leopard (NMR)] refers to Greece, which persisted (MNMRT) impudently in making harsh decrees, saying to Israel, "Write on the horn of an ox that you have no share in the God of Israel."

GG. "After this I saw in the night visions, and behold, a fourth beast, terrible and dreadful and exceedingly strong; [and it had great iron teeth; it devoured and broke in pieces and stamped the residue with its feet. It was different from all the beasts that were before it; and it had ten horns]" (Dan. 7:7).

HH. This refers to Edom [Rome].

II. Daniel saw the first three visions on one night, and this one he saw on another night. Now why was that the case?

JJ. R. Yohanan and R. Simeon b. Laqish:

KK. R. Yohanan said, "It is because the [terror caused by the fourth beast, that is, Rome] would be greater than [the terror caused by] the other three [together]."

LL. And R. Simeon b. Laqish said, "It outweighed them."

MM. R. Yohanan objected to R. Simeon b. Laqish, "'Prophesy, therefore, son of man, clap your hands [and let the sword come down twice; yea, thrice. The sword for those to be slain; it is the sword for the great slaughter, which encompasses them]' [Ez. 21:14-15]. [So the single sword of Rome weighs against the three others]."

NN. And how does R. Simeon b. Laqish interpret the same passage? He notes that [the threefold sword] is doubled (Ez. 21:14), [thus outweighs the three swords, equaling twice their strength].

9. A. Moses foresaw what the evil kingdoms would do [to Israel].

B. "The camel, rock badger, and hare" (Deut. 14:7). [Compare: "Nevertheless, among those that chew the cud or part the hoof, you shall not eat these: the camel, because it chews the cud but does not part the hoof, is unclean to you. The rock badger, because it chews the cud but does not part the hoof, is unclean to you. And the hare, because it chews the cud but does not part the hoof, is unclean to you, and the pig, because it parts the hoof and is cloven-footed, but does not chew the cud, is unclean to you" (Lev. 11:4-8).]

C. The camel (GML) refers to Babylonia, [in line with the following verse of Scripture: "O daughter of Babylonia, you who are to be devastated!] Happy will be he who requites (GML) you, with what you have done to us" (Ps. 147:8).

D. "The rock badger" (Deut. 14:7) — this refers to Media.

E. Rabbis and R. Judah b. R. Simon.

F. Rabbis say, "Just as the rock badger exhibits traits of uncleanness and traits of cleanness, so the kingdom of Media produced both a righteous man and a wicked one."

G. Said R. Judah b. R. Simon, "The last Darius was Esther's son. He was clean on his mother's side and unclean on his father's side."

H. "The hare" (Deut 14:7) — this refers to Greece. The mother of King Ptolemy was named "Hare" [in Greek: lagos].

I. "The pig" (Deut. 14:7) — this refers to Edom [Rome].

J. Moses made mention of the first three in a single verse and the final one in a verse by itself (Deut. 14:7, 8). Why so?

K. R. Yohanan and R. Simeon b. Laqish.

L. R. Yohanan said, "It is because [the pig] is equivalent to the other three."

M. And R. Simeon b. Laqish said, "It is because it outweighs them."

N. R. Yohanan objected to R. Simeon b. Laqish, "'Prophesy, therefore, son of man, clap your hands [and let the sword come down twice, yea thrice]'" (Ez. 21:14).

O. And how does R. Simeon b. Laqish interpret the same passage? He notes that [the threefold sword] is doubled (Ez. 21:14).

10. A. (Gen. R. 65:1:) R. Phineas and R. Hilqiah in the name of R. Simon: "Among all the prophets, only two of them revealed [the true evil of Rome], Assaf and Moses.

B. "Assaf said, 'The pig out of the wood ravages it' (Ps. 80:14).

C. "Moses said, 'And the pig, [because it parts the hoof and is cloven-footed but does not chew the cud]' [Lev. 11:7].

D. "Why is [Rome] compared to a pig?

E. "It is to teach you the following: Just as, when a pig crouches and produces its hooves, it is as if to say, 'See how I am clean [since I have a cloven hoof],' so this evil kingdom acts arrogantly, seizes by violence, and steals, and then gives the appearance of establishing a tribunal for justice."

F. There was the case of a ruler in Caesarea, who put thieves, adulterers, and sorcerers to death, while at the same time telling his counselor, "That same man [I] did all these three [crimes] on a single night."

11. A. Another interpretation: "The camel" (Lev. 11:4).

B. This refers to Babylonia.

C. "Because it chews the cud (MLH\GRH) [but does not part the hoof]" (Lev. 11:4).

D. For it brings forth praises [(MQLS) with its throat] of the Holy One, blessed be he. [The Hebrew words for "chew the cud" — bring up cud — are now understood to mean "give praise." GRH is connected with GRWN, throat, hence, "bring forth (sounds of praise through) the throat."]

E. R. Berekhiah and R. Helbo in the name of R. Ishmael b. R. Nahman: "Whatever [praise of God] David [in writing a psalm] treated singly [item by item], that wicked man [Nebuchadnezzar] lumped together in a single verse.

F. "'Now I, Nebuchadnezzar, praise and extol and honor the King of heaven, [for all his works are right and his ways are just, and those who walk in pride he is able to abase' [Dan. 4:37].

G. [Nebuchadnezzar said only the word], "'Praise' — [but David devoted the following entire Psalm to praise]: 'O Jerusalem, praise the Lord' [Ps. 147:12].

H. "'Extol' — 'I shall extol you, O Lord, for you have brought me low' [Ps. 30:2].

I. "'Honor the king of heaven' — 'The Lord reigns, let the peoples tremble! [He sits enthroned upon the cherubim, let the earth quake]' [Ps. 99:1].

J. "'For all his works are right' — 'For the sake of thy steadfast love and thy faithfulness' [Ps. 115:1].

K. "'And his ways are just' — 'He will judge the peoples with equity' [Ps. 96:10].

L. "'And those who walk in pride' — 'The Lord reigns, he is robed in majesty, [the Lord is robed, he is girded with strength]' [Ps. 93:1].

M. "'He is able to abase' — 'All the horns of the wicked he will cut off'" (Ps. 75:11).

N. "The rock badger" (Lev. 11:5) — this refers to Media.

O. "For it chews the cud" — for it gives praise to the Holy One, blessed be he: "Thus says Cyrus, king of Persia, 'All the kingdoms of the earth has the Lord, the God of the heaven, given me'" (Ezra 1:2).

P. "The hare" — this refers to Greece.

Q. "For it chews the cud" — for it gives praise to the Holy One, blessed be he.

R. Alexander the Macedonian, when he saw Simeon the Righteous, said, "Blessed be the God of Simeon the Righteous."

S. "The pig" (Lev. 11:7) — this refers to Edom.

T. "For it does not chew the cud" — for it does not give praise to the Holy One, blessed be he.

U. And it is not enough that it does not give praise, but it blasphemes and swears violently, saying, "Whom do I have in heaven, and with you I want nothing on earth" (Ps. 73:25).

12. A. Another interpretation [of GRH, cud, now with reference to GR, stranger:]

B. "The camel" (Lev. 11:4) — this refers to Babylonia.

C. "For it chews the cud" [now: brings up the stranger] — for it exalts righteous men: "And Daniel was in the gate of the [Babylonian] king" (Dan. 2:49).

D. "The rock badger" (Lev. 11:5) — this refers to Media.

E. "For it brings up the stranger" — for it exalts righteous men: "Mordecai sat at the gate of the king [of Media]" (Est. 2:19).

F. "The hare" (Lev. 11:6) — this refers to Greece.

G. "For it brings up the stranger" — for it exalts the righteous.

H. When Alexander of Macedonia, [a Greek,] saw Simeon the Righteous, he would rise up on his feet. They said to him, "Can't you see Jews [elsewhere], that you stand up before this Jew [and honor him]?"

I. He said to them, "When I go forth to battle, I see something like this man's visage, and I conquer."

J. "The pig" (Lev. 11:7) — this refers to Rome.

K. "But it does not bring up the stranger" — for it does not exalt the righteous.

L. And it is not enough that it does not exalt them, but it kills them.

M. That is in line with the following verse of Scripture: "I was angry with my people, I profaned my heritage; I gave them into your hand, [you showed them no mercy; on the aged you made your yoke exceedingly heavy]" (Is. 47:6).

N. This refers to R. Aqiba and his colleagues.

13. A. Another interpretation [now treating "bring up the cud" (GR) as "bring along in its train" (GRR)]:

B. "The camel" (Lev. 11:4) — this refers to Babylonia.

C. "Which brings along in its train" — for it brought along another kingdom after it.

D. "The rock badger" (Lev. 11:5) — this refers to Media.

E. "Which brings along in its train" — for it brought along another kingdom after it.

F. "The hare" (Lev. 11:6) — this refers to Greece.

G. "Which brings along in its train" — for it brought along another kingdom after it.

H. "The pig" (Lev. 11:7) — this refers to Rome.

I. "Which does not bring along in its train" — for it did not bring along another kingdom after it.

J. And why is it then called "pig" (HZYR)? For it restores (MHZRT) the crown to the one who truly should have it [namely, Israel, whose dominion will begin when the rule of Rome ends].

K. That is in line with the following verse of Scripture: "And saviors will come up on Mount Zion to judge the Mountain of Esau [Rome], and the kingdom will then belong to the Lord" (Ob. 1:21).

MAKING MATCHES FOR MARRIAGE

LEVITICUS RABBAH VIII:I

1. A. "The Lord said to Moses, 'This is the offering which Aaron and his sons shall offer [to the Lord on the day when he is anointed]'" (Lev. 6:13 [RSV: 6:19]).

   B. R. Levi bar Hita opened [discourse with the following verse:] "'For God is judge. This one he humbles, and that one he lifts up'" (Ps. 75:6).

2. A. A Roman lady asked R. Yosé b. Halputa, saying to him, "In how many days did the Holy One, blessed be he, create his world?"

   B. He said to her, "In six days, as it is written, 'For in six days the Lord made heaven and earth'" (Ex. 31:17).

   C. She said to him, "What's he been doing since then?"

   D. He said to her, "He's been sitting and making matches, assigning Mr. So-and-so's daughter to Mr. Such-and-such, the wife of Mr. So-and-so [deceased] to Mr. Such-and-such, the estate of Mr. So-and-so to Mr. Such-and-such."

   E. She said to him, "You know I have quite a number of slave boys and slave girls, and in a brief moment I can match them up too."

   F. He said to her, "If it's such an easy thing to you, it's a very hard thing before the Omnipresent, [as difficult] as splitting the Red Sea, as it is written, 'God brings bachelors to dwell in a home [with a wife]'" (Ps. 68:7).

   G. R. Yosé b. Halputa went along home. What did the lady do? She sent and called a thousand slave boys and a thousand slave girls and set them up in rows. She said to them, "X marry Y, and W marry Z." [In Aramaic:] In the morning they came to her. One had a broken head, another a blind eye, a third a broken hand, a fourth a broken foot, a fifth said, "I don't want this one," and a sixth said, "I don't want that man."

   H. She sent a message to him, "Your Torah indeed is praiseworthy."

   I. He replied to her, "Did I not tell you, if it is such an easy thing in your eyes, it is a very hard thing before the Omnipresent, [as difficult] as splitting the Red Sea, as it is written, 'God brings bachelors to dwell in a home [with a wife]';

   J. "'he brings out prisoners into prosperity (BKWSRWT)' [Ps. 68:7].

   K. "What is the meaning of the word for prosperity? Weeping and singing (BKW\SYRWT). These are weeping, and those are singing.

   L. "What does the Holy One, blessed be he? He brings them willy-nilly and matches them up."

   M. R. Berekhiah told the story in the following version: "R. Yosé b. Halputa answered the woman 'He sits and makes ladders, bringing this one down and raising that one up, lowering this one and exalting that one, as it is written, "For God is judge. This one he humbles, and that one he lifts up"'" (Ps. 75:6).

PROHIBITED MARRIAGES

LEVITICUS RABBAH XXXII:V

1. A. "A garden locked is my sister, my bride, a garden locked, a fountain sealed" (Song 4:12).

   B. [Regarding the sister as Israel, and the locked garden as evidence that Israelite women did not commit sexual relations with Egyptians], said R. Phineas, "'A garden locked' refers to the virgins. 'A garden locked' refers to women who had had sexual relations. 'A fountain sealed' refers to the males."

   C. It was taught in the name of R. Nathan, "'A garden locked, a garden locked' — these refer to two modes of sexual relations, frontwards, backwards."

2. A. Another interpretation: "A garden locked" (Song 4:12):

   B. R. Phineas in the name of R. Hiyya bar Abba: "Because the Israelites locked themselves up [and avoided] licentious sexual behavior with the Egyptians, they were redeemed from Egypt.

   C. "On that account was 'Your being sent forth' [lit.: Your shoots are an orchard of pomegranates, with all choicest fruits] [Song 4:13].

   D. "That interpretation is in line with the following: 'And it came to pass, when Pharaoh sent forth . . . ' [Ex. 13:17]. [The 'shoots' of Song 4:13 calls to mind the 'sending forth' of Pharaoh, and the Israelites were sent forth by virtue of the fact that they had protected the integrity of their 'shoots,' their offspring.]"

3. A. R. Huna in the name of R. Hiyya bar Abba: "Sarah went down to Egypt and fenced herself off from sexual licentiousness and all the other [Israelite] women were kept fenced off on account of the merit that she had attained.

   B. "Joseph went down to Egypt and fenced himself off from sexual licentiousness, and all the other [Israelite] men kept fenced off on account of the merit that he had attained."

   C. Said R. Hiyya bar Abba, "It was truly worthy that through the fence that kept people from licentious behavior, Israel should be redeemed."

4. A. R. Huna in the name of Bar Qappara: "It was on four counts that the Israelites were redeemed from Egypt:

   B. "Because they did not change their names [from Jewish to Egyptian ones], because they did not change their language, because they did not gossip, because they did not go beyond the bounds of sexual decency.

   C. "Because they did not change their names: Reuben and Simeon — whoever went down Reuben and Simeon came up bearing the same names.

   D. "They did not call Reuben, Rufus, Judah, Julian, Joseph, Justus, or Benjamin, Alexander.

   E. "Because they did not change their language: Elsewhere it is written, 'And a refugee came and told Abram the Hebrew' [Gen.

14:13]. Here it is written, 'The God of the Hebrews has met with us' [Ex. 3:18].

F. "And it is written, 'For my mouth it is that speaks with you' [Gen. 45:12]. That was in the holy language.

G   "Because they did not gossip: For it is written, 'Speak into the ears of the people [and let them ask . . . jewels or silver from their neighbors]' [Ex. 11:2]. Now you find that this matter [of taking away the wealth of Egypt] had been set in trust with them for twelve months [prior to the actual exodus], but not a single one of them turned out to have revealed the secret, and not a single one of them squealed on his fellow [Jews].

H. "Because they did not go beyond the bounds of sexual decency: You may find evidence that that was the case, for there was only a single [Israelite] woman who actually did so, and Scripture explicitly identified her: 'And the name of his mother was Shulamit, daughter of Dibri, of the tribe of Dan' [Lev. 24:11]. [So she was the only one who bore a child to an Egyptian man.]"

5. A. "Shulamit" (Lev. 24:11).

B. R. Levi said, "It was because she went around chattering, 'Peace (SLM) to you! Peace to you! Peace to you!'"

C. "Daughter of Dibri" (Lev. 24:11).

D. R. Isaac said, "It was because she brought disaster (DBR) on her son."

E. "Of the tribe of Dan" (Lev. 24:11).

F. It was a disgrace to him, a disgrace to his mother, a disgrace to his family, a disgrace to his tribe, from which he came forth.

XXXII:VI

1. A. Said R. Simeon b. Laqish, "[Though called by the same name or title,] some are named and [blessed 'may he] rest in peace'], others are named [and cursed 'may his bones] rot.'

B. "Named and blessed: 'Behold, I have called by name Bezalel, son of Uri, son of Hur, of the tribe of Judah' [Ex. 31:2].

C. "Named and cursed: 'Achan, son of Karmi, son of Zabdi, son of Zarhi, of the tribe of Judah' [Josh. 7:1].

D. "Named and blessed: 'Now there was a certain man of Ramathaim-zophim of the hill country of Ephraim' [1 Sam. 1:1].

E. "Remembered and cursed: 'Now there was a man of the hill country of Ephraim, whose name was Micah' [Jud. 17:1].

F. "Remembered and blessed: 'Remember the children of Levi' [Num. 3:15].

G   "Remembered and cursed: 'I remember what Amalek did' [1 Sam. 15:2].

H. "Remembered and blessed: 'Remember what the Lord your God did to Miriam' [Deut. 24:9].

I. "Remembered and cursed: 'Remember what Amalek did to you' [Deut. 25:17].

J.   "Remembered and blessed: 'And David was the son of an Ephraimite man' [1 Sam. 17:12].

K.   "Remembered and cursed: 'Jeroboam son of Nabat, the Ephraimite' [1 Kgs. 11:26].

L.   "Remembered and blessed: 'There was a Jewish man in Susa, the capital [. . . Mordecai]' [Est. 2:5].

M.   "Remembered and cursed: 'A man, an adversary, and an enemy . . . [Haman]' [Est. 7:6].

N.   "Remembered and blessed: 'For Mordecai, the Jew . . . ' [Est. 10:3].

O.   "Remembered and cursed: 'For Haman, son of Hammedatha the Amalekite' [Est. 9:24].

P.   "Remembered and blessed: 'And with him was Oholiab, son of Ahisamach, of the tribe of Dan' [Ex. 38:23].

Q.   "Remembered and cursed: 'And the name of his mother was Shulamit, daughter of Dibri, of the tribe of Dan'" (Lev. 24:11).

2. A.   Rab said, "Under no circumstances does a mamzer live more than thirty days."

B.   Said R. Hunia, "Once every sixty or seventy years, the Holy One, blessed be he, brings a great pestilence over the world and wipes out the mamzers, but he takes the people of valid pedigree with them [Y. Yeb. 8:3.V.M.:] [so as not to publicize the sins of the sinners]. What is the Scriptural proof for that statement? 'Yet he also is wise and brings evil' [Is. 31:2].

C.   "Now it was hardly necessary for the verse of Scripture to say more than, 'He brings good.' [Why then does it add that God is wise?] It is to teach you that even the evil that he brings to the world is brought through [his] wisdom."

D.   "'And his word (DBR) he does not call back' [Is. 31:2]. He does not call back his pestilence (DBR).

E.   "Why so? 'He will rise against the house of evildoers and against the court of those that do evil'" (Is. 31:2).

F.   That [statement above, that God wipes out valid and invalid folk alike, so as not to publicize the sin of the sinners], accords with what R. Simeon b. Laqish said, "'In the place in which the burnt offering is killed shall the sin offering be killed, before the Lord' (Lev. 6:25).

G.   "Why so? This is so as not to publicize the sins [of the sinners]."

XXXII:VII

1. A.   When R. Zeira came up here, he heard people saying, "Mamzer boy" and "Mamzer girl." He said to them, "[Why is this? Lo, note] that which R. Huna stated, 'A mamzer does not live more than thirty days.'"

B.   Said to him R. Jacob bar Aha, "I was with you when R. Ba and R. Huna in the name of Rab stated, 'A mamzer does not live more than thirty days. Under what circumstances? When the matter is not known. But if the matter is known, he may live [a good long life].'"

2. A. That accords with what happened in the time of R. Berekhiah. A Babylonian came up here, and it was known of him that he was a mamzer. He came to him. He said to him, "Rabbi, give me [charity]."

B. R. Berekhiah said to him, "Go, but tomorrow appear in the congregation, and I shall publicly provide you something from the community chest."

C. The next day he came to him and found him in session expounding lessons in the synagogue. He waited until he finished. When he had finished his exposition, he came to him. Then R. Berekhiah said to them, "Brethren, provide for this one, who is a mamzer." They allotted him [what he needed].

D. When the congregation had gone out, he said to him, "Rabbi, I asked you for sustenance for this life, and you have cut off the life of that man [me]."

E. He said to him, "By your life! I have given you life. For R. Ba in the name of R. Huna in the name of Rab stated, 'A mamzer lives only thirty days. Under what circumstances? When the matter is not known. But if the matter is public, he lives a good long life.'"

3. A. R. Meir and R. Yosé:

B. R. Meir says, "Mamzers will never be clean in the world to come. What is the proof text? 'A mongrel people [mamzer] shall dwell in Ashdod' [Zech. 9:6]. They bring mud to a muddy place and thorns to thorns."

C. R. Yosé said, "They will be clean in the world to come. Lo, Scripture says, 'I will sprinkle clean water upon you, and you shall be clean' [Ez. 36:25].

D. Said to him R. Meir, "Lo, it says, 'And you shall be clean from [some of] all your uncleannesses, and from all your idols I will cleanse you'" (Ez. 36:25).

E. Said to him R. Yosé, "Rabbi, if Scripture had said, ' . . . all your uncleannesses and from all your idols,' and then nothing more, I should have ruled in accord with your view. When Scripture says, 'I shall clean you,' it means, even from the mamzers."

F. Said R. Huna, "If the law is not in accord with R. Yosé, generations to come will be destitute."

XXXII:VIII

1. A. "But I returned and considered all the oppressions [that are practiced under the sun. And behold, the tears of the oppressed, and they had no one to comfort them]" (Qoh. 4:1).

B. Hanina the tailor interpreted the cited verse to speak of mamzers: "'But I returned and considered all the oppressions' — this refers to mamzers.

C.   "'And behold, the tears of the oppressed' — the mothers of these people committed a transgression, and as a result [people] put these [poor folk] away.

D.   "The father of this one had sexual relations with a woman of prohibited pedigree. But what did this one do? And what does it matter to this one?

E.   "'And they had no one to comfort them.' Rather: 'On the side of their oppressors there was power' [Qoh. 4:1].

F.   "This refers to Israel's great Sanhedrin, which comes against [mamzers] with the power of the Torah and puts [mamzers] away, on the count of the following verse: 'A mamzer shall not enter the congregation of the Lord' [Deut. 23:3].

G.   "'And they had no one to comfort them.' Said the Holy One, blessed be he, 'It is my task to comfort them.'

H.   "For in this world, there may be dross, but in the world to come, said Zechariah, 'I have seen them all gold, [that is,] pure gold.'"

2. A.   "And he said to me, 'What do you see,' and I said, 'I see, and behold, a wholly golden candelabrum, with a bowl [guleh] on top of it'" (Zech. 4:2).

B.   What is the meaning of the phrase, "And a guleh on top of it"?

C.   Two Amoras: One of them said, "[Guleh, to be read as] golah, exile."

D.   The other said, "Goalah, meaning, redeemer."

E.   In the view of the one who said that it is to be read, golah, exile, the Israelites were exiled to Babylonia, and the Presence of God went into exile with them [at their head]. That is in line with the following verse: "On your account I have been sent to Babylonia" (Is. 43:14).

F.   The one who said that it is to be read goalah, meaning redeemer, or savior, [cites the following verse]: "Our Redeemer, the Lord of hosts is his name" (Is. 47:4).

G.   "The breaker is gone up [before them, they have broken forth and passed on, by the gate, and are gone out from it; and their king passed on before them, and the Lord at the head of them]" (Mic. 2:13). [The operative phrase is at the end, "The Lord is at the head of them."]

PROVIDING FOR THE FUTURE

LEVITICUS RABBAH XXV:III

2. A.   Hadrian (may his bones be ground up) was walking through the paths of Tiberias. He saw an old man standing and digging holes to plant trees. He said to him, "Old man, old man, if you got up early [to do the work, when you were young], you would not have stayed late [to plant in your old age]."

B. He said to him, "I got up early [and worked in my youth] and I stayed late [working in my old age], and whatever pleases the Master of heaven, let him do."

C. He said to him, "By your life, old man! How old are you today?"

D. He said to him, "I am a hundred years old."

E. He said to him, "Now you are a hundred years old, and you are standing and digging holes to plant trees! Do you honestly think that you're going to eat the fruit of those trees?"

F. He said to him, "If I have the merit, I shall eat it. But if not, well, just as my forefathers labored for me, so I labor for my children."

G. He said to him, "By your life! If you have the merit of eating of the fruit of these trees, be sure to let me know about it."

H. After some time the trees produced figs. The man said, "Lo, the time has come to tell the king."

I. What did he do? He filled a basket with figs and went up and stood at the gate of the palace.

J. [The guards] said to him, "What is your business here?"

K. He said, "To come before the king."

L. When he had gone in, he said to him, "What are you doing here?"

M. He said to him, "I am the old man you met. I was the one who was digging holes to plant trees, and you said to me, 'If you have the merit of eating the fruit of those trees, be sure to let me know.' Now I in fact did have the merit, and I ate of their fruit, and these figs here are the fruit of those trees."

N. Then said Hadrian, "I order you to bring a chair of gold for him to sit on.

O. "I order you to empty this basket of his and fill it with golden denars."

P. His servants said to him, "Are you going to pay so much respect to that old Jew?"

Q. He said to him, "His Creator honors him, and should I not honor him?"

R. The wife of the neighbor [of that man] was wicked. She said to her husband, "Son of darkness, see how the king loves figs and trades them for golden denars."

S. What did [the man] do? He filled a sack with figs and went and stood before the palace.

T. They said to him, "What is your business here?"

U. He said to them, "I heard that the king loves figs and trades them for golden denars."

V. They went and told the king, "There is an old man standing at the gate of the palace carrying a sackful of figs. When we asked him, 'What are you doing here,' he told us, 'I heard that the king loves figs and trades them for golden denars.'"

W. [The king] said, "I order you to set him up before the gate of the palace. Whoever goes in and out is to throw [a fig] in his face."

X.   Toward evening they freed him and he went home. He said to his
     wife, "For all the honor [that I got], I owe you!"
Y.   She said, "Go and boast to your mother that they were figs and not
     etrogs, that they were soft and not hard!"

SEXUAL TRANSGRESSION

LEVITICUS RABBAH **XXIII:X**

1. A.   There are three who fled from committing a transgression, and the
        Holy One, blessed be he, joined his name to theirs.
   B.   And these are they: Joseph, Jael, and Palti.
   C.   How do we know it in the case of Joseph: "He appointed it in
        Jehoseph for a testimony" (Ps. 81:6).
   D.   What is the meaning of adding the h to the name of Joseph [hence,
        YH]? It means that the Lord [YH] himself gives testimony in his
        behalf that he never laid a hand on the wife of Potiphar.
   E.   How do we know it in the case of Jael? "And Jael went out to meet
        Sisera . . . and she covered him with a blanket [semikhah]" (Jud.
        4:18).
   F.   What is the meaning of the word, semikhah?
   G.   The rabbis here [in the land of Israel] say, "It means that she covered
        him with a scarf."
   H.   Rabbis from over there [in Babylonia] say, "It was with a cloak."
   I.   Said R. Simeon b. Laqish, "We have searched through the entire
        Scripture and found no object that is called a semikhah [SMY\KH].
        Then what is the meaning of the word? It is written with a shin,
        hence [SMY\KH], Shemi\koh: 'My name is here.'"
   J.   "'[Attaching] my name gives testimony concerning her that she
        did not lay a hand on that wicked man.'"
   K.   How do we know it in the case of Palti?
   L.   One verse of Scripture says, "And Saul gave Michal his daughter
        to Palti" (1 Sam. 25:44).
   M.   And another verse of Scripture says, "And Ishbosheth sent and
        took her from the man, from Paltiel" (2 Sam. 3:15).
   N.   [In one place] he is called Palti, and [in the other] Paltiel.
        [Accordingly, God's name was attached to his.] Who then took
        away the name Palti and handed over the name Paltiel?
   O.   It is God who gives testimony concerning him that he never laid a
        hand on David's wife."

XXIII:XI

1. A.   Said R. Yosé, "There are three who were overwhelmed by sexual
        desire, but who made an oath [to resist]: Joseph, David, and Boaz.
   B.   "How do we know it in the case of Joseph?
   C.   "'How shall I do such a great wickedness and sin against God'"
        (Gen 39:9).

D. R. Huna in the name of R. Idi: "This verse of Scripture does not say, 'And sin against the Lord,' but rather, ' . . . against God.' [The meaning is that] he imposed an oath on his passion, 'By God! I shall not sin and I shall not do this evil thing!'"

2. A. [Yosé continues:] "How do we know it in the case of David? 'But David said to Abishai, . . . As the Lord lives, the Lord will smite him . . . ' [1 Sam. 26:9-10]."

3. A. To whom did he take the oath?

B. R. Yohanan and R. Simeon b. Laqish:

C. R. Yohanan said, "He took the oath to his passion."

D. R. Simeon b. Laqish said, "He took the oath to Abishai:

E. "'As the Lord lives! If you touch him, I shall mix your blood with his.'

F. "That is in line with the following verse of Scripture: 'But David said to Abishai, Do not destroy him, [for who can put forth his hand against the Lord's anointed and be guiltless?']" (1 Sam. 26:9).

3. A. [Yosé continues:] "How do we know it in the case of Boaz?

B. "'As the Lord lives! Lie down until the morning'" (Ruth 3:13).

4. A. R. Yudan and R. Honia:

B. R. Yudan said, "For that entire night, his passion kept him in distress and enticed him with arguments, saying to him, 'You are unmarried, and she is unmarried, you are looking for a wife, and she is looking for a husband. Go and have sexual relations with her, and let her be acquired for you as a wife through an act of sexual relations.'

C. "He took an oath to his passion: 'As the Lord lives!'

D. "And to the woman he said, 'Lie down until the morning.'"

E. Said R. Honia, "'A wise man is strong (BWZ)' [Prov. 24:5]: A wise man was Boaz (BWZ).

F. "'A man of knowledge increases strength' [Prov. 24:5]: for he overcame his passion through an oath."

XXIII:XII

1. A. "The eye of the adulterer also waits for the twilight, [saying, 'No eye shall see me,' and he [God] who dwells in secret puts on a face]" (Job 24:15).

B. Said R. Simeon b. Laqish, "You should not say that [only one who] actually commits adultery is called an adulterer. But one who commits adultery merely with his eyes also is called an adulterer,

C. "as it is said, 'The eye of the adulterer waits for the twilight.'"

2. A. Now the adulterer sits and watches, [saying,] "When will twilight come, when will evening come?"

B. "In the twilight, in the evening of the day" (Prov. 7:9).

C. But he does not know that he who sits in the secret place of the world, the Holy One, blessed be he, so shapes the features of the embryo's face as to expose him [as the father of the child].

D. This is in line with what Job says, "'Does it seem good to you to oppress [and to despise the work of your hands and favor the designs of the wicked]?' [Job 10:3].

E. "This one [the woman's husband] supports and feeds [the wife], but [God] shapes the features of the embryo's face in the other man's likeness!

F. "'To despise the work of your hands' [Job 10:3]. Since you have labored all those forty days [to make the embryo] now will you go and spoil it?

G. "'And favor the designs of the wicked' [Job 10:3]. Is this appropriate to your dignity, to stand between the adulterer and adulteress?"

H. Said to him the Holy One, blessed be he, "Job, you really do owe me an apology. But will people say as you have said, 'Do you have eyes of flesh' [Job 10:4]?

I. "But," said the Holy One, blessed be he, "Lo, I shall so shape the features of the embryo's face in the other's likeness as to expose him [the adulterer, as the father of the child]."

3. A. Said R. Levi, "The matter may be compared to the case of an apprentice of a potter, who stole a lump of potter's clay, and his master found out about the theft.

B. "What did [the master] do?

C. "He went and made it into a utensil and left it before [the disciple].

D. "Why did he do this? To let him know that his master had detected the theft.

E. "So said the Holy One, blessed be he, 'Lo, I shall so shape the features of the embryo's face in his likeness as to expose [the adulterer as the father of the child].'"

4. A. R. Judah b. R. Simon in the name of R. Levi b. Parta: "It is written, 'The Rock that formed you have you weakened (teshi)' [Deut. 32:18].

B. "You have exhausted (hittastem) the strength of the Creator.

C. "The matter may be compared to an artist who was sitting and drawing the features of the king.

D. "Just as he was finishing his drawing, they came and told him, 'The king has been changed.'

E. "Forthwith the artist's hands trembled. He said, 'Whose [picture] shall we make, the one of the former or the one of the new [king]?'

F. "So too for all forty days the Holy One, blessed be he, is engaged in shaping the embryo. At the end of the forty days the mother goes and plays around with someone else. Forthwith: 'The hands of the Creator tremble. He says, 'Whose [likeness] shall we make, the one of the former or the one of the new [father]?'

G. "This is an example of the statement, 'The Rock that formed you have you weakened.' You have exhausted the strength of the Creator."

H. In the word teshi (TSY) the Y is written smaller than the other letters. [There is no similar instance in Scripture.]

5. A. Said R. Isaac, "We find that in the case of all those who commit transgression, the thief benefits, and the victim loses, the robber benefits, and the victim loses.

B. "But here both of them benefit!

C. "Who then is the victim? It is as if it were the Holy One, blessed be he, who [has to] destroy the marks of identification [that he has already given to the embryo]."

XXIII:XIII

1. A. R. Miasha, grandson of R. Joshua b. Levi, said, "We find that whoever sees [a woman's] private parts and does not feast his eyes on them acquires sufficient merit to receive the face of the Presence of God.

B. "What is the Scriptural proof of that proposition?

C. "'He who shuts his eyes from looking upon evil' [Is. 33:15]. What is written immediately afterward? 'Your eyes will see the king in his beauty'" (Is. 33:17).

8

Ruth Rabbah

PROPER CONDUCT OF ISRAELITE WOMEN

RUTH RABBAH XX:I

1. A. "But Ruth said, 'Entreat me not to leave you or to return from following you'":
   B. What is the meaning of "entreat me not to leave you"?
   C. This is what she said to her, "Do not sin against me. Do not take your troubles from me." [The words for "entreat" and "troubles" share the same consonants.]
2. A. "...to leave you or to return from following you, for where you go I will go, and where you lodge I will lodge; your people shall be my people, and your God my God":
   B. "Under all circumstances I intend to convert, but it is better that it be through your action and not through that of another."
3. A. When Naomi heard her say this, she began laying out for her the laws that govern proselytes.
   B. She said to her, "My daughter, it is not the way of Israelite women to go to theaters and circuses put on by idolators."
   C. She said to her, "Where you go I will go."
   D. She said to her, "My daughter, it is not the way of Israelite women to live in a house that lacks a mezuzah."
   E. She said to her, "Where you lodge I will lodge."
   F. "...your people shall be my people":
   G. This refers to the penalties and admonitions against sinning.
   H. "...and your God my God":
   I. This refers to the other religious duties.
4. A. Another interpretation of the statement, "for where you go I will go":

B.   to the tent of meeting, Gilgal, Shiloh, Nob, Gibeon, and the eternal
     house.
C.   "...and where you lodge I will lodge":
D.   "I shall spend the night concerned about the offerings."
E.   "...your people shall be my people":
F.   "so nullifying my idol."
G.   "...and your God my God":
H.   "to pay a full recompense for my action."

9

Pesiqta deRab Kahana

CHILDLESSNESS

PESIQTA DERAB KAHANA XXII:I

3. A. For we have learned in the Mishnah:

   B. **If one has married a woman and lived with her for ten years and not produced a child, he is not allowed to remain sterile [but must marry someone else]. If he has divorced her, he is permitted to marry another. The second is permitted to remain wed with her for ten years. If she had a miscarriage, one counts from the time of the miscarriage. The man bears the religious duty of engaging in procreation but the woman does not. R. Yohanan b. Beroqah says, "The religious duty pertains to them both, for it is said, *And God blessed them* (Gen. 1:28)" [M. Yeb. 15:6].**

4. A. There was a case in Sidon of one who married a woman and remained with her for ten years while she did not give birth.

   B. They came to R. Simeon b. Yohai to arrange for the divorce. He said to her, "Any thing which I have in my house take and now go, return to your father's household."

   C. Said to them R. Simeon b. Yohai, "Just as when you got married, it was in eating and drinking, so you may not separate from one another without eating and drinking."

   D. What did the woman do? She made a splendid meal and gave the husband too much to drink and then gave a sign to her slave girl and said to her, "Bring him to my father's house."

   E. At midnight the man woke up. He said to them, "Where am I?"

   F. She said to him, "Did you not say to me, 'Any thing which I have in my house, take and now go, return to your father's household.' And that is how it is: I have nothing more precious than you."

G.   When R. Simeon b. Yohai heard this, he said a prayer for them,
     and they were visited [with a pregnancy].

H.   The Holy One, blessed be He, visits barren women, and the
     righteous have the same power.

I.   "And is it not an argument a fortiori: if in the case of a mortal, to
     whom rejoicing comes, the person rejoices and gives joy to
     everyone, when the Holy One, blessed be He, comes to give joy to
     Jerusalem, all the more so! And when Israel looks forward to the
     salvation of the Holy One, blessed be He, all the more so!

J.   *"I will greatly rejoice in the Lord, [my soul shall exult in my God;*
     for he has clothed me with the garments of salvation, he has covered
     me with the robe of righteousness, as a bridegroom decks himself
     with a garland, and as a bride adorns herself with her jewels. For
     as the earth brings forth its shoots, and as a garden causes what
     is sown in it to spring up, so the Lord God will cause righteousness
     and praise to spring forth before all the nations] (Isaiah 61:10-
     11)."

KEEPING THE COMMANDMENTS

PESIQTA DERAB KAHANA XII:I

1. A.   R. Judah bar Simon commenced discourse by citing the following
        verse: "Many daughters show how capable they are, but you excel
        them all. [Charm is a delusion and beauty fleeting; it is the God-
        fearing woman who is honored. Extol her for the fruit of her toil
        and let her labors bring her honor in the city gate] (Prov. 31:29-
        31):

   B.   "The first man was assigned six religious duties, and they are: not
        worshipping idols, not blaspheming, setting up courts of justice,
        not murdering, not practicing fornication, not stealing.

   C.   "And all of them derive from a single verse of Scripture: And the
        Lord God commanded the man, saying, 'You may freely eat of
        every tree of the garden, [but of the tree of the knowledge of good
        and evil you shall not eat, for in the day that you eat of it you shall
        die]' (Gen. 2:16).

   D.   "And the Lord God commanded the man, saying: this refers to
        idolatry, as it is said, For Ephraim was happy to walk after the
        command (Hos. 5:11).

   E.   "The Lord: this refers to blasphemy, as it is said, Whoever curses
        the name of the Lord will surely die (Lev. 24:16).

   F.   "God: this refers to setting up courts of justice, as it is said, God
        [in context, the judges] you shall not curse (Ex. 22:27).

   G.   "the man: this refers to murder, as it is said, He who sheds the
        blood of man by man his blood shall be shed (Gen. 9:6).

   H.   "saying: this refers to fornication, as it is said, Saying, will a man
        divorce his wife... (Jer. 3:1).

I.   "You may freely eat of every tree of the garden: this refers to the prohibition of stealing, as you say, but of the tree of the knowledge of good and evil you shall not eat.

J.   "Noah was commanded, in addition, not to cut a limb from a living beast, as it is said, But as to meat with its soul – its blood you shall not eat (Gen. 9:4).

K.   "Abraham was commanded, in addition, concerning circumcision, as it is said, And as to you, my covenant you shall keep (Gen. 17:9).

L.   "Isaac was circumcised on the eighth day, as it is said, And Abraham circumcised Isaac, his son, on the eighth day (Gen. 21:4).

M.   "Jacob was commanded not to eat the sciatic nerve, as it is said, On that account the children of Israel will not eat the sciatic nerve (Gen. 32:33).

N.   "Judah was commanded concerning marrying the childless brother's widow, as it is said, And Judah said to Onen, Go to the wife of your childless brother and exercise the duties of a levir with her (Gen. 38:8).

O.   "But as to you, at Sinai you received six hundred thirteen religious duties, two hundred forty-eight religious duties of commission [acts to be done], three hundred sixty-five religious duties of omission [acts not to be done],

P.   "the former matching the two hundred forty-eight limbs that a human being has.

Q.   "Each limb says to a person, 'By your leave, with me do this religious duty.'

R.   "Three hundred sixty-five religious duties of omission [acts not to be done] matching the days of the solar calendar.

S.   "Each day says to a person, 'By your leave, on me do not carry out that transgression.'"

TORAH STUDY

PESIQTA DERAB KAHANA XV:V

4. A.   R. Huna, R. Jeremiah in the name of R. Hiyya bar Abba: "It is written, 'Me have they abandoned' (Jer. 16:11).

B.   "'Is it possible that they have kept my Torah? Would that they would abandon Me but keep my Torah.

C.   "For if they had abandoned Me but kept my Torah, then in the course of their study of the Torah, the yeast that is in it would have brought them back to Me.'"

5. A.   R. Huna said, "Study Torah even though it is not for its own sake,

B.   "for while you are studying Torah not for its own sake, since you are occupied with it, you will go and do it for its own sake."

6. A.   Said R. Joshua b. Levi, "Every day an echo comes forth from Mount Horeb and says, 'Woe for you, created beings [of the world], because of the disgrace that has come to the Torah.'"

7. A. Said R. Abba bar Kahana, "No philosophers in the world ever arose of the quality of Balaam ben Beor and Abnymos of Gadara. The nations of the world came to Abnymos of Gadara. They said to him, 'Do you maintain that we can make war against this nation?'

   B. "He said to them, 'Go and make the rounds of their synagogues and their study houses. So long as there are there children chirping out loud in their voices [and studying the Torah], then you cannot overcome them. If not, then you can conquer them, for so did their father promise them: 'The voice is Jacob's voice' (Gen. 27:22), meaning that when Jacob's voice chirps in synagogues and study houses, The hands are not the hands of Esau [so Esau has no power].

   C. "'So long as there are no children chirping out loud in their voices [and studying the Torah] in synagogues and study houses, The hands are the hands of Esau [so Esau has power].'"

8. A. Samuel said, "'The host was given over to it together with the continual burnt-offering through transgression' (Dan. 8:12).

   B. "It is through the transgression against the Torah.

   C. "So long as the Israelites toss words of the Torah to the earth, this wicked kingdom makes decrees and succeeds in carrying them out.

   D. "What verse of Scripture indicates it? 'And the truth is thrown to the ground' (Dan. 8:12).

   E. "And the word truth refers only to teachings of Torah, as it is said, 'Acquire truth and do not sell it' (Prov. 23:23)."

9. A. Said R. Judah bar Pazzi, "'Israel has cast off that which is good, the enemy shall pursue him' (Hos. 8:3).

   B. "The word good refers only to words of Torah, in line with this verse: 'I have given you a good doctrine, my Torah, do not forsake it' (Prov. 4:2).

   C. "And so Scripture says, 'As the stubble devours the tongue of fire [Hebrew text: As the tongue of fire devours stubble'] (Is. 5:24). Now does the stubble consume the fire? Is it not the way of fire to consume stubble, and yet you say, As the stubble devours the tongue of fire!

   D. "But in this case, the word stubble refers to the house of Esau, which is compared to stubble, as it is said, 'The house of Esau is for stubble' (Ob. 1:18).

   E. "And the tongue of fire refers to the house of Jacob, which is compared to fire, as it is said, 'The tongue the House of Jacob shall be a fire' (Ob. 1:18).

   F. "'And the house of Joseph shall be a flame' (Ob. 1:18):

   G. "And as the chaff is consumed in the flame (Is. 5:24) refers to the house of Joseph, which is compared to a flame in the following verse: 'And the house of Joseph shall be a flame' (Ob. 1:18).

   H. "'Their root shall be as rottenness' (Is. 5:24) refers to the patriarchs, who are the root of Israel.

I. "'And their blossom shall go up as dust' (Is. 5:24) refers to the tribes, who are the blossoms of Israel.

J. "On what account? 'Because they have rejected the Torah of the Lord of hosts' (Is. 5:24)."

10. A. Said R. Yudan, "Because they have rejected the Torah of the Lord of hosts (Is. 5:24) refers to the Torah that is in writing.

B. "'...and condemned the word of the Holy One of Israel' (Is. 5:24) refers to the Torah that is oral."

10

The Fathers According to Rabbi Nathan

How to Die

The Fathers According to R. Nathan

XXV:I.1 A. Ben Azzai says, "Whoever has a serene mind on account of his learning has a good omen for himself, and who does not have a serene mind on account of his learning has a bad omen for himself.

B. "Whoever has a serene mind on account of his impulse, has a good omen for himself, but if his mind is distressed because of his impulse, it is a bad sign for him.

C. "For him with whom the sages are satisfied at the hour of death it is a good sign, and for him with whom sages are not satisfied at the hour of death it is a bad sign.

D. "For whoever has his face turned upward [at death] it is a good sign, and for whoever has his face turned toward the bed it is a bad sign.

E. "If one is looking at people, it is a good sign, at the wall, a bad sign.

F. "If one's face is glistening, it is a good sign, glowering, a bad one."

XXV:II.1 A. At the time that Rabban Yohanan ben Zakkai was departing from this life, he raised up his voice and wept. His disciples said to him, "Lord, tall pillar, eternal light, mighty hammer, why are you weeping?"

B. He said to them, "Now am I going to appear before a mortal king, who, should he be angry with me, is angry only in this world, and if he should imprison me, imposes imprisonment only in this world, and if he should put me to death, imposes death only in this world, and not only so, but whom I can appease with words and bribe with money?

C. "Lo, I am going to appear before the King of kings of kings, the Holy One, blessed be he, who, should he be angry with me, is angry both in this world and in the world to come, whom I cannot appease with words or bribe with me.

D. "And furthermore, before me are two paths, one to the Garden of Eden, the other to Gehenna, and I do not know on which road, whether I shall be drawn down to Gehenna or whether I shall be brought into the Garden of Eden."

E. And in this regard it is said, "Before him shall be sentenced all those who go down to the dust, even he who cannot keep his soul alive" (Ps. 22:30).

XXV:III.1 A. [Ben Azzai] would say, "If one dies in a serene mind, it is a good omen from him, in derangement, it is a bad omen.

B. "...while speaking, it is a good omen, in silence, a bad omen.

C. "...in repeating words of the Torah, it is a good omen for him, in the midst of discussing business, it is a bad omen.

D. "...while doing a religious duty, it is a good omen, while involved with a trivial matter, it is a bad omen.

E. "...while happy, it is a good omen, while sad, a bad omen.

F. "...while laughing, a good omen, while weeping, a bad omen.

G. "...on the eve of the Sabbath, a good omen, at the end of the Sabbath, a bad omen.

H. "...on the eve of the Day of Atonement a bad omen, at the end of the Day of Atonement a good omen.

THE IMPULSE TO DO EVIL

THE FATHERS ACCORDING TO R. NATHAN

XVI:V. 1 A. R. Reuben b. Astrobuli says, "How can someone escape from the evil impulse in his guts, for the very first drop [of semen] that a man puts into a woman is the evil impulse.

B. "And the impulse to do evil is located only at the gates of the heart. For it is said, 'Sin couches at the door' (Gen. 4:7).

C. "It says to a person while still an infant in the cradle, 'Someone wants to kill you,' [and] the infant wants to pull out his hair.

D. "When an infant in the cradle puts its hand on a snake or a scorpion and gets bitten, is it not the impulse to do evil that is the cause?

E. "[If the infant] puts its hand on coals and is burned, is it not the evil impulse in his guts that is the cause?

F. "For the evil impulse is what drives him headlong.

G. "But come and see the case of a kid or a lamb: when it sees a well, it jumps backward, because there is no evil impulse in a beast.

XVI:V.2A. R. Simeon b. Eleazar says, "I shall draw a comparison, to what is the impulse to do evil to be likened? To iron that one tossed into the fire.

    B.   "So long as it is in the fire, people can shape it any way they want.

    C.   "So is the impulse to do evil: its remedy lies only in teachings of the Torah, which are like fire,

    D.   "For it is said, 'If your enemy is hungry, give him bread to eat, and if he is thirsty, give him water to drink, for you will heap coals of fire upon his head, and the lord will reward you' (Prov. 25:21f).

    E.   "In place of the letters that read will reward you, read will put him at peace with you."

XVI:V.3A.   R. Judah the Patriarch says, "I shall give you a parable. To what is the impulse to do evil to be compared? To the case of two men who went to an inn. One of them was arrested as a bandit. They said to him, 'Who is with you?'

    B.   "He could have said, 'No one is with me.'

    C.   "But he says, 'If I am going to be put to death, let my fellow be put to death with me.'

    D.   So it is with the impulse to do evil: 'Since I am going to perish in the world to come, so I shall make the entire body perish with me.'"

THE IMPULSE TO DO EVIL IS OLDER THAN THE IMPULSE TO DO GOOD

THE FATHERS ACCORDING TO RABBI NATHAN

XVI:III.1   A.   **Desire of bad things:** how so?

    B.   The impulse to do evil is thirteen years older than the impulse to do good.

    C.   From the mother's womb it grows and develops with a person.

    D   If one began to profane the Sabbath, it does not stop him. If he wanted to kill, it does not stop him. If he goes to commit a transgression [of a sexual character], it does not stop him.

    E.   After thirteen years the impulse to do good is born. When the man then violates the Sabbath, it says to him, "Empty head, lo, Scripture says, 'Those who profane it will surely die' (Ex. 31:11)."

    F.   When the man then kills, it says to him, "Empty head, lo, Scripture says, 'One who sheds man's blood by man his blood will be shed' (Gen. 9:6)."

    G   When he goes to commit a transgression, it says to him, "Empty head, lo, Scripture says, 'The adulterer and the adulteress will surely die' (Lev. 20:10)."

XVI:III.2   A.   When a man arouses himself and goes to commit fornication, all of his limbs obey him, because the impulse to do evil is king over the two hundred and forty-eight limbs.

    B.   But when he goes to carry out a religious duty, all his limbs begin to drag, because the impulse to do evil from the womb is king over the two hundred and forty-eight limbs that are in a man.'

    C.   The impulse to do good is only like one who is imprisoned, as it is said, "For out of prison he came forth to be king" (Qoh. 4:14), referring to the impulse to do good.

LOVING KINDNESS

THE FATHERS ACCORDING TO R. NATHAN

IV:V.1 A. ...on deeds of loving kindness: how so?

B. Lo, Scripture says," For I desire mercy and not sacrifice, [and the knowledge of God rather than burnt offerings]" (Hos. 6:6).

C. To begin with the world was created only on account of loving kindness.

D. For so it is said, "For I have said, the world is built with loving kindness, in the very heavens you establish your faithfulness" (Ps. 89:3).

IV:V.2 A. One time [after the destruction of the Temple] Rabban Yohanan ben Zakkai was going forth from Jerusalem, with R. Joshua following after him. He saw the house of the sanctuary lying in ruins.

B. R. Joshua said, "Woe is us for this place which lies in ruins, the place in which the sins of Israel used to come to atonement."

C. He said to him, "My son, do not be distressed. We have another mode of atonement, which is like [atonement through sacrifice], and what is that? It is deeds of loving kindness.

D. "For so it is said, 'For I desire mercy and not sacrifice, [and the knowledge of God rather than burnt offerings]' (Hos. 6:6)."

IV:V.3 A. So we find in the case of Daniel, that most desirable man, that he carried out deeds of loving kindness.

B. And what are the deeds of loving kindness that Daniel did?

C. If you say that he offering whole offerings and sacrifices, do people offer sacrifices in Babylonia?

D. And has it not in fact been said, "Take heed that you not offer your whole offerings in any place which you see but in the place which the Lord will select in the territory of one of the tribes. There you will offer up your whole offerings" (Deut. 12:13-14).

E. When then were the deeds of loving kindness that Daniel did?

F. He would adorn the bride and make her happy, join a cortege for the deceased, give a penny to a pauper, pray three times every day,

G. and his prayer was received with favor,

H. for it is said, "And when Daniel knew that the writing was signed, he went into his house — his windows were open in his upper chamber toward Jerusalem — and he kneeled upon his knees three times a day and prayed and gave thanks before his God as he did aforetime" (Dan. 6:11).

STUDY THE TORAH IN YOUTH

THE FATHERS ACCORDING TO R. NATHAN

XXIII:III.1 A. He used to say, "Do not treat anyone contemptuously, and do not regard anything as impossible,"

B.   as it is said, "Whoever despises the word shall suffer from it, but whoever fears the commandment shall be rewarded" (Prov. 13:13).

XXIII:IV.1   A.   He used to say, "He who studies the Torah in his youth — to what is he likened? To a calf subdued when young, as it is said, 'Ephraim is a heifer well broken, that loves to thresh'(Hos. 10:11).

B.   "But he who studies the Torah in his old age — to what is he likened? To a full-grown cow that has been subdued only in its old age, as it is said, 'For Israel is stubborn as a rebelling old beast' (Hos. 4:16)."

XXIII:IV.2   A.   He used to say, "He who studies the Torah in his youth is like a woman who kneads using hot water. And one who studies the Torah in his old age is like a woman who kneads using cold water."

XXIII:IV.3   A.   R. Eliezer b. Jacob says, "One who studies the Torah in his youth is like writing incised on clean paper. One who studied the Torah in his old age is like writing incised on used paper."

B.   Rabban Gamaliel adds to his statement: "He who studies the Torah in his youth is like a youngster who married a virgin who is suitable for him and he for her, and she is drawn to him and he to her.

C.   "He who studies the Torah in his old age is like an old man who married a virgin. She is suitable for him, but he is not suitable for her. She is drawn to him, but he is repelled from her,

D.   "as it is said, 'Like arrows in the hand of a hero are the children of one's youth' (Ps. 127:4), and immediately afterward: 'Happy is the man who has his quiver full of them, and they shall not be put to shame when they speak with their enemies in the gate' (Ps. 127:5)."

XXIII:IV.5   A.   R. Simeon b. Eleazar says, "He who studies the Torah in his youth is like a physician to whom people present a wound for which he has a scalpel for cutting and also drugs for healing.

B.   "He who studies the Torah in his old age is like a physician to whom people present a wound who has a scalpel for cutting but no drugs for healing.

C.   "So should the teachings of the Torah should be clearly distinguished for you from one another,

D.   "clearly distinguished for you beside one another.

E.   "For it is said, 'Bind them on your fingers, write them on the table of your heart' (Prov. 7:3), and also, 'Bind them continually upon your heart, tie them around your neck' (Prov. 6:21)."

STUDY THE TORAH IN YOUTH AND IN OLD AGE

THE FATHERS ACCORDING TO R. NATHAN

III:IV.1   A.   R. Dosa b. R. Yannai says, "If you went ahead and sowed seed during the early rains, again go and sow in the later rains, for it is entirely possible that a hail may come down and destroy the earlier crop, while the later crop [still in the ground and not yet sprouted] will survive.

B. "'For you do not know which will prosper, the one or the other, or perhaps both of them will survive, and they shall both turn out well' (Qoh. 11:6), as it is said, 'In the morning sow your seed and in the evening keep it up' (Qoh. 11:6).

C. "If you went ahead and sowed seed during the early rains and again during the later rains, again go and sow in the final rains, for a blight may descend and ruin the first crops, while the later ones may survive.

D. "'For you do not know which will prosper, the one or the other, or perhaps both of them will survive, and they shall both turn out well' (Qoh. 11:6), as it is said, 'In the morning sow your seed and in the evening keep it up' (Qoh. 11:6)."

III:IV.2A. R. Ishmael says, "If you have studied the Torah in your youth, do not conclude, 'I shall not study the Torah in my old age.' 'Study the Torah, For you do not know which will prosper, the one or the other.'

B. "If you have studied the Torah in a time of prosperity, do not let up in a time of need, if you have studied the Torah in a time of satisfaction, do not let up in a time of famine, if you have studied the Torah in a time of plenty, do not let up in a time of penury,

C. "for better for a person is one thing in distress than a hundred in ease.

D. "For it is said, 'In the morning sow your seed and in the evening keep it up' (Qoh. 11:6)."

III:IV.3A. R. Aqiba says, "If you have studied the Torah in your youth, do not conclude, 'I shall not study the Torah in my old age.' Study the Torah, 'For you do not know which will prosper, the one or the other, or perhaps both of them will survive, and they shall both turn out well' (Qoh. 11:6)

B. "And [If you have raised disciples in your youth, raise disciples in your old age also,] as it is said, 'In the morning sow your seed and in the evening keep it up' (Qoh. 11:6).

III:IV.4A. R. Meir says, "If you have studied the Torah with one master, do not say, 'That is enough,' but go to another sage and study the Torah.

B. "But do not go to just anyone, but rather, go to someone to whom to begin with you have an affinity.

C. "So it is said, 'Drink waters out of your own cistern and running water out of your own well' (Prov. 5:15)."

11

The Talmud of the Land of Israel

YERUSHALMI NEDARIM 3:9

[A] [If he said,] "Qonam if I derive benefit from the uncircumcised," he is permitted [to derive benefit] from uncircumcised Israelites, but prohibited [from deriving benefit] from circumcised gentiles.

[B] "Qonam if I derive benefit from the circumcised" — he is prohibited [to derive benefit] from uncircumcised Israelites and permitted [to derive benefit] from circumcised gentiles.

[C] For the word "uncircumcised" is used only as a name for gentiles, as it is written, "For all the nations are uncircumcised, and the whole house of Israel is uncircumcised at heart" (Jer. 9:26).

[D] And it says, "This uncircumcised Philistine" (1 Sam. 17:36).

[E] And it says, "Lest the daughters of the Philistines rejoice, lest the daughters of the uncircumcised triumph" (2 Sam. 1:20).

[F] R. Eleazar b. Azariah says, "The foreskin is disgusting, for evil men are shamed by reference to it, as it is written, 'For all the nations are uncircumcised.'"

[G] R. Ishmael says, "Great is circumcision, for thirteen covenants are made thereby."

[H] R. Yosé says, "Great is circumcision, since it overrides the prohibitions of the Sabbath, which is subject to strict rules."

[I] R. Joshua b. Qorha says, "Great is circumcision, for it was not suspended even for a moment for the sake of Moses, the righteous."

[J] R. Nehemiah says, "Great is circumcision, for it overrides the prohibition [against removing the marks of] nega'im."

[K] Rabbi says, "Great is circumcision, for, despite all the commands which Abraham our father carried out, he was called complete and whole only when he had circumcised himself as it is said, 'Walk before me and be perfect' (Gen. 17:1).

[L] "Another matter: Great is circumcision, for if it were not for that, the Holy One, blessed be he, would not have created his world, since it says, 'Thus says the Lord: But for my covenant day and night, I should not have set forth the ordinances of heaven and earth'" (Jer. 33:25).

[I:1 A] Said R. Yohanan bar Mareh, "It is written, 'On that day [38b] the Lord made a covenant with Abram, saying 'To your descendants I give this land, from the river of Egypt to the great river, the river Euphrates' (Gen. 15 :18); 'But I will establish my covenant with Isaac, [whom Sarah shall bear to you at this season next year]' (Gen. 18:21). There are thirteen covenants" [cf. M. 3:9G].

[I:2 A] "And on the eighth day the flesh of his foreskin shall be circumcised" (Lev. 12:3) — even on the Sabbath.

[B] How then am I to interpret: "[You shall keep the Sabbath, because it is holy for you;] every one who profanes it shall be put to death" (Ex. 31:14)? Even by reason of circumcision.

[C] How then am I to interpret:". . . on the eighth day the flesh of his foreskin shall be circumcised" (Lev. 12:3)? Except for the Sabbath.

[D] Scripture says,". . . on the day . . ." — even on the Sabbath.

[I:3 A] In the Torah, in the Prophetic Writings, and in the Writings, we find that the Sabbath is weighed in the balance opposite all of the other commandments in the Torah.

[B] In the Torah, as it is written, "[And the Lord said to Moses,] 'How long do you refuse to keep my commandments and my laws?'" (Ex. 16:28).

[C] And it is written, "See! The Lord has given you the Sabbath, [therefore on the sixth day he gives you bread for two days]" (Ex. 16:29).

[D] In the prophets, it is written: "But the House of Israel rebelled against me in the wilderness; they did not walk in my statutes [but rejected my ordinances, by whose observance man shall live;] and my Sabbaths they greatly profaned" (Ezek. 20 :13).

[E] In the Writings, as it is written, "Thou didst come down upon Mount Sinai, [and speak with them from heaven and give them right ordinances and true laws, good statutes and commandments,] and thou didst make known to them thy holy Sabbath" (Neh.9:13-14).

[F] Said R. Eleazar b. R. Abinah, "The word 'commandments' [of the Sabbath] is written out fully, to tell you that it is weighed in the balance against all of the other commandments of the Torah. Yet circumcision overrides [the requirements of the Sabbath]."

[G] One may compare the matter to two women who were standing on steps, one above the other, so that you do not know which of them is taller than the other. If this one appears to be coming down the steps before her friend, you know that her friend is taller than she.

[H] The most stringent of all of them is the commandment concerning the prohibition of idolatry: "But if you err, and do not observe all these commandments which the Lord has spoken to Moses, [. . . all the congregation shall offer one young bull for a burnt offering]" (Num. 15:22).

[I] Said R. Judah b. Pazzi, "The profanation of God's name is the most stringent of all of them."

[J] That is in line with that which is written, "As for you, O house of Israel, thus says the Lord God: Go serve every one of you his idols, now and hereafter, if you will not listen to me; but my holy name you shall no longer profane with your gifts and your idols" (Ezek. 21:39).

[I:4 A] Because Moses was slow in getting circumcised, the angel sought to kill him.

[B] That is in line with the following: "[At a lodging place on the way] the Lord met him and sought to kill him" (Ex. 4:24).

[C] Said R. Yosé, "Heaven forbid! Moses was not slow about getting circumcised. But [in Midian] he wondered to himself whether to fulfill his obligation and get circumcised, and so to undergo the danger, or to postpone it.

[D] "The Holy One, blessed be he, said to him, '[And the Lord said to Moses in Midian,] "Go back to Egypt; [for the men who were seeking your life are dead]' ' (Ex. 4:19).

[E] "But it was because he was slow on account of taking care of a lodging place before he undertook the circumcision [that the angel sought to kill him]."

[F] "That is in line with these words: 'At a lodging place on the way [the Lord met him and sought to kill him]'" (Ex. 4:24).

[G] And Rabban Simeon b. Gamaliel said, "Heaven forbid! The angel did not seek to kill Moses, but the child.

[H] "Come and see: Who was called, 'groom'? Moses or the baby?"

[I] *There are Tannaim who teach that* Moses was called the groom.

[J] *There are Tannaim who teach that* the child was called the groom.

[K] *He who said that* Moses was called the groom: "A bridegroom of blood" (Ex. 4:25) is sought from your hand.

[L] *And he who said that* the child was called the groom: "A bridegroom of blood" (Ex. 4:25) stands for me.

[M] "Then Zipporah took a flint and cut off her son's foreskin, and touched Moses' feet with it, and said, 'Surely you are a bridegroom of blood to me!'" (Ex. 4:25).

[N] R. Judah, R. Nehemiah, and rabbis:

[O] *One said,* "It was at the feet of Moses."

[P] *The next said,* "It was at the feet of the angel."

[Q] *The third said,* "It was at the feet of the child."

[R] *He who said that it was at the feet of Moses:* "There, that which is a sin for you has been cut away."

[S] *He who said it was at the feet of the angel:* "Lo, you have done your duty."

[T] *He who said it was at the feet of the child [maintains that]* she touched the body of the child. 7 I

U] "So he let him alone. Then it was that she said, 'You are a bridegroom of blood,' [because of the circumcision]" (Ex. 4:26).

[V] On the basis of this statement we learn that there are two acts of circumcision, one for the actual circumcision, the other for uncovering the corona, one for the act of circumcision, the other to remove the trimmings.

[I:5A] "And on the eighth day the flesh of his foreskin shall be circumcised" (Lev. 12:3) — even though there is a bright spot there.

[B] How then do I interpret the following: "Take heed, in an attack of leprosy, to be very careful to do according to all that the Levitical priests shall direct you'" (Deut. 24:8)?

[C] Even in the case of circumcision.

[D] How then shall I interpret: "And on the eighth day the flesh of his foreskin shall be circumcised"? When there is no bright spot.

[E] Scripture says,"... flesh ..." — even though there is a bright spot there.

[F] *In the view of R. Jonah,* who has said that a commandment to do a deed overrides a commandment not to do a deed, even though the latter is not stated alongside the former, this poses no problems.

[G] *But in the view of R. Yosé,* who has said, "A commandment to do a deed does not override a commandment not to do a deed unless the latter is stated right alongside the former, [how is this to be explained]?

[H] Since it is written, "The flesh of his foreskin," it is as if it were written right alongside.

RABBI'S DEATH AND HIS LAST WISHES. THE DEATH OF OTHER SAGES

YERUSHALMI KETUBOT 12:3

[I:2 A] When Rabbi lay dying, he gave instructions in three matters: "Let my widow not be moved from my house. Do not make a lamentation for me in the villages. He who took care of me while I was alive should take care of me after I have died."

[B] "My widow should not be moved from my house."

[C] [35a] *Is this not a Mishnaic teaching:* **A widow who said, "I don't want to move from my husband's house" [M. 12:3A].** [Why did Rabbi have to say so?]

[D] *Said R. Dosa, "It was so that they should not say to her, 'It is the palace of the patriarch and indentured to the patriarchate [Gamaliel, my son, who then may live here].'"*

[E] Said R. Eleazar b. Yosé, "It is in line with that which is taught: [In Tosefta's version:] **A woman whose husband has died dwells in the rooms [of her house] just as she did when her husband was alive. She makes use of the man slaves and woman slaves, of silver utensils and golden utensils, just as she made use of them when her husband was alive,** and she will be supported, just as she did when her husband was alive. **[For thus does he write for her, 'You will dwell in my house and enjoy support from my property so long as you spend your widowhood in my house']** [T. Ket. 11: 5]."

[F] "Do not make a lamentation for me in the villages": This is to prevent contention.

[G] "He who took care of me while I was alive should take care of me after I have died" Said R. Haninah of Sepphoris, "For example, Joseph of Ephrat, Yosé Hopni."

[H] R. Hezekiah added, "'Do not provide elaborate shrouds for me, and let my bier be open to the ground.'"

[I] *There is a saying implying that* Rabbi was buried in only a single wrapping.

[J] For Rabbi said, "It is not in the garb in which a man goes [to the grave] that he comes [from the grave, at the resurrection of the dead]."

[K] But rabbis say, "Just as a man goes to the grave does he come from it."

[L] *It has been taught in the name of R. Nathan,* "In the garment with which a man goes to the grave he comes up from it."

[M] *What is the scriptural basis for this statement?*

[N] "It is changed like clay under the seal, and it is dyed like a garment" (Job 38 :14).

[O] Antoninus asked Rabbi, "What is the meaning of the following verse of Scripture: 'It is changed like clay under the seal'" (Job 38 :14)?

[P]   He said to him, "He who will bring the generation [back to life] is the one who will clothe [it, at the resurrection of the dead]."

[I:3 A]   *R. Yohanan gave instructions, "Shroud me in scarlet, which is neither white nor black. If I end up among the righteous, I shall not be ashamed, and if I end up among the wicked, I shall not be ashamed."*

[B]   *R. Josiah gave instructions, "Shroud me in hemmed white shrouds."*

[C]   *They said to him, "Are you better than your master [Yohanan]?"*

[D]   *He said to them, "And should I be ashamed of the things I have done?"*

[E]   *R. Jeremiah gave instructions, "Shroud me in white shrouds. Dress me in my slippers, and put my sandals on my feet, and place my staff in my hand, and bury me by the side of a road. If the Messiah comes, I shall be ready."*

[I:4 A]   *The Sepphoreans said, "Whoever tells us that Rabbi has died shall we kill."*

[B]   *Bar Qappara approached them, with his head covered, and his clothing torn.* "The angels and the mortals have laid hold of the tablets, and the angels got the upper hand and have seized the tablets."

[C]   *They said to him, "Rabbi has died."*

[D]   *He said to them, "You have said so." Then they tore their clothes, and the noise of their tearing of their clothes reached Papa, three mils away.*

[E]   R. Nathan in the name of R. Mana: "There were miracles done that day. It was the eve of the Sabbath, and all the villagers assembled to make a lamentation for him. *They put down the bier eighteen times en route to burial to mourn him, and they accompanied him down to Bet Shearim. The daylight was protracted* until each one of them had reached his home [in time for the Sabbath] and had time to fill up a jug of water and light the Sabbath lamp. When the sun set, the cock crowed, *and the people began to be troubled, saying, 'Perhaps we have violated the Sabbath.'*

[F]   *"But an echo came to them,* 'Whoever did not refrain from participation in the lamentations for Rabbi may be given the good news that he is going to enjoy a portion in the world to come,

[G]   *"'except for the launderer [who used to come to Rabbi day by day, but did not bother to participate in his funeral].' When he heard this, he went up to the roof and threw himself down and died. Then an echo went forth and said, 'Even the laundryman [will enjoy the life of the world to come].'"*

[I:5 A]   *Rabbi lived in Sepphoris seventeen years and he cited the following verse in his own regard:* "And Jacob lived in the land of Egypt seventeen years; [so the days of Jacob, the years of his life, were a hundred and forty-seven years]" (Gen. 47: 28).

[B] Thus: And Judah lived in Sepphoris for seventeen years, *and of that time he spent thirteen years suffering from a toothache.*

[C] Said R. Yosé b. R. Bun, "During that entire period of thirteen years, a woman in labor never died in the land of Israel, nor was there ever a miscarriage in the land of Israel."

[D] *And why did he suffer from pain in the teeth?*

[E] *One time he was passing by and saw a calf being taken to the slaughter. It lowed in terror, but Rabbi said to her, "Go, for this is the purpose for which you were created."*

[F] *And in the end [when the pain was made to cease] how was he healed? They saw how they were killing a nest of mice, and he said to them, "Let them be. It is written, '[The Lord is good to all,] and his compassion is over all that he has made'"* (Ps. 145: 9).

[I:6 A] *Rabbi was very humble and he said, "Whatever anyone tells me to do shall I do, except for what the elders of Batera did in behalf of my forefather, for they gave up their position and appointed him in their place [the reference being to Bathyrans' giving way before Hillel and making him patriarch].*

[B] *"If the exilarch, R. Huna, should come here, I should seat him above me, because he comes from the tribe of Judah, while I come from the tribe of Benjamin, because he derives from the male line, and I from the female line."*

[C] *One time R. Hiyya the Elder came to him. He said to him, "Lo, R. Huna is here." Rabbi's face blanched. He said to him, "It is his bier."*

[D] *He said to him, "Go see who wants you outside." He went out and found no one there, and he knew that Rabbi was angry with him. R. Hiyya then did not go to see Rabbi for thirty days.*

[E] *Said R. Yosé b. R. Bun, "During those thirty days Rab learned from R. Hiyya all of the principles of the Torah."*

[F] *At the end of the thirteen years and thirty days, Elijah came to him [= to Rabbi] in the guise of R. Hiyya the Elder. He said to him, "How does my lord do?"*

[G] *He said to him, "I have a tooth which is painful to me."*

[H] *He said to him, "Show me."*

[I] *And he showed it to him. [Elijah] put his finger on the tooth and healed it.*

[J] *The next day R. Hiyya the Elder came to him. He said to him, "How does my lord do? As to your teeth, how are they doing?"*

[K] *He said to him, "From that moment at which you put your finger on it, it has been healed."*

[L] At that moment [Hiyya] said, "Woe for you, women in childbirth in the Land of Israel! Woe for you, pregnant women in the Land of Israel!"

[M] *[Hiyya] said, "It was not I [who healed you, but Elijah did it]."*

[N] *From that moment onward Rabbi began to pay respect to Hiyya.*

[O] *When he would come into the meetinghouse, he would say, "Let R. Hiyya the Elder go in before me."*

[P] Said to him R. Ishmael b. R. Yosé, "Even before me?"

[Q] He said to him, "Heaven forfend! But R. Hiyya the Elder is within, but R. Ishmael b. R. Yosé is innermost."

[R] *Rabbi was praising R. Hiyya the Elder in the presence of R. Ishmael b. R. Yosé. One time he saw him in the bathhouse and [Hiyya] did not rise to pay his respects [to Ishmael].*

[S] *Ishmael said to [Rabbi], "Is this the one whom you were praising to me?"*

[T] *He said to him, "What did he do to you?"*

[U] *He said to him, "I saw him in the bathhouse, and he did not rise to pay his respects to me."*

[V] *He said to [Hiyya], "Why did you behave in such a way?"*

[W] *He said to him, "May a terrible thing happen to me, if I even noticed him. I knew nothing about it. At that time I was reviewing the aggadic traditions of the whole book of Psalms."*

[X] *From that time [Rabbi] assigned to him two disciples to accompany him so that he would not get into trouble because of his concentration on his own thoughts.*

[I:7 A] *R. Yosa fasted eighty fasts in order to see R. Hiyya the Elder [in a dream]. He finally saw him, and his hands trembled and his eyes grew dim.*

[B] *Now if you say that R. Yosa was an unimportant man, [and so was unworthy of such a vision, that is not the case]. For a weaver came before R. Yohanan. He said to him, "I saw in my dream that the heaven fell, and one of your disciples was holding it up."*

[C] *He said to him, "Will you know him [when you see him]?"*

[D] *He said to him, "When I see him, I shall know him." Then all of his disciples passed before him, and he recognized R. Yosa.*

[E] *R. Simeon b. Laqish fasted three hundred fasts in order to have a vision of R. Hiyya the Elder, but he did not see him.*

[F] *Finally he began to be distressed about the matter. He said, "Did he labor in learning of Torah more than I?"*

[G] They said to him, "He brought Torah to the people of Israel to a greater extent than you have, *and not only so, but he even went into exile [to teach on a wider front]."*

[H] *He said to them, "And did I not go into exile too?"*

[I] *They said to him, "You went into exile only to learn, but he went into exile to teach others."*

[J] *When R. Huna, the exilarch, died, they brought his bones up here. They said, "If we are going to bury him properly, let us place him near R. Hiyya, because he comes from there."*

[K] *They said, "Who is worthy of placing him there?"*

[L] *Said to them R. Haggai, "I shall go up and place him there."*

[M] *They said to him, "You are looking for an excuse, for you are an old man, so you want to go up there and die and be buried there next to Hiyya."*

[N] *He said to them, "Tie a rope to my feet, [35b] and if I delay there too long you can drag me out."*

[O] *He went in and found three biers.*

[P] [He heard,] "Judah, my son, is after you, and no one else. Hezekiah, my son, is after you, and no one else. After you, Joseph, son of Israel, and no one else."

[Q] *He raised his eyes and looked. One said to him, "Lower your face."*

[R] *Said R. Hiyya the Elder, "Judah, my son, make room for R. Huna."*

[S] *He made a place for him, but [Huna] did not accept being buried [next to Hiyya the Elder, out of modesty]*

[T] *[They] said, "Just as [out of modesty] he did not accept being buried next to him, so may his seed never die out."*

[U] R. Haggai left that place at the age of eighty years, and they doubled the number of his years, [so that he lived another eighty years].

[I:8 A] It is written, ""You shall carry me out of Egypt and bury me in their burial ground" (Gen. 47:30): as to Jacob, wherever he was located [in death] — what loss would he sustain? [Granted that sinners benefit from burial in the Land of Israel, which atones for sin, since Jacob was entirely righteous, what difference did it make to him to be buried there rather than in Egypt (PM)]?

[B] R. Eleazar said, "There is something hidden here."

[C] Hanina said, "There is something hidden here."

[D] What is the meaning of "There is something hidden here"?

[E] R. Simeon b. Laqish said, "'I shall walk before the Lord in the lands of the living' (Ps. 116:9) — and is it not the fact that the lands of the living are only Tyre and Caesarea and their surroundings [so reference cannot be made to this world, since in this world life is most abundant in the cities that are named, and places like them]. There is everything, there is abundance."

[F] [Rather,] R. Simeon b. Laqish in the name of Bar Qappara [said], "It is the land where the dead will be the first to return to life in the time of the Messiah.. What is the scriptural foundation for that view? 'Thus says God, the Lord, who created the heaven and stretched them out, who spread forth the earth and what comes from it, who gives breath to the people upon it, and spirit to those who walk in it' (Is. 42:5)."

[G] If that is the case [that in the land of Israel the dead rise first,] then our masters who are located in Babylonia lose out!

[H] Said R. Simai, "The Holy One, blessed be he, opens the ground before them, and they roll to the land like leather bottles, and once they get their, their soul comes back to them."

[I] What is the Scriptural basis for that view?

[J]   "And I will place you on the land of Israel and I will put my spirit within you and you shall live" (Ez. 37:14).

[K]   R. Berekiah asked R. Helbo, R. Helbo asked R. Immi, R. Immi asked R. Eleazar, and R. Eleazar, R. Hanina; and there are those who say, R. Haninah asked R. Joshua, "And is that the case even of Jeroboam and his allies?"

[L]   He said to him, "'The whole land burned by sulfur and salt, unsown, and growing nothing, where no grass can spurt, an overthrow like that of Sodom and Gomorrah, Admah and Zeboiim, which the Lord overthrew in his anger and his wrath' (Dt. 29:22)."

[M]   Said R. Berekiah, "Even though everyone asked someone else, in the end we have not learned a thing on this question! What's the point of this verse? Since the land of Israel was burned, the attribute of justice was applied to them, in line with the verse, 'And he shall make a strong covenant with many for one week' (Dan. 9:27)." [They have suffered and atoned, and they too will rise from the dead.]

[N]   *It has been taught as a Tannaite statement in the name of R. Yudah,* "'For seven years sulfur and salt prevailed in the land of Israel. *That is in line with what is written,* 'And he shall make a firm covenant with many for one week" (Dan. 9:27).

[O]   As to the Samaritans that were in the land during this time — what did they do?

[P]   It was burned in strips, [and they lived in the strips that were not burning].

[Q]   It is written, "And you, Pashhur, and all who dwell in your house shall go into captivity, to Babylon you shall go and there you shall die and there you shall be buried" (Jer. 20:6).

[R]   R. Abba said R. Helbo, and R. Hama bar Hanina — one said, "If one died there and was buried there, he has two [sins against him,] and the other said, "If one died there and was buried here, he has only one." The other said, "Burial atones for their death there."

[S]   *R. Jonah in the name of R. Hama bar Hanina, "A man's feet are what bring him anywhere where he wants [to die],* as it is said, 'And the Lord said, Who will entice Ahab that he may go up and fall at Ramoth-Gilead?' [And one said one thing and another said another]'" (1 Kings 22: 20). But he died in his own house, not there."

[T]   *Elihoref and Ahaiah, two scribes of Solomon, saw the angel of death staring at them and grinding his teeth. Solomon said a word, and they were raised up into the air, and he went and took them from there. [The angel of death] came and laughed at Solomon. He received him. He said to him, "A while ago you were grinding your teeth, and now you are smiling!"*

[U]   *He said to him, "The All-merciful told me to take Elihoref and Ahaiah from the air, and I said, 'Who is going to put them there, from which place I have been sent to take them?' And he moved*

*you to do it for me. [It was your own deed, therefore] which made
it possible for me to carry out my mission, so I went and I took
care of them."*

[V] *As to the two sons of R. Reuben bar Istrobili, the disciples of R.
Hama, the angel of death laid eyes on them and was grinding his
teeth.*

[W] *He said, "Let us send them into exile into the south. Perhaps the
suffering of exile will atone for their sins and they will not be
taken."*

[X] *The angel of death went and took them from them.*

[I:9 A] *Ulla, who went down into exile, was dying there. He began to cry.
They said to him, "Why are you crying? Will we not bring your
body to be buried there?"*

[B] *He said to him, "And what good does it do me, if I lose my pearl
[my soul] in an unclean land? It is not the same when one sucks in
the bosom of one's mother as when he sucks in the bosom of an
alien woman."*

[I:10 A] *R. Meir lay dying in Asia. He said, "Tell the sons of the land of
Israel that your Messiah is coming [home, for burial]."*

[B] *And even so, he said to them, "Place my bier at the seashore, for
it is written,* 'He has founded it upon the seas, and established it
upon the rivers'" (Ps. 24: 2).

[C] Seven seas surround the land of Israel, the *Great Sea, the Sea of
Tiberias, the Sea of Kub, the Salt Sea, the Sea of Helath, the Sea of
Shilhath, the Sea of Apamaea.*

[D] And as to the Sea of Hamas, Diocletian stopped up rivers and
made it.

[E] It is written, "[And from Bamoth to the valley lying in the region
of Moab by the top of Pisgah,] which looks down upon the desert"
(Num. 21: 20).

[F] Said R. Hiyya bar Ba, "Whoever goes up to the Mountain of
Yeshimon overlooking the desert, and who saw a kind of small
sieve in the Sea of Tiberias — that is the well of Miriam."

[G] *Said R. Yohanan bar Marah, "The rabbis surveyed it, and lo, it is
directly opposite the center door of the ancient synagogue of the
town of Sarognin in the land of Israel."*

[I:11 A] *Rabbah bar Qaria and R. Eleazar were strolling in the road and
saw biers which were being brought from abroad to the land.*

[B] Said Rabbah bar Qaria to R. Eleazar, "What have these profited? I
recite concerning them, '[And I brought you into a plentiful land
to enjoy its fruits and its good things. But when you came in you
defiled my land,] and made my heritage an abomination' (Jer. 2:
7). That you did while you were alive, and will you come and
impart corpse uncleanness to my land now that you are dead?"

[C] He said to him, "Once they reach the land, they take a clump of ~4
dirt and place it on their bier, in accord with that which is written,

'[Praise his people, O you nations;] for he avenges the blood of
his servants, [and takes vengeance on his adversaries, and makes
expiation for the land of his people]'" (Deut. 32: 43).

PRECEDENCE OF MASTER OVER FATHER, MAN OVER WOMAN

YERUSHALMI HORAYOT 3:4

**[A] [When the priest faces a choice on tending to two or more
animals that have been designated as offerings, then:]
Whatever is offered more regularly than its fellow takes
precedence over its fellow, and whatever is more holy
than its fellow takes precedence over its fellow.**

**[B] [If] a bullock of an anointed priest and a bullock of the
congregation [M. 1:5] are standing [awaiting sacrifice]—**

**[C] the bullock of the anointed [high priest] takes precedence
over the bullock of the congregation in all rites pertaining
to it.**

**[D] The man takes precedence over the woman in the matter
of the saving of life and in the matter of returning lost
property [M. B.M. 2:11].**

**[E] But a woman takes precedence over a man in the matter
of [providing] clothing and redemption from captivity.**

**[F] When both of them are standing in danger of defilement,
the man takes precedence over the woman.**

[II:3A] The man takes precedence over the woman.

[B] Now that is the rule **if one had this one to save and that one to
save, this one to clothe and that one to clothe [M. Hor. 3:4D,
E].** [That is, when all things are equal, the man takes precedence
in the one instance, the one in the other.]

[C] Lo, if one had this one to restore to life and that one to clothe,
[what is the rule]?

[D] *Let us infer the rule from that which* R. Joshua b. Levi said in the
name of R. Antigonos: "[If there is a choice of] providing a garment
for the wife of an associate, and saving the life of an ordinary
person, the garment for the wife of the associate takes precedence
over saving the life of the ordinary person, on account of the honor
owing to the associate."

[E] Now the rule has been stated only with regard to providing a
garment for the wife of an associate in the lifetime of the associate.
But if it was a case of saving this one [48b] and clothing that one,
saving the live takes precedence.

**[F] [If one has the choice of retrieving] that which he has lost and
that which his father has lost, his own takes precedence. [If he
has a choice of retrieving] that which he has lost and that which
his master has lost, his own takes precedence. [If he has a choice**

of retrieving] that which his father has lost and that which his master has lost, that of his master takes precedence [over that of his father]. For his father has brought him into this world, but his master, who taught him wisdom, has brought him into the life of the world to come [M. B.M. 2:11A-H].

[G] [Now under discussion is] his master who taught him the Mishnah, not his master who taught him Scripture.

[H] Now if his father was the equal of his master, his father takes precedence.

[I] What is the difference favoring [the father]?

[J] "It is a case in which," said R. Yosé b. R. Bun, "half of his learning came from this one, and half of his learning came from that one[, so the father's having brought him into the world now registers]."

[K] [If it is a choice of retrieving] that which his father, from whom he had acquired half of his learning, has lost, and that which his mother, whom his father has divorced, has lost, who takes precedence?

[L] Is it the father who takes precedence?

[M] Or [do we give the father precedence] only when the whole of the man's learning has derived from the father?

[N] [If there is a choice of retrieving] that which his master has lost, from whom the man has derived half of his learning, and the object that his mother, the divorced wife of his father, has lost, which one takes precedence?

[O] Is it his master who takes precedence, or [do we say that that is the case] only when all of his learning has come from the master?

[P] [If it is a choice of retrieving] that which he *has* lost, that *which* his mother *has* lost, that which his father has lost, and that which his master has lost, that which he has lost takes precedence over that which his father has lost, that which his father has lost takes precedence over that which his mother has lost, and that which his mother has lost takes precedence over that which his master has lost.

[Q] *Now is this teaching not made explicit in the Mishnah:*

[R] **The man takes precedence over the woman in the matter of the saving of life and in the matter of returning lost property [M. B.M. 2: 11 = M. Hor. 3:4D]***?*

[S] They had in mind to rule that that is the case when his master is not present at all. So this teaching comes along to tell you that the rule applies even when his master is present.

[T] **He, his mother, his master, his father are standing in captivity [and awaiting ransom]:**

[U] **he takes precedence over his mother, and his mother over his master, and his master takes precedence over his father. [So ransoming] his mother takes precedence over all other people [T. Hor. 2:5A].** *Now does not the Mishnah say this explicitly:* **A woman takes precedence over a man in the matter of providing clothing and redemption from captivity [M. Hor. 3:4E]?**

[V] *One might consider ruling that the Mishnah speaks of a case in which his master is not present. So the Mishnah comes to tell you that that is the rule even if his master is present.*

[W] **Who is one's master?**

[X] **"He is the one who has taught him wisdom [and not the master who has taught him a trade].**

[Y] **"He is anyone who started him off first," the words of R. Meir.**

[Z] **R. Judah says, "He is anyone from whom he has gained the greater part of his learning."**

[AA] **R. Yosé says, "He is anyone who has enlightened his eyes in his repetition of traditions" [T. Hor. 2:5G-H].**

[BB] R. Abbahu came [and taught] in the name of R. Yohanan: "The law is in accord with the position of the one who says, 'It is anyone from whom he has gained the greater part of his learning.'"

[CC] (Now why did he not simply interpret the Mishnah-pericope by saying "The law is in accord with R. Judah"?

[DD] *[Because there are] repeaters of traditions who will get confused and switch [matters about].)*

[EE] R. Eliezer would make a tear in mourning on the demise of someone who had simply opened his education at the outset [but was not his principal teacher (= Z)].

[FF] Samuel removed his phylacteries on the news of the demise of one who had enlightened his eyes in his learning of the Mishnah [= BB].

[GG] And what is the case of one's "enlightening his eyes in his learning of the Mishnah"?

[HH] Said R. Yosé b. R. Bun, "It is one who taught merely so brief a passage as the following: **[The two keys] — one goes down into the lock as far as its armpit, and one opens the door forthwith [M. Tam. 3:6E]."**

[II] (Now what is the meaning of **One goes down into the lock as far as its armpit?** That it would go down for a cubit before it would open the door.)

[JJ] *R. Hananiah was walking, leaning on the shoulder of R. Hiyya bar Ba in Sepphoris. He saw all the people running. He asked him, "Why do all the people run?"*

[KK] *He said to him, "It is because R. Yohanan is in session and expounding Torah in the schoolhouse of R. Benaiah, and all the people are running to hear what he has to say."*

[LL] *He said to him, "Blessed be the All-Merciful, who has shown me the fruits of my labor while I am still alive."*

[MM] *For all of the Aggadah had he [Hananiah] laid forth before him [Yohanan], except for Proverbs and Ecclesiastes.*

[III:1 A] When both of them are standing in danger of [sexual] defilement, the man takes precedence over the woman:

[B] Why is this the rule?

[C] Because the woman is accustomed to such treatment, but the man is not accustomed to such treatment.

[III:2 A] **M'SH B: R. Joshua went to Rome. They told him about a child from Jerusalem who was ruddy, with beautiful eyes and a handsome face, and his locks were curled, and he was in danger of being put to shame. R. Joshua went to examine him When he came to the door, [standing outside] he recited this verse: "Who gave up Jacob to the power of his enemies?"**

[B] **That child answered and said, "'Was it not the Lord against whom we have sinned, in whose ways they would not walked, and whose law they would not obey' (Is. 42:24)?"**

[C] **At that instant R. Joshua's eyes filled with tears, and he said, "I call the heaven and the earth to testify against me, that I shall not move from this spot until I shall have redeemed this child!"**

[D] **He redeemed him for a huge sum of money and sent him to the land of Israel.**

[E] **And concerning him [Ishmael] Scripture has said, "The precious sons of Zion, worth their weight in fine gold, how they are reckoned as earthen pots, the work of a potter's hands" (Lam. 4:2) [T. Hor. 2:5L].**

HUSBANDS AND WIVES

YERUSHALMI KETUBOT 5: 6

[A] **These are the kinds of labor which a woman performs for her husband:**

[B] **she grinds flour, bakes bread, does laundry, prepares meals, feeds her child, makes the bed, works in wool.**

[C] **[If] she brought with her a single slave girl, she does not grind, bake bread, or do laundry.**

[D] **[If she brought] two, she does not prepare meals and does not feed her child.**

[E] **[If she brought] three, she does not make the bed for him and does not work in wool.**

[F] **If she brought four, she sits on a throne.**

[G] **R. Eliezer says, "Even if she brought him a hundred slave girls, he forces her to work in wool,**

[H] **"for idleness leads to unchastity. "**

[I] **Rabban Simeon b. Gamaliel says, "Also: He who prohibits his wife by a vow from performing any labor puts her away and pays off her marriage contract.**

[J] **"For idleness leads to boredom. "**

[I:1 A] **The kinds of work which a woman does for her husband —**

[B]   *it has been taught as a Tannaite statement:* **seven basic categories of labor did they enumerate.**

[C]   **And the rest did not require enumeration [M. 5:6A-B] [T. Ket. 5:4A-C].**

[II:1A]   **She feeds her child [M. 5:6B].**

[B]   Said R. Haggai, "It says only, 'her child' [in the singular]. Lo, in a case of twins, she is not [required to suckle both]."

[C]   And why does it say, "her child"?

[D]   It is so that she should not nurse her friend's child.

[E]   *That is in line with the following, which is taught:*

[F]   **The husband cannot force his wife to give suck to the child of his fellow.**

[G]   **And the wife cannot force her husband to permit her to give suck to the child of her girl friend [T. Ket. 5:5G-H].**

[H]   **[If] she took a vow not to give suck to her child —**

[I]   **the House of Shammai say, "She pulls her teats from his mouth."**

[J]   **And the House of Hillel say, "He forces her to give suck to her child."**

[K]   [If] she was divorced, however, they do not force her to give suck to him [T. Ket. 5:5A-D].

[L]   Under what circumstances? In a case in which the infant does not recognize the mother.

[M]   But if he recognizes her, they force her and pay her a wage to nurse her child.

[N]   And how old would he be so as to recognize her?

[O]   R. Jeremiah in the name of Rab: "Three months."

[P]   Now [when he made that statement], R. Zeira cast his gaze at him.

[Q]   *He said to him, "Why are you staring at me? Shall I tell you what Samuel said? For Samuel said, 'Three days.'"*

[R]   *Samuel is consistent with opinions expressed elsewhere.*

[S]   *Samuel said, "I recognized the midwife who delivered me [right after I was born]."*

[T]   *R. Joshua b. Levi said, "I recognized the ritual circumciser who performed the circumcision on me."*

[U]   *R. Yohanan said, "I recognized the women who kept my mother company [during labor]."*

[V]   *It has been taught:* **"An infant continues to suckle all twenty-four months. From that point onward, he is like one who sucks [from] an abomination," the words of R. Eliezer**

[W]   **And R. Joshua says, "The infant continues to suck even for four or five years [Y. lacks: and he is permitted to do so]. If he separated from the teat, they do not return him to it" [T. Nid. 2:3/I-J].**

[X]   How long [a time is deemed to mark the child's actually separating from the teat and giving up nursing, so that the child then is prohibited from returning to nursing]?

[Y]   R. Jacob b. R. Aha, R. Jeremiah in the name of Rab: "After twenty-four hours."

[Z]   R. Hezekiah, R. Abbahu in the name of R. Joshua b. Levi: "No longer than three days, reckoned from the moment of the last feeding. [So it depends on the status of the infant.]"

[AA]   *It was taught,* "After twenty-four hours." [= The baraita is in accord with Rab].

[BB]   R. Hezekiah the elder: "Under what circumstances? In a case in which he gave up the teat while in a state of good health. But if he did so while in a state of illness, they do bring him back to the teat forthwith. [Now this rule applies, moreover,] in the case of an infant who is in no danger [by reason of sickness], but in the case of an infant whose life is endangered [by sickness], forthwith do they return him to the teat even after some time as soon as [the need is recognized]."

[III:1 A]   **If she brought [with her a single slave girl, etc. (M. 5:6C-F)].** Said R. Samuel bar R. Isaac, "It is not the end of the matter that she actually brought [the slave girls with her]. But even if she was in a position to do so [but did not actually bring them in, the same law applies]."

[B]   *This is in line with what is taught:* **His wife goes up with him, but she does not go down with him [T. Ket. 5:9B].** [She rises in status and perquisites, but does not lose what she already has if she marries down.]

[C]   A widow and her children go down but do not go up.

[D]   Workers go up but do not go down.

[E]   A daughter neither goes up nor goes down.

[III:2 A]   [Since the Mishnah specifies the work of the several slave girls, M. 5: 6C-F, we now ask:] And let her bring a slave girl to do all the work?

[B]   Said R. Hiyya bar Judah, "It is for the welfare of the slave girl [who should not be overworked]. [That is why the slave girl has a specified set of tasks, and the mistress of the household must do the rest of them.]"

[C]   Said R. Bun, "It is because these sorts of work are menial that they assigned them to the slave girl."

[D]   Said R. Judah b. R. Bun, "[The reason sages assigned the remainder of the work to the woman] is that it is not usual for a woman to sit idly in her husband's household."

[III:3 A]   R. Huna said, "Even if she brought in to the marriage a hundred slave girls, he may force her to perform for him certain tasks best done in private."

[B]   What are these tasks best done in private?

[C]   She anoints his body with oil, washes his feet, and mixes his cup.

[D]   What is the reason? Is it because she is obligated to do these things, or is it because it is not appropriate to make use of a slave girl to do them?

[E] *What is the practical difference between these two reasons?*

[F] A case in which she brought slave boys into the marriage.

[G] If you say that these are not tasks for which it is appropriate to make use of a slave girl, lo, she has brought slave boys into the marriage [who may do these tasks].

[H] *Accordingly, the reason is only on the count that* she is liable to do these things for him.

[I] *R. Abodema in Sepphoris raised the question before R. Mana, "Is it not reasonable to suppose that* the reason is only on the count of her being liable to do these things for him?"

[J] *He said to him, "I, too, maintain that view."*

[III:4   A] *It is taught [in the Tosefta's version]:* **R. Judah says, "Also: He cannot force her to work in flax, for it makes the mouth swell and cuts the lips" [T. Ket. 5: 4G].**

5:7

[A] **He who takes a vow not to have sexual relations with his wife—**

[B] **the House of Shammai say, "[He may allow this situation to continue] for two weeks."**

[C] **And the House of Hillel say, "For one week. "**

[D] **Disciples go forth for Torah study without [the wife's] consent for thirty days.**

[E] **Workers go out for one week.**

[F] **"The sexual duty of which the Torah speaks [Ex. 21:10]: (1) those without work [of independent means] — every day; (2) workers — twice a week; (3) ass-drivers — once a week; (4) camel-drivers — once in thirty days; (S) sailors — once in six months, " the words of R. Eliezer.**

[I:1 A] He who takes a vow not to have sexual relations with his wife—

[B] the House of Shammai say, "[He may remain married] for two weeks,

[C] "equivalent to the period of uncleanness after the birth of a female."

[D] And the House of Hillel say, "One week,

[E] "equivalent to the period of uncleanness after the birth of a male,

[F] "and equivalent to the menstrual period" [T Ket. 5:6A-F].

[II:1 A] Disciples go forth for Torah study without [the wife's] consent for thirty days [M. 5:7D].

[B] Lo, with their wives' consent, [they may go forth] even for any period of time.

[II:2A] R. Samuel bar Nahman in the name of R. Jonathan: "'And he sent them to Lebanon, ten thousand a month in relays; [they would be a month in Lebanon and two months at home]'" (I Kings 5 :14).

[B] Said R. Abin, "The Holy One, blessed be he, preferred procreation over [30b] the building of the house of the sanctuary."

[C] *What is the scriptural basis for this opinion?*

[D] "They would be a month in Lebanon and two months at home" (1 Kings 5 :14).

[E] Rab said, "'the divisions that came and went, month after month throughout the year'" (1 Chr. 27:1).

[III:1 A] With reference to M. 5:7E, **Workers go out for one week,** as against M. 5:7F, **Workers, twice a week:**] Here you say once a week, and there you say twice a week?

[B] *Bar Qappara taught,* "Workers go out to their usual labor without permission of their wives for a week at a time. [They have the right to vary from their normal procedure for a week. For any longer spell they must have the agreement of their wives.]"

[IV:1 A] **The sexual duty of which the Torah speaks [M. 5:7F]:** *There are Tannaim who teach* [with reference to Ex. 21:10: "He shall not diminish her S'R, her clothing, and her 'WNH," with the words given in consonants translated at RSV: her food, her marital rights, respectively], that S'R refers to sexual relations, and 'WNH refers to food. *And there are Tannaim who teach:* 'WNH refers to sexual relations, [and] S'R refers to food.

[B] *He who says that* S'R refers to sexual relations cites in evidence the following verse: "None of you shall approach anyone near (S'R) of kin to him to uncover nakedness" (Lev. 18: 6). 'WNH in the sense of food is found in the following verse: "And he humbled you and let you hunger and fed you with manna" (Deut. 8: 3).

[C] *He who says that* S'R refers to food cites in evidence the following verse: "He rained flesh (S'R) upon them like dust, winged birds like the sand of the seas" (Ps. 78: 27). 'WNH in the sense of sexual relations is seen in the following: "If you ill-treat ('NH) my daughters, or if you take wives besides my daughters" (Gen. 31: 50). This refers to sexual relations.

[D] *R. Eliezer b. Jacob interpreted the verse in this way:* "Food and clothing [referred to at Ex. 21: 10] means that the clothing should be in accord with her body, that he should not give what is suitable for a girl to an old woman, nor what is suitable for an old woman to a girl. 'Her clothing and her marital rights' — this means that the clothing should be appropriate to the season, so he should not give her summer clothes in the rainy season or clothes for the rainy season in the summer."

[E] *Now what is there to be said about food [since the verse is interpreted in such wise that the obligation to provide food is omitted] ?*

[F] Now if matters on which life does not depend the husband has not got the right to hold back from the wife, matters on which the life depends, is it not an argument a fortiori that he may not withhold such things from her?

[G] *Now what is there to be said about marital rights?*

[H]   Now if matters on account of which she did not have to get married from the very outset he has not got the right to hold back from her, matters for which she got married to begin with, is it not an argument a fortiori [that he may not hold back such things from her]?

[I]   It is from the present that Jacob, our father, sent to Esau, his brother, that R. Eliezer derived his lesson:

[J]   "For he sent the gifts in an appropriate way: 'Two hundred she-goats and twenty he-goats,' — one to ten — 'two hundred ewes and twenty rams,' — one to ten — 'thirty milch camels and their colts'" (Gen.32:14-15).

[K]   (Said R. Berekiah, "It is because the camel is modest when he has sexual relations that the Scripture did not mention him.")

[L]   "Forty cows and ten bulls," — one to four, for they are workers — "twenty she-asses and ten he-asses" — one to two for they are workers (Gen. 32 :15).

[V:1 A]   **[As to M. 5:7D, disciples, and M. 5:7F, those of independent means:]** *R. Jeremiah raised the question, "As to these disciples of sages, is it not reasonable that we should treat them as equivalent to those who have independent means [and have sexual relations every day]?"*

[B]   *Said R. Mana, "Is it not yet more reasonable to treat them as equivalent to those who harvest crops [that is, very hard workers indeed], for they work harder [in their learning, than anyone else]."*

[V:2 A]   Rab said, "[When M. 5:11 says that the wife] eats with him on Sabbath nights, the Mishnah uses a euphemism [for sexual relations]."

5:8

[A]   **She who rebels against her husband [declining to perform wifely services [M. 5: 6] —**

[B]   **they deduct from her marriage contract seven denars a week.**

[C]   **R. Judah says, "Seven tropaics. "**

[D]   **How long does one continue to deduct?**

[E]   **Until her entire marriage contract [has been voided].**

[F]   **R. Yosé says, 'He continues to deduct [even beyond the value of the marriage contract], for an inheritance may come [to her] from some other source, from which he will collect what is due him. "**

[G]   **And so is the rule for the man who rebels against his wife [declining to do the husband 's duties (M. 5: 5)] —**

[H]   **they add three denars a week to her marriage contract.**

[I]   **R. Judah says, "Three tropaics."**

[I:1 A]   *Here you state [that they deduct]* **seven [M. 5: 8B],** *and there you state [that they add]* **three [M. 5:8H]!**

[B] Said R. Yosé bar Haninah, "As to her, since she is obligated to him for seven [sorts of labor], he deducts from her marriage settlement seven, while in his case, since he is obligated to her for three [acts of labor], he adds three to her contract."

[C] But take note of the following: If she brought slaves into the marriage [as specified above], she should not owe him a thing.

[D] Further take note of the case in which he stipulated with her that he will not owe her food, clothing, or marital relations — in such a case, lo, he should not owe her a thing!

[E] *Why so [that there should be seven obligations for a woman, three for a man]?*

[F] *It is in line with what* R. Yohanan said, "The anguish of a man is greater than that of a woman [in being deprived of wifely services]."

[G] *There is a pertinent verse of Scripture:* "And when she pressed him hard with her words day after day, and urged him, [his soul was vexed to death]" (Judg. 16 :16).

[H] What is the meaning of, "and urged him"?

[I] Said R. Isaac bar Eleazar, "She would pull herself out from under him."

[J] "His soul was vexed to death," but her soul was not vexed to death.

[K] And there are those who say that she found the necessary satisfaction with other men.

[L] All the more so that she desired sexual relations!

[M] [The rule under discussion is in line with what] R. Nahman said in the name of R. Nahman: "That certain organ — if she starves it, she makes it satisfied. The more she satisfies it, the more she makes it hungry" [cf. Jastrow, 2:1485].

[I:2 A] And in accord with the view of R. Eliezer, an ass driver [and the other professionals, who, according to Eliezer at M. 5: 7, have different obligations to their wives, from whom they may be absent for brief periods], how much does he diminish [the marriage contract, when the wife rebels]?

[B] *Let us derive the answer from the following: R. Hiyya taught,* "[Even in the case of] a betrothed girl, a sick woman, a menstruating woman, and a deceased childless brother's widow — they write for him a writ of rebellion as a charge against her marriage contract."

[C] *Now how do we interpret this matter?* If it was a case in which she rebelled against him [refusing to have sexual relations], and she is already in her menstrual period, it is the Torah that has required her to rebel against him. *But thus must we interpret the matter:* It is a case in which she rebelled against him [refusing to have sexual relations] before her menstrual period had begun. Now [the argument continues], when in fact she comes to her menstrual period, she is no longer in a position to rebel, and yet you say that [nonetheless] he writes such a writ of rebellion against her marriage contract. Now, along these same lines [here in the case of an ass driver, etc.], one likewise deducts [the sum from her marriage settlement, even though, in point of fact, the husband bears no obligation to have sexual relations with her and is not going to do so. The fact that she has rebelled suffices to set in motion the process of reducing her marriage settlement.]

[I:3 A]   What does one deduct? Is it from the property she brought him into the marriage over and above the dowry?

[B]   *Let us derive the answer from the following:* **R. Yosé says, "He continues to deduct even beyond the value of the marriage contract, for an inheritance may come to her from some other source, from which he will collect what is due him " [M. 5:8F].** It has stated only that he may collect from an inheritance, *something that is not commonplace.* That means that he may even deduct from the property she brought him into the marriage over and above the dowry.

[I:4 A]   R. Zeira in the name of Samuel: "They write a writ of rebellion as a charge against the marriage contract in the case of a betrothed woman, but they do not write a rebellion as a charge against the marriage contract of a deceased childless brother's widow."

[B]   *And has not R. Hiyya taught:* "Even in the case of a menstruating woman, a sick woman, a betrothed girl, and a deceased childless brother's widow, they write a writ of rebellion as a charge against her marriage contract"?

[C]   *The former statement [Hiyya's] accords with the former version of the Mishnah, the latter [Samuel's] accords with the final version of the Mishnah.*

[D]   Said R. Yosé bar Bun, "Even if you say that this, too, refers to the final version of the Mishnah, [Samuel's statement applies to a case in which the levir wants to enter into levirate marriage. They do not force him to do so if he prefers to undergo the rite of removing the shoe. Hiyya's statement speaks of a case in which the woman wants neither to enter into levirate marriage nor to undergo the rite of removing the shoe.]"

[I:5 A]   [In the Tosefta's version:] **Our rabbis ordained that a court should warn her four or five consecutive weeks, twice a week.**

[B]   **[If she persists] any longer than that — even if her marriage contract is a hundred *maneh,* she has lost the whole thing [T. Ket. 5:7C-D].**

[I:6 A]   R. Haninah in the name of R. Ishmael b. R. Yosé: "She who goes forth because she has a bad name has no claim on indemnity [for the wear or ruin of things which she brought into the marriage along as her property]. She who rebels [and leaves the marriage on that count] does have such a claim."

[B]   R. Simon in the name of R. Joshua b. Levi: "She who rebels and she who goes forth because of having a bad name have no claim either for support or for indemnity."

[C]   Said R. Yosé, "In the case of those who write in the marriage settlement, 'If he should hate,' 'If she should hate,' [in which case

there may be a provision contrary to that just now stated] — this is
a stipulation concerning a monetary matter, and such a stipulation
remains in effect [despite the circumstances of the breakup of the
marriage]."

MOURNING RITES: THE MOURNER'S CONDUCT

YERUSHALMI BERAKHOT 3:1

[A] **He whose deceased relative is lying before him [not yet
buried], is exempt from the obligations to recite the
Shema' and to wear Tefillin.**

[B] **The [first set of] pallbearers, and the [next people] who
replace them, and the [next people] who replace their
replacements — whether they go [in the procession to
the cemetery] before the bier, or they go behind the bier
—**

[C] **If they are needed to [carry] the bier, they are exempt
[from reciting the Shema' and wearing Tefillin].**

[D] **And if they are not needed to [carry] the bier, they are
obligated [to recite the Shema' and to wear Tefillin].**

[E] **Both are exempt from [reciting] the Prayer [of Eighteen
blessings].** [Y. printed ed. continues here with M. 3:2-6, given
below at the appropriate places.]

[I:1 A] *It was taught,* **[He whose deceased relative is not yet buried, is]
exempt from [the obligations to recite the Shema' and to wear]
Tefillin. [M. 3:1A].** A mourner does not put on Tefillin on the first
day of mourning. On the second day he may put on Tefillin.
Throughout the entire seven days of mourning, if a new person
comes [to console him,] he removes [the Tefillin while that person
remains with him because it is as though the presence of a new
person renews the mourner's grieving]," the words of R. Eliezer.

[B] R. Joshua says, "On the first and second days he does not put on
Tefillin. On the third day he puts on Tefillin. And if a new person
comes [to console him] he does not remove them."

[C] [Now, to raise a question:] If on the second day he does not put on
Tefillin [in accord with Joshua], *do we need to say* **[in M. 3:1A]
He whose deceased relative is not yet buried is exempt
from...Tefillin?**

[D] *[The answer is, it is redundant. However,] because they taught [in
the M.] the rule concerning the [recitation by a mourner of the]
Shema', they taught [together with it the rule] concerning the
Tefillin as well.*

[E] R. Zeira, R. Jeremiah in the name of Rab, "The law follows R.
Eliezer with regard to putting on Tefillin [i.e., he may put them on
the second day]. And [the law follows] R. Joshua with regard to

taking them off [i.e., from the third day he does not have to remove them if someone new comes to console him]."

[F] *R. Zeira asked,* "What if he puts on Tefillin on the second day in accord with R. Eliezer's rule? Can he act in accord with R. Joshua and not remove them [if someone new comes to console him] while [at the same time] he follows R. Eliezer [and wears them on the second day]?" [This appears to be a self-contradictory position.]

[G] Said R. Yosé b. R. Bun, "In truth, the law follows R. Eliezer with regard to putting on Tefillin [i.e. he may do so] on the second day. And while following R. Eliezer, we act in accord with R. Joshua and do not remove them on the second day either."

[H] *Then why, if this is true, do we not just say,* "The law follows R. Eliezer [with regard to putting them on]?" [Then we could infer that the law follows Joshua and that one does not remove them following the third day. It would be clearer for Rab (E) to say only that we follow Eliezer with regard to putting on Tefillin. This then would imply that we do not follow his opinion with regard to taking them off. Why does Rab also add that we follow Joshua's view, thereby leaving unresolved the issue of what the practice is on the second day? The Talmud leaves this objection unresolved.]

[I:2 A] Said R. Bun, "It is written, 'That all the days of your life you may remember the day when you came out of the Land of Egypt' [Deut. 16:3]. On days when you are taking care of the living [you must recite the Shema' and remember the exodus], but not on days when you are taking care of the dead." [The verse is used to support the exemption of a mourner from the obligation to recite the Shema'.]

[C] *It was taught,* "If he [a mourner] wished to be strict with himself [and recite the Shema'] they do not allow him to." Why? Is it out of respect for the dead or because there will be no one else to bear his burden [assisting in the interment while he recites]?

[D] *What is the difference [with regard to the law between these two explanations]?*

[E] [The difference is apparent in a case where] there was another to bear his burden for him. If you say the reason he may not recite [the Shema'] is out of respect for the dead, [in this case] he is still forbidden to recite. But if you say the reason is because no one else will bear his burden, lo, [in this case] there is someone who will bear his burden [and he should be permitted to recite].

[F] *But it was taught,* "[A mourner] is exempt from taking the lulab." [They do not perform a burial on the festival day. Accordingly, he could not be exempt from taking the lulab on account only of his involvement in the burial. This proves that one is exempt from the obligation to recite out of respect for the dead.]

[G] [This is not probative.] We may explain that this refers to [a case of one who is exempt from taking the lulab on an intermediate day of the festival [on which burial is permitted. It could be that he is

exempt out of respect for the dead or because of his involvement
in the burial. This case is no proof one way or the other.]

[H] *But it was taught,* "[A mourner] is exempt from the obligation of
hearing the blasts of the shofar." *In this case can you say* it refers
to an intermediate day? No, it must refer to a festival day [because
the shofar is sounded on the New Year festival days only.
Accordingly, the reason one does not recite the Shema' must be
out of respect for the dead, and not because he is involved with the
burial.]

[I] Said R. Haninah, "[From this case of the shofar on the New Year
there is still no proof one way or the other.] Because [even on the
festival] one is obliged to bring a coffin and shrouds [for the
deceased] *in accord with that which we learned* [**M. Shab. 24:2**]:
**They may await nightfall at the Sabbath limit to see to the
business of a bride or of a corpse, to bring for it a coffin and a
shroud, flutes and weepers.**

[J] "[Even on the festival day, as on the Sabbath, he may have tasks to
do for the deceased. It is no different from an ordinary case of] one
who has a burden to bear [for the burial. On the New Year festival
either reason for the exemption from his obligation may apply and
we have no proof one way or the other.]" [The question remains
unresolved. If there is someone who will attend to his tasks for
him, we do not know whether or not the mourner is exempt.]

[I:3 A] When do they turn over the beds [making it lower to the floor in a
house of mourning, as a sign of mourning]?

[B] "When the body is taken out through the courtyard gate," the words
of R. Eliezer.

[C] And R. Joshua says, "When the stone is set in place [closing the
burial chamber]."

[D] When R. Gamaliel died, as soon as they went out through the
courtyard gate [with the body,] R. Eliezer said to his students,
"Turn over the beds."

[E] When the stone was set in place R. Joshua said, "Turn over the
beds."

[F] They said to him, "We have already turned them over in accord
with [the words of the] Elder [Eliezer]."

[G] On the Sabbath eve one turns the beds upright [again] and after
the Sabbath one turns them over [since they do not permit one to
show signs of mourning on the Sabbath].

[H] *It was taught:* The state-bed [a low bed] may be left upright and
need not be turned over.

[I] R. Simeon b. Eleazar says, "One detaches the straps [from the
bed], and that is enough [of a sign of mourning]."

[J] R. Yosa in the name of R. Joshua b. Levi, "The law follows R.
Simeon b. Eleazar."

[K] R. Jacob bar Aha in the name of R. Yosé, "In the case of a bed with
a curtain frame, it is enough [of a sign of mourning] to detach it."

[L]   What is the difference between a bed [mth] and a state-bed [drgs]?

[M]   Said R. Jeremiah, "A bedstead on which the girths [interlaced straps] are drawn over the frame is called a bed. And a bedstead [which is lower] on which the girths are not drawn over the frame [but are attached in another way] is called a state-be]."

[N]   *But have we not learned as a Tannaite statement:* **The bed and cot [become susceptible to uncleanness] after they are rubbed over with fish skin [to smooth them? Before that time, they cannot be used, because they are too rough.] [M. Kel. 16:1.]** If they are girded over the top [of the frame, thus covering the top of the frame,] what purpose is served by rubbing [the bed frame to smooth it]?

[O]   *Said R. Eleazar, "We may solve this problem [as follows: Mishnah refers to] those cots from Caesarea which have openings [for the straps to go through. Since the top of the frame is exposed, rubbing it with skin serves the purpose of finishing it for use.]"*

[P]   What is the basis for [the custom of] turning over the beds?

[Q]   R. Qerispa in the name of R. Yohanan, "[They justify the practice based on the verse] 'And they sat with him near to the ground' [Job 2:13]. It does not say, 'On the ground' but, 'Near to the ground,' implying they sat on something close to the ground. From here we see that they slept on beds which were turned over."

[R]   Bar Qappara [explained the custom as follows], "[God] says, 'I had a fine likeness of myself in your house and you caused me to turn it over [to the ground, to die, through your sins]. Now [as a sign for this] you shall turn over your beds.'"

[S]   [Some interpret this explanation of Bar Qappara differently: Not, "You caused me to turn it over,"] but, "You forced [his likeness from the world]." As in the saying, "May the agent of sin be forced [away]." [So now you are forced to turn over your beds. P.M. explains that this is just a semantic difference.]

[T]   R. Jonah and R. Yosé both [taught] in the name of R. Simeon b. Laqish: One said, "Why does one sleep on an overturned bed? So that if he should awaken at night, he will remember that he is a mourner."

[U]   And the other said, "Since he sleeps on an overturned bed, he will awaken at night and remember that he is a mourner."

[I:4 A]   A mourner must eat at the house of his fellow until the corpse of his deceased relative is buried. And if he has no fellow [with whom he can eat], he should eat in a stranger's house. And if he has no stranger's house [nearby in which to eat] he should construct a partition [in his own house] and eat there. And if he cannot construct a partition, he should turn his face to the wall [of his own house] and eat.

[B]   And he [the mourner before the body is buried] may neither recline and eat, nor eat and drink a full meal, nor eat meat, nor drink wine.

And they do not [count him in the quorum] to extend the invitation [to recite the blessing over the meal as a group]. And if he recited the blessing [over the meal], others do not respond [to it] "Amen." And [when he hears] blessings of others, he does not respond [to them] "Amen."

[C] All of these [rules] apply during the week. But on the Sabbath he may recline and eat, and he may eat meat and drink wine, and he may eat and drink a full meal, and they may [count him to establish the needed quorum in order] to extend the invitation to recite the blessing of the meal, and if he recited a blessing, others may respond "Amen," and for the blessings of others, he may respond "Amen."

[D] Said Rabban Simeon b. Gamaliel, "Once I have permitted [the mourner] to do all this, I may as well obligate him to keep all the commandments of the Torah. For if I permit him [to partake fully] of temporal life [by eating and drinking on the Sabbath], should I not surely permit him [to partake fully] of eternal life [by keeping all the commandments on the Sabbath]?"

[E] R. Judah b. Pazzi in the name of R. Joshua b. Levi, "The law follows Rabban Simeon b. Gamaliel."

[F] Once it [the body] has been given over to the [burial] association, [the mourner] may eat meat and drink wine. Once it was given over the corpse-bearers, it is as if it was given over to the [burial] association.

[G] *When R. Yosa died, R. Hiyya bar Wawa [i.e. Abba] took it upon himself to mourn [for his teacher]. Even so he ate meat and drank wine [before the body was buried].*

[H] *When R. Hiyya bar Abba died, R. Samuel bar R. Isaac took it upon himself to mourn [for his teacher]. Even so he ate meat and drank wine [before the body was buried].*

[I] *When R. Samuel bar R. Isaac died, R. Zeira took it upon himself to mourn [for his teacher]. But he ate [only] lentils. That tells us that we act according to the custom [of a place. What one eats if he accepts upon himself mourning for his teacher is not fixed by law.]*

[J] *As R. Zeira was dying he instructed his disciples saying, "Do not take it upon yourselves to mourn for me today but wait until tomorrow to begin mourning. [He wanted to delay them to be sure that they would not get carried away in their mourner's meal, get drunk, and act foolishly, as in the following story.]*

[K] *R. Isaac the son of Rab [R: son of R. Hiyya] at Toba suffered an untimely bereavement. R. Mana and R. Yudan went up [to console him], and they had some good wine, and they drank until they became silly.*

[L] *The next day when they wished to visit him [Isaac] again, he said to them, "Rabbis, is this how a person acts toward his associate? The only thing we missed yesterday was to get up and to dance [and we would have had a time of festivity rather than of mourning]."*

[I:5 A] It was taught: **They drink ten cups [of wine] in a house of mourning — two before the meal, and five during the meal, and three after the meal.**

[B] **Regarding these three after the meal — over the first [they recite] the blessings following the meal, over the second [they recite a blessing concerning the] acts of loving kindness [of those who came to console the mourners], and over the third [they recite a blessing] to console the mourners themselves. [T. 3:23-24. T.'s version refers to two blessings: "Comforting the mourners" and "Merciful works." The present text directs that one recite each of these blessings over a cup of wine.]**

[C] When Rabban Gamaliel died they added another three [cups] — one for the Hazzan [sexton] of the Congregation, one for the Head of the Congregation [to praise them for their public service], and one for Rabban Gamaliel [because he permitted people to perform a simple inexpensive funeral].

[D] And when the court saw that people were getting drunk [on account of the extra three cups], they issued a decree forbidding [people to drink] these cups, and [the custom] reverted to its previous state [i.e. ten cups].

[I:6 A] May a priest render himself unclean [by coming into proximity or contact with a corpse, by participating in his teacher's funeral] out of honor to his master?

[B] *R. Yannai the younger's father-in-law died. He had been both his father-in-law and his master. He [Yannai] asked R. Yosé [whether he could take part in the funeral and render himself unclean]. And [R. Yosé] forbade him.*

[C] R. Aha heard this and said, "His students may become unclean on his account." [He considered one's master to be equivalent to one's father.]

[D] R. Yosé [died and his] students became unclean on his account [by taking part in his funeral], and [before the funeral] they ate meat and drank wine.

[E] *Said R. Mana to them, "You cannot have it both ways. If you are mourners, why did you eat meat and drink wine? And if you are not mourning, why did you render yourselves unclean?"*

[F] May a priest render himself unclean in order to honor [i.e. study] the Torah?

[G] *R. Yosé was sitting and teaching, and a corpse was brought up [to the study hall for a eulogy]. To [all those priests studying there] who went out, so as not to become unclean, he did not say anything. And to all those who remained seated, he did not say anything. [For he was in doubt about this matter.]*

[H] *R. Nehemiah, son of R. Hiyya bar Abba said, "My father would not pass under the arch at Caesarea [even though this was the* shortest way for him to go to study Torah, for the arch could transmit the uncleanness of a corpse as a tent]." R. Ammi [L omits: would pass under the arch].

[I] R. Hezekiah and R. Kohen and R. Jacob bar Aha were walking in the plazas of Sepphoris [R: Caesarea]. When they reached the arch, R. Kohen separated from them. And when they reached a clean area, he rejoined them.

[J] He [Kohen] said to them, "What were you discussing [in my absence]?"

[K] R. Hezekiah said to R. Jacob bar Aha, "Do not tell him anything."

[L] [And this story does not prove anything because we do not know] whether [he instructed Jacob to remain silent] because he was angry that he [R. Kohen] left, because [a priest] is permitted to become unclean in order to study Torah, or whether [Hezekiah told Jacob to be silent] because [he did not wish to be detained by a lengthy] discussion. [S.H.: He wanted to go ahead to finish his own lesson.]

[I:7 A] **It was taught: A priest is permitted to go out of the Land of Israel, and thereby render himself unclean, for monetary judgments, for capital judgments, for sanctifying the new moon, for intercalating the year, and to save a field from seizure by a gentile. And he may go out even with a claim to contest [the seizure]. [The principle is that all lands outside of Israel are unclean with a form of uncleanness decreed by the rabbis.]**

[B] **[And a priest may leave Israel] to study Torah and to get married. R. Judah says, "If he has somewhere to study [in Israel] he may not render himself unclean [by leaving the Land]."**

[C] **R. Yosé says, "Even if he [the priest] has somewhere to study [in Israel], he may render himself unclean [and leave Israel to study]. For one may not be worthy enough to learn from all persons. [He may need a different teacher.]"**

[D] **They said concerning Joseph the priest that he used to go out and defile himself [by leaving the Land of Israel] to follow his teacher to Sidon.**

[E] **But they said: a priest should not leave the Land of Israel [to get married on the chance that he may find a wife. He may leave] only if he was promised a bride [in a place outside of the Land of Israel] [T. A.Z. 1:8-9].**

[I:8 A] May a priest render himself unclean in order to recite the priestly blessing [in a synagogue in which there is uncleanness]?

[B] Magbilah the brother of R. Abba bar Kohen said in the presence of R. Yosé in the name of R. Aha, "A priest may render himself unclean to make the priestly blessing."

[C] R. Aha heard this and said, "I never told him any such thing."

[D] He [Aha] retracted, "It could be that he heard me teach [and misinterpreted] that which R. Judah b. Pazzi said in the name of

R. Eleazar, 'Any priest who stands in the synagogue and does not
raise his hands [to recite the priestly blessing] violates a positive
commandment.' And he [Yosé] concluded that to perform this
positive commandment [to bless the people] one may override a
negative commandment [to avoid uncleanness]. [But this is a grave
error.] *I never said any such thing. Bring him before me and I
shall flog him."*

[E] *R. Abbahu was sitting and teaching in the synagogue of the city
gate in Caesarea.*

[F] *And there was [in the synagogue] a corpse [for a funeral]. When
it came time [to recite] the priestly blessing [his students who
were priests] did not ask him [whether they should stop studying
to recite the blessing. For once they stopped studying they would
then have to leave, since they thought one may continue to render
himself unclean in the presence of a corpse only to study Torah,
but not in order to recite the priestly blessing.] When it came time
for eating they asked him [whether or not to stop studying].*

[G] *He said to them, "You did not ask me [whether to stop studying]
for the priestly blessing! You now ask me [whether to stop studying]
in order to eat?"*

[H] *When they heard this, they ran.*

[I] Said R. Yannai, "A priest may defile himself in order to see the
emperor. *When the emperor Diocletian came here, they saw R.
Hiyya bar Abba [a priest] walking over Tyrian graves in order to
see him."*

[J] [This accords with the following teaching:] R. Hezekiah and R.
Jeremiah in the name of R. Yohanan [said], "It is an obligation to
see great royalty [even a Gentile king], so that when the royalty of
the House of David [the Messiah] comes, one will know how to
distinguish between one kind of royalty and another [i.e. between
the ordinary king and the Messiah]."

[K] May a priest render himself unclean in honor of a patriarch [by
attending his funeral]?

[L] *When R. Judah the patriarch died, R. Yannai announced,* "For
today, the [prohibition against becoming unclean applicable to
members of the] priesthood is suspended [i.e. priests may come to
the funeral]."

[M] *When R. Judah II the patriarch, grandson of Judah I the patriarch,
died, R. Hiyya bar Abba pushed R. Zeira into the synagogue in the
vineyard near Sepphoris [where the funeral was held], and
rendered him unclean. [The room transmitted the corpse-
uncleanness as a "tent."]*

[N] *When Nehorai, the sister of R. Judah II the patriarch, died, R.
Haninah sent for R. Mana [a priest, to attend the funeral], and he
did not come.*

[O] He [Mana] said to him, "If we do not render ourselves unclean on
their account when they are alive [i.e. we remove ourselves from

having relations with women when they menstruate], all the more so [shall we take care not to render ourselves unclean on account of women] when they are dead."

[P] Said R. Nasa, "[When a woman of stature such as a sister of the patriarch dies] we may render ourselves unclean for her, just as [we may render ourselves unclean] for a neglected corpse for which we are obliged to defile ourselves. [So a priest may render himself unclean for the sister of the patriarch.]

[Q] May a priest render himself unclean in order to honor his father or mother [in their lifetime, e.g. to visit them outside the Land of Israel]?

[R] *[This case may clarify the matter.] R. Yosa heard that his mother was going to Bozrah. He went to ask R. Yohanan whether he may go out [of the Land of Israel with her].*

[S] He said to him, "If you wish to go [to protect her] on account of the dangers of the road [in her travels], then go. If you wish to go in order to honor your mother, then I do not know whether to allow you to go or not."

[T] *Because [Yosa] pressured R. Yohanan [about this issue] he said,* "If you have decided to go, then come back in peace."

[U] *Said R. Samuel bar R. Isaac, "R. Yohanan is still in doubt concerning this issue."*

[V] R. Eleazar heard this and said, "You could not have better permission than that [which Yohanan gave to Yosa saying, 'Come back in peace']."

[W] May a priest render himself unclean for the public honor?

[X] [This will clarify the question.] *It was taught:* If there were two alternative routes [for going to console a mourner], one longer [and through an area which is] clean, the other shorter but [passing through] unclean [precincts] — if the majority of people goes by way of the longer route, he [a priest] should go by way of the longer route. And if not, he may go by the way of the shorter [unclean] route out of deference to the public honor.

[Y] This is the case for uncleanness ordained by the rabbis. But [how do we know the same law applies in] a case of uncleanness ordained in Scripture?

[Z] *Based on that which R. Zeira said,* "The public honor is so important. In some instances it [even temporarily] overrides prohibitions [against becoming unclean]. As in the case [for instance, of the obligation to bury an unknown corpse]. *That is to say,* [for the sake of the public honor one may render himself unclean] even with [a form of uncleanness] prohibited by Scripture."

[I:9 A] R. Jonah, R. Yosé the Galilean, in the name of R. Yasa bar R. Hanina, "They do not inquire into decisions of law in the presence of a coffin of the dead." [This is disrespectful to the dead, for they can no longer learn.]

[B] *[This case appears to contradict the following ruling:] But lo, R.
Yohanan inquired of R. Yannai in the presence of the coffin of R.
Samuel b. Yosedeq,* "If one consecrated to the Temple treasury his
[animal previously designated for a] burnt-offering [what is the
outcome]? [Must he pay its value to the treasury? Or did he have
no right to consecrate an animal which was already sanctified for
use as a sacrifice on the altar? Clearly this is a question requiring
a decision of law.]

[C] *And he [Yannai even] answered him! We may say that [in this
case] they were far [from the bier], or that they already had
completed the service.*

[D] *But lo, [another apparent contradiction:] R. Jeremiah inquired of
R. Zeira [about a legal ruling] in the presence of the coffin of R.
Samuel bar R. Isaac [and he answered him]!*

[E] *We may say that [when he asked him a question while] he was far
[from the coffin], he answered him. [When he asked him a question
while] he was close [to the coffin], he would not answer him.*

[F] *It was taught:* The pallbearers are prohibited to wear sandals, lest
the [strap of the] sandal of one of them break and as a result he be
prevented from performing his obligation [of carrying the bier].

[G] *R. Zeira fainted while speaking. They came and tried to lift him up
and found he was too weak.*

[H] *They said to him, "What is causing this?"*

[I] *He said to them, "Because we came to [study laws which deal
with the subject of death and mourning, I became weak,] in accord
with the verse,* '[It is better to go to the house of mourning than to
go to the house of feasting; for this is the end of all men,] and the
living will lay it to heart' [Qoh. 7:2]. [When I study these subjects,
it makes my heart faint.]"

MOURNING RITES: SPECIAL RULES

YERUSHALMI MOED QATAN 3:5

[A] He who buries his dead three days before the festival —
the requirement of the seven days of mourning is nullified
for him.

[B] [He who buries his dead] eight days [before the festival]
— the requirement of the thirty days of mourning is
nullified for him.

[C] For they have said, "The Sabbath counts [in the days of
mourning] but does not interrupt [the period of
mourning], [while] the festivals interrupt [the period of
mourning] and do not count [in the days of mourning]."

[I:1 A] The requirement of the seven days of mourning covers use of
sandals and having a haircut.

[B] The requirement of the thirty days of mourning encompasses stitching the rent in garments of mourning, laundering clothing, and getting a haircut [none of which may be done in the period of thirty days from death].

[C] What is the meaning of laundering clothing?

[D] This applies to woolen garments when they are new, and to white linen garments when they are laundered.

[I:2 A] R. Helbo, R. Huna in the name of Rab: "If the eighth day [after burial] coincided with the Sabbath, one gets a haircut on the eve of the Sabbath."

[B] *How is such a thing possible? [Was the deceased buried on the Sabbath? Surely not.]*

[C] Interpret the passage to speak of a case in which a wild beast dragged a man off, and [it was on the Sabbath that] they despaired of finding him [in which case that is the point at which the counting of the days begins].

[D] *And so it has been taught:* Lo, he whom a wild beast dragged off — at what time do they begin to count [the days of bereavement, from burial]?

[E] It is once they have given up hope of finding him.

[F] If they found him limb by limb, they begin counting for him from the day on which his head and the greater part of his body are found.

[G] R. Judah says, "The backbone and the skull constitute the greater part."

[H] Said R. Abun, "Interpret [the earlier statement, A, to deal with a case in which] the grave was sealed on the eve of the Sabbath at sunset."

[I] *How is such a thing possible?*

[J] Said R. Aha, "Interpret the case to speak of a burial in which gentiles sealed the grave."

[K] *There is he who wished to propose:* we deal with a case [A] in which the news of a bereavement reached one on the Sabbath.

[I:3 A] *R. Immi [82b] had a case in which he ruled that* someone may cut his hair on the thirtieth day. *Rab had a case in which he ruled that* someone may cut his hair on the thirty-first day.

[B] *Said R. Zeriqan, "It is from the following passage of the Mishnah that R. Immi derived his [confused] view of the law, for we have learned there:*

[C] **He who took a Nazirite vow for two spells cuts his hair for the first on the thirty-first day, and for the second on the sixty-first day [M. Naz. 3:2A]** [and, Immi maintained, if he wanted to cut it on the thirtieth day, he may do so].

[D] *Said R. Yosé, "[That proves nothing.] There we deal with a case in which the ruling is post facto. But here do we deal with a ruling that is de novo?"*

[E] *R. Jeremiah instructed R. Isaac Atoshayya, and some say he instructed R. Hiyya bar R. Isaac Atoshayya* to have the haircut on the thirtieth day, *on the basis of the following passage of the Mishnah:*

[F] **[He who buries his dead three days before the festival — the requirement of the seven days of mourning is nullified for him. He who buries his dead] eight days before the festival — the requirement of the thirty days of mourning is nullified for him, [for they have said, "The Sabbath counts in the days of mourning, but one does not interrupt the period of mourning, while the festivals interrupt the period of mourning and do not count ii the days of mourning"] [M. 3:5].**

[G] The eighth day is [equivalent to] the thirtieth day. [That is, part of the day is deemed equivalent to the whole of it, and likewise here.]

[H] Said R. Yosé, "[No, it is not for that reason at all.] The case there is different; it is on account of the honor owing to the festival. [So M. M.Q. 3:5 supplies no relevant evidence on the disposition of part of the final day.]

[I] "You should know that that is so, for R. Helbo bar Huna said in the name of R. Yohanan, 'If the eighth day of the mourning should come out on the Sabbath, he may get a haircut on the eve of the Sabbath.'

[J] "Now if you say that it is not because of the honor owing to the festival, would they have permitted doing so in that wise?

[K] "If that is the case, then even if the Nazir's thirtieth day should coincide with the Sabbath, he should be able to cut his hair on the eve of the Sabbath.

[L] *"And further evidence [that part of the day is not equivalent to the whole of it] derives from the following which has been taught:* 'On account of all of one's deceased he makes a tear after seven days, and he mends it after thirty days.'"

[M] And let him make a tear on the seventh day and mend it on the thirtieth day?

[N] *Said R. Haggai, "That is his tradition on the matter [of disposing of part of a day], while we have our [different] tradition [on the same matter]."*

[I:4 A] [With reference to the view that part of a day is treated as equivalent to the whole of it,] *it has been taught,* "This is the opinion of Abba Saul."

[B] R. Judah in the name of Samuel, R. Abbahu in the name of R. Yohanan: "The law is in accord with Abba Saul."

[C] *And so it has been taught:* The law is in accord with his view.

[D] R. Ba in the name of Rab: "In the view of Abba Saul, both the restrictions [the formal observances of mourning] and the days of mourning are nullified [by the advent of the festival].

[E] But in the view of sages, while the observance of the days of mourning is nullified, the restrictions are not nullified.

[F] *What is at issue between them?*

[G] R. Huna said, "The status of the eve of the festival *is at issue between them.*

[H] "If one has gotten a haircut on the eve of the festival, he may get a haircut after the festival.

[I] "If he did not get a haircut on the eve of the festival, let him not get a haircut after the festival [since he is still subject to the restrictions of the thirty days]."

[J] R. Yohanan said, "Even though he did not get a haircut on the eve of the festival, he may get a haircut after the festival."

[K] R. Eleazar gave a decision to R. Simeon bar Ba that he might get a haircut after the festival. *But we do not know whether this was in accord with the view of Abba Saul or whether it was in accord with the view of rabbis, representing the opinion of all parties.*

[L] *R. Eleazar instructed Simeon bar Ba,* "The days of the festival count in the total of thirty [required for mourning]."

[M] *Said R. Yosé, "It turns out that* the thirty days take precedence over the seven days of mourning?"

[I:5 A] **He who buries his dead three days before a festival — the requirement of the seven days of mourning is nullified for him [M. 3:5A].**

[B] The law has stated only that that is so if it is three days before. Lo, if it is only two, that is not the case.

[C] *That which you have stated applies to* matters pertaining to him personally. But the community does not deal with him [as a mourner during the festival].

[D] *And so it has been taught [in T.'s version:]* **[If he buries his dead] with three days left of the festival week itself, he counts seven [days of mourning] after the festival.**

[E] **For the first four, the public takes care of him. For the other three, the public does not take care of him.**

[F] **For they have said that the days of mourning that took place on the festival go to his credit so that the public must take care of him.**

[G] **And his work is done by others.**

[H] **His male slaves and female slaves work in private for other people [T. Moed 2:7].**

[I] What is the law as to visiting him [without undertaking the rite of comforting him, on the specified days on which the public does not take care of him]?

[J] R. Jacob bar Idi in the name of R. Haninah: "And have they not ruled, 'There is no mourning on the Sabbath'? On what account did they give that ruling? Was it to visit him? Was it not on account of paying all due respect? Here too [they visit him] in order to pay all due respect."

[K] *And along these same lines,* if the burial was one day prior to the festival, the restrictions of two days are removed from him.

[I:6 A] [M. Ber. 3:1: **He whose dead still lies before him (unburied) is free of the obligation of saying the Shema and of tefillin:**] "A mourner on the first day does not put on *tefillin*. On the second day he does put on *Tefillin*. But if new faces [comforters] come, he removes them, for all seven days" — the words of R. Eliezer.

[B] R. Joshua says, "On the first and on the second day, he does not put on *Tefillin*. On the third day, he does put on *Tefillin*, but if new faces come, he does not remove them."

[C] If on the third day after death, the mourner does not put on *Tefillin, is* it necessary to say that he whose dead lies unburied [does not put on *Tefillin]?* [That is self-evident.]

[D] *But since the teacher of the passage wished to refer to this [the Shema], he referred also to that [the putting on of Tefillin].*

[E] R. Zeira, Mar Uqban in the name of Samuel —

[F] R. Zeira, R. Jeremiah in the name of Rab [stated], "The law follows R. Eliezer as to putting on *[Tefillin]* and R. Joshua as to removing them."

[G] *R. Zeira raised the following question:* "If a mourner put on *Tefillin* on the second day, in conformity with the view of R. Eliezer, how does the law accord the position of R. Eliezer with the view of R. Joshua as to taking them off? [That is, Eliezer says one puts them on on the second day, but takes them off if new comforters appear. Joshua says that he does not put them on on the second day. But on the days on which he does put them on, if new comforters arrive, he also does not remove them. So the area of puzzlement is putting them on, in accord with Eliezer, and not removing them, in accord with Joshua.]"

[H] *Said R. Yosé b. R. Bun, "And that in fact is the case:* If he put them on on the second day in accord with R. Eliezer, the law, done in accord with R. Eliezer, then follows the view of R. Joshua that one does not take them off. [Accordingly, on the second day, in accord with Eliezer, one puts them on. But if new mourners arrive, one nonetheless does not take the *Tefillin* off.]"

[I] *If that were the case, then we should say,* "The law accords with R. Eliezer." [What need is there to mention Joshua at all? If in fact even on the second day one does not remove the *Tefillin,* then there is no need to speak of Joshua's views as to the later days.]

[I:7 A] If the mourner had nothing to eat, on the first day and on the second day he does not perform an act of labor in that regard. On the third day he does so discretely.

[B] But they have said, "May a curse come upon his neighbors that made it necessary for him to do so."

[C] Bar Qappara said, "Even on the third day he should not do any act of labor."

[D] *Bar Qappara is consistent with his other views, for* Bar Qappara has said, "Mourning retains its power over the mourner for only three days."

[E] *R. Abba son of R. Pappi, R. Joshua of Sikhnin in the name of R. Levi: "For the first three days after death, the soul flutters over the body, thinking that she will return to it. When she sees that the appearance of the corpse deteriorates, she leaves the body and goes her way."*

[F] After three days the belly explodes over the face and says to the deceased, "Here is what you have stolen and seized and given to me."

[G] *R. Haggai in the name of R. Josiah proves that proposition from the following verse of Scripture:* "[Behold, I will rebuke your offspring, and] spread dung upon your faces, the dung of your offerings [and I will put you out of my presence]" (Mal. 2:3).

[H] At that moment: "He feels only the pain of his own body, and he mourns only for himself" (Job 14:22).

[I:8 A] The sharecroppers of the land [of the mourner], those who rent land for a fixed proportion of the crop and those who contract [to work for the mourner], do labor [during the memorial period since they work for themselves, not for him]. Those who do day labor for him, those who lead his camels and his barges do not work [since they are his employees].

[B] R. Joshua b. Levi said, "If he had a cow rented by others in the town for its milk — lo, this one continues to do work."

[C] *Said to him R. Yosé, "That which you have said applies in the case of one who already was obligated to him. Lo, so far as making such arrangements at the outset, it is forbidden."*

[I:9 A] In the case of two brothers, two partners, two butchers, two shopkeepers, to one of whom a misfortune happened — lo, these both must lock their shop.

[B] One's sharecroppers and workers labor in a discrete way in some other location.

[I:10 A] With regard to a mourner, so long as his deceased is lying [unburied] before him, he eats with a fellow.

[B] If he has no fellow, he eats in some other house.

[C] If he has no other house, he sets up a partition and eats.

[D] If he cannot set up a partition, he turns away and faces the wall and eats.

[E] In any event he does not recline and eat, nor does he eat to satiety, nor does he drink to satiety,

[F] nor does he eat meat or drink wine.

[G] They do not include him in a quorum for grace after meals.

[H] If he said a blessing, they do not say after him, "Amen."

[I] And as to others who said a blessing, he does not say after them, "Amen."

[J] Under what circumstances do these rules apply?

[K] In the case of an ordinary day.

[L] But on the Sabbath he reclines and eats, he eats to satiety, he drinks to satiety, he eats meat and drinks wine, they include him in a quorum for saying grace, and if he said a blessing, they answer, "Amen," after him. If others said a blessing, he answers after them, "Amen."

[M] Said R. Simeon b. Gamaliel, "Since you have permitted him to do all these things, why not declare him obligated to carry out all the other commandments of the Torah?

[N] "Matters affecting life of the moment have you permitted to him. As to matters affecting eternal life — is it not an argument a fortiori [that you should permit him]?"

[O] R. Judah bar Pazzi in the name of R. Joshua b. Levi: "The law is in accord with the view of Rabban Simeon b. Gamaliel."

[P] If the deceased was handed over to the community [for burial], [the mourner] may then eat meat and drink wine.

[Q] Once the deceased has been handed over to the pallbearers, it is as if he has been handed over to the community [for burial].

[R] On the first Sabbath [after burial] the mourner does not go to the synagogue. On the second Sabbath he goes to the synagogue but does not sit in his usual place. On the third Sabbath he sits in his usual place, but does not speak with others. On the fourth he is equivalent to everyone else.

[S] R. Judah says, "It surely is not possible to speak of the first Sabbath in any event, since the community takes care of him.

[T] "But the second Sabbath in fact is the first [in the synagogue], the third is the second, the fourth is the third."

[U] R. Simeon [82c] says, "On the first Sabbath [after burial of the deceased] the mourner goes to the synagogue, but he does not sit in his usual place. On the second, he sits in his usual place, but does not talk. On the third, he is equivalent to all others."

[V] R. Joshua b. Levi said, "The law accords with the view of him who adds days [to the period at which the mourner is equivalent to all others, that is, Simeon."

[I:11   A] Lo, if one came home and found mourning in his house, if this is on the second and on the third days, he completes the week of mourning with the others. If it is on the fourth day [after the mourning week has begun for the others], he counts [days of mourning] for himself.

[B] R. Simeon says, "Even if it is on the fourth day, he completes [the week of mourning] with them."

[C] R. Joshua b. Levi said, "The law accords with the view of R. Simeon."

[D] This is in the case that the one who has come home is not the eldest in the family. But if he was the eldest of the family, he counts [the entire mourning week] for himself.

[E] *That is in line with the following: R. Mana instructed R. Armenayya,* "Since you are the eldest in your family, you should count [the days of mourning] for yourself."

[F] [When we say that if one came after three days, he counts for himself,] that applies when the majority of those who will come to comfort the mourners have yet to make their appearance. But if the majority of those who will come to comfort the mourners already have made their appearance, [if he comes even on the seventh day, with the week over,] he still may go and take a bath [since the week is now over for all concerned, including the latecomer].

[G] *That is in line with the following: R. Huna instructed the brother of R. Judah bar Zabedi that* since the majority of those who would come to comfort the mourners had made their appearance, he might go off and take a bath.

[I:12 A] Lo, if they were bringing the deceased from one place to another—

[B] *for instance, those whom they bury in Beth Sharaii —*

[C] *there is a Tannaite authority who teaches:* Those who are here count the days of mourning from the time at which the deceased has gone forth, and those who are there count the days of mourning from the time that the stone has been rolled over onto the grave.

[D] *There is a Tannaite authority who teaches:* Both these and those begin to count the days of mourning from the moment at which the stone is rolled over onto the grave.

[E] R. Simon in the name of R. Joshua b. Levi: "All follows the status of the eldest in the family. [When he counts, they begin.]"

[F] R. Jacob bar Aha in the name of R. Assi: "This is to impose the strict rule."

[G] What is the meaning of that statement?

[H] If the eldest in the family were here, those who are here count the days of mourning from the time at which the deceased went forth, and those who are there count the days from the time at which the stone was rolled over onto the grave.

[I] If the eldest of the family were there, these and those begin to count the days of mourning from the time at which the stone was rolled over the grave.

[J] *This is in line with the following: The sister of Gamaliel Zugga was smitten. Hillel, his brother, went up with him [later on]. Said to him [Hillel] R. Mana, "Since you are the eldest of your family, when you go out to your brother, remove your shoe [as a sign of mourning]. [That is the point at which the mourning week begins for all concerned.]"*

[K] Lo, if they were moving the deceased from one grave to another:

[L] *There is a Tannaite authority who teaches:* Once the stone is rolled over onto the first grave[, the mourning rites begin].

[M] *There is a Tannaite authority who teaches:* Once the stone is rolled over the second grave[, the mourning rites begin].

[N] *R. Jonah had a case. He asked R. Hananiah, associate of the rabbis, who said to him,* "It is once the stone has rolled over the first grave [that the mourning begins]."

[O]   *Jeremiah had a case. He asked R. Zeira [and] R. Ammi. He said to him,* "Once the stone has been rolled over the second grave [the rites of mourning commence]."

[P]   *He came to him. He said to him, "He gave you a strict rule."*

[Q]   *[As to this problem of moving the deceased and the rites of mourning,] R. Jonah and R. Yosé both maintain, "That which you have said applies* during the seven days of mourning [after the original burial], but after those seven days, the period of mourning already has passed.

[R]   "[It further applies] when they had decided [at the outset] to move the body. But if [at the time of burial] he had not decided at the outset to move the body, the mourning rites begin after the first grave has been sealed."

[S]   *This is in line with the following: Gamaliel of Quntiah was buried by the people of Kursai in their place. After three days they reconsidered the matter [and wished to bury him in his own town]. They came and asked R. Simeon.*

[T]   R. Simeon said to them in the name of R. Joshua b. Levi, "Since you did not give thought to moving him once burial had taken place, the rites of mourning are counted from the time at which the original grave was sealed."

[U]   *Jeshua, brother of Dorai, had a case. He came and asked R. Abbahu. He said to him,* "The rites of mourning commence once the second grave has been sealed."

[V]   Said to him R. Jacob bar Aha, "I was with you when you asked that question to R. Abodemi of Haifa, who said, 'It is when the first grave has been sealed.'"

[W]   *He said to him, "Well, now, for my part, I never heard that teaching. If you heard it, go and teach it."*

[I:13 A]   Whence in the Torah do we derive the rites of mourning?

[B]   As to the observance of seven days: "And he made a mourning for his father seven days" (Gen. 50:10).

[C]   Do they derive a law from evidence pertaining to the period prior to the giving of the Torah?

[D]   *R. Jacob bar Aha in the name of R. Zeira: "Derive the rule from the following:* 'At the door of the tent of meeting you shall remain day and night for seven days, performing what the Lord has charged, lest you die' (Lev. 8:35).

[E]   "Just as the Holy One, blessed be he, kept watch over his world for seven days, so you must keep watch for your brothers for seven days."

[F]   And how do we know that the Holy One, blessed be he, kept watch over his world for seven days?

[G]   "And after seven days the waters of the flood came upon the earth" (Gen. 7:10).

[H]   But do they mourn prior to the death of the deceased [before the flood]?

[I] But the answer is simple: In the case of mortal man, who does not know what is going to happen, one undertakes the rites of mourning only after the person has died.

[J] But in the case of the Holy One, blessed be he, who knows what is going to happen, he kept watch over his world from the very beginning [even before the world perished in the flood].

[K] *There is he who proposes to state:* This refers to the seven days of mourning for Methuselah, the righteous.

[L] Said R. Hoshaiah, "'[And do not go out from the door of the tent of meeting, lest you die;] for the anointing oil of the Lord is upon you. [And they did according to the word of Moses]' (Lev. 10:7). Just as you have been anointed with the anointing oil for seven days, so you must keep watch for your [deceased] brethren for seven days."

[M] R. Abbahu in the name of R. Yohanan: "'Let her not be as one dead[, of whom the flesh is half consumed when he comes out of his mother's womb. And Moses cried to the Lord, Heal her, O God, I beseech thee]' (Num. 12:12-13). Let her be shut up. Just as the days of mourning for the deceased are seven, so the days of shutting up [for the inspection of leprosy signs] are to be seven."

[N] *A disciple repeated this statement of R. Yohanan before R. Simeon b. Laqish, who did not accept it. He said, "Here you deal with a case of shutting up, while there you deal with a case of certifying that a person is unclean."*

[O] For R. Yohanan in the name of R. Yannai: "'Let her not be as one dead' (Num. 12:12). Just as the seven days of mourning for the deceased do not count [toward the days of observing the Nazirite vow], so the days of being certified unclean do not count [toward the thirty days of observance of the Nazirite vow]."

[P] R. Jeremiah and R. Hiyya in the name of R. Simeon b. Laqish, R. Abbahu, R. Yosé b. Haninah in the name of R. Simeon b. Laqish: "'And the people of Israel wept for Moses in the plains of Moab thirty days; then the days of weeping and mourning for Moses were ended' (Deut. 34:8). 'The days' refers to the seven days of mourning. 'Weeping' is two. 'Mourning' is thirty."

[Q] *And there are those who revise the matter as follows:* "Days" is two, "weeping" is seven, and "mourning" is thirty.

[R] R. Yosé, R. Hiyya in the name of R. Simeon b. Laqish, R. Jonah and R. Hiyya and R. Simeon b. Laqish in the name of R. Yudan the Patriarch: "'I will turn your feasts into mourning [and all your songs into lamentation; I will bring sackcloth upon all loins and baldness on every head; I will make it like the mourning for an only son, and the end of it like a bitter day]' (Amos 8:10). Just as the days of the Festival [of Tabernacles] are seven, so the days of mourning are seven."

[S]   Said R. Ammi to R. Hiyya bar Ba, "Perhaps we may say, 'Just as the days of the Festival [of Tabernacles] are eight, so the days of mourning are eight'?"

[T]   He said to him, "The eighth day is a festival day unto itself [and not part of the Festival of Tabernacles]."

[U]   "Then may we argue, 'Just as the Eighth Day of Assembly is a single day, so mourning should be a single day'?"

[V]   He said to him, "It is from that argument that we derive a rule concerning conduct when news of a death arrives from a distant place."

[W]   *And so has it been taught:* When news of a death arrives from a nearby place, the death is subject to a period of seven days of mourning and a further thirty days of observance. But when it comes from a distant place, it is not subject to either seven or thirty days of mourning.

[X]   *There is a Tannaite authority who teaches:* News of a death arriving from a nearby place is defined as that which comes during thirty days after the death. That from a distant place is defined as that which comes thirty days after the death of the deceased.

[Y]   *There is a Tannaite authority who teaches:* News of a death falls into the category of that which comes from nearby if it is during twelve months after the death of the deceased, and it is deemed to fall into the category of a distant place if it comes twelve months after the death.

[Z]   R. Abbahu in the name of R. Yohanan: "The law is in accord with the view of him who says, 'News of a death coming from nearby is that which comes during thirty days after death, and from a distant place is what comes after thirty days.'"

[I:14 A]   Lo, if on a festival one heard that he had suffered a bereavement, but the days of the festival did not end before the thirty days [from the death of the deceased] were completed,

[B]   associates say, "Since he heard the news during the thirty days [following the death of the deceased], he counts seven days [of mourning even] after the thirty days have passed."

[C]   Said to them R. Yosé, "Since he heard the news at a time at which he was not able to undertake the rites of mourning, he is like one who heard the news thirty days after the death itself, and he is subject to engage in the rites of mourning only for a single day."

[D]   R. Iddi of Caesarea in the name of R. Yohanan: "If the news came from a nearby place on the Sabbath, he makes a tear in his garment on the next day and goes into a period of mourning."

[E]   Said R. Hananel, "He does not undertake rites of mourning."

[F]   Said to him [E] R. Mana, "Is there the possibility of tearing the garments as a sign of mourning, without actually undertaking the rites of mourning thereafter?"

[G]   [Yes, there is such a case,] for if he should hear news of the death of his father or his mother, even on the next day he is liable to make a tear in his garment [although the news may be so late that he is not liable to mourn in other ways].

[I:15 A] R. Abbahu in the name of R. Yohanan: "Even one who is secondary to the one involved in the bereavement is forbidden to get a haircut. [For instance, if one's grandson died and he is assisting the son in the burial, he is subject to the rules.]"

[B] *It is pertinent to the following: R. Mana was in Caesarea. He heard that the son of his son had died, and he went and got a haircut. They said to him, "And did our master not teach us: 'Even one who is secondary to the one involved in the bereavement is forbidden to get a haircut'?"*

[C] *He said to them, "That applies to those who are with the bereaved. But we are not actually with the bereaved."*

[D] [82d] R. Abodemi bar Tobi in the name of R. Abbahu: "And even one who is secondary to the one involved in the bereavement is liable to tear his clothing as a sign of mourning."

[I:16 A] There is that which R. Abbahu said: "'Sigh, but not aloud; [make no mourning for the dead]. [Bind on your turban, and put your shoes on your feet; do not cover your lips, nor eat the bread of mourners]'" (Ezek. 27:17). On the strength of this verse [we learn] that a mourner is supposed to express his sorrow out loud [in crying aloud].

[B] "'Make no mourning for the dead — on the strength of this verse [we learn] that one has to undertake the rites of mourning."

[C] "Bind on your turban": *There is he who wishes to say,* "This refers to the *Tefillin." There is he who wishes to say,* "This refers to laundering a linen garment."

[D] *He who said,* "This refers to the *Tefillin"* [then deals with the following inference]: Just as *Tefillin* [are not put on by the mourner] for two days, so mourning lasts for only two days.

[E] *He who said,* "This refers to laundering a linen garment" [then deals with the following inference]: Just as the prohibition against laundering a linen garment is for thirty days, so the rites of mourning apply for thirty days.

[F] "Put your shoes on your feet" — on the strength of this verse [we learn] that a mourner is forbidden to put on a sandal.

[G] "Do not cover your lips" — on the strength of this verse [we learn] that the mourner has to cover up his mouth.

[H] And let him cover it up below [but not the entire mouth]?

[I] *Said R. Hisda, "It is so that people will not say, 'He has a pain in his mouth' [and that is why he covers it up]."*

[J] "Nor eat the bread of mourners" — on the strength of this verse [we learn] that the less important people go to the more important people [to provide food on the occasion of mourning].

[K] And on the basis of what verse of Scripture do we learn that the more important people go to the less important ones [as well]?

[L]   Said R. Samuel bar R. Isaac, "It is written 'For thus says the Lord: Do not enter the house of mourning, or go to lament, or bemoan them; for I have taken away my peace from this people, says the Lord, my steadfast love and mercy'" (Jer. 16:5).

[I:17 A]   *It has been taught:* These are the things that are forbidden for a mourner all seven days [after the burial of the deceased: washing, anointing, putting on sandals, having sexual relations, getting a haircut, laundering clothing, reading in the Torah, speaking about the exegesis of Scriptures, laws, and lore, greeting someone, and doing work.

[B]   *Who taught that* a mourner is forbidden to wash all seven days?

[C]   It is R. Nathan.

[D]   *R. Ammi had a case. He asked R. Hiyya. He came and instructed him,* "It is for all seven days, in accord with the view of R. Nathan."

[E]   *R. Yosé had a case. He sent to R. Ba bar Kohen. He said to him, "And did my lord not teach us?"*

[F]   *R. Ammi had a case. He sent to R. Ba bar Kohen. He said to him, "And did not my lord teach us?"*

[G]   *R. Ammi had a case. He asked R. Simeon b. Laqish, who instructed him,* "The prohibition continues for seven days, in accord with the view of R. Nathan."

[H]   *He said to him, "And were there two cases?"*

[I]   *He said to him, "We state the matter in line with the case involving R. Hiyya bar Abba [D], and you state it in accord with R. Simeon b. Laqish [G]."*

[J]   *And there is further: R. Hama, father of R. Hoshaiah, had a case. He asked rabbis, and they prohibited [washing during the mourning week].*

[K]   *R. Yosé asked, "Which rabbis? Rabbis from here or rabbis from the south? If you say we refer to the rabbis from here, there are no problems. If you say it was the rabbis from the south, there are great authorities here [in the north], and are you going to ask the minor authorities [of the south]?!"*

[L]   *"If, further, you say that they were the rabbis from here, there is no problem. But if you say they were the rabbis from the south, you [here] declare it permitted, while do they declare it forbidden?"*

[M]   *For it has been taught:* In a place in which they are accustomed to wash after [returning from] the bier, they wash. And in the south, they wash.

[N]   Said R. Yosé b. R. Bun, "He who permits washing treats it as equivalent to eating and drinking."

[O]   *That which you say* [regarding washing as prohibited] applies to washing merely for pleasure. But as to washing not for pleasure, it is in any event permitted.

[P]   Ulcers came up on Samuel bar Abba. *They came and asked R. Yosé, "What is the law on his washing?"*

[Q]   *He said to them, "If he does not wash, he will die."*

[R] If so, even on the ninth of Ab, and even on the Day of Atonement [it will be permitted in an equivalent circumstance].

[S] R. Yosé b. Haninah: "If people saw the mourner washing, and if it was on account of [purifying himself from] his seminal emission [from before the bereavement], whether it was to cool off his body [they do not know], for washing in cold water is not regarded as washing."

[T] *R. Ba bar Kohen taught in accord with this latter opinion [that washing in cold water is permitted].*

[U] *R. Aha taught concerning him* who comes in from a trip, with his feet aching, that it is permitted to wash them in water.

[I:18 A] It has been taught: A mourner and one who has been excommunicated who are going on a trip are permitted to wear shoes. When they reach a town, they then take them off.

[B] So is the rule on the ninth of Ab, and so is the rule in connection with a public fast.

[I:19 A] It has been taught: In a place in which it is the custom to greet mourners on the Sabbath, they greet them. And in the south they greet them.

[B] *R. Hoshaiah the Elder went to a certain place. He saw mourners on the Sabbath and greeted them.* He said to them, "I do not know the custom in this place of yours, but I greet you with a greeting of peace in accord with the custom of our place."

[C] *R. Meir praised R. Yosé b. R. Halapta before the people of Sepphoris:* "A great man, a holy man, a modest man."

[D] *One time [Yosé] saw mourners on the Sabbath and greeted them. The people said to [Meir], "Rabbi, is this the one whom you were praising to us?"*

[E] *He said to them, "What has he done?"*

[F] *They said to him, "He saw mourners on the Sabbath and greeted them."*

[G] *He said to them, "He wanted you to know the full extent of his authority.* He came to inform us that the laws of mourning do not apply on the Sabbath, *in line with that which is written,* 'The blessing of the Lord makes rich, and he adds no sorrow with it' (Prov. 10:22).

[H] "'The blessing of the Lord' refers to the blessing of the Sabbath. 'And he adds no sorrow with it' refers to mourning, in line with that which you recite in Scripture: 'So the victory that day was turned into mourning for all the people; for the people heard that day, the king is grieving for his son' (2 Sam. 19:2)."

[I:20 A] Samuel said, "[With regard to the Sabbath, a mourner's] uncovering the head, turning of the tear of the garment, and setting the bed right-side up are obligatory, while putting on sandals, having sexual relations, and washing of hands are optional."

[B]   *A disciple of Samuel had sexual relations [on the Sabbath during
      a bereavement]. Samuel heard about it and was angry at him, and
      he died.*

[C]   [Explaining his attitude and its consequences,] Samuel] said, "That
      statement [that sexual relations are optional and may then be carried
      out on the Sabbath, while on the weekdays a mourner is prohibited
      from doing so] was stated for the purposes of legal theory, but
      surely not for the purposes of actual practice!"

[D]   Rab said, "[On the Sabbath] turning of the tear of the garment and
      setting the bed right-side up are obligatory, while uncovering the
      head and putting on sandals are optional."

[E]   *The two sons of Rab went out [on the Sabbath during bereavement],
      one with his head uncovered but without sandals, and one with
      his head covered but wearing sandals.*

[F]   *R. Jonah went up to R. Gurion. He went out to him wearing sandals.
      He said to him, "What are you thinking? That we shall derive a
      precedent from your behavior? A precedent surely does not derive
      from the action of such an unimportant person."*

[I:21 A] As to the prohibition of reading in the Torah during mourning:

[B]   Said R. Yohanan, "'And they sat with him on the ground seven
      days and seven nights, and no one spoke a word to him, for they
      saw that his suffering was very great' (Job 2:13). And no one
      speaking a word to him means, even a word of Torah."

[C]   *Said to him R. Simeon b. Laqish, "The very essence of the matter
      demands this conclusion: Had he repeated [Mishnah traditions]
      he would not have died!"*

[D]   *What is the upshot of the matter?*

[E]   *It is in accord with that which* R. Judah bar Pazzi said in the name
      of R. Yohanan, "That [prohibition (at Job 2:13) of speaking]
      applied, for they did not know how to open the discourse with
      him, whether with regard to his person, his property, or the life of
      his sons and daughters."

[F]   *[Proving that while one is studying Torah, the angel of death cannot
      touch a person, the following is told:] A disciple of R. Hisda fell
      sick. R. Hisda sent two disciples to him, so that they would repeat
      Mishnah traditions with him. [The angel of death] turned himself
      before them into the figure of a snake, and they stopped repeating
      traditions, and [the sick man] died.*

[G]   *A disciple of Bar Pedaiah fell ill. He sent to him two disciples to
      repeat Mishnah traditions with him. [The angel of death] turned
      himself before them into a kind of star, and they stopped repeating
      Mishnah traditions, and he died.*

[H]   *It was taught:* A mourner repeats traditions in a passage with which
      he is not familiar.

[I]   *That would be illustrated by the following: R. Yosé had [a
      bereavement]. R. Yohanan sent him two disciples to repeat Mishnah
      traditions with him. We do not know whether that is because it is*

> *permitted to do so, or because they repeated traditions for him in
> a passage with which he is not familiar.*

[J]   *And is R. Yosé not familiar [with the whole of the Torah]?*

[K]   *But [they repeated traditions], for example, concerning those
statements of a rabbi in which a man would have to investigate
deeply, and these would be passages in which one is not familiar.*

[L]   *R. Yosé bar Petros, father-in-law of R. Joshua b. Levi by reason of
[Joshua's] first wife, had a bereavement. Bar Qappara sent him
two disciples to repeat Mishnah traditions with him.*

[M]   *We do not know whether he did so because it is permitted to do so
or because [the mourner] yearned after Torah.*

[N]   *And so we have learned:* If the mourner thirsted after the Torah, it
is permitted [to him to study Torah during his bereavement].

[I:22 A]   On account of every relationship stated in the Torah for which a
priest contracts uncleanness [in burying the corpse], an Israelite
undertakes the rites of mourning.

[B]   [For both priest and Israelite] they added: his brother and sister on
his mother's side, his sister who is married.

[C]   [In these instances both] undertake the rites of mourning and enter
the status of one who has suffered a bereavement but whose dead
is not yet buried, but [a priest] does not contract uncleanness for
them.

[D]   As to a woman whom one has betrothed [but not yet married], one
does not undertake rites of mourning, or enter the status of one
who has suffered a bereavement but who has not yet buried his
dead, nor does a priest contract corpse-uncleanness.

[E]   *It has been taught:* In the case of all those who undertake rites of
mourning for a person, these same people undertake the rites of
mourning along with that same person. [That is, if one would be
obligated to mourn *for* a person, he is obligated to mourn with that
person, if the latter suffers a bereavement.]

[F]   *When Rab's sister was smitten, he instructed Hiyya, his son, saying
to him, "When you come to me, take off your sandal."*

[G]   *The sons of R. Haninah, brother of R. Mana, died. They came
[83a] and asked R. Yosé,* "What is the law [as to Mana's having] to
overturn the bed."

[H]   He said to them, "It is not necessary."

[I]   "What is the law as to his having to sleep on an overturned bed?"

[J]   He said to them, "It is not necessary."

[K]   "What is the law as to his reciting the *Shema* and saying the Prayer?"

[L]   *He said to them, "Let us derive the answer from the following:*
'Lo, if someone was busy with a corpse in a grave, and the time for
saying the *Shema* came, he should go up to a clean place and put
on his *Tefillin* and recite the *Shema* and say the Prayer.' [So he
must do so.]"

[I:23 A]   At what time do they overturn the beds [as a sign of mourning]?

[B] "When the corpse is taken out the door of the courtyard," the opinion of R. Eliezer.

[C] And R. Joshua says, "When the stone is rolled over onto the grave."

[D] Now when Rabban Gamaliel died, when the corpse had been taken out of the gate of the courtyard, R. Eliezer said to his disciples, "Turn over the beds [in the house]."

[E] When the stone was rolled over the mouth of the grave, said R. Joshua to the disciples, "Turn over the beds."

[F] They said to him, "They already have turned them over, on the instructions of the elder."

[G] On the eve of the Sabbath one sets his beds aright. At the end of the Sabbath, he turns them over again.

[H] *It has been taught:* A footstool is set upright and not turned over.

[I] R. Simeon b. Eleazar says, "One removes its frame, and that suffices."

[J] R. Yosé in the name of R. Joshua b. Levi: "The law follows the view of R. Simeon b. Eleazar."

[K] R. Jacob bar Aha in the name of R. Yosé, "As to a bed, the poles of which are put together and taken apart with it — one removes them, and that suffices."

[L] What is a bed and what is a footstool?

[M] Said R. Jeremiah, "Any on the outside of the frame of which one stretches the net is a bed, and any on the outside of which one does not spread the net is a footstool."

[N] *Lo, we have learned:* **A bed and a cot [become susceptible to uncleanliness as completely manufactured and ready for use] when one will have rubbed them with fish skin [M. Kel. 16:1D].**

[O] Now if one weaves the webbing for the bed on the outside of its frame, for what purpose will one rub on the fish skin [since the wood, covered with ropes, cannot be sandpapered anyhow]?

[P] *Said R. Eleazar, "Interpret the passage to speak of cribs that come from Caesarea, which have holes [through which the thongs for the webbing are inserted, and hence have an outer surface that requires smoothing]."*

[I:24 A] How do we know from Scripture that it is required to turn over the beds as a sign of mourning?

[B] R. Qerispai in the name of R. Yohanan: "'And they sat with him at the ground [seven days and seven nights, and no one spoke a word to him, for they saw that his suffering was very great]' (Job 2:13).

[C] "'On the ground' is not written here, but rather, 'at the ground.' That means something that is near the ground. On that basis we learn that they slept on beds that had been turned over."

[D] Bar Qappara said, "'I had one good likeness of myself [God] in your house, and you made me turn it over [and bury it, namely, your children], so you turn over your bed.'"

[E] *And there are those who derive the meaning of the expression from the following:* "Let the agent [of sin] be overpowered [by mourning ceremonies]"

[F] Both R. Jonah and R. Yosé, both of them citing R. Simeon b. Laqish [explain the matter].

[G] *One said,* "On what account does a mourner sleep on a bed that has been turned upside down? It is so he will wake up during the night and be reminded that he is a mourner."

[H] *The other said,* "Since he is sleeping on a bed turned upside down, he will wake up by night and be reminded that he is a mourner."

[I] If one said, "I am not going to turn the bed upside down. Lo, I shall sleep on a stool instead" — they do not listen to him, for he has said, "I am not going to turn the bed upside down."

[J] But if he said, "Lo, I shall turn the bed upside down," they do listen to him[, and he may sleep on the stool anyhow].

[I:25 A] *Now has not the Mishnah made this point? [With reference to M. San. 2:2F-G:]* **And when they provide him with the funeral meal, [all the people sit on the ground, while he sits on a stool]** —

[B] that refers to the high priest.

[C] Lo, with regard to an ordinary priest, that is not the case.

[D] *And the Mishnah speaks of* a public meal. Lo, when the high priest eats by himself, he does not [sit on a stool].

[E] *And in any event they do not do things this way.*

[I:26 A] As to turning over the beds, there are occasions on which one does it six days, five, four, or three.

[B] [If the bereavement is] on Friday, one does it six days.

[C] If it is on Friday at sunset, one does it five.

[D] If it is on a festival day that comes after the Sabbath, one does it four days.

[E] If it is on the two days of the New Year, one does it three days.

[F] *A disciple of R. Mana instructed one of the relatives of the patriarch that,* when he had set the bed upright again [for the Sabbath], he need not overturn it again.

[G] How many days of mourning had he already observed prior to the Sabbath?

[H] R. Jacob bar Aha in the name of R. Yosé, "He had already observed two days prior to the Sabbath."

[I] R. Ba, R. Ammi, R. Jacob bar Zabedi in the name of R. Isaac: "Three days."

[J] R. Hinenah bar Pappi gave instructions to turn it over even for one day [if there was only a single day lacking, then, even after the Sabbath, the mourner had to turn the bed over. The following verse appeared to him in a dream]":

[K] "And he cried to the man of God who came from Judah, 'Thus says the Lord, Because you have disobeyed the word of the Lord, and have not kept the commandment which the Lord your God commanded you'" (1 Kings 13:21).

[I:27 A]   *It has been taught:* He who dwells in a shop — they do not
            require him to turn his bed over,

[B]   so that people should not say that he is a wizard.

[I:28 A]   Lo, if one's father-in-law or mother-in-law or any of the relatives
            of his wife died, he does not have the right to require his wife to
            make up her eyes or do her hair as usual.

[B]   But he behaves with her just as she behaves [in observing the
       rites of mourning].

[C]   And so a woman whose father-in-law or mother-in-law or other
       relatives of her husband died, she does not make up her eyes or
       do her hair, but she behaves with him just as he behaves.

[D]   Said Samuel, "That teaching has been applied only in the case of
       one's father-in-law or mother-in-law. But as to one of the other
       relatives, it does not apply at all."

[E]   R. Ba bar Kohen said before R. Yosé, R. Judah bar Pazzi in the
       name of R. Yohanan: "It applies when [the relative] is living with
       him."

[F]   *R. Yosé dealt with R. Judah bar Pazzi, and he said to him, "Have
       you heard this teaching from your father?"*

[G]   *He said to him, "Father did not explicitly say so. But the brother
       of the wife of Bar Nehemiah died. They came and asked him, 'What
       is the law as to turning the bed over?' He said to them, 'It is not
       necessary.'*

[H]   "What is the law as to reciting the *Shema* and saying the Prayer?'

[I]   *"He said, 'Let us derive the answer from the following:* If one was
       occupied with a corpse in the grave, and the time for reciting the
       Shema came, lo, this one goes off to a clean place and puts on his
       Tefillin and recites the *Shema* and says the Prayer.'"

[II:1A]   For they have said, "The Sabbath counts in the days of
           mourning, but does not interrupt the period of mourning, while
           the festivals interrupt the period of mourning, and do not count
           in the days of mourning" [M. 3:5C].

[B]   "[The festivals do not count,]" R. Simon in the name of R. Yohanan
       [explained], "Because one is permitted on them to have sexual
       relations."

[C]   *R. Jeremiah dealt with R. Judah b. R. Simon, saying to him, "Do
       all the disciples of R. Yohanan report this tradition? Not one person
       has ever heard this tradition from him, except for your father!"*

[D]   *Said to him R. Jacob, "If it was said, it was said only by those who
       say, 'Thus and so is the matter' [without knowing what they are
       talking about]!*

[E]   "For R. Joshua b. Levi said, 'Lo, [on the festival] it is forbidden
       [for a mourner] to have sexual relations.'"

[F]   For R. Simon said in the name of R. Joshua b. Levi, "Have they
       not said, 'A mourning does not apply on a festival, but people
       observe mourning discretely'?"

[G] What is the context for this discretion? It has to do with sexual relations [which are not to be performed on the festival by a mourner].

[H] [Reverting to the discussion broken off at B:] *They objected,* "Lo, in the case of the festival, lo, the mourner is prohibited from having sexual relations, and yet it does not count [toward the days of mourning]. Also in regard to the Sabbath, since a mourner is forbidden to have sexual relations, the Sabbath should not count [among the days of mourning, and yet it does, so the reason proposed at B is not likely]."

[I] Said R. Ba, "It is possible that seven days can pass without a festival, but it is not possible that seven days can pass without a Sabbath[, and if the Sabbath does not suspend the rites of mourning, there will be eight days of mourning, and not seven] ."

Yerushalmi Moed Qatan 3:7

[A] **They do not tear their clothing, bare the shoulder, or provide food for mourners, except the near relatives of the deceased.**

[B] **And they do not provide mourners food except on an upright couch.**

[C] **They do not bring [food] to a house of mourning on a tray, salver, or flat basket, but in plain baskets.**

[D] **And they do not [in Grace after meals] say the blessing for mourners during the intermediate days of the festival.**

[E] **But [the mourners] do stand in a line and offer consolation and dismiss those that have gathered together.**

[I:1 A] Said R. Jeremiah, "[As to M. 3:7A,] that is on condition that they are relatives who are appropriate to undertake the rites of mourning."

[B] [83b] *There is that which is taught:* A sage who died — all are regarded as his near relatives, and that applies even to relatives who [otherwise] are not suitable to undertake the rites of mourning on his account.

[C] *There is the following: R. Abun died on the intermediate day of the festival, and R. Mana did not then pay his respects to him. The Sepphoreans were saying, "This hatred surpasses even death."*

[D] *After the festival he paid him all due respect. He went up and said before them, "'As to a sage who has died, all are regarded as his near relatives.' That applies to those who are with him. But we were not with him."*

[I:2 A] He who makes a tear in his clothing at a part that was hemmed together, basted, or at the edges picked up by cross-stitch or ladder stitch — this is not regarded as a valid tear in the clothing. If it is a part that had been rejoined [in a seam], lo, this is regarded as a valid tear.

[B] What is the meaning of "a part that had been rejoined"?

[C] Said R. Aha, "Any, the place of which is not visible [is regarded as a seam that has been stitched together]."

[I:3 A] Ten occasions of making a tear are forbidden in respect to tearing a part that had been rejoined in a seam [for this would be insufficient]: He who tears on account of the death of his father, mother, master who has taught him wisdom, the patriarch, head of the court, bad news, hearing the Name of God cursed, the burning of a Torah, for Jerusalem, and for the sanctuary.

[B] How do we know that that is the case on account of his father, mother, and master who taught him wisdom?

[C] "And Elisha saw it and he cried, 'My father, my father! The chariots of Israel and its horsemen!' And he saw him no more" (2 Kings 2:12).

[D] *R. Matun asked before R. Yohanan,* "Do we derive a lesson of Torah from the case of Elisha [for Elijah did not die]?"

[E] He said to him, "Matun, Matun, just as in the case of the deceased, once it is taken away, one does not see it any more, so in the case of this one, once he was removed, people did not see him any longer. [That is, even though Elijah did not die, the mourning procedures are adequate precedent as if he had.]"

[I:4 A] Just as they make a tear for sages, so they make a tear for their disciples.

[B] What is the definition of a disciple of a sage?

[C] Hezekiah said, "It is any one who has learned laws and [their basis in the law of Torah] in addition."

[D] *Said to him R. Yosé, "That which you have said applies in the beginning.* But as to nowadays, even if one has learned only laws [, it suffices to apply to such a person the title of a disciple of a sage]."

[E] R. Abbahu in the name of R. Yohanan: "It is any who sets aside his worldly affairs on account of his learning of Mishnah."

[F] *It was taught:* It is anyone of whom they ask a question and who can answer it.

[G] *Said R. Hoshaiah, "Take us, for example, for our masters inspect our learning, and we are able to answer them."*

[H] Said R. Ba bar Mamel, "It is anyone who knows how to explain what he has learned in the Mishnah. *But as to us, even our masters do not know how to explain the Mishnah that we have learned."*

[I:5 A] [In T.'s version:] **Who is one's master?**

[B] [Y. omits:] **"It is the one who has taught him wisdom [and not the master who has taught him a trade].**

[C] **"It is anyone who started him off first," the words of R. Meir [Y.: Eliezer].**

[D]   **R. Judah says, "It is anyone from whom he has gained the greater part of his learning."**

[E]   R. Yosé says, "It is anyone who has enlightened his eyes in his repetition of traditions" [T. Hor. 2:5C-H], **even in one thing only.**

[F]   R. Abbahu in the name of R. Yohanan: "The law is in accord with the position of the one who says, 'It is anyone from whom he has gained the greater part of his learning.'"

[G]   Now why did he not simply interpret the Mishnah pericope by saying, "The law is in accord with R. Judah"?

[H]   *[Because there are] repeaters of traditions who will become confused and switch [matters about].*

[I]   R. Eliezer would make a tear in mourning on the demise of someone who had simply opened his education at the outset [but was not his principal teacher (C)].

[J]   Samuel removed his phylacteries on the news of the demise of one who had enlightened his eyes in his learning of the Mishnah [E].

[K]   And what is the case of one's "enlightening his eyes in his learning of the Mishnah"?

[L]   It is one who taught merely so brief a passage as the following: **[The two keys] — one goes down into the lock as far as its armpit, and one opens the doorforthwith [M. Tam. 3:6E].**

[M]   (Now what is the meaning of, **One goes down into the lock as far as its armpit?** That it would go down for a cubit before it would open the door.)

[I:6 A]   On account of the patriarch, head of the court, and bad news: How do we know [from the Torah] that one tears his garment on these occasions?

[B]   It is from the following verse: "Then David took hold of his clothes and tore them; and so did all the men who were with him; and they mourned and wept and fasted until evening for Saul and for Jonathan his son" (2 Sam. 1:12).

[C]   "For Saul" — this represents the patriarch.

[D]   "And for Jonathan his son" — this represents the head of the court.

[E]   "And for the people of the Lord and for the house of Israel, because they had fallen by the sword" (2 Sam. 1:12) — this refers to bad news.

[F]   And how do we know that one tears his garment when hearing a curse of the Name of God?

[G]   "When King Hezekiah heard it, he rent his clothes, and covered himself with sackcloth, and went into the house of the Lord" (2 Kings 19:1).

[I:7 A]   What is the law as to tearing one's garment because he has heard the Name of God cursed by a gentile?

[B]   Let us derive the law from the following:

[C]   "When King Hezekiah heard the words of Rabshakeh, he tore his clothes and covered himself with sackcloth" (2 Kings 19:1).

[D] What is the law as to tearing one's clothes on hearing the curse of an idolater [of the Name of God]?

[E] *He who says that* Rabshakeh was an idolater, holds that they do tear their clothes at the blasphemy of an idolater.

[F] *One who said that* he was a Jew holds that they do not tear their clothes when an idolater curses God.

[G] *R. Hoshaiah taught:* "All the same is the law for one who hears the cursing of the divine name on the part of an Israelite and one who hears the cursing of the divine name on the part of an idolater: one is liable to tear one's clothes."

[H] *What is the scriptural basis for that statement?*

[I] "The word of the Lord came to Jeremiah: 'Behold, I am the Lord, the God of all flesh; is anything too hard for me?'" (Jer. 32: 27).

[I:8 A] What is the law as to tearing one's garments in this time?

[B] R. Yosé, R. Jeremiah in the name of R. Hiyya bar Ba, R. Hezekiah, R. Jeremiah in the name of R. Yohanan: "Once blasphemers became many, they have ceased from tearing their garments upon hearing blasphemy."

[C] What is the law as to tearing one's garments at this time upon hearing God cursed through euphemisms?

[D] *Let us derive the answer to that question from the following:*

[E] R. Simeon b. Laqish was riding along on the road. *A Samaritan crossed his path, and was cursing, and [Simeon] tore his clothes, and again the Samaritan cursed, and again [Simeon] tore his clothes.*

[F] *[Simeon] got off his ass and gave the Samaritan a punch in the chest.*

[G] *He said to him, "Evil one! Does your mother have enough new clothes to give me [for your causing me to tear mine]?"*

[H] *From this story it is clear that* they do tear their clothing when they hear God cursed through euphemisms, and they also do tear their clothing at this time [after the destruction of the Temple].

[I:9 A] And how do we know that they tear clothing in mourning on account of the burning of the Torah?

[B] "As Jehudi read three or four columns, the king would cut them off with a penknife and throw them into the fire in the brazier, until the entire scroll was consumed in the fire that was in the brazier" (Jer. 36:23).

[C] What is the meaning of "three or four columns"?

[D] Three or four verses.

[E] When he came to the fifth verse: "Her foes have become the head, her enemies prosper, because the Lord has made her suffer for the multitude of her transgressions; her children have gone away, captives before the foe" (Lam. 1:5).

[F] Forthwith: "The king would cut them off with a penknife" (Jer. 36:23).

[G] "Now after the king had burned the scroll with the words that Baruch wrote at Jeremiah's dictation, the word of the Lord came to Jeremiah" (Jer. 36:27).

[I:10 A] He who sees a disciple of a sage who has died is as if he sees a scroll of the Torah that has been burned.

[B] Said R. Abbahu, "May a bad thing happen to me, if I tasted any food all that day [on which I saw a deceased disciple of a sage]."

[C] *R. Jonah was in Tyre when he heard that the son of R. Abbahu had died. Even though he had eaten cheese and drunk water, he undertook a fast for the rest of the day.*

[D] *R. Ba and R. Huna bar Hiyya were in session. An ostrich came along and snatched the Tefillin of R. Huna bar Hiyya.* R. Ba trapped the bird and strangled it. Said to him R. Huna bar Hiyya, "Had matters gone a bit further, we should have been in a situation in which the Torah would have been burned [and we should have had to mourn for it]."

[E] He said to him, "Do you still maintain [so strict a view]? Thus did R. Jeremiah say in the name of Rab, 'They do not make a tear as an act of mourning except in the case of a scroll of the Torah which an Israelite king burned by force, for example, Jehoiakim, the son of Josiah, king of Judah, and his associates.'"

[F] Ulla Biria, R. Eleazar in the name of R. Haninah: "He who sees a scroll of the Torah that has been burned is liable to make a tear for the parchment by itself and for the writing by itself.

[G] *"What is the scriptural basis for that view?* 'Now after the king had burned the scroll with the words that Baruch wrote at Jeremiah's dictation, the word of the Lord came to Jeremiah' (Jer. 36:27).

[H] "'The scroll' refers to the parchment, and 'with the words' refers to the writing."

[I:11 A] R. Berekhiah, R. Helbo, Ulla Biria, R. Eleazar in the name of R. Hanina: "In the future, the Holy One, blessed be he, is going to be made the chief dancer among the righteous in the age to come.

[B] *"What is the scriptural basis for this view?* 'Consider well her ramparts' (Ps. 48:13). It is written, 'Her dance.'"

[C] "And the righteous will point to him with their finger [so saluting him], and say, 'That this is God, our God for ever and ever. He will be our guide forever'" (Ps. 48:14).

[D] [Since the word 'forever' is written ' LMWT, we consider the following meanings of that word:] It means "strength," "quickness," and "like those maidens."

[E] Aqilas Athena Sira translated: "A world in which is no death."

[F] And the righteous will point to him with their fingers and say, "That this is God, our God for ever and ever. He will be our guide forever" (Ps. 48:14).

[G] He will lead us in this world, and he will lead us in the world to come.

[I:12 A]   And for Jerusalem and for the Temple: "Eighty men arrived from Shechem and Shiloh and Samaria, with their beards shaved and their clothes torn, and their bodies gashed, bringing cereal offerings and incense to present at the temple of the Lord" (Jer. 41:5).

[B]   All the same are he who has heard that Jerusalem has been destroyed and he who sees Jerusalem in her ruin. Both are liable to make a tear in mourning.

[C]   He who sees Jerusalem from Mount Scopus is liable to make a tear.

[I:13 A]   *There is a Tannaite authority who teaches:* One adds to the tear.

[B]   *There is a Tannaite authority who teaches:* A tear to begin with is a handbreadth, and an addition to it is any length of further tear at all.

[C]   *There is, further, a Tannaite authority who teaches:* The tear to begin with is a handbreadth, and an addition to it is three fingers in breadth.

[D]   R. Yosé, R. Jeremiah in the name of R. Hiyya bar Ba, R. Hezekiah, R. Jeremiah in the name of R. Yohanan: "The law accords with the view of him who said that a tear to begin with is a handbreadth, and an addition to it is any length at all."

[E]   What is the law as to separating the hem [and so regarding that as a tear]?

[F]   [83c] R. Jeremiah, R. Hiyya in the name of R. Simeon b. Laqish: "'Then David took hold of his clothes and rent them; and so did all the men who were with him' (2 Sam. 1:11). There is no 'taking hold' less than a handbreadth."

[G]   "And rent them" — R. Simon in the name of R. Joshua b. Levi: "On the basis of that statement we learn that it is necessary to separate the hem."

[I:14 A]   If one suffered a bereavement, he makes a tear. If he suffered yet another bereavement, even if he heard that it was his father, mother, or teacher who had taught him wisdom, he suffices with a single tear for all of them.

[B]   R. Judah b. Tema says, "He makes a tear on account of this one by himself, and on account of that one by himself."

[C]   And that is on condition that he not treat the one for his father or for his mother as merely a supplement to the others.

[D]   *But that statement does not pertain to what has gone before.*

[E]   Rather: It is that he not add to the tear for his father or the one for his mother.

[F]   R. Helbo and R. Mattena, Yosé bar Menassia in the name of Rab: "The law accords with the view of R. Judah b. Tema."

[G]   If one suffered a bereavement, he makes a tear. If he suffered yet another bereavement, he adds to the tear he originally made, thereby making a tear [for the other bereavement].

[H]   To what extent?

[I]   Said R. Haninah, "Until he reaches the belly button."

[J]   *An elder taught before R. Zeira,* "Even if he had set aside a different garment for each day of the seven days of mourning, he is liable to make a tear in each one."

[K]   *Said to him R. Zeira, "That which you say applies to the case of* other relatives. But if he heard the news of his father's or mother's death, even after a long time, he is liable to make a tear."

[L]   If one suffered a bereavement, he makes a tear. If he suffered yet another bereavement, he makes a tear three fingerbreadths away from the first.

[M]   If the front part of the garment is fully torn, he begins a tear on the other side. If the top part of the garment is fully torn, he begins at the bottom.

[N]   If these and those are fully torn —

[O]   R. Hiyya son of R. Ada of Jaffa said, "He is treated as one who is fully exposed [in ragged garments, and no further tearing is possible]."

[I:15 A]   *R. Hinenah bar Pappi went up to R. Tanhum bar Hiyya. He came out to him dressed in his upper garments [street dress, though he was in mourning].*

[B]   *(What was this "upper garment"? It is a garment without a tear.)*

[C]   *He said to him, "How do you know [that it is permitted to wear such a garment during a bereavement]?"*

[D]   *He said to him, "This is what R. Simon, my teacher, did."*

[E]   He said to him, "Pray for us."

[F]   He said to him, "May your breach go away [that is, the loss you have suffered]."

[G]   For during the entire year [in which a bereavement is suffered by a family], the attribute of justice points toward the family [that has suffered a loss].

[H]   For R. Yohanan has said, "For the entire period of seven days of mourning, a sword is unsheathed. For the first thirty days it spins about. After twelve months it goes back to its sheath.

[I]   "To what is the matter compared? To a pile of stones. When one of them falls loose, all of them spill out."

[J]   And R. Eleazar said, "If a male child is born to that family, the entire family is healed."

[I:16 A]   How do we know that a mourner is liable to make a tear [as a sign of mourning] while standing up?

[B]   It is written, "Then Job arose, and rent his robe, and shaved his head[, and fell upon the ground, and worshiped]" (Job 1:20).

[C]   R. Judah bar Pazzi in the name of R. Yohanan: "On the strength of that passage it is clear that a mourner is liable to make a tear [as a sign of mourning] while standing up."

[I:17 A]   Said R. Yohanan, "R. Yosé gave instructions to baste the rent on the next day."

[B]   *When R. Yosé died, R. Hiyya bar Ba gave instructions* to close the tear on the same day.

[C] *Said R. Zeira, "And they do not differ. He who said* one should baste the tear on the next day will agree to close it up on the next day. *And he who said* to close it up on the same day will concur that it may be basted on the same day."

[I:18 A] If people said to someone, "Reuben has died," and he made a tear, and afterward they said to him, "Simeon has died," lo, he already has carried out his obligation to make a tear in mourning.

[B] If they told him, "Reuben has died," and he made a tear, and afterward they said to him, "At that time he was alive, but he now has died —

[C] *there is a Tannaite authority who teaches that* he has carried out his obligation to make a tear in mourning.

[D] *And there is a Tannaite authority who teaches that* he has not.

[E] *He who maintains that* he has already carried out his obligation to make a tear points out that he indeed has already made a tear.

[F] *He who maintains that* he has not carried out his obligation to make a tear notes that, lo, he has made a tear [only] for a living person.

[G] *There is a further relevant passage:*

[H] If one made a tear, and the person began to breathe again, [and then died,] if this was forthwith, the mourner does not have to make another tear. If it was after a while, he does have to make another tear.

[I] How long an interval is regarded as "forthwith"? Sufficient time for an exchange of speech.

[J] And how long is "sufficient time for speech"? R. Simon in the name of R. Joshua b. Levi: "Sufficient time for one person to greet another."

[K] Abba bar bar Hannah in the name of R. Yohanan: "Sufficient time for a master and a disciple to greet one another, and for the disciple to say to the master, 'Peace be to you, my lord.'"

[I:19 A] *R. Yohanan was leaning on R. Jacob bar Iddi, and R. Eleazar [a Babylonian] saw him and avoided him. [Yohanan] said, "Lo, now there are two things that that Babylonian has done to me! One is that he did not even bother to greet me, and the other is that he did not cite a tradition of mine in my name."*

[B] *[Jacob] said to him, "That is the custom over there, that the lesser party does not greet the more important authority. For they carry out the following verse of Scripture:* 'The young men saw me and withdrew, and the aged rose and stood'" (Job 29:8).

[C] *As they were going along, they saw a certain schoolhouse.*

[D] *[Jacob] said to him, "Here is where R. Meir used to go into session and expound the law. And he stated traditions in the name of R. Ishmael, but he did not state traditions in the name of R. Aqiba."*

[E] *[Yohanan] said to him, "Everybody knows that R. Meir was the disciple of R. Aqiba [so he did not have to cite him]."*

[F] *[Jacob] said to him, "Everybody knows that R. Eleazar is the disciple of R. Yohanan."*

[G] *As they were going along, [they passed by a procession in which an idol was carried, and Jacob asked Yohanan,] "What is the law as to passing a procession in which an idol is being carried?"*

[H] *He said to him, "And do you pay respect to the idol? Go before it and blind its eyes."*

[I] *[Jacob] said to him, "Well did R. Eleazar do to you, for he did not pass by you [since that would have required an inappropriate gesture]."*

[J] *[Yohanan] said to him, "Jacob bar Iddi, you know very well how to make peace [between quarreling people]."*

[K] R. Yohanan wanted traditions to be stated in his name, for David too prayed for mercy [for the same purpose], saying, "Let me dwell in thy tent forever! Oh to be safe under the shelter of thy wings!" (Ps. 61:4).

[I:20 A] R. Phineas, R. Jeremiah in the name of R. Yohanan: "And did it enter David's mind that he would live forever? But this is what he said: 'May I have the merit of having my words repeated in synagogues and schools.'"

[B] *And what made this important to him?* Bar Tira said, "He who says a tradition in the name of the person who originally said it — [the latter's] lips move in the grave."

[C] What is the scriptural foundation for this statement? "And your kisses like the best wine that goes down smoothly, gliding over lips and teeth" (Song 7:9).

[D] *R. Hinenah bar Pappi and R. Simon — one said, "It is comparable to one who drinks spiced wine," and the other said, "It is comparable to one who drinks old wine."*

[E] *That is, even though [in the one case or the other] he has drunk the wine, the taste lingers in his mouth.*

[F] Now there is not a generation in which there are no scoffers What did the arrogant of that generation do? They went under David's windows and cried out, "When will the Temple be built? When shall we go up to the house of our Lord?"

[G] And he would say, "Even though they are trying [83d] to make me mad, may a curse come on me if I am not happy in my heart: 'I was glad when they said to me, "Let us go to the house of the Lord!" '" (Ps. 122:1).

[H] "When your days are fulfilled to go to be with your fathers, I will raise up your offspring after you" (1 Chron. 17:11).

[I] Said R. Samuel bar Nahman, "Said the Holy One, blessed be he, to David, 'David, I shall count out for you a full complement of days. I shall not give you less than the full number. Will Solomon, your son, not build the Temple in order to offer sacrifices in it? But more precious to me are the just and righteous deeds that you do than the offerings [that will be made in the Temple].'"

[J] What is the relevant verse of Scripture?

[K] "To do righteousness and justice is more acceptable to the Lord than sacrifice" (Prov. 21:3).

OBLIGATIONS OF PARENTS AND CHILDREN

YERUSHALMI QIDDUSHIN 1: 7

[A] **For every commandment concerning the son to which the father is subject— men are liable, and women are exempt.**

[B] **And for every commandment concerning the father to which the son is subject, men and women are equally liable.**

[C] **For every positive commandment dependent upon time, men are liable, and women are exempt.**

[D] **And for every positive commandment not dependent upon time, men and women are equally liable.**

[E] **For every negative commandment, whether dependent upon time or not dependent upon time, men and women are equally liable.**

[F] **except for "not marring the corners of the beard, not rounding the corners of the head " (Lev. 19: 27), "and not becoming unclean because of the dead " (Lev. 21:1).**

[G] **[The cultic rules of] laving on of hands, waving, drawing near, taking the handful. burning the incense, breaking the neck of a bird, sprinkling, and receiving [the blood]**

[H] **apply to men and not to women.**

[I] **except in the case of a meal offering of an accused wife and of a Nazirite girl, which they wave.**

[I. A] **What is a commandment pertaining to the father concerning the son [M. 1: 7A]?**

[B] **To circumcise him, to redeem him, and to teach him Torah, and to teach him a trade, and to marry him off to a girl.**

[C] **And R. Aqiba says, "Also to teach him how to swim" [T. Qid. 1: 1 1E-G].**

[D] To circumcise him, in line with the following verse of Scripture: "And on the eighth day the flesh of his foreskin shall be circumcised" (Lev. 12: 3).

[E] To redeem him, in line with the following verse of Scripture: "Every first born of man among your sons you shall redeem" (Ex. 13:13).

[F] To teach him Torah, in line with the following verse of Scripture: "And you shall teach them to your children [talking of them when you are sitting in your house, and when you are walking by the way, and when you lie down, and when you rise]" (Deut. 11:19).

[G] To teach him a trade: R. Ishmael taught, "[I call heaven and earth to witness against you this day, that I have set before you life and death, blessing and curse;] therefore choose life. [that you and your descendants may live]" (Deut. 30 :19).

[H] "This [refers to] learning a trade."

[I] To marry him off to a girl, in line with the following verse of Scripture: "[Only take heed, and keep your soul diligently, lest you forget the things which your eves have seen, and lest they depart from your heart all the days of your life;] make them known to your children and your children's children" (Deut. 4: 9).

[J] In what circumstances do you have the merit [of seeing] children and grandchildren? When you marry your children off when they are young.

[K] **R. Aqiba says, "Also to teach him how to swim,"** in line with the following verse of Scripture: "[I call heaven and earth to witness against you this day, that I have set before you life and death, blessing and curse; therefore choose life,] that you and your descendants may live" (Deut. 30 :19).

[I:2 A] What [is the status of the statement about the father's obligations]? Is it a supererogatory religious duty, or are these absolute requirements, [which a person is compelled to carry out, with special reference to marrying off the son]?

[B] *Let us derive the answer from the following case:*

[C] *Bar Tarimah came to R. Immi. He said to him, "Persuade father to get me a wife."*

[D] *He went and tried to persuade him, but the father was not agreeable [to the project].*

[E] *That is to say that it is a mere religious duty, for if you say that it was an absolute requirement, he should have forced him to comply.*

[F] How do we know that, if his father did not do his duty, the son is liable to do it for himself?

[G] Scripture states, "Every firstborn of man among your sons you shall redeem."

[H] "You shall be circumcised [in the flesh of your foreskin, and it shall be a sign of the covenant between me and you]" (Gen. 17: 11).

[I] "And you shall teach them to your children."

[J] "And make them known to your children."

[K] "That you and your descendants may live."

[I:3 A] *There we have learned:.* **the father endows his child with beauty, strength, riches, wisdom. and length of years [M. Ed. 2: 9].**

[B] How do we know beauty?

[C] "Let thy work be manifest to thy servants, [and thy glorious power to their children]" (Ps. 90:17).

[D] Strength: "His descendants will be mighty in the land; [the generation of the upright will be blessed]" (Ps. 112: 2).

[E] Riches: "I have been young and now I am old; yet I have not seen the righteous forsaken or his children begging bread" (Ps. 37: 25).

[F] Wisdom: "And you shall teach them to your children, speaking of them . . ." (Deut. 11:19).

[G] Years: "That your days and the days of your children may be multiplied in the land which the Lord swore to your fathers to give them" (Deut. 11: 20).

[H] And just as the father endows his children with five traits, so the children are liable to him in five regards, and these are they: food, drink, clothing, shoes, and guidance.

[I] This is in line with what is written, "May it fall upon the head of Joab, [and upon all his father's house; and may the house of Joab never be without] one who has a discharge, or who is leprous, or who holds a spindle, or who is slain by the sword, or who lacks bread" (2 Sam. 3: 29).

[J] "One who has a discharge" is weak.

[K] "One who is leprous" is abandoned [on account of ugliness].

[L] "One who holds a spindle" is feebleminded.

[M] "Who is slain by the sword" is short-lived.

[N] "Who lacks bread" is poor.

[I:4 A] *When Solomon came to kill Joab, [Joab] said to him, "Your father made five evil decrees against me [those at 2 Sam. 3: 29]. You accept them, and I shall accept the death penalty from you. Solomon accepted them, and all of them were fulfilled in the house of David."*

[B] "One who has a discharge" applies to Rehoboam: "And King Rehoboam made haste to mount his chariot, to flee to Jerusalem" (1 Kings 12 :18).

[C] There is he who says he had a discharge, and there is he who says he was spoiled.

[D] As to "a leper," this is Uzziah: 'And King Uzziah was a leper to the day of his death, [and being a leper dwelt in a separate house, for he was excluded from the house of the Lord]" (2 Chr. 26: 21).

[E] "One who holds a spindle" applies to Joash: "[Though the army of the Syrians had come with few men, the Lord delivered into their hand a very great army, because they had forsaken the Lord, the God of their fathers.] Thus they executed judgment on Joash" (2 Chr. 24: 24).

[F] R. Ishmael taught, "This teaches that they set up against him sadists, who had never known a woman in their lives, and they inflicted suffering on him as they inflict suffering on a woman."

[G] This is in line with what is written, "The pride of Israel testifies to his face; [Israel and Ephraim shall stumble in his guilt; Judah also shall stumble with them]" (Hos. 5: 5). [The meaning is,] they tormented the pride of Israel in his face.

[H] "One who is slain by the sword" refers to Josiah, in line with the following verse of Scripture: "And the archers shot King Josiah;

[and the king said to his servants, 'Take me away, for I am badly wounded']" (2 Chr. 35: 23).

[I]   R. Yohanan says, "This teaches that they made his body into a sieve."

[J]   R. Ishmael taught, "Three hundred arrows did they shoot into the anointed of the Lord."

[K]   "Who lacks bread" refers to Jehoiachin, as it is written, "[And every day of his life he dined regularly at the king's table;] and for his allowance, a regular allowance was given him [by the king, every day a portion, as long as he lived]" (2 Kings 25: 30).

[I:5 A]   *There we have learned:* **If [before the start of the Sabbath] they began, they do not interrupt the process] [M. Shab. 1: 5].**

[B]   What is the point at which the bath begins?

[C]   R. Zeriqan in the name of R. Haninah: "Once he has removed his belt."

[D]   Rab said, "Once he has removed his sandal."

[E]   *R. Joshua b. Levi would hear the lesson of his grandson every Friday afternoon. One time he forgot and went into the bath of Tiberias. Now he was leaning on the shoulder of R. Hiyya b. Ba. He remembered while he was in the bath [that he had not heard the child's lesson] and he went out of the bath. What happened?*

[F]   *R. Daromi said, "It was this way. R. Eleazar b. Yosé said, 'He had already removed his garments.'"*

[G]   *Said to him R. Hiyya bar Ba, "Did not Rabbi teach us, '**If before the start of the Sabbath they began, they do not interrupt?**'"*

[H]   He said to him, "Hiyya, my son, is it a small thing in your eyes that whoever hears a passage of Torah from his grandson is as if he hears it from Mount Sinai? *What is the scriptural basis for this statement?* 'Make them known to your children and your children's children— how on the day that you stood before the Lord your God at Horeb' (Deut. 4: 9-10). That is to say, 'It is like the day on which you stood before the Lord your God at Horeb.'"

[I:6 A]   R. Hezekiah b. R. Jeremiah, R. Hiyya in the name of R. Yohanan: "If you can trace the authority behind a tradition to Moses, do so, and if not, put the first [name you hear] first, and the last last."

[B]   Gidul said, "Whoever says a tradition in the name of the one who said it should see himself as if the one who is the authority for the tradition is standing before him."

[C]   What is the scriptural basis for that statement?

[D]   "Surely a man goes about as a shadow! [Surely for naught are they in turmoil] man heaps up, and knows not who will gather]"

[E]   "Many a man proclaims his own loyalty, but a faithful man who can find?" (Prov. 20: 6).

[F]   *This refers to R. Zeira, for R. Zeira said, "We pay no attention to the traditions of R. Sheshet, [which he says in the names of those who originally said them,] because he is blind [and may err in identifying the voices]."*

[G] *And R. Zeira said to R. Yosa. "Do you know Bar Pedaiah. that you cite traditions in his name?"*

[H] *He said to him, "R. Yohanan said them in his name."*

[I] *Said R. Zeira to R. Ba, bar Zabeda, "Does mv lord know Rab, that you cite traditions in his name?"*

[J] *He said to him, "R. Ada bar Ahva said them in his name."*

[II:1 A] **Every commandment concerning the father to which the son is liable [M. 1: 7B]:**

[B] **What is the way one expresses reverence for the father?**

[C] **He does not sit in his place or speak in his place, he does not contradict him.**

[D] **And what is the form of honor owing to the father?**

[E] **Giving him food to eat and something to drink and clothing him and covering him and taking him out and bringing him in and washing his face, his hands, and his feet[T. Qid. 1:1 IB].**

[F] *Whose [food and the like must be given to the father]? [Does the son have to provide it?]*

[G] Hunah bar Hiyya said, "It is the old man's."

[H] *And there are those who wish to say, "It is his [the son's]."*

[I] Did not R. Abbahu say in the name of R. Yosé b. R. Haninah, "How do we know that even if the father said to him, 'Throw this purse into the sea,' the son must listen to him?" [So the son bears unlimited obligations.]

[J] That applies to a case in which the father has another such purse, and in which the son gives pleasure to the father by doing what he wants.

[II:2 A] **All the same are husband [61b] and wife, but the husband has sufficient means to do these things [for the aged parent], and the wife does not have sufficient means to do them, or others have power over her [T. Qid. 1: 1].**

[B] If the daughter was widowed or divorced, she enters the status of one who has sufficient means to carry out what is required.

[II:3 A] To what extent does the requirement of honoring the father and mother extend?

[B] He [Eleazar, Y. Pe. 1:1] said to them, "Are you asking me? Go and ask Damah b. Netinah. He was the chief of the *patroboule* of his town. One time his mother was slapping him before the entire council, and the slipper she was beating him with fell from her hand, and he got down and gave it back to her, so that she would not be upset."

[C] Said R. Hezekiah, "He was a gentile from Ashkelon, and head of the *patroboule* of his town. Now if there was a stone on which his father had sat, he would never sit on it. When [his father] died, he made the stone into his god."

[D] One time the Benjamin-jewel in the high priest's breastplate was lost [cf. Jastrow, p. 601]. *They said, "Who has one as fine as that one? They said that Damah b. Netinah had one. They went to him and made a deal with him to buy it for a hundred denars. He went to get it for them, and he found that his father was sleeping [on the box containing the jewel].*

[E] *And some say that the key to the box was on the finger of his father, and some say that his foot was stretched out over the jewel cask.*

[F] *He went down to them and said, "I can't bring it to you." They said, "Perhaps it is because he wants more money." They raised the price to two hundred, then to a thousand. Once his father woke up from his sleep he went up and got the jewel for them.*

[G] *They wanted to pay him what they had offered at the end, but he would not accept the money from them. He said, "Shall I sell you [at a price] the honor I pay to my father? I shall not derive benefit by reason of the honor I pay to my father."*

[H] How did the Holy One, blessed be he, reward him?

[I] Said R. Yosé b. R. Bun, "That very night his cow produced a red cow, and the Israelites paid him its weight in gold and weighed i[[for use for producing purification water in line with

[J] Said R. Shabbetai, "It is written, '[The Almighty — we cannot find him; he is great in power and justice,] and abundant righteousness he will not violate' (Job 37:23). The Holy One, blessed be he, will not long delay the reward that IS coming to gentiles for the good they do."

[II:4 A] The mother of R. Tarfon went down to take a walk in her courtyard on the Sabbath, and her slipper fell off, and R. Tarfon went and placed his two hands under the soles of her feet, so that she could walk on them until she got to her couch.

[B] One time sages went to call on him. She said to them, "Pray for Tarfon, my son, who pays me altogether too much honor."

[C] *They said to her, "What does he do for you?" She repeated the story to them.*

[D] *They said to her, "Even if he did a thousand times more than this, he still would not have paid even half of the honor of which the Torah has spoken."*

[II:5 A] The mother of R. Ishmael went and complained to the rabbis about him. She said, "Rebuke Ishmael, my son, because he does not pay respect to me."

[B] At that moment the faces of our rabbis grew dark. *They said, "Is it at all possible that R. Ishmael does not pay honor to his parents?"*

[C] *They said to her, "What did he do to you?"*

[D] *She said, "When he comes home from the council house, I want to wash his feet in water and drink the water, and he does not let me do it."*

[E] *They said, "Since that is what she deems to be the honor she wants for herself, that indeed is just the kind of honor he must pay to her."*

[F] *Said R. Mana, "Well do the millers say, 'Everyone's merit is in his own basket.' [That is, there is a different way of doing good for every man. The mother of R. Tarfon said one thing to them, and they responded thus, and the mother of R. Ishmael said something else to them, and they responded so."*

[II:6 A] *R. Zeira was distressed, saying, "Would that I had a father and a mother, whom I might honor, and so inherit the Garden of Eden." When he heard these two teachings [about Tarfon and Ishmael], he said, "Blessed be the All-Merciful, that I have no father and mother. I could not behave either like R. Tarfon or like R. Ishmael."*

[B] Said R. Abin, "I am exempt from the requirement of honoring father and mother."

[C] They say that when his mother became pregnant, his father died, and when his mother gave birth, she died.

[II:7 A] There is he who feeds his father fattened [birds] and inherits Gehenna. and there is he who ties his father to the millstones [to pull them] and inherits the Garden of Eden.

[B] How does one feed his father fattened [birds] and inherit Gehenna? *There was a man who gave his father fattened chickens to eat. One time the father said to him, "My son, how do you come by these things?" He said to him, "Old man, eat and shut up, just like dogs that eat and shut up." So he turns out to feed his father fattened [birds] and to inherit Gehenna.*

[C] How does he tie his father to the millstones and inherit the Garden of Eden? *There was a man who was a miller, pulling the stones. The government orders came to the millers [for the corvée]. He said to him, "Father, go and pull the wheel in my place. If the [labor for the government] should be dishonorable, it is better that I do it and not you, and if there should be floggings, it is better that I get them and not you." So he turns out to tie his father to the millstones and inherits the Garden of Eden.*

[II:8 A] "Every one of you shall revere his mother and his father, [and you shall keep my Sabbaths]" (Lev. 19: 3).

[B] And it is said, "You shall fear the Lord your God; [you shall serve him and swear by his name]" (Deut. 6 :13).

[C] Scripture so compares the reverence owing to father and mother to the reverence owing to the Omnipresent.

[D] It is said, "Whoever curses his father or his mother shall be put to death" (Ex. 21:17).

[E] And it is said, "[And say to the people of Israel,] 'Whoever curses his God shall bear his sin'" (Lev. 25: IS).

[F] Scripture so compares the penalty for cursing the father and mother to the penalty for cursing the Omnipresent.

[G] But it is not possible to introduce the matter of smiting Heaven.

[H] But these [C, F] are reasonable, for the three of them are partners.

[II:9 A] What is the way one expresses reverence for the father? He does not sit in his place or speak in his place, he does not contradict him.

[B] And what is the form of honor owing to the father?

[C] **Giving him food to eat, something to drink, clothing him, and covering him and taking him out and bringing him in and washing his face, his hands, and his feet** [T. Qid. 1:1].

[D] *Whose [food and the like must be given to the father]? [Does the son have to provide it?]*

[E] Huna bar Hiyya said [that the father must supply what is needed for himself].

[F] *The following saying of R. Hiyya bar Ba differs, for R. Hiyya bar Ba [said], "R. Judah, son of the daughter of R. Simeon b. Yohai taught that R. Simeon b. Yohai taught:* 'Great is the honor owing to father and mother, for the Holy One, blessed be he, gave preference to it, even over the honor owing to God.' Here is stated, 'Honor your father and mother, [that your days may be long in the land which the Lord your God gives you]' (Ex. 20 :12). And elsewhere it is stated, 'Honor the Lord with your substance [and with the firstfruits of all your produce]' (Prov. 3: 9). How then do you honor God? It is with your substance. You set aside gleanings, the forgotten sheaf, and the corner of the field. You set aside heave offering and first tithe, second tithe and poor man's tithe, dough offering, you make a tabernacle [for the festival of Sukkot], and take a lulab, a shofar, phylacteries and show fringes, feed the hungry and give drink to the thirsty. Now if you have enough, you are liable for all these things, and if you do not have, you are not liable for any one of them. But when it comes to the matter of honoring father, and mother, whether you have sufficient or whether you do not have, you must honor your father and mother, even if you have to go begging at doorways."

[II:10 A] R. Aha in the name of R. Abba bar Kahana, "It is written, 'She does not take heed to the path of life. her ways wander and she does not know it' (Prov. 5: 6). The Holy One, blessed be he, took [and kept to himself] the reward that is coming to those who carry out their religious duties, so that they should do them in true faith [and without expecting a reward]."

[B] R. Aha in the name of R. Isaac, "'Keep your heart with all vigilance; for from it flows the springs of life' (Prov. 4: 23). [The meaning is this:] 'As to all the things about which I spoke to you in the Torah, keep [and do them all], for you do not know from which of them the springs of life will flow to you.'"

[C] Said R. Abba bar Kahana, "The Scripture has compared the easiest of all the religious duties to the most difficult of them all. The easiest of them all is sending forth the dam from the fledglings. The most difficult of them all is honoring father and mother. Yet in regard to both of them, the same reward is specified: 'that your days may be long.'"

[D] Said R. Abun, "Now if in respect to a matter that is tantamount to paying back a debt [that is, the debt one owes one's father and mother], it is written, '[You shall walk in all the way which the Lord your God has commanded you, that you may live,] and that it may go well with you, and that you may live long in the land which you shall possess' (Deut. 5: 33), as to a matter that involves a loss of money and endangerment to life [as some religious duties may require], how much the more so [will there be the reward of long life]."

[E] Said R. Levi and an [unnamed] rabbi. "A matter that is tantamount to paying back a debt is still greater than a matter that is not tantamount to paying back a debt."

[F] *It was taught as a Tannaite rule:* R. Simeon b. Yohai says. "Just as the reward that is coming for doing the two of them is equivalent, so the punishment applying to not doing the two of them is the same: 'The eye that mocks a father and scorns to obey a mother will be picked out by the ravens of the valley and eaten by the vultures' (Prov. 30:17). The eye that has ridiculed the notion of honoring the father and mother and that scorns [61c] the duty of not taking the dam with the fledglings. 'will be picked out by the ravens of the valley': Let the raven come, which is cruel, come and pluck it, but not derive benefit from it. 'and eaten by the vultures': Let the vulture come, which is merciful, and eat it and derive benefit from it."

[G] *R. Yannai and R. Jonathan were in session. Someone came and kissed the feet of R. Jonathan. R. Yannai said to him, "What is the meaning of this [honor that] he pays you today?"*

[H] *[Jonathan] said to him, "One time he came to complain to me about his son, so that the son would support him. I said to him to go to the synagogue and get some people to rebuke him [and tell him to support his father]."*

[I] *[Yannai] said to him, "And why did you not force [the son to do so, by court order]?"*

[J] *He said to him, "And do they force [children to do so]?"*

[K] *[Yannai] said to him, "And are you still [in doubt about] that?"*

[L] *They say that R. Jonathan reverted and established the tradition on the matter in his [Yannai's] name.*

[M] *[So too did] R. Jacob bar Aha come [and give evidence].*

[N] R. Samuel b. Nahman said in the name of R. Jonathan that they force the son to support the father.

[O] Said R. Yosé, "Would that all the traditions I know were so clear and self-evident to me as this one, that they do force the son to support the father. "

[III:1 A] What is a positive commandment dependent upon the time [of year, for which men are liable and women are exempt] [M. Qid. 1:7C]?

[B] For example, building the sukkah, taking the lulab, putting on Tefillin.

[C] What is a positive commandment not dependent upon the time [of year] [M. Qid. 1: 7D]?

[D] For example, restoring lost property to its rightful owner, sending forth the bird, building a parapet, and putting on Sisit [show-fringes].

[E] R. Simeon declares women exempt from the requirement of wearing Sisit [show-fringes], because it is a positive commandment dependent upon time [T. Qid. 1:10].

[F] Said to them R. Simeon, "Do you not concur with me that it is a positive commandment dependent upon time? For lo, one's nightgown is exempt from the requirement of having Sisit."

[G] *Said R. Hila, "The reasoning behind the position of the rabbis is that if [the garment] was designated by him for use by day and by night, it would be liable for Sisit."*

[III:2 A] Said R. Eleazar, "The Passover offering to be prepared for women is a matter of optional performance, [and even so] if they set aside the restrictions of the Sabbath."

[B] R. Jacob bar Aha in the name of R. Eleazar, "The Passover offerings to be prepared for women and slaves are a matter of optional performance."

[C] Then [shall we say] all the more so do they override the restrictions of the Sabbath on their account? [Obviously not.] That is the status of unleavened bread prepared for them?

[D] He said to him, "It is an obligation."

[E] R. Zeira said, "That is subject to dispute."

[F] R. Hila said, "That is a matter of unanimous opinion."

[G] *There is a Tannaite teaching that supports the position of this party, and there is a Tannaite teaching that supports the position of that party.*

[H] *There is a Tannaite teaching that supports the position of R Zeira.* Lettuce, unleavened bread, and the Passover lamb— on the first night, [eating them] is an obligation. And on the other days, it is optional matter. R. Simeon says, "For men it is an obligation, and for women it is an optional matter" [T. Pisha 2: 22].

[I] *The following Tannaite teaching supports the position of R. Hila:* It is said, "You shall eat no leavened bread with it; seven days you shall eat it with unleavened bread, the bread of affliction— [for you came out of the land of Egypt in hurried flight— that all the days of your life you may remember the day when you came out of the land of Egypt]" (Deut. 16: 3). One who is subject to the requirement not to eat leaven, lo, he is subject to the positive requirement of eating unleavened bread. Now lo, since women are subject to the negative commandment of not eating leaven, lo, they are subject to the positive commandment of eating unleavened bread.

[J] *Now we have learned:* **For every positive commandment dependent upon the time, men are liable, and women are exempt [M. 1: 7C].** [That would seem to contradict the conclusion just now reached, since the positive commandment of eating unleavened bread depends upon the time of year.]

[K] Said R. Mana, "A more strict rule applies to a positive commandment that comes in the wake of a negative commandment."

[III:3 A] [What follows relates to M. Hal. 4 :11, which states, **Joseph the Priest also brought his sons and household to keep the Lesser Passover (Num. 9: 10ff.) in Jerusalem, and they turned him back, lest it should be established as an obligation.**]

[B] *Now this accords with the view of him who says,* "The Passover offering of women ['his household'] is an optional matter." [Offering the Passover offering on the first Passover is an optional matter. On the second Passover they turned him back. Why? For on the second Passover women do not make the offering at all (E). That is, to do it at its normal time is optional, and to do it at the later time is not permitted at all.]

[C] *It was taught as a Tannaite rule:* "[The woman's obligation on the first Passover is firm, and therefore] a woman prepares the Passover offering on the first Passover for herself, and on the second. she is ancillary to others [but shares their Passover offering]. [But it is optional for her to observe the second Passover, if she has missed the first one,]" the words of R. Meir.

[D] R. Yosé says, "A woman prepares the Passover offering on the second Passover for herself [as a matter of obligation]. It is hardly necessary to specify that she does the same on the first."

[E] R. Eleazar b. Simeon says, "A woman prepares the Passover offering on the first Passover as an ancillary matter [joining in the Passover offering done for males], and she does not prepare a Passover offering on the second Passover, [should she miss the first one,] at all."

[F] *What is the scriptural basis for the position of R. Meir [C]?*

[G] "Tell all the congregation of Israel that on the tenth day of this month they shall take every man a lamb according to their fathers' houses, [a lamb for a household]" (Ex. 12: 2~. [House is understood to mean wife.] Then, if they wished, [they do it] for the wife, [who has the right to do it for herself].

[H] *What is the scriptural basis for the position of R. Yosé?*

[I] "A lamb according to their fathers' houses"— all the more so for his house [his wife].

[J] What is the scriptural basis for the position of R. Eleazar b. R. Simeon?

[K] "Man"— not a woman.

[L] How do the other rabbis interpret the language "man"?

[M] "Man"— not a minor.

[N] Said R. Jonah, "Even in accord with the one who said that it is an obligation [for a woman to keep the Passover the first time around,

[O] the present case is different.

[P] "For the matter was based on a limited consideration: So that the matter [as done by Joseph the Priest] should not be established as an obligation. "

[IV:1 A] **Except for not marring the corners of the beard. not rounding the corners of the head [Lev. 19: 27], and not becoming unclean because of the dead [Lev. 21:1].**

[B] Issi says, "[Women are also not liable for transgressing the prohibition of] 'They shall not make bald spots upon their heads.'"

[C] *What is the scriptural basis for this?* "They shall not make bald spots upon their heads nor shave off the edges of their beards" [Lev. 21: 5].

[D] One who is subject to the negative commandment against marring the corners of the beard is subject to the prohibition of a bald spot.

[E] Women, who have no beards, are exempt from the negative commandment regarding a bald spot.

[F] And there is yet a further matter: "Sons" not daughters.

[IV:2 A] Said R. Eleazar, "Women are liable not to make a bald spot."

[B] *What is the scriptural basis for this position?*

[C] "For you are a holy people to the Lord your God, [and the Lord has chosen you to be a people for his own possession, out of all the peoples that are on the face of the earth]" (Deut. 14: 2).

[D] All the same are men and women.

[E] How does R. Eleazar interpret the reference to "sons"?

[F] When Israel does the will of the Holy One, blessed be he, they are called his children, and when Israel does not do the will of the Holy One, blessed be he, they are not called his children.

[G] *Rab instructed the members of the household of R. Ahi, R. Hamnuna gave instructions to the associates: "Tell your wives that when they are standing before the deceased, they should not tear out their hair, so that they should not produce a bald spot, [which they are forbidden to do, just like men]. "*

[IV:3 A] *How large is a bald spot?*

[B] *There is a Tannaite authority who teaches, "Any size at all."*

[C] *And there is a Tannaite authority who teaches, "The size of a bean."*

[D] *One who says it is of any size at all derives that from the language* "bald spot," *which indicates any size at all.*

[E] *One who says it is the size of a bean proves it as follows:* "Bald spot" is mentioned in two different contexts, both in regard to the present prohibition and in respect to the appearance of leprosy

[Lev. 13: 12]. Just as "bald spot" stated later is one the size of a bean. so the one here is the size of a bean.

[F]   R. Yosé bar Mamel: "A priest girl is permitted to go abroad."

[G]   'What is the scriptural basis for that position?

[H]   [Lev. 21:1 says,] "Say to the priests," and not to the priest girls.

[I]   [That must be the case,] for if you do not say so, shall we conclude that, since she is subject to the general decree, she should not go abroad? If you say so, you turn out to set aside the entire chapter dealing with the matter of uncleanness. [Women in general are not subject to the prohibitions of uncleanness in the Temple cult, for they do not participate in the cult. So the proposed conclusion is the only possible one.]

[V:1 A]   **[With reference to M. 1: 7I: Except in the case of a meal of offering of an accused wife and of a Nazirite girl, which they wave:]** The priest puts his hand under hers and she waves [the offering].

[B]   Is that not a disgrace [that the priest should touch the woman]?

[C]   He brings a cloth.

[D]   But it will not sufficiently interpose.

[E]   They bring an old priest.

[F]   And even if you say it is a young priest [that poses no problem], for concupiscence will not be troublesome for that brief moment.

[G]   *R. Hiyya taught as a Tannaite rule:* "If the accused wife has no arms, two priests come and wave the offering in her behalf."

PRAYERS OF SAGES

YERUSHALMI BERAKHOT 4:2

[A]   **R. Nehunia b. Haqqaneh used to recite a short Prayer when he entered the study hall and when he exited.**

[B]   **They said to him, "What is the nature of this Prayer?"**

[C]   He said to them, "When I enter, I pray that I will cause no offense. And when I exit, I give thanks for my portion."

[I:1 A]   When he enters [the study hall] what does he say? "May it be thy will, Lord my God, God of my fathers that I shall not be angry with my associates, and that my associates shall not be angry with me; that we not declare the clean to be unclean, that we not declare the unclean to be clean; that we not declare the permissible to be forbidden, that we not declare the forbidden to be permissible; lest I find myself put to shame in this world and in the world to come [for rendering a wrong decision]."

[B]   And when he exits [the study hall] what does he say? "I give thanks to thee, Lord my God, God of my fathers, that you cast my lot with those who sit in the study hall and the synagogues, and you did not cast my lot with those who sit in the theaters and circuses. For I toil and they toil. I arise early and they arise early. I toil so that I shall inherit [a share of] paradise [in the world to come] and they toil [and shall end up] in a pit of destruction. As it says, 'For thou dost not give me up to Sheol, or let thy godly one see the pit' [Ps. 16:10]."

[I:2 A]   R. Pedat in the name of R. Jacob bar Idi, "R. Eleazar used to recite three prayers after his recitation of the Prayer [of Eighteen]. What did he say? 'May it be thy will, Lord my God, and God of my fathers, that no person come to hate us, nor that we come to hate any person, and that no person come to envy us, not that we come to envy any person. And let [the study of] your Torah be our occupation all the days of our lives. And let our words be supplications before you.'"

[B]   R. Hiyya bar Abba adds [to this prayer recited after the recitation of the Prayer of Eighteen], "And unite our hearts to fear your name. And keep us far from that which you despise. And bring us near to that which you love. And deal justly with us for the sake of your name."

[C]   The house of R. Yannai says, "When one wakes up from his sleep, he must say, 'Blessed are you Lord who resurrects the dead. My master, I have sinned before you. May it be thy will, Lord my God, that you give to me a good heart, a good portion, a good inclination, a good associate, a good name, a good eye, and a good soul, and a humble soul and a modest spirit. And do not allow your name to be profaned among us. And do not make us the subject of [evil] talk among your creatures. And do not lead us in the end to destruction. And [do not turn] our hope to despair. And do not make our welfare depend on gifts from other people. And do not make us depend for sustenance on other people. For the beneficence of others is small and their hatred is great. And set our portion with your Torah, with those who do your will. Rebuild your house, your [Temple] courtyard, your city, and your Temple speedily in our days."

[D]   R. Hiyya bar Abba [Wawa] prayed, "May it be thy will, Lord our God, and God of our fathers, that you put in our hearts [the ability] to repent fully before you so that we not be put to shame in the presence of our forefathers in the world to come [after our death, on account of our sins]."

[E]   *R. Yudan b. R. Ishmael established the practice that his spokesman say this [Hiyya's Prayer above] after he recited the portion [of Torah].*

[F]   R. Tanhum bar Scholasticus prayed, "And may it be thy will, Lord my God, God of my fathers, that you break the yoke of the evil inclination and vanquish it from our hearts. For you created us to do your will. And we are obligated to do your will. You desire [that we do your will]. And we desire [to do your will]. And what prevents us? That bacteria [the evil inclination] which infect us [lit.: the yeast which makes the dough rise]. It is obvious to you that we do not have the strength to resist it. So let it be thy will,

Lord my God, and God of my fathers, that you vanquish it from before us, and subdue it, so that we may do thy will as our own will, with a whole heart."

[G]   R. Yohanan used to pray, "May it be thy will, Lord my God, and God of my fathers that you imbue our portion [of life] with love and brotherhood, peace and friendship. And bring [our lives] to a happy end and [fulfill] all our hopes. And fill our dominion with disciples. And grant that we may enjoy our portion in paradise [in the world to come]. And provide for us a good heart and a good associate. And grant that we may rise early and find [each day] our hearts' desires. And let our souls' yearnings come before you for [our future] good."

[II:1 A]   And when I exit I give thanks for my portion [M. 4:2]. Said R. Abun, "[I give thanks to] the God who has bestowed upon me understanding and good works."

12

The Talmud of Babylonia

ACCOUNTING FOR LONG LIFETIMES

BAVLI MEGILLAH 4:3 /27B-28A

II.2 A. R. Zakkai's students asked him: Through what have you attained long life.

B. He said to them: In my [entire] life, I never urinated within four cubits of prayer; and I never called my fellow a nickname; and I never missed the daytime Qiddush [prayer of sanctification of the Sabbath day].

II.3 A. I had a grandmother.

B. Once she sold the cap off her head and brought me [wine for] the daytime Qiddush.

C. *One learned:* When she died, she left him three hundred socks of wine. When he died, he left his sons three thousand socks of wine.

II.4 A. *Rav Huna was girded in straw and standing before Rav.*

B. *He [Rav] said to him: What is this?*

C. *He [Rav Huna] said to him: I did not have [wine for] Qiddush [prayer of sanctification of the Sabbath day], so I pawned my belt and obtained for it [some wine for] Qiddush.*

D. *He [Rav] said to him: May it be [His] will that you will be clothed in silk.*

E. *When his son, Rabbah, was betrothed, Rav Huna, [who] was short, was in bed. His daughters and daughters-in-law came; they threw their garments on him until he was covered in silk.*

F. *Rav heard and remembered.*

G. *He said: When I blessed you, why did you not say: The same to you?*

II.5 A. R. Eleazar ben Shamua's students asked him: Through what have you attained long life?

B. He said to them: In my [entire] lifetime, I never took a shortcut through the synagogue; and I never trod on the heads of the holy people; and I never raised my hands without [saying] a blessing.

II.6 A. R. Pereidah's students asked him: Through what have you attained long life?

B. He said to them: In my [entire] lifetime, no one ever preceded me at the academy; **[28a]** and I never recited a blessing before a priest; and I never ate from an animal whose [priestly] gifts were not removed, for

C. Said R. Isaac, said R. Yohanan: It is forbidden to eat from an animal from which the [priestly] gifts were not removed.

D. And said R. Isaac: Anyone who eats from an animal from which the [priestly] gifts were not removed is like one who eats produce from which tithes have not been removed.

E. And the halakhah is not according to him.

II.7 A. "And I never recited a blessing before a priest" — is that to say that this is better?

B. And said R. Yohanan: Any scholar before whom anyone, even an ignorant high priest, recites a blessing, is worthy of death, as is said, "all of my enemies loved death" (Prov. 8:36). Do not read *mesane'ai,* "my enemies" [i.e., those who hate me], but *maseni'ai,* "those who make me hate."

C. *When he said this, [it was] about equals.*

II.8 A. R. Nehunia ben HaQaneh's students asked him: Through what have you attained long life?

B. He said to them: In my [entire] lifetime, [1] I was never honored through my fellow's embarrassment; [2] and my fellow's curse never followed me to bed; [3] and I was generous with my money.

C. "I was never honored through the embarrassment of my fellow..." *Similarly, when Rav Huna was carrying a hoe on his shoulder, Rav Hanna bar Hanilai came along and took it from him. He [Rav Huna] said to him: If you regularly carry [one] in your town, carry [it]; and if not, I am uncomfortable being honored through your degradation.*

D. "And my fellow's curse never followed me to bed..." *Similarly, when Mar Zutra climbed into his bed, he would say: I forgive everyone who has pained me.*

E. "And I was generous with my money," as a master said: Job was generous with his money, since he used to leave a coin (*perutah*) for the storekeeper from his money.

II.9 A. R. Aqiba asked R. Nehunia HaGadol: Through what have you attained long life?

B. *He said to him: The attendants came and beat him.*

C. *He climbed and stayed on the top of a date palm.*

D. He [Aqiba] said to him: My master, if "lamb" is mentioned [in Num. 28:4], why is "one" [also] mentioned?

E. *He [Nehunia] said to him: He is a student of the rabbis; leave him alone.*

F. He said to him [Aqiba]: "One" [means] unique in its flock.

G. He [Nehunia] said to him: In my entire lifetime, [1] I never received gifts, [2] and I never stood on my dues [lit.: insisted on retribution]; [3] [and] I was generous with my money.

H. ..."I never received gifts." *Similarly R. Eleazar. When they gave him gifts from the Patriarch's house, he did not take [them]. When they invited him, he did not go. He said to them: Are you not comfortable if I live, as is written,* "One who hates gifts will live" (Prov. 15:27).

I. *When they sent R. Zeira [gifts] from the Patriarch's house, he did not take [them]. When they invited him, he went. He said: They honor themselves through me.*

J. ..."And I never stood on my dues," *as Raba said:* Anyone who passes over (*ha-ma'avir 'al*) his dues, they remove from him (*ma'avirim mi-*) all his sins, as is said, "...[who] forgives evil and passes over ('*over 'al*) sin." To whom does he forgive evil? To he who passes over sin [done to him]."

II.10 A. R. asked R. Joshua ben Qorha: Through what have you attained long life?

B. He said to him: Are you hostile to my life? [Cf. Gen. 27:46.]

C. He said to him: R., it is Torah, and I must learn [it].

D. He said to him: In my [entire] lifetime, [1] I never looked at the image of an evil man, for said R. Yohanan: It is forbidden for one to look at the visage of an evil man, as is said, "Were it not for the face of Jehoshafat, King of Judah, I swear I would not look at you or see you" (2 Kings 3:14).

E. R. Eleazar said: His eyes were dim, as is said, "And when Isaac was old, his eyes dimmed" (Gen. 27:1), because he looked at Esau, the evil one.

F. *And did this [really] cause it [i.e., the weakness of his eyes]?*

G. For, said R. Isaac: Never take the curse of a commoner lightly, because Abimelekh cursed Sarah, and it was fulfilled through her seed, as is said, "...behold it is for you as a covering (*kesut*) of the eyes" (Gen. 20:16). Do not read *kesut*, "covering," read *kesiyat*, "closing."

H. *[Both] this and that caused it [i.e., the weakness of his eyes].*

I. Raba said from here: "Tolerating (*se'et*) the face of an evil person is not good" (Prov. 18:5).

J. At the time of his death, he said to him: R., bless me.

K. He said to him: May it be [His] will that you reach to half of my days.

L. He said to him: But not to all of them?

M. He said to him: Will those who come after you herd cattle [and not have a chance to be scholars]?

N. *Abbahu bar Ihi and Minyamin bar Ihi:* One said: May it [i.e., the blessing] come to me, because I have not looked at a Kuthean [literally a Samaritan, but here probably substituted for any non-Jew].

O. *And one said: May it [i.e., the blessing] come to me,* because I have not made any partnership with a Kuthean.

II.11 A. R. Zeira's students asked him: Through what have you attained long life?

B. He said to them: In my [entire] lifetime, [1] I never got angry in my house; [2] and I never walked in front of someone greater than myself; [3] and I never thought [holy thoughts] in unclean alleys; [4] and I never walked four cubits without Torah or without Tefillin; [5] and I never slept in the academy, neither soundly nor dozing; [6] and I never rejoiced at the misfortune of my fellow; [7] and I never addressed my fellow by his insulting nickname, some say, not even by his [regular] nickname.

BEHAVIOR IN THE PRESENCE OF THE CORPSE.
THE SOUL VISITING THE SICK

BAVLI SHABBAT 23:6 152A-B

I.34 A. **Said R. Judah, "In the case of a deceased for whom there is no survivor to be comforted, ten people go and sit in the place in which he died [and do the obsequies]."**

B. *There was the case of someone who died in the neighborhood of R. Judah. There was no survivor to be comforted.* [152B] *Every day Rab Judah assembled ten men and they sat in his place. After seven days the deceased appeared to him in a dream and said to him, "May your mind be at rest, for you set my mind at rest."*

I.35 A. **Said R. Abbahu, "Whatever they say in the presence of the deceased he knows until the sealing stone closes his grave."**

B. *There was a dispute in this matter between R. Hiyya and R. Simeon b. Rabbi. One said,* "Until the sealing stone is placed over his grave," *the other said,* "until the flesh rots away."

C. *And as to the other, who said,* "until the flesh rots away," "But his flesh upon him has pain and his soul within him mourns."

D. *As to the one who said,* "Until the sealing stone is placed over his grave," "and the dust return to the earth as it was and the spirit returns to God" (Qoh. 12:7).

I.36 A. *Our rabbis have taught on Tannaite authority:*

B. "And the dust return to the earth as it was and the spirit returns to God" (Qoh. 12:7) —

C. Give it back to him: Just as it was given to you, in purity, so give it back to him in purity.

D. The matter may be compared to the case of a mortal king who divided up royal garments among his staff. The intelligent ones among them folded them up and laid them away in a chest. The stupid ones went and did their daily work in them. Some time later the king wanted his garments back. The intelligent ones among them returned them to him immaculate. The stupid ones returned them dirty. The king was pleased to great the intelligent ones but angry with the stupid ones. To the intelligent ones he said, "Let the garments be sent back to storage, and they will go home in peace." On the stupid ones he said, "Let the garments be sent to the laundry, and let them be sent to prison."

E. So the Holy One, blessed be He, concerning the bodies of the righteous, says, "He enters into peace, they rest in their beds" (Isa. 57:2). Concerning their souls, he says, "Yet the soul of my lord shall be bound up in the bundle of life with the Lord your God" (1 Sam. 25:29). But of the bodies of the wicked he says, "There is no peace, says the Lord, for the wicked" (Isa. 58:22), and of their souls: "And the souls of your enemies, them shall he sling out, as from the hollow of a sling" (1 Sam. 25:29).

I.37 A. **It has been taught on Tannaite authority:**

B. R. Eliezer says, "The souls of the righteous are hidden away under the throne of glory: 'Yet the soul of my lord shall be bound up in the bundle of life with the Lord your God' (1 Sam. 25:29). And those of the wicked are kept in prison. One angel stands at one end of the world, and another angel stands at the other end of the world, and they sling their souls from one to the other: 'And the souls of your enemies, them shall he sling out, as from the hollow of a sling' (1 Sam. 25:29)."

C. *Said Rabbah to R. Nahman, "So what about the middling ones?"*

D. *He said to him, "If I'd not died, I couldn't have told you this fact: This is what* Samuel said, 'These and those [the souls of the middling and of the wicked] are handed over to Dumah. These get rest, those get no rest."

I.38 A. *Said R. Mari, "The righteous are destined to be dust:* 'And the dust return to the earth as it was' (Qoh. 12:7)."

I.39 A. *Some grave-diggers were digging in the earth at R. Nahman's. R. Ahai bar Josiah snorted at them. They came and told R. Nahman, "Somebody snorted at us." He came and said to him, "Who are you?"*

B. *He said to him, "I am Ahai bar Josiah."*

C. *He said to him, "Well, didn't R. Mari say, 'The righteous are destined to be dust'?"*

D. *He said to him, "So who's Mari? I know nothing of him!"*

E. *He said to him, "But there is a verse of Scripture that makes the point: 'And the dust return to the earth as it was' (Qoh. 12:7)."*

F. *He said to him, "So whoever taught you the Scriptures of Qohelet didn't teach you the Scriptures of Proverbs, where it is written,* 'but envy is the rottenness of the bones' (Prov. 14:30): Whoever has envy in his heart — his bones rot. Whoever has no envy in his heart — his bones don't rot."

G. *[Nahman] touched him and saw that he was substantial. He said to him, "May the master rise and come to my house?"*

H. *He said to him, "You've shown that you haven't even studied the prophets:* 'And you shall know that I am the Lord when I open your graves' (Ezek. 37:13)."

I. *He said to him, "But isn't it also written,* 'for dust you are and to dust you shall return' (Gen. 3:19)?"

J. *He said to him, "That applies a moment before the resurrection of the dead."*

I.40 **A.** **Said a Sadducee to R. Abbahu, "You people say, the souls of the righteous are hidden under the throne of glory. Then how did the necromancer working with bones bring up Samuel through his necromancy (1 Sam. 28:7)?"**

B. *He said to him, "It was done within twelve months of death."*

C. *For it has been taught on Tannaite authority:*

D. **For the full twelve months after death, the body still endures, and the soul goes up and goes down. After twelve months, the body is null, [153A] and the soul goes up but doesn't go down again.**

I.41 **A.** **Said R. Judah b. R. Samuel bar Shila in the name of Rab, "On the basis of the funeral eulogy of a person, it is known whether he is destined to the world to come or not."**

B. *Well, now, is that so? But didn't Rab say to R. Samuel bar Shila, "Be enthusiastic in my eulogy, for I'll be standing right there on the spot!"*

C. *No problem, in the one case a warm-hearted eulogy is given and is found moving, in the other, a warm-hearted eulogy is given and is not found moving.*

I.42 **A.** ***Said Abbayye, "For instance, the master, whom everybody in Pumbedita loathes — who in the world is going to give a moving eulogy for you?"***

B. *He said to him, "You and Rabbah bar R. Hanan will be quite sufficient, thank you very much."*

I.43 **A.** **R. Eleazar asked Rab, "Who is a person destined for the world to come?"**

B. He said to him, "'And your ears shall hear a word behind you, saying, This is the way, walk in it; when you turn to the right hand and when you turn to the left' (Isa. 30:21)."

C. R. Hanina said, "It is any one with whom our masters are pleased."

I.44 **A.** **"And the mourners go about the streets" (Qoh. 12:5) —**

B. *The Galileans say,* "Do things [Freedman: that will be lamented] in front of your bier."

C. *The Judeans say,* "Do things [Freedman: that will be lamented] behind your bier."

    D.   *But there really is no conflict. The one spoke in accord with local custom, so did the other.*

I.45 A.   *We have learned in the Mishnah there:* R. Eliezer says, "Repent one day before you die" [M. Abot 2:10D].

    B.   His disciples asked R. Eliezer, "So does someone know just what day he'll die?"

    C.   He said to them, "All the more so let him repent today, lest he die tomorrow, and he will turn out to spend all his days in repentance."

    D.   And so, too, did Solomon say, "Let your garments be always white and don't let your head lack ointment" (Qoh. 9:8).

I.46 A.   **["Let your garments be always white and don't let your head lack ointment" (Qoh. 9:8)] — said R. Yohanan b. Zakkai, "The matter may be compared to the case of a king who invited his courtiers to a banquet, but he didn't set a time. The smart ones among them got themselves fixed up and waited at the gate of the palace, saying, 'Does the palace lack anything?' [They can do it any time.] The stupid ones among them went about their work, saying, 'So is there a banquet without a whole lot of preparation?' Suddenly the king demanded the presence of his courtiers. The smart ones went right before him, all fixed up, but the fools went before him filthy from their work. The king received the smart ones pleasantly, but showed anger to the fools. He said, 'These, who fixed themselves up for the banquet, will sit and eat and drink. Those, who didn't fix themselves up for the banquet, will stand and look on.'"**

    B.   R. Meir's son in law in the name of R. Meir said, "They, too, would appear as though in attendance. But, rather, both parties sit, the one eating, the other starving, the one drinking, the other in thirst: 'Therefore thus says the Lord God, behold, my servants shall eat, but you shall be hungry, behold, my servants shall drink, but you shall be thirty, behold, my servants shall rejoice, but you shall be ashamed; behold, my servants shall sing for joy of heart, but you shall cry for sorrow of heart' (Isa. 65:13-14)."

    C.   Another matter: "Let your garments be always white and don't let your head lack ointment" (Qoh. 9:8) —

    D.   "Let your garments be always white": This refers to show fringes.

    E.   "And don't let your head lack ointment": This refers to phylacteries.

CELEBRATING THE BRIDE

BAVLI KETUBOT 2:1 17A-B

I.9 A.   *Our rabbis have taught on Tannaite authority:*

    B.   What do they say when dancing before a bride?

    C.   **The House of Shammai say, [17A] "You praise the bride just as she is."**

    D.   The House of Hillel say, "They say, 'Beautiful and graceful bride.'"

E. Said the House of Shammai to the House of Hillel, "So if she was lame or blind, are they going to say before her, 'Beautiful and graceful bride'? But the Torah has said, 'From a false matter keep your distance' (Ex. 23:7)!"

F. Said the House of Hillel to the House of Shammai, "Well, in accord with your opinion, if somebody makes a bad purchase in the market, should one praise it to him or denigrate it to him? You have to say, one should praise it to him."

G. In this connection sages have said, "A person should always show sympathy to other people."

I.10 A. *When R. Dimi said, "This is what they sing before a bride in the West: 'No powder, no paint, no hairdo – and still a graceful gazelle.'"*

I.11 A. *When rabbis laid hands in ordination on R. Zira, they sang this to him: 'No powder, no paint, no hairdo – and still a graceful gazelle.'"*

B. *When rabbis laid hands in ordination on Ammi and R. Assi, they sang to them: "Anyone like this, anyone like that, ordain for us, but don't ordain for us counterfeiters or babblers," and some say, "half-baked scholars or third-cooked scholars."*

I.12 A. *When R. Abbahu would come from the court session to the palace of Caesar, slave girls of Caesar's household would come toward him singing this to him: "Lord of his people, spokesman of his nation, bright light, blessed is your coming in peace!"*

I.13 A. They said concerning R. Judah bar Ilai that he would take a branch of a myrtle and dance before the bride, saying, "Beautiful and graceful bride."

B. *R. Samuel bar R. Isaac would dance with three of them.*

C. *Said R. Zira, "The elder puts us to shame."*

D. *When [Samuel] died, a pillar of flame made a barrier between him and everyone else, and there is a tradition that a pillar of fire does something like that only for one or two people in an entire generation. Said R Zira, "The twig has rewarded the elder," or, some say, "His habit has rewarded the elder." And some say, "The foolishness has rewarded the elder."*

I.14 A. *R. Aha would put the bride on his shoulder and dance. Rabbis said to him, "What is the rule on our doing the same thing?"*

B. *He said to them, "If a bride resting on you is no more than a beam of wood, well and good, but if not, you'd better not do it."*

I.15 A. Said R. Samuel bar Nahman said R. Jonathan, "It is permitted to gaze upon the face of the bride all seven days of the celebration, so as to make her all the more beloved to her husband."

B. *But the law is not in accord with him.*

I.16 A. *Our rabbis have taught on Tannaite authority:*

B. The funeral procession gives way before the bridal procession, and both of them before the king of Israel.

C. They said about King Agrippas that he gave way before a bridal procession, and sages praised him.

D. *They praised him? Then it would follow that he did the right thing! But lo, R. Ashi said, "Even in the view of him who has said, 'If the patriarch forgives an insult to his honor, the insult to his honor is forgiven,' nonetheless, a kind who gave up the honor owing to him – the honor owing to him nonetheless is not to be given up"! For a master has said, "'You shall surely set him as king over you' (Deut. 17:15) – that reverence for him will be upon you" [M. San. 2:5C].*

E. *It was at a crossroad.*

I.17 A. *Our rabbis have taught on Tannaite authority:*

B. They cancel a Torah study session in order to bring out a corpse and bring in a bride.

C. They say about R. Judah b. R. Ilai that he cancelled the study of the Torah in order to bring out a corpse and bring in a bride.

D. Under what circumstances may this be done? When the corpse or bride does not have a sufficient company, but if there is a sufficient company, they do not cancel Torah study.

I.18 A. **And how big is a sufficient company?**

B. *Said R. Samuel bar Ini in the name of Rab, "Twelve thousand men and six thousand shofars."*

C. *There are those who say, "Twelve thousand men, with, among them, six thousand shofars."*

D. *Ulla said, "For example, when people form a funeral procession from the gate of the city to the burial place."*

I.19 A. **[With special reference to the death of a sage,] R. Sheshet, and some say, R. Yohanan, said, "Removing [the Torah contained in the sage] must be like the giving of the Torah: just as the giving of the Torah involved six hundred thousand, so taking away the Torah involves six hundred thousand.**

B. *"But this is with regard to one who has recited Scripture and repeated Mishnah traditions. [17B] But in the case of one who repeated Tannaite statements to others, there is no upper limit at all."*

I.20 A. …she went forth to music:

B. *What is the meaning of music?*

C. *Surhab bar Pappa in the name of Zeiri said, "A canopy of myrtle."*

D. *R. Yohanan said, "A veil under which she may slumber."*

CHASTITY AND ADULTERY

BAVLI NEDARIM 2:5 20A

II.2 A. **R. Aha b. R. Josiah says, "Whoever stares at women in the end will fall into transgression, and whoever stares at a woman's heel will have children who behave improperly."**

B. Said R. Joseph, "That applies also to one's wife when she is menstruating."

C. *Said R. Simeon b. Laqish, "The sense of 'heel' in that Tannaite statement is euphemistic, namely,* the place that becomes unclean, which is opposite the heel [when the woman squats]."

II.3 A. **It has been taught on Tannaite authority: "And Moses said to the people, do not fear, for God is come to prove you, that fear of him may be before your faces" (Ex. 20:17) – this refers to shamefacedness.**

B. "That you do not sin" (Ex. 20:17) – this teaches that shamefacedness leads to fear of sin.

C. On this basis, sages have said, "A good trait of someone is that he should be somewhat bashful."

D. Others say, "Any man who is bashful will not readily sin."

E. And of one who is not shamefaced one may be certain that his fathers did not stand at Mount Sinai.

II.4 A. **Said R. Yohanan b. Dehabai, "There are four matters that the ministering angels told me:**

B. "Children are born lame because [the parents] turned their table upside down [having sex other than missionary style];

C. "...dumb, because they practice cunnilingus;

D. "...deaf, because they talk during sex;

E. "...blind, because they stare at 'that place.'"

F. *By way of contradiction:* **They asked Imma Shalom, "How come [20B] your children are so beautiful?"**

G. She said to them, "He 'talks' with me not at the beginning of the night nor at the end of the night but at midnight. And when he 'talks,' he thumps up and down so as to uncover a handbreadth and cover a handbreadth, and he is as though compelled by a demon.

H. "So I said to him, 'How come?'

I. "And he said to me, 'So that I won't ever "look at" any other women, and my children end up in the status of *mamzerut* [that is, lest I produce children with a woman whom I am not legally permitted to wed].'"

J. *No problem, the one refers to chatter about sex [which is o.k.], the other, anything else.*

II.5 A. **Said R. Yohanan, "That represents the position of Yohanan b. Dehabai, but sages have said, 'The law is not in accord with Yohanan b. Dehabai. Rather, Whatever someone wants to do with his wife in sexual relations he should do.**

B. "The matter may be compared to meat that comes from the slaughterhouse [which is permitted for eating]. If one wants to eat it salted, he eats it that way; roasted, he eats it that way; boiled, he eats it that way; seethed, he eats it that way; so, too, fish from the fish store."

II.6 A. *Said Amemar, "Who are these 'ministering angels' anyhow? They are rabbis. For if you should say that they really were*

ministering angels, then how come R. Yohanan said, 'The law
is not in accord with Yohanan b. Dehabai'? *Lo, the ministering
angels are really better informed about the formation of the foetus
than we are! And how come he referred to them as ministering
angels? Because they are as distinguished as ministering angels.* "

II.7 A. *A woman came before Rabbi. She said to him,* "My lord, I set
'the table' but he turned it over.'"

B. He said to her, "My daughter, the Torah has permitted you to him,
and as for me, what can I do for you?"

II.8 A. *A woman came before Rab. She said to him,* "My lord, I set 'the
table' but he turned it over.'"

B. *He said to her, "So how is it different from fish [which can be
prepared any which way]?"*

II.9 A. "And that you seek not after your own heart" (Num. 15:39):

B. On this basis Rabbi said, "Someone should not drink from this
cup while looking at another cup."

C. *Said Rabina, "That rule applies even if both of them are his wives."*

II.10 A. "And I will purge out from among you the rebels and those
that transgress against me" (Ezek. 20:38):

B. Said R. Levi, "This refers to children in the following nine
classifications: children born of a rape of a husband by a wife;
rape; a wife one hates; a woman under a ban; a woman confused
with some other; of strife, drunkenness during intercourse, a woman
one has decided to divorce, children of promiscuity, and children
of a brazen woman [who demands sex]."

C. Is that so? But didn't R. Samuel bar Nahmani say R. Jonathan
said, "Any man whose wife calls him to sexual relations will have
children of the like of which the generation of our lord, Moses,
didn't have, as it is said, 'Take you wise men and understanding
and known among your tribes and I will make them rulers over
you' (Deut. 1:13); and 'So I took the chiefs of your tribes, wise
men and known' (Deut. 1:15) — without reference to
'understanding.' But it is written, 'Issachar is a large-boned ass'
(Gen. 49:14), and elsewhere, 'and of the children of Issachar, who
were men that had understanding of the times' (1 Chr. 12:33)."
[Freedman: This was Leah's reward, proving that it is meritorious
for a woman to demand sexual relations.]

D. *That applies when the woman is seductive.*

CONVERSION IN GENERAL

BAVLI YEBAMOT 4:1'2 45B-46A

18. A. Said R. Hama bar Guria said Rab, "He who buys a slave from a
gentile, and the slave went ahead on his own and immersed, so as
to acquire the status of a freed man — he has acquired title to
himself as a free man. *How come?* [46A] *The gentile has no title*

to the person of the slave, and what he transfers to the Israelite is
only what he owns. Now since the slave went ahead on his own
and immersed, so as to acquire the status of a freed man, *the slave
has removed from himself his indenture as a slave.*"

B.   *That accords with Raba, for* said Raba, "The act of sanctification
[of something to the altar that has already been mortgaged],
leavened food [held by an Israelite during Passover but pledged to
a gentile for a debt], and the freeing of a slave that is mortgage
nullify a mortgage." [Slotki: similarly here, the immersion of the
slave cancels his obligations to the gentile and the Jewish master
only represents the gentile and has no greater claim to the slave
than the gentile.]

C.   *Objected R. Hisda,* "There was the case of Beluria, the convert,
the slaves of whom went ahead and immersed before her. The case
came before sages, and they ruled, 'They have acquired title to
themselves as free men.' *So if it was before her that they did so,
but if it was after she did, then it is not the case.*" [Slotki: thus it
has been shown that if the owner is an Israelite, immersion does
not procure the slave's freedom, and that contradicts what Hama
said in Rab's name.]

D.   Said Raba, "If it was before her doing so, then they acquire title to
themselves whether they did so without further explanation of their
intent or whether they made explicit what their purpose was; but if
it was after her, then if it was done in full articulation of their
purpose, they acquire title to themselves, but if not, they do not."

E.   Said R. Avayya, "They have stated this rule [that immersion frees
the slave] only in the case of one who buys a slave from a gentile.
*But the gentile himself [if he sold himself] transfers title [to the
Israelite purchaser], as it is written,* 'And also from the children
of strangers who sojourn among you, of them you may buy' (Lev.
25:45) — you buy from them, but they do not buy from you, and
they do not buy from one another, and they do not buy from you."

F.   *Now for what purpose can this statement be made? If we say that
it refers to manual work, then may not a gentile buy an Israelite to
do manual work? Is it not written,* "Or to the offshoot of a stranger's
family" (Lev. 25:47), and a master has said, "'...a stranger's family'
refers to a gentile"? So does it not refer to the person [so that a
gentile may not acquire the person of the Israelite, but only his
labor], *and the All-Merciful has said,* "you may buy of them,"
even their persons!

G.   *R. Aha questioned this:* "[Permitting the purchase of the person
of a gentile] may refer to purchase by means of money and
immersion." [Slotki: as a slave of a Jew; but what proof is there
that a gentile does not acquire his freedom if he performed
immersion with the object in particular of gaining his manumission
thereby?]

H.   *That's a problem.*

19. A.   Said Samuel, "[When one immerses a gentile slave to initiate him into Judaism], it is necessary to hold him firmly in the water."

B.   *That was done with Minyamin, slave of R. Ashi, whom [Ashi] wanted to immerse. He handed him over to Rabina and R. Aha b. Raba. He said to the, 'See to it that I shall claim him from you [if anything goes wrong].' They put a chain around his neck, loosened it, and tightened it. They loosened it so that there would be no interposition between the water and his skin, and they tightened it again so that he could not go ahead and declare,* "Lo, I immerse myself so as to gain my freedom."

C.   *As he was raising his head from the water, they put on him a bucket of clay on his head and said to him, "Go, carry this bucket to the house of your master."*

20. A.   *Said R. Pappa to Raba, "Has the master seen how the members of the household of Pappa bar Abba lay out money in behalf of people for their head taxes and then force them into working for them. Once they have served out their indenture, do they have to have a deed of freedom or not?"*

B.   *He said to him, "So if I were dead, I could not have said this ruling to you — this is what R. Sheshet said, 'The surety for these people is deposited in the government archive, and the government has made the law that whoever does not pay his head tax serves as a slave for him who pays it for him.' [So a deed of emancipation is required.]"*

21. A.   *R. Hiyya bar Abba came to Gabla. He saw Israelite women who had become pregnant by gentiles who had been circumcised but not immersed. He saw Israelite wine that gentiles had mixed, being drunk by Israelites. He saw lupines boiled by gentiles and eaten by Israelites. And he said nothing whatsoever to them.*

B.   *He came before R. Yohanan.* He said to him, "Go and proclaim concerning their children that they are mamzers, their wine that that it is subject to prohibition by reason of being libation-wine, their lupines that they are subject to prohibition by reason of having been cooked by gentiles, for the people are not disciples of the Torah."

C.   "their children that they are mamzers:" *R. Yohanan is consistent with views expressed elsewhere, for* said R. Yohanan, "A person is not deemed a proselyte until he is circumcised and immersed, *and if he has not immersed, he remains a gentile.*

D.   And said Rabbah bar bar Hannah said R. Yohanan, "A gentile or a slave who had sexual relations with an Israelite woman — the offspring is a mamzer."

E.   ["their wine that that it is subject to prohibition by reason of being libation-wine:"] He made a decree against their wine as libation wine, on the principle, on the principle of, "We say to a Nazirite, 'keep off, *go around the vineyard and do not approach it.'"*

F.   "their lupines that they are subject to prohibition by reason of having been cooked by gentiles, for the people are not disciples of the Torah:" *is the operative consideration that* the people are not disciples of the Torah? *Then had they been disciples of the Torah, would the lupines have been permitted? Has not* R. Samuel b. R. Isaac said Rab said, "Whatever is eaten as is, fresh, is not subject to prohibition by reason of having been cooked by gentiles"? And lo, lupines cannot be eaten raw, so the prohibition of food cooked by gentiles does pertain.

G.   *R. Yohanan takes the position of the following version of the same matter, for* R. Samuel b. R. Isaac said Rab said, "Whatever is not served on kings' tables as a relish with bread is not subject to prohibition by reason of having been cooked by gentiles."

H.   *So, as a matter of fact, the operative consideration that* the people are not disciples of the Torah, *and had they been disciples of the Torah, would the lupines have been permitted.*

22. A.   *Our rabbis have taught on Tannaite authority:*

B.   A proselyte who was circumcised but did not immerse —

C.   R. Eliezer says, "Lo, this one is a valid proselyte. For so we find in the case of our fathers that they circumcised themselves but did not immerse."

D.   If he immersed but did not circumcise —

E.   R. Joshua says "Lo, this one is a proper proselyte, for so we find in the case of our mothers that they immersed but did not circumcise."

F.   And sages say, "If he immersed but did not circumcise, circumcise but did not immerse, he is no proselyte — until he both circumcises himself and immerses.

23. A.   *Now why does R. Joshua not invoke the analogy of the fathers, or R. Eliezer the analogy of the mothers? And should you say, we do not invoke an analogy concerning what is possible from what is not possible, and has it not been taught on Tannaite authority:*

B.   R. Eliezer says, "How on the basis of Scripture do we know the rule covering the Passover offering, that it derives only from unconsecrated animals? We find a reference to the offering of a Passover offering to be presented in Egypt, and a reference to the offering of a Passover offering for generations to come. Just as the Passover offering that was presented in Egypt could derive only from what was unconsecrated, so the Passover offering that was to be presented in generations to come might derive only from what was unconsecrated."

C.   Said to him R. Aqiba, "But is it right to derive the rule governing what is possible from a case involving what is not possible [Cashdan, *Menahot* to 82A: for at that time the law of the second tithe had not been promulgated, and even later, when it was given, it came into force only when the Israelites had entered the promised land. So in Egypt there was no possibility of presenting the Passover offering from a beast designated as second tithe.]"

D. He said to him, "Even though it was not possible, it does represent probative evidence, so that we should derive the rule from that case."

E. Rather, **[46B]** *in the case of one who has immersed and not circumcised himself, all concur. Where they differ concerns the case of circumcision without immersion. R. Eliezer derives the governing analogy from the case of the fathers. R. Joshua maintains that in the case of the fathers too, immersion was done.*

F. *So how does he know it? If we say it is from the verse,* "Go to the people and sanctify them today and tomorrow and have them wash their garments" (Ex. 19:10), now if in a case in which washing the clothing is not required [e.g., after an involuntary ejaculation], immersion is required [Lev. 15:16], in a case in which washing the garments is required [Israel's receiving the Torah is their conversion], how much the more so should immersion be required! *but that may have had as its consideration the matter of cultic cleanness [not conversion].*

G. Rather, it is from the following: "And Moses took the blood and sprinkled it on the people" (Ex. 24:8), *and there is a tradition that sprinkling is done only where there has been immersion.*

H. *And how does R. Joshua know that the mothers immersed?*

I. *It stands to reason, for otherwise,* how could they have come under the wings of the Presence of God [through their conversion]?

24. A. Said R. Hiyya bar Abba said R. Yohanan, "Under no circumstances does a man become a full proselyte until he both is circumcised and also immersed in a ritual pool."

B. *So what else is new? Where you have a dispute between* a named opinion and an unattributed majority, the decided law accords with the position of the majority *[that is, sages in the context of Eliezer and Joshua]!*

C. *But who are "sages" here? R. Yosé. For it has been taught on Tannaite authority:*

D. "Lo, if someone came and said, 'I circumcised myself but did not immerse,' they immerse him, and it makes no difference [that the circumcision was done earlier]," the words of R. Judah.

E. R. Yosé says, "They do not immerse him."

F. Therefore "They immerse a proselyte on the Sabbath," the words of R. Judah.

G. R. Yosé says, "They do not immerse on the Sabbath." [Slotki: thus it has been shown that the author of the vie that both immersion and circumcision are required is Yosé.]

25. A. The master has said: Therefore "They immerse a proselyte on the Sabbath," the words of R. Judah —

B. *That is obvious. Since R. Judah takes the view that one of the two actions, either immersion or circumcision, suffices, isn't it self-evident that, if the circumcision has been performed in our presence, he is permitted to immerse? So why say* "therefore..."?

C.   *What might you otherwise have supposed? That from R. Judah's perspective, immersion is principal, so that immersion is not to take place on the Sabbath, since in that way a person improves his situation [and one may not change one's status on the Sabbath]. So we are informed that R. Judah requires either the one or the other equally.*

26. A.   R. Yosé says, "They do not immerse on the Sabbath" —

B.   *That is obvious. Since R. Yosé takes the view that we require both actions in connection with conversion, immersion may not take place, since in that way a person improves his situation [and one may not change one's status on the Sabbath].*

C.   *What might you otherwise have supposed? That from R. Yosé's perspective, circumcision is principal, and there the operative consideration is that the circumcision was not performed in our presence; but if circumcision were done in our presence, one might have supposed that, under such conditions, the convert may immerse even on the Sabbath. So we are informed that R. Yosé requires both actions equally.*

27. A.   *Said Rabbah, "There was a case at the household of R. Hiyya bar Rabbi — and R. Joseph repeated it as R. Oshaia b. Rabbi, and R. Safra repeated it as R. Oshaia bar Hiyya — in which a convert came before him who had circumcised himself but not immersed. He said to him, 'Wait here until tomorrow, and we shall immerse you.'"*

B.   *There are three rulings that are to be deduced from that case:*

C.   A proselyte has to have a court of three men.

D.   A proselyte achieves conversion only through circumcision and immersion.

E.   They do not immerse a proselyte at night.

F.   *Well, why not draw the inference that expert scholars are required?*

G.   *Maybe that was sheer coincidence.*

28. A.   Said R. Hiyya bar Abba said R. Yohanan, "A proselyte's conversion-rite must be done in the presence of three men, for 'law' is written in that connection" [Num. 15:16].

29. A.   *Our rabbis have taught on Tannaite authority:*

B.   If someone came along and said, "I am a convert," might one suppose that we accept that statement?

C.   Scripture says, "...with you..." (Lev. 19:33), meaning, it is only when he is well known to you.

D.   If he came with witnesses as to his status with him, how do we know the rule that he is accepted forthwith?

E.   Scripture states, "And if a proselyte sojourn...in your land" (Lev. 19:33).

F.   [47A] I know that that is so only within the land of Israel. How do I know that the same rule applies overseas?

G.   Scripture says, "with you," meaning, wherever you may be.

H. "If so, why is it said, 'in the land'?

I. "In the land it is necessary to produce proof. Abroad it is not necessary to produce proof," the words of R. Judah.

J. And sages say, "Whether in the land or abroad, it is necessary to produce proof."

30. A. "If he came with witnesses as to his status with him, how do we know the rule that he is accepted forthwith?"

B. How come I need a verse of Scripture to make this point?

C. *Said R. Sheshet, "If they say, 'We heard that he was accepted as a convert in such and such a court,' it might have entered your mind not to accept that testimony. So we are informed that you do."*

31. A. Scripture states, "And if a proselyte sojourn...in your land" (Lev. 19:33). I know that that is so only within the land of Israel. How do I know that the same rule applies overseas?"

B. Scripture states, "with you," meaning, wherever he is with you.

C. *But this language* "with you" *has already been expounded for another purpose?*

D. One lesson derives from "with you" in the singular (Lev. 19_33) the other, "with you" in the plural (Lev. 19:34).

32. A. And sages say, "Whether in the land or abroad, it is necessary to produce proof:"

B. But lo it is written, "In your land" (Lev. 19:33)!

C. *That is required to make the point that even in the Land of Israel they accept converts. For it might have entered your mind to suppose that, because of the advantages of the Land of Israel, they became proselytes, and at the present time, when there is no advantage [the land being poor], they still might be attracted by the consideration of collecting a share of the gleanings, forgotten sheaf, corner of the field, and poorman's tithe. So we are told that, nonetheless, they are accepted.*

33. A. Said R. Hiyya bar Abba said R. Yohanan, "The decided law is that whether in the land or abroad, it is necessary to produce proof."

B. *So what else is new?!* Where there is an opinion attributed to a single individual and one that appears without attribution and so in the name of the majority, the law accords with the majority.

C. *What might you have supposed? That R. Judah's position stands to reason, because a variety of verses of Scripture support him? So we are informed that that is not the case.*

34. A. *Our rabbis have taught on Tannaite authority:*

B. "And judge righteously between a man and his brother and the proselyte that is with him" (Dt. 1:16):

C. On this basis said R. Judah, "A proselyte who converts in court, lo, this is a valid proselyte; but one who converts all by himself is not regarded as a proselyte."

35. A. There was a case in which someone came before R. Judah and said to him, "I converted while all by myself."

B. Said to him R. Judah, "Do you have witnesses?"

C. He said to him, "No."

D. "Do you have children?"

E. He said to him, "Yes."

F. He said to him, "You are trusted to invalidate yourself, but you are not believed to invalidate your children." [The offspring of the union of a gentile and an Israelite woman are mamzerim.]

36. A. Did R. Judah say that a convert is not believed as regards his children? *Has it not been taught on Tannaite authority:*

B. "He shall acknowledge the firstborn" (Dt. 21:17) — even to others [letting the know who is firstborn].

C. In this connection said R. Judah, "A man is believed to state, 'This son of mine is firstborn.' And just as he is believed to state, 'This son of mine is firstborn,' so he is believed to state, 'This son of mine is the son of a divorcée or the son of a woman who has performed the rite of removing the shoe.'"

D. And sages say, "He is not believed."

E. *Said R. Nahman bar Isaac, "This is the sense of what he said to him:* 'In accord with what you have said, you are a gentile, and a gentile cannot give testimony.'"

F. *Rabina said, "This is the sense of what he said to him:* 'Do you have children?' 'Yes.' 'Do you have grandchildren?' 'Yes.' 'You are believed to invalidate your children, but you are not believed to invalidate your grandchildren.'"

G. *So too it has been taught on Tannaite authority:* R. Judah says, "A person is believed to say concerning his minor son [what his status is], but he is not believed to say concerning his grown-up son."

H. And said R. Yohanan, "The meaning is not actually 'the minor' or 'the adult,' but the minor who has children is regarded as an adult, and an adult who has no children is regarded as a minor."

I. *And the decided law is in accord with R. Nahman bar Isaac.*

J. *But has it not been taught on Tannaite authority in accord with Rabina?*

K. *That has been stated in connection with the rule governing acknowledgment. [An Israelite can testify that his son is firstborn, etc.]*

37. A. *Our rabbis have taught on Tannaite authority:*

B. A person who comes to convert at this time — they say to him, "How come you have come to convert? Don't you know that at this time the Israelites are forsaken and harassed, despised, baited, and afflictions come upon them?" If he said, "I know full well, and I am not worthy [of sharing their suffering]," they accept him forthwith. And they inform him about some of the lesser religious duties and some of the weightier religious duties. He is informed about the sin of neglecting the religious duties involving gleanings, forgotten sheaf, corner of the field, and poorman's tithe. They further inform him about the penalty for not keeping the commandments.

C. They say to him, "You should know that before you came to this lot, if you ate forbidden fat, you would not be penalized by extirpation. If you violated the Sabbath, you would not be put to death through stoning. But now if you eat forbidden fat, you are punished with extirpation. If you violate the Sabbath, you are punished by stoning."

D. And just as they inform him about the penalties for violating religious duties, so they inform him about the rewards for doing them. They say to him, "You should know that the world to come is prepared only for the righteous, and Israel at this time is unable to bear [47B] either too much prosperity or too much penalty."

E. They do not press him too hard, and they do not impose too many details on him.

F. If he accepted all this, they circumcise him immediately. If any shreds that render the circumcision invalid remain, they do it a second time.

G. Once he has healed, they immerse him right away.

H. And two disciples of sages supervise the process and inform him about some [more] of the lesser religious duties and some of the weightier religious duties.

I. He immerses and comes up, and lo, he is an Israelite for all purposes.

J. In the case of a woman, women sit her in the water up to hear neck, and two disciples of sages stand therefor her outside, and inform her about some [more] of the lesser religious duties and some of the weightier religious duties.

K. All the same are a proselyte and a freed slave.

L. And in a place in which a woman immerses a proselyte and a freed slave immerse.

M. And whatever would be deemed an invalidating interposition in the case of an immersion is deemed an invalidating interposition in the case of a proselyte and a freed slave.

38. A. The master has said: A person who comes to convert at this time — they say to him, "How come you have come to convert? Don't you know that at this time the Israelites are forsaken and harassed, despised, baited, and afflictions come upon them?" If he said, "I know full well, and I am not worthy [of sharing their suffering]," they accept him forthwith. And they inform him about some of the lesser religious duties and some of the weightier religious duties. He is informed about the sin of neglecting the religious duties involving gleanings, forgotten sheaf, corner of the field, and poorman's tithe. They further inform him about the penalty for not keeping the commandment—

B. *How come?*

C. *So that if he goes his way, he goes his way.*

D. for said R. Helbo, ""proselytes are as hard for Israel as a scab: 'And the proselyte shall join himself with them and they shall cleave to the house of Jacob' (Is. 14:1)."

39. A. He is informed about the sin of neglecting the religious duties involving gleanings, forgotten sheaf, corner of the field, and poorman's tithe:

    B. *How come?*

    C. Said R. Hiyya bar Abba said R. Yohanan, "A child of Noah would rather be put to death on account of something worth less than a penny rather than spend as much as a penny that he cannot get back."

40. A. They do not press him too hard, and they do not impose too many details on him:

    B. Said R. Eleazar, "What verse of Scripture makes that point? It is written, 'And when she saw that she was steadfastly minded to go with her, she left off speaking to her' (Ruth 1:18).

    C. "She said to her, 'It is forbidden for us to go beyond the Sabbath boundary.'

    D. "She said to her, 'Where you go, I will go' (Ruth 1:16)."

    E. "'It is forbidden to us to be alone with men.'

    F. "'Where you spend the night, I will spend the night.'

    G. "Six hundred thirteen commandments have been assigned to us.'

    H. "'Your people will be my people' (Ruth. 1:16).

    I. "'We are forbidden to worship idols.'

    J. "'And your God, my God.'

    K. **"'Four modes of inflicting the death penalty have been assigned to the court' [M. San. 7:1A].'**

    L. "'Where you die, I will die.'

    M. "'Two graveyards have been assigned for the use of the court.'

    N. "'And there I will be buried.'

    O. "'When she saw that she was steadfastly minded....'"

41. A. If he accepted all this, they circumcise him immediately:

    B. *How come?*

    C. *In no way do we postpone carrying out a religious duty.*

42. A. If any shreds that render the circumcision invalid remain, they do it a second time:

    B. *So we have learned in the Mishnah:* **These are the shreds [of the foreskin, if they remain] which render the circumcision invalid: flesh which covers the greater part of the corona — and such a one does not eat heave offering. And if he was fat [so the corona appears to be covered up], one has to fix it up for appearance's sake. [If] one circumcised but did not tear the inner lining [the cut did not uncover the corona, since the membrane was not split and pulled down], it is as if he did not perform the act of circumcision [M. Shab. 19:6].** And said R. Jeremiah bar Abba said Rab, "It is flesh that covers the greater part of the height of the corona."

43. A. Once he has healed, they immerse him right away:

    B. *Only after he is healed by not before? how come?*

    C. *Water irritates the wound.*

44. A. And two disciples of sages supervise the process and inform him about some [more] of the lesser religious duties and some of the weightier religious duties:

B. But lo, said R. Hiyya said R. Yohanan, "A proselyte's conversion has to have three men present"?

C. *But lo, said R. Yohanan to the Tannaite authority: "Repeat: three."*

45. A. He immerses and comes up, and lo, he is an Israelite for all purposes:

B. *For what practical purpose is this decided law set forth?*

C. *If he retracted but then betrothed an Israelite woman, he is regarded as a faithless Israelite, but his act of betrothal remains valid.*

46. A. All the same are a proselyte and a freed slave:

B. *Assuming that the comparison pertaining to the proselyte and the slave applies to the acceptance of the yoke of the commandments [both having to know some of them at the time of the immersion], a contradiction is to be raised:* At the time of the immersion, a proselyte has to declare that he accepts the commandments, but a freed slave does not have to do so [since at the time he became an Israelite's slave, he is immersed].

C. Said R. Sheshet, there really is no contradiction. The one represents the position of R. Simeon b. Eleazar, the other of rabbis. For it has been taught on Tannaite authority:

D. "'And bewail her father and her mother' (Dt. 21:13) — under what circumstances? When she did not accept the yoke of the commandments. But if she has accepted the yoke of the commandments, from the moment of immersion, he is permitted to marry her immediately.

E. "R. Simeon b. Eleazar says, 'Even though she did not accept the yoke of the commandments, one forces her to be immersed for the sake of becoming a female slave, then another immersion for the sake of being freed from that status, and he then frees her **[48A]** and is permitted to marry her forthwith.'"

F. *Said Raba, "What is the scriptural basis for the position of R. Simeon b. Eleazar?* 'Every man's slave that is bought for money' (Ex. 12:44) — does this mean the slave of a man and not the slave of a woman? Rather: the slave of a man may be circumcised against his will, but no son of a man may be circumcised against his will. [Slotki: the son of a gentile who is not a slave or the son of a proselyte if he is of age may not be forcibly circumcised.]"

G. And rabbis?

H. Said Ulla, "Just as you cannot forcibly circumcise the son of a man against his will, so you may not forcibly circumcise a slave of a man against his will."

I. But it is written, "Every man's slave"!

J. *That is required to make the point of Samuel, for* said Samuel, "He who declares his slave to be ownerless property — the slave goes forth to freedom and does not require a writ of emancipation, as it is said, 'Every man's slave that is bought for money' (Ex. 12:44)

— does this mean the slave of a man and not the slave of a woman? Rather: a slave whose master exercises possession of him is called a slave, but one the master of whom does not exercise possession of him is not called a slave."

K.   *Objected R. Pappa, "Might I say that rabbis heard [the rule that one does not forcibly convert someone to Judaism] in regard to 'the woman of goodly form' (Dt. 21:11) because to her do not pertain religious duties. But a slave, to whom religious duties do pertain, even rabbis would concur [that he does not have to state his acceptance and may be required to keep the religious duties]. For lo it has been taught on Tannaite authority:* all the same are a convert and a slave bought from a gentile — they have to make a verbal acceptance of the religious duties. Lo, one that is bought from an Israelite does not have to make such a declaration. *Now who can be the authority behind this ruling? It cannot be R. Simeon b. Eleazar, for* has he not said, 'One purchased from a gentile also does not have to make such a declaration'? *So is it not rabbis? And it would then follow that* a slave that is purchased from a gentile has to make a declaration of accepting the commandments, but a slave purchased from an Israelite does not have to do so? *And that then poses a problem to the statement:* All the same are a proselyte and a freed slave."

L.   *That Tannaite formulation was set forth only with regard to immersion.*

47. A.   *Our rabbis have taught on Tannaite authority:*

B.   "...and she shall trim her hair, pare her nails:"

C.   R. Eliezer says, "She should cut them.

D.   R. Aqiba says, "She should let them grow."

E.   Said R. Eliezer, "Here 'paring' is said, and elsewhere, 'paring the nails.' Just as 'paring' stated in connection with the head means that one cuts it, so 'paring' here means that one cuts the nails."

F.   R. Aqiba says, "'Paring' is stated in connection with the head, and 'paring' is stated in connection with the nails. Just as in connection with the head, the sense is to make the head ugly and disheveled, so in connection with the nails, it means the same."

G.   Proof for R. Eliezer's view: "And Mephibosheth, son of Saul, came down to meet the king, and he had neither dressed his feet nor trimmed his beard" (1 Sam. 19:25) [Sifré Dt. CCXII:I.2].

H.   *What is the meaning of* "doing"? Removing.

48. A.   *Our rabbis have taught on Tannaite authority:*

B.   "And bewail her father and her mother" (Dt. 21:13) —

C.   **[48B] "That is, 'her father and her mother,' meant literally," the words of R. Eliezer.**

D.   R. Aqiba says, "'Her father and mother' refers only to idolatry, as it is said, 'Saying to a piece of wood, you are my father' (Jer. 2:27)."

E.   "…a month's time:"

F.   Thirty days [Sifré to Dt. CCXIII:I.2-3]

G.   R. Simeon b. Eleazar says, "Ninety days: 'a month' — thirty days; 'full' — thirty days; 'and after that' — thirty days."

H.   *Objected Rabina, "Then say:* 'a month' — thirty days; 'full' — thirty days; 'and after that' — *equivalent to the foregoing [sixty, thus one hundred twenty in all]."*

I.   *That's a question?!*

49. A.   *Our rabbis have taught on Tannaite authority:*

B.   "People may keep uncircumcised slaves," the words of R. Ishmael.

C.   R. Aqiba says, "People may not keep uncircumcised slaves."

D.   Said to him R. Ishmael, "Lo, it is written, 'And the son of your handmaid may be refreshed' (Ex. 23:12)."

E.   "That speaks of a slave bought at twilight, when there was not enough time to perform the act of circumcision."

F.   *But all parties concur, in any event, that* "And the son of your handmaid may be refreshed" (Ex. 23:12) *refers to an uncircumcised slave. On what basis?*

G.   *It is on the basis of that which has been taught on Tannaite authority:*

H.   "your manservant or your maidservant:"

I.   This refers to those who are within the covenant [that is, Israelites].

J.   You maintain that this refers to those who are covered by the covenant. But perhaps reference is to an uncircumcised slave?

K.

L.   When Scripture says, "And the son of your slave-girl and the stranger may be refreshed" (Ex. 23:12), lo, the uncircumcised slave is covered.

M.   You say that it refers to the uncircumcised slave. But perhaps it refers only to a circumcised slave?

N.   When Scripture says, "So that your manservant and your maidservant may rest as well as you," the circumcised slave has been covered. Then to what does the phrase, "And the son of your slave-girl and the stranger may be refreshed" (Ex. 23:12), refer?

O.   It must be to an uncircumcised slave.

P.   "And the stranger,"

Q.   This refers to a resident alien.

R.   But perhaps it refers to the righteous proselyte?

S.   "nor your stranger who is within your gates" lo, this refers to the righteous proselyte. So to what does the phrase "And the stranger" refer? I must address the resident alien [Mekhilta 53: Bahodesh 7/ LIII.1.14-15]

50. A.   Said R. Joshua b. Levi, "He who buys a slave from a gentile and did not want to circumcise him may postpone the matter for twelve months. If he has not circumcised him by that time, he goes and resells him to gentiles."

B. *This was stated by rabbis before R. Pappa: "In accord with whose position? It cannot accord with that of R. Aqiba. For if it were R. Aqiba's, has he not said,* 'People may not keep uncircumcised slaves'?"

C. *Said to them R. Pappa, "You may even say that it represents the view of R. Aqiba. The statement made by R. Aqiba pertains to a case in which the slave never gave permission to be circumcised* [and to accept the obligations of an Israelite slave (Slotki)], *but in a case in which he assented to the matter, he has assented"* [and one may keep the slave for twelve months, assuming he will assent again (Slotki)].

D. *Said R. Kahana, "I stated this tradition before R. Zebid of Nehardea. He said to me, 'If so, then, instead of R. Aqiba's replying [to Ishmael's objection] that the text speaks of a slave that has been bought at twilight, he should have given this reply!"*

E. *He stated to him one of two possible reasons for his position.*

F. *Rabin sent in the name of R. Ilai,* "And all my masters have stated the matter to me in his name: 'What is the definition of an uncircumcised slave that one may retain? It is one that was purchased by his master with the intention of not circumcising him."

G. *Rabbis stated this before R. Pappa: "In accord with which authority? For if it were R. Aqiba's, has he not said,* 'People may not keep uncircumcised slaves'?"

H. *Said to them R. Pappa, "You may even say that it represents the view of R. Aqiba. The statement made by R. Aqiba pertains to a case in which he made no stipulation with the slave [that he would not circumcise him]. But in a case in which such a stipulation was made, that stipulation governs."*

I. *Said R. Kahana, "I stated this tradition before R. Zebid of Nehardea. He said to me, 'If so, then, instead of R. Aqiba's replying [to Ishmael's objection] that the text speaks of a slave that has been bought at twilight, he should have given this reply!"*

J. *Even so, he stated to him one of two possible reasons for his position.*

51. A. *R. Hanina bar Pappi, R. Ammi, and R. Isaac Nappaha happened to go into session in the doorway of R. Isaac Nappaha, and in session they stated:* "There was a town in the Land of Israel, where the slaves did not want to be circumcised, and after postponing the matter for twelve months, they went and resold them to gentiles. *Now in accord with which authority did they act in this manner? It is in accord with the Tannaite authority responsible for that which has been taught as a Tannaite formulation:* He who buys a slave from a gentile and did not want to circumcise him may postpone the matter for twelve months. If he has not circumcised him by that time, he goes and resells him to gentiles. R. Simeon b. Eleazar says, 'They do not postpone the matter involving him when

the case is in the Land of Israel, on account of the loss of food requiring preparation in conditions of cultic cleanness [which will be made unclean by his touch]. But in a town near the frontier, they do not postpone the matter concerning him for a single moment, lest he hear something and go and tell his gentile friend.'"

52. A. *It has been taught on Tannaite authority:*

B. R. Hanania b. Rabban Gamaliel says, "How come gentiles at this time are harassed, and suffering comes upon them? Because they have not carried out [even] the seven religious duties assigned to the children of Noah."

C. R. Yosé says, "A proselyte at the moment of conversion is like a new-born baby. So why are they harassed? Because they are not expert in the details of the religious duties as Israelites are."

D. Abba Hanan says in the name of R. Eleazar, "It is because they do [their religious duties] not out of love of God but out of fear of God."

E. Others say, "Because they postponed coming under the wings of the Presence of god."

F. *Said R. Abbahu and some say R. Hanina, "What is the pertinent verse of Scripture?* 'The Lord recompense your work and be your reward complete from the Lord, the God of Israel, under whom you have come to take refuge' (Ruth 2:12)."

DAUGHTERS AND WIVES, WITH SPECIAL REFERENCE TO HOSEA

BAVLI PESAHIM 8:1 / 87A-B

2. A. "And it shall be at that day says the Lord that you will call my 'My man,' and not 'My master'" (Hos. 2:18) —

B. Said R. Yohanan, "Like a bride in the household of her father-in-law, not like a bride in the household of her father."

3. A. "We have a little sister, and she has no breasts" (Song 8:8):

B. R. Yohanan said, "This refers to Elam, which had sufficient inherited merit to learn but didn't have sufficient inherited merit to teach."

4. A. "I am a wall and my breasts are like towers" (Song 8:10).

B. Said R. Yohanan, "'I am a wall' refers to the Torah, 'and my breasts are like towers' refers to disciples of the sages."

C. And Raba said, "'I am a wall' refers to the community of Israel, 'and my breasts are like towers' refers to houses of assembly and houses of study."

5. A. Said R. Zutra bar Tobiah said Rab, *"What is the meaning of the verse of Scripture,* 'We whose sons are as plants grown up in their youth, whose daughters are as corner pillars carved after the fashion of the Temple' (Ps. 144:12)? 'We whose sons are as plants grown up in their youth' refers to Israelite youngsters, who have never tasted the flavor of sin. '...whose daughters are as corner pillars carved aft her the fashion of the Temple' refers to Israelite girls,

who seal their doors to save them for their husbands, and so Scripture says, 'and they shall be filled like the basins, like the corners of the altar' (Zech. 9:15). *And if you wish, I shall say that the same proposition derives from here:* 'Whose garners are full, affording all manner of store' (Ps. 144:13). 'carved after the fashion of the Temple' (Ps. 144:12) — to both the one and the other is regarded by Scripture as though the Temple were built in their times."

6. A. "The word of the Lord that came to Hosea son of Beeri in the days of Uzziah, Jotham Ahaz, and Hezekiah, kings of Judah" (Hos. 1:1):

   B. Four prophets prophesied in the same period, but the greatest of them all was Hosea, for it is said, "The Lord spoke first with Hosea" (Hos. 1:2). But did he speak first of all with Hosea? Is it not the fact that, from Moses to Hosea, there were numerous prophets?

   C. Said R. Yohanan, "'first,' means, he was the first of the four prophets who prophesied at that same time, and these are they: Hosea, Isaiah, Amos, and Micah.

   D. "Said the Holy One, blessed be he, to Hosea, 'You sons of sinned,' and he should have said, 'They are your sons, the sons of those you have favored, the sons of Abraham, Isaac, and Jacob. So turn your mercies to them.' Now it wasn't enough that that's not what he said, but he said before him instead, 'Lord of the world, all the world is yours, exchange them for some other nation.'

   E. "Said to him the Holy One, blessed be he, 'Then what shall I do with this old man? I'll instruct him, "Go, marry a whore and have children of a whore for yourself," and then I'll order him, "Send her away from you." If he can send her away, so then I'll send Israel away.' For it is said, 'And the Lord said to Hosea, Go take yourself a wife of harlotry and children of harlotry' (Hos. 1:2), and it is written, 'So he went and took Gomer the daughter of Diblaim' (Hos. 1:3)."

7. A. "Gomer:"

   B. said Rab, "For everybody finished up on her."

   C. "'Daughter [87B] of Diblaim:'

   D. "woman of bad name daughter of a woman of bad name."

   E. And Samuel said, "She was sweet in everybody's mouth as a cake of figs."

   F. And R. Yohanan said, "Because everybody 'walked' on her as a cake of figs is pressed down."

8. A. Another interpretation: "Gomer:"

   B. Said R. Judah, "It is because they wanted to destroy the capital of Israel in her time."

   C. R. Yohanan said, "They despoiled and finished it up: 'For the king of Aram destroyed them and made them like the dust in threshing' (2 Kgs. 13:7)."

9. A. "And she conceived and bore him a son. And the Lord said to him, Call his name Jezreel, for yet a little while and I will visit the

blood of Jezreel on the house of Jehu and will cause to cease the kingdom of the house of Israel. And it shall come to pass at that day that I will break the bow of Israel in the valley of Jezreel.' And she conceived again, and bore a daughter, and he said to him, 'Call her name Lo ruhamah' [she has not obtained compassion], for I will no more have compassion upon the house of Israel, that I should in any wise pardon them...and she conceived and bore a son, and he said, Call his name Lo-ammi [not my people], for you are not my people and I will not be yours'" (Hos. 1:3-6, 8-9):

B. After two sons and a daughter were born to him, said the Holy One, blessed be he to Hosea, "Shouldn't you have learned the lesson from your lord, Moses? As soon as I spoke with him, he desisted from sexual relations with his wife. You too, desist from sexual relations with her."

C. He said to him, "Lord of the world, I have children by her, and I can't expel her or divorce her."

D. Said to him the Holy One, blessed be he, "Now you, with a whore for a wife and with children of harlotry, and not knowing whether your children are yours or belong to someone else, are the way you are, then Israel, who really are my children, the children of those whom I have favored, Abraham, Isaac, and Jacob; who are one of the four possessions that I have acquired in this world" —

E. the Torah is one possession: "The Lord acquirement me as the beginning of his way" (Prov. 8:22);

F. "heaven and earth are one possession: "God Most High who possesses heaven and earth" (Gen. 14:19);

G. the Temple is one: "This mountain, which his right hand has acquired" (Ps. 78:54);

H. Israel is one: "This people that you have gotten" (Ex. 15:16) —

I. — "and you can use such language as, ' exchange them for some other nation.'?!"

J. When he realized that he had sinned, he sought mercy for himself. Said to him the Holy One, blessed be he, "Instead of seeking mercy for yourself, seek mercy for Israel, for I have made three decrees against them on account of you."

K. He went and sought mercy, and he annulled the decrees.

L. He began to bless them: "Yet the number of the children of Israel shall be as the sand of the sea...and it shall come to pass that, instead of that which was said unto them, You are not my people, it shall be said unto them, you are the children of the living God. And the children of Judah and the children of Israel shall be gathered together. And I will sow her to me in the land and I will have compassion upon her that has not obtained compassion and I will say to them that were not my people, you are my people" (Hos. 2:1-2, 25).

10. A. Said R. Yohanan, "Woe to a government that buries the one who possesses it, for you don't have a single prophet who didn't outlive

four kings in his own lifetime: 'The vision of Isaiah the son of Amoz, which he saw concerning Judah and Jerusalem in the days of Uzziah, Jotham, Ahaz, and Hezekiah, kings of Judah' (Is. 1:1)."

11. A. Said R. Yohanan, "On what basis did Jeroboam son of Joash, king of Israel, have the unearned grace of being counted with the kings of Judah? Because he didn't accept gossip against Amos.

B. "How do we know that he was counted with them? 'The word of the Lord that came to Hosea son of Beeri in the days of Uzziah, Jotham Ahaz, and Hezekiah, kings of Judah' Hos. 1:1).

C. "And how do we know that he didn't accept gossip? 'Then Amaziah priest of Beth el sent to Jeroboam king of Israel, saying, Amos has conspired against you' (Amos 7:10); 'for thus Amos said, 'Jeroboam shall die by the sword' (Amos 7:11). Said Jeroboam, 'God forbid, that that righteous man could have said any such thing! But if he did say it, what can I do to him, since the Presence of God said it to him.'"

12. A. Said R. Eleazar, "Even at the time of the wrath of the Holy One, blessed be he, he remembers mercy: 'for I will no more have compassion upon the house of Israel' (Hos. 1:6)."

B. R. Yosé bar Hanina said, "It derives from here: 'that I should in any wise pardon them' (Hos. 1:6)."

13. A. And said R. Eliezer, "The Holy One, blessed be he, exiled the Israelites among the nations only so that converts should join them: 'And I will sow her unto me in the land' (Hos. 2:25). Certainly someone sows a seah of seed to harvest many kor of seed."

B. R. Yohanan derived the same proposition from the following: "And I will have compassion upon her who has not obtained compassion" (Hos. 2:25).

14. A. Said R. Yohanan in the name of R. Simeon b. Yohai, "What is the meaning of the verse of Scripture: 'Don't slander a servant to his master, lest he curse you and you be found guilty' (Prov. 30:10)? And it is written, 'a generation that curse their father and do not bless their mother' (Prov. 30:11)? Is the sense, because they curse their father and don't bless their mother, don't slander? But the sense is, even if the slaves are a generation that curse their father and don't bless their mother, don't slander them. On what basis do we know that fact? From Hosea."

THE EXILE AND HOSEA'S PROPHECY

15. A. Said R. Oshayya, "What is the meaning of the verse of Scripture: 'Even the righteous acts of his ruler in Israel' (Judges 5:11)? The Holy One, blessed be he, did an act of righteousness with Israel when he scattered them among the nations."

B. *That is in line with what a certain heretic said to R. Hanina, "We are better than you. Concerning you it is written, 'for Joab and all Israel remained there six months, until he had cut off every male in Edom' (1 Kgs. 11:16), while you have been with us many years and we haven't done a thing to you."*

C. He said to him, "If you like, let a disciple deal with you."

D. R. Oshayya dealt with him. *He said to him, "It is because you don't know how to behave. If you want to destroy all of them, they're not all among you, being scattered. If you want to destroy those who are among you, then you'll be called a kingdom of murderers."*

E. *He said to him, "By the Roman capitol! We worry about this when we lie down, and we worry about this when we get up"* [Freedman: how to destroy you without incurring odium].

16. A. *R. Hiyya taught on Tannaite authority, "What is the meaning of the verse of Scripture:* 'God understood her way and he knew her place' (Job 28:23)? The Holy One, blessed be he, knew that the Israelites wouldn't be able to take the Romans' persecution, so he drove them to Babylonia."

17. A. And said R. Eleazar, "The Holy One, blessed be he, exiled Israel to Babylonia only because it is as deep as hell: 'I shall ransom them from the power of the netherworld, I shall redeem them from death' (Hos. 13:14)."

B. R. Hanina said, "It is because their language is near the language of the Torah."

C. R. Yohanan said, "It is because he sent them back to their mother's house. The matter may be compared to the case of someone who got made at his wife. Where does he send her? To her mother's house."

D. *That's in line with what R. Alexandri stated:* "Three went back to the place where they were planted, and these are they: Israel, the wealth of Egypt, and the writing of the tablets.

E. "Israel: as we just said.

F. "the wealth of Egypt: 'And it came to pass in the fifth year of King Rehoboam, that Shishak king of Egypt came up against Jerusalem and he took away the treasures of the house of the Lord' (1 Kgs. 14:25).

G. "and the writing of the tablets: 'And I broke them before your eyes' (Dt. 9:17)."

18. A. *A Tannaite statement:*

B. The tablets broke, and the letters flew up.

19. A. Ulla said, "They were sent into exile so that they might eat [88A] dates and have the free time to get busy with the Torah."

20. A. *Ulla came to Pumbedita. They offered him a basket of dates. He said to them, "How many of these do you get for a zuz?"*

B. *"Three for a zuz."*

C. *"A basketful of honey for a zuz, and yet the Babylonians don't engage in the study of the Torah?!"*

D. *That night the dates upset his belly. He said, "A basketful of deadly poison costs a zuz in Babylonia, and yet the Babylonians study the Torah?!"*

21. A. And said R. Eleazar, "What's the meaning of the verse of Scripture, 'And many people shall go and say, Come and let's go up to the mountain of the Lord, to the house of the god of Jacob' Is. 2:3)? The God of Jacob, not the God of Abraham or Isaac? But we shall not be like Abraham, in whose regard 'mountain' is written: as it is said to this day, in the mountain where the Lord is seen' (Gen. 22:14), nor like Isaac, in regard to whom 'field' is written, 'And Isaac went out to meditate in the field at eventide' (Gen. 24:63), but let us be like Jacob, who called him 'home,' 'and he called the name of that place Beth El' [God is a home]' (Gen. 28:19)."

22. A. Said R. Yohanan, "The ingathering of the exiles is as great as the day on which heaven and earth were created: 'And the children of Judah and the children of Israel shall be gathered together, and they shall appoint themselves one head and shall go up out of the land, for great shall be the day of Jezreel' (Hos. 2:2), and 'and there was evening and there was morning, one day' (Gen. 1:4)."

DEATHS OF VARIOUS SAGES AND HOW THEIR MASTERY OF THE TORAH AFFORDED THEM SPECIAL STANDING AFTER DEATH

BAVLI MOED QATAN 3:7-8/28A

5. A. *Our rabbis have taught on Tannaite authority:*
   B. If someone died suddenly, that is classified as "being caught up."
   C. If someone died after an illness of one day, that is classified as "being rushed out."
   D. R. Hanania b. Gamaliel says, "That is death by a stroke: 'Son of man, behold I take away from you the desire of your eyes with a pestilential stroke' (Ez. 24:16), and then, 'So I spoke to the people in the morning, and at evening my wife died' (Ez. 24:18)."
   E. If someone lingered for two days and then died, this is classified as a precipitous death.
   F. After three — this is classified as a death of reproof.
   G. After four — this is classified as a death of rebuff.
   H. After five — this is classified as a routine death.
   I. *Said R. Hanina, "What verse of Scripture indicates it?* 'Lo, your days are approaching that you must die' (Dt. 31:14). 'Behold' *is one,* 'your days,' *two more,* 'are approaching' *represents two more."*
   J. "Behold" makes one because the Greek word for one is *hen* [which is the Hebrew word for "behold"].
   K. [Continuing from H:] If one died at under fifty years of age — this is classified as death by extirpation.
   L. If one died at fifty-two — this is classified as the death of Samuel of Ramah.
   M. If one died at sixty — this is classified as death at the hand of Heaven.

N. *Said Mar Zutra, "What verse of Scripture indicates it?* 'You shall come to your grave in ripe age' (Job 5:26), *and the numerical value of the word for in ripe age is sixty."*

O. If one died at the age of seventy — this is classified as the hoary head.

P. If one died at the age of eighty — this is classified as the vigorous old man: "The days of our years are three score and ten, or even by reason of strength, four score" (Ps. 90:10).

R. Said Rabbah, "If one died from age fifty to age sixty, that is classified as death by extirpation, *and the reason that is not stated explicitly is out of respect to Samuel of Ramah."*

6. A. *When R. Joseph reached the age of sixty, he made for the rabbis a festival day, saying, "I have now emerged from the age at which my death would have marked punishment by extirpation."*

B. *Said to him Abbayye, "Granted that you have now passed the limit of the age at which extirpation would have been the case, have you escaped the limit at which death would mark dying out of a sudden illness on a single day?"* [That is, If someone died suddenly, that is classified as "being caught up."]

C. *He said to him, "Anyhow, grab half of whatever you can get."*

7. A. *R. Huna died suddenly. The rabbis were worried about it. Zoga of Adiabene repeated to them the following Tannaite statement:* "What we learned as the rule pertains only if one has not attained eighty years of age, but if one has attained the age of eighty, sudden death is the same as dying by a kiss."

8. A. *Said Raba, "How long you live, how many children you have and how much money you make depend on not merit but one's star."*

B. *For lo, Rabbah and R. Hisda were both upright rabbis. One master prayed for rain and it rained, the other prayed for rain and it didn't come.*

C. *R. Hisda lived to ninety-two, Rabbah to forty.*

D. *In R. Hisda's household sixty marriage feasts were celebrated, in Rabbah's house sixty funerals were held.*

E. *At R. Hisda's house they fed first-rate wheat bread to the dogs and it went to waste. At Rabbah's house all they had was barley bread for human beings, and even that they didn't have.*

F. *And said Raba, "I asked these things of Heaven, two were granted, one not. I prayed to have the learning of R. Huna and the wealth of R. Hisda, which I got, and I prayed for the humility of Rabbah b. R. Huna, but that I didn't get."*

The topic of the sequence of composites now shifts to dealing with the angel of death; this composite does not exhibit connections to the foregoing.

9. A. *R. Seorim, brother of Raba, was sitting before Raba at his deathbed, and saw him falling into a coma. Raba said to him, "Tell [the angel of death] not to torment me as I die."*

B.   *He said to him, "But aren't you his good buddy?"*

C.   *He said to him, "Since my star has been handed over into his control, he doesn't pay any attention to me any more."*

D.   *He said to him, "Show yourself to me in a dream." [Raba] did so.*

E.   *He asked him, "Did you suffer when you were dying?"*

F.   *He said to him, "No more than the prick of the leech."*

10. A.   *Raba was sitting before R. Nahman at his deathbed, and saw him falling into a coma. He said to him, "Tell [the angel of death] not to torment me as I die."*

B.   *He said to him, "But aren't you an eminent authority?"*

C.   *He said to him, "So who is eminent, who is regarded, who is treated as distinguished [by the angel of death]?"*

D.   *He said to him, "Show yourself to me in a dream." He did so.*

E.   *He asked him, "Did you suffer when you were dying?"*

F.   *He said to him, "No more than taking a piece of hair out of the milk, and, I have to tell you, if the Holy One, blessed be he, said to me, 'Now go back to that world as you were before,' I wouldn't do it, for the fear of death is too much to take."*

11. A.   *R. Eleazar was engaged in eating food in the status of priestly rations [which have to be protected from corpse-uncleanness] at the moment at which the angel of death made his appearance. He said to him, "Am I not eating food in the status of priestly rations? And is this not classified as Holy Things?!"*

B.   *So the hour passed.*

12. A.   *The angel of death made his appearance to R. Sheshet in the market place. He said to him, "Are you going to take me in the market place like a dumb cow? Come to me at my home!"*

13. A.   *The angel of death made his appearance to R. Ashi in the market place. He said to him, "Give me thirty days' more so I can review my learning, since you say up there, 'Happy is he who comes up here bringing his learning all ready at hand.'"*

B.   *So he came along thirty days later. He said to him, "So what's the rush?"*

C.   *He said to him, "R. Huna bar Nathan is on your heels, and 'no regime may impinge upon its fellow, even by so much as a hair's breadth.'"*

14. A.   *The angel of death could not overcome R. Hisda, because his mouth never ceased to recite his learning. He went out and sat on a cedar tree by the house of study. The branch of the cedar cracked, R. Hisda stopped, and the other overcame him.*

15. A.   *The angel of death could not get near R. Hiyya. One day he appeared to him in the form of a poor beggar. He came and knocked on the door, saying, "Bring out some food for me." Others brought it out to him.*

B.   *He said to R. Hiyya, "Aren't you, my lord, going to treat with mercy this man who is standing outside?"*

C.   *He opened the door to him, and he showed him a fiery rod and made him give up his soul.*

DEFINITION OF A MINOR

BAVLI HAGIGAH 1:2 5B-6A

VII.1 A.   **What is the definition of a minor? "Any who cannot ride on the shoulder of his father to go up from Jerusalem to the Temple mount," the words of the House of Shammai.** And the House of Hillel say, **"Any who cannot hold his father's hand to go up from Jerusalem to the Temple mount, as it is written, 'Three [festivals, involving a pilgrimage] by foot' [regalim=feet] (Ex. 23:14):"**

B.   *Objected R. Zira,* **[6A]** *"So who carried him up to now?"* [Abraham: from his house to Jerusalem; the fact that he could travel to Jerusalem shows that he is old enough to do without his mother; at that age he is also old enough to be able to go up from Jerusalem to the Temple Mount by holding his father's hand; what point is there in defining a minor as one who is unable even with the aid of his father to go up from Jerusalem to the Temple mount, when the prior journey to Jerusalem shows that he is old enough to do this and therefore no longer a minor?]

.   *Said to him Abbayye, "Up to now, because his mother was obligated in regard to the rejoicing offering, his mother brought him; from this point,* **if he can go up from Jerusalem to the Temple Mount holding his father's hand,** *he is obligated, and if not, he is exempt."*

2. A.   Rabbi [better: Raba] responded in behalf of the House of Hillel to the House of Shammai as follows: "'But Hannah didn't go up, for she said to her husband, until the child is weaned, when I'll bring him up' (1 Sam. 1:22). [That would be at the end of two years.] *But Samuel was perfectly ready to ride on his father's shoulders."*

B.   His father [better: Abbayye] said to him, *"But by your reasoning, the case of Hannah herself should present a problem! Wasn't Hannah obligated to rejoice on the festival* [so she should have gone up to the sanctuary and taken Samuel even before he was weaned (Abraham]*! Rather, Hannah realized that Samuel was exceptionally frail and was concerned on account of Samuel's frailty in respect to making such a trip."*

3. A.   *R. Simeon raised this question:* "As to a lame minor in the position of the House of Shammai, or a blind minor in respect to both views, what is the law?"

B.   *So how are we to understand the case? Should we say the question concerns a lame one who cannot ever walk, or a blind one who cannot ever see? Then in such cases an adult is exempt, so can there be an issue about a minor?*

C.   *Not at all, the question concerns* a lame child who can some day walk and a blind child who can some day see. *What is the law?*

D.   *Said Abbayye, "In any case in which an adult is obligated by the law of the Torah, then by the authority of rabbis we also educate a minor, and in any case in which an adult is exempt from the obligation by the law of the Torah, by the rule of rabbis a minor also is exempt.*

DIVORCE/THE EVILS OF DIVORCE, PARTICULARLY OF AN AGING WIFE

BAVLI SANHEDRIN 2:5 22A-B

I.3A.   Said R. Eliezer, "Whoever divorces his first wife — even the altar weeps tears on that account, for it is said, 'And this further did you do, you cover the altar of the Lord with tears, with weeping and with sighing, in so much that he regards not the offering any more, nor receives it with good will at your hand' (Mal. 2:13). And it is written, 'Yet you say, Why? Because the Lord has been witness between you and the wife of your youth, against whom you have dealt treacherously, though she is your companion and the wife of your covenant' (Mal. 2:14)."

I.4 A.   Said R. Yohanan, and some say, R. Eleazar, "A man's wife dies only if people ask for money from him and he does not have it, as it is said, 'If you have not wherewith to pay, why should he take away the bed from under you' (Prov. 22:27)."

B.   And R. Yohanan said, "Any man whose first wife dies is as if the Temple was destroyed in his day. For it is said, 'Son of man, behold I take away from you the desire of your eyes with a stroke, yet you shall not make lamentation nor weep, neither shall your tears run down.' And it is written, 'And I spoke to the people in the morning, and at evening my wife died.' And it is written, 'Behold I will profane my sanctuary, the pride of your power, the desire of your eyes' (Ez. 24:16-18)."

C.   Said R. Alexandri, "For every man whose wife dies in his lifetime the world grows dark, as it is said, 'The light shall be dark because of his tent and his lamp over him shall be put out' (Job 18:6)."

D.   R. Yosé bar Hanina said, "His steps grew short, as it is said, 'The steps of his strength shall be straightened' (Job 18:7)."

E.   R. Abbahu said, "His good sense fails, as it is said, 'And his own counsel shall cast him down' (Job 18:7)."

I.5 A.   Said Rabbah bar bar Hannah said R. Yohanan, "It is as difficult to match people up as it is to split the Red Sea, as it is said, 'God sets the solitary in families, he brings prisoners into prosperity' (Ps. 68:7)."

B.   Is that really the accepted view? And did not Rab Judah say Rab said, "Forty days prior to the formation of the foetus, an echo goes forth and proclaims, 'The daughter of Mr. So-and-so is assigned to Mr. Such-and-such, [the house of Mr. So-and-so is assigned to

Mr. Such-and-such, the field of Mr. So-and-so is assigned to Mr. Such-and-such.'"]

C. *There is no contradiction between the implications of the cited views. The former refers to the first marriage, the latter to the second.*

I.6 A. Said R. Samuel bar Nahman, "Everything can be replaced except for the wife of one's youth,

B. "as it is said, 'And a wife of one's youth, can she be rejected?' (Is. 54:6)."

I.7 A. *R. Judah repeated on Tannaite authority to his son, R. Isaac,* "A man finds true serenity only with his first wife, as it is said, 'Let your fountain be blessed and have joy of the wife of [22B] your youth' (Prov. 5:18)."

B. *He said to him, "Such as whom?"*

C. *He said to him, "Such as your mother."*

D. *Is this so? And did not R. Judah recite for R. Isaac, his son, the verse of Scripture,* "And I find more bitter than death the woman whose heart is snares and nets" (Qoh. 7:26)?

E. *And he said to him, "Such as whom?"*

F. *He said to him, "Such as your mother."*

G. *She was easy to anger but easy to appease with a good word.*

I.8 A. Said R. Samuel bar Onia in the name of Rab, "A woman is unformed, and she makes a covenant only with him who turns her into a utensil, as it is said, 'For your maker is your husband, the Lord of hosts is his name' (Is. 54:5)."

B. *It has been taught on Tannaite authority:*

C. A man dies only for his wife, and a woman dies only for her husband.

D. A man dies only for his wife, as it is said, "And Elimelech, Naomi's husband, died" (Ruth 1:3).

E. And a woman dies only for her husband, as it is said, "And as for me, when I came from Padan, Rachel died for me" (Gen. 48:7).

DYING WITHOUT SONS

BAVLI BABA BATRA 8:2 116A

3. A. Said R. Yohanan in the name of R. Simeon b. Yohai, "Whoever does not leave a son to inherit his estate — the Holy One, blessed be he, is full of anger against him. Here it is written, 'And you shall cause his inheritance to pass' (Num. 27:8), and there, "That day is a day of wrath' (Zeph. 1:15) [and the words for cause to pass and wrath use the same consonants].

4. A. "Such as have no changes and do not fear God" (Ps. 55:20) —

B. R. Yohanan and R. Joshua b. Levi —

C. One said, "This refers to one who leaves no son."

D. And the other said, "This refers to one who leaves no disciple."

E. *You may draw the conclusion that it is R. Yohanan who said,*
    "...disciple," for said R. Yohanan, "This is the bone of my tenth
    son."

F. *You may indeed drawn the conclusion that it is R. Yohanan who*
    made reference to a disciple, and since R. Yohanan made reference
    to a disciple, it must be that R. Joshua b. Levi said that it is a son.

G. *But lo, R. Joshua b. Levi would go to a house of mourning only in*
    the case of someone who had gone off without children, in line
    with the verse, "Weep bitterly for the one who goes away, for he
    shall return no more nor see his native country" (Jer. 22:10).

H. And said R. Judah said Rab, "That refers to one who goes away
    with no male child."

I. *Rather, It is R. Joshua b. Levi who said that the verse refers to a*
    disciple, and since R. Joshua b. Levi is the one who said that the
    verse refers to a disciple, it must be R. Yohanan who said that it
    refers to a son.

J. *And that yields a contradiction between the two statements of R.*
    Yohanan.

K. *There really is no contradiction between the two statements of R.*
    Yohanan. The one statement belongs to him [and he concurs with
    Joshua], the other statement belongs to his master [and he has
    merely repeated it].

5. A. Expounded R. Phineas b. Hama, *"What is the meaning of the verse*
        of Scripture, 'And when Hadad heard in Egypt that David slept
        with his fathers and that Joab the captain of the host was dead' (1
        Kgs, 11:21)? Why refer to David as 'sleeping' but refer to Joab as
        'dead'? Of David, who left a son, 'sleeping' is said, of Joab, who
        left no son, 'death' is said."

   B. But is it the fact that Joab left no son? Isn't it written, "Of the sons
        of Joab Obadiah the son of Jehiel" (Ezra 8:9)?

   C. But of David, who left a son like himself, "sleeping" is said, but of
        Joab, who left no son like himself, "death" is said.

6. A. Expounded R. Phineas b. Hama, "Poverty in one's own home is
        harder to take than fifty lashes: 'Have pity on me, have pity upon
        me, O you, my friends, for the hand of God has touched me' (Job
        19:21). *And note what his friends say to him:* 'Take heed, regard
        not iniquity, for this have you chosen rather than poverty' (Job
        36:21)."

7. A. Expounded R. Phineas b. Hama, "Whoever has a sick person in
        his house should go to a sage to seek mercy: 'The wrath of a king
        is as messengers of death, but a sage will pacify it' (Prov. 16:14)."

HONOR OF MOTHER AND FATHER

BAVLI QIDDUSHIN 1:7 30B-31A

II.2 A. *Our rabbis have taught on Tannaite authority:*

B.   It is said, "Honor your father and your mother" (Ex. 20:12), and it is further said, "Honor the Lord with your wealth" (Prov. 3:9).

C.   Scripture thereby establishes an analogy between the honor of father and mother and the honor of the Omnipresent.

D.   It is said, "He who curses his father or his mother will certainly die" (Prov. 20:20), and it is said, "Any person who curses his God will bear his sin" (Lev. 24:15).

E.   Scripture thereby establishes an analogy between cursing father and mother and cursing the Omnipresent.

F.   But it is not possible to refer to smiting Heaven [in the way in which one is warned not to hit one's parents].

G.   And that is entirely reasonable, for all three of them are partners [in a human being] [Sifra Qedoshim CXCV:II.3].

II.3 A.   *Our rabbis have taught on Tannaite authority:*

B.   Three form a partnership in the creation of a human being, the Holy One, blessed be He, one's father and one's mother. When someone honors father and mother, said the Holy One, blessed be He, "I credit it to them as though I had lived among them and they honored me."

II.4 A.   *It has been taught on Tannaite authority:*

B.   **Rabbi says, "It is perfectly self-evident to the One who spoke and brought the world into being that the son honors his mother more than his father, because [31A] she influences him with kind words. Therefore the Holy One, blessed be He, gave precedence to honoring the father over honoring the mother. But it also is perfectly self-evident before the One who spoke and brought the world into being that the son fears the father more than the mother, because he teaches him Torah. Therefore the Holy One, blessed be He, gave priority to fear of the mother over fear of the father."**

II.5 A.   *A Tannaite authority repeated before R. Nahman:* **"When someone gives anguish to his father or his mother, said the Holy One, blessed be He, 'I did well in not living among them, for if I lived among them, they would have given me anguish, too.'"**

II.6 A.   **Said R. Isaac, "Whoever secretly carries out a transgression is as though he stepped on the feet of the Presence of God: 'Thus said the Lord, the heaven is my throne, and the earth is my footstool' (Isa. 66:1)."**

II.7 A.   **Said R. Joshua b. Levi, "It is forbidden to walk about stiffly erect, even for four cubits, for it is written, 'The whole earth is full of his glory' (Isa. 6:3)."**

B.   R. Huna b. R. Joshua wouldn't walk four cubits bareheaded. He said, "The Presence of God is above my head."

II.8 A.   **A widow's son asked R. Eliezer, "If father says, 'Give me a glass of water,' and mother says, 'Give me a glass of water,' to which of them do I give precedence?"**

B. He said to him, "Ignore the honor owing to your mother and carry out the act of respect owing to your father, for you and your mother are equally obligated to pay respect to your father."

C. He came before R. Joshua, who said the same to him.

D. "My lord, if she is divorced, what is the law?"

E. He said to him, "From the character of your eyelids, it's obvious that you're a widow's son. Pour out some water for them in a basin and cackle for them like chickens."

II.9 A. *Ulla the elder gave this exposition at the gate of the patriarch: "What is the meaning of Scripture,* 'All the kings of the earth shall praise you, Lord, for they have heard the words of your mouth' (Ps. 138:4)? What is stated is not, 'the word of your mouth,' but 'the words of your mouth.' So when the Holy One, blessed be He, said, 'I am the Lord your God' 'you shall have no other Gods before me,' (Ex. 20:2-3), said the nations of the world, 'All he wants is his own self-aggrandizement.'When he said, 'Honor your father and your mother' (Ex. 20:12), they retracted and confessed to the validity of the first statements as well."

B. *Raba said, "From the following verse [the same point can be drawn, namely:]* 'The beginning of your word is true' (Ps. 119:160) – the beginning but not the end? But what comes at the end of your word – the truth of the beginning of your word is understood."

II.10 A. *They asked R. Ulla, "To what extent is one obligated to honor father and mother?"*

B. He said to them, "Go and observe how a certain gentile has treated his father in Ashkelon, and Dama b. Netinah is his name. On one occasion sages wanted to do business with him in the amount of six hundred thousand but the keys were lying under his father's pillow, and he would not disturb him."

C. Said R. Judah said Samuel, "They asked R. Eliezer, to what extent is one obligated to honor one's father and one's mother? He said to them, 'Go and observe how a certain gentile has treated his father in Ashkelon, and Dama b. Netinah is his name. On one occasion they wanted to buy from him precious stones for the ephod, in the amount of six hundred thousand *(R. Kahana repeated as the Tannaite version,* eight hundred thousand) but the keys were lying under his father's pillow, and he would not disturb him. Another year the Holy One, blessed be He, gave him his reward, for a red cow was born to him in his corral, and sages of Israel came to him. He said to them, "I know full well of you that if I should demand of you all the money in the world, you will give it to me. But now I ask of you only that sum of money that I lost in honor of my father."'"

D. And said R. Hanina, "Now if someone who is not subject to commandments acts in such a way, then if someone who is subject to the commandment acts in such a way, all the more so! For said

R. Hanina, 'Greater is he who is commanded and acts on that account than he who is not commanded and acts on that account.'"

II.11 A. *Said R. Joseph, "To begin with, I thought that if someone said to me, the decided law accords with R. Judah, that a blind person is exempt from the obligation of the commandments, I should have made a big party for all the rabbis, since I'm not obligated to do them but I do them anyhow. But now that I've heard the statement of R. Hanina,* 'Greater is he who is commanded and acts on that account than he who is not commanded and acts on that account,' *to the contrary, if someone will tell me that the decided law is not in accord with R. Judah, I'll make a big party for all the rabbis."*

II.12 A. *When R. Dimi came,* he said, "Once [Dama] was dressed in a gold embroidered silk coat, sitting among the Roman nobles, and his mother came along and tore it from him and hit him on the head and spat in his face, but he did not in any way answer back to her."

II.13 A. *A Tannaite statement of Abimi b. R. Abbahu:* There is he who feeds his father pheasant to eat but this drives the son from the world, and there is he who binds his father up to the grinding wheel, [31B] and this brings the son into the world to come. [Someone fed the father pheasants but when the father asked how he could afford them, said, "It's none of your business, chew and eat." By contrast, someone was grinding on a mill and the father was summoned for the corvée, so the son said to the father, "You grind for me and I'll go in your place."]

II.14 A. Said R. Abbahu, "For instance, my son Abimi carried out in an exemplary manner the religious duty of honor of parents."

B. *Abimi had five ordained sons when his father was yet alive, but when R. Abbahu came and called at the gate, he ran and opened for him, saying, "Coming, coming," until he got there.*

C. *Once he said to him, "Bring me a glass of water." Before he got there, the father dozed off. So he bent over him until he woke up. This brought it about that Abimi succeeded in explaining "a song of Asaph"* (Ps. 79:1).

II.15 A. *Said R. Jacob bar Abbuha to Abbayye, "How about someone like me? For when I come home from the household of the master, father pours a cup for me, and mother mixes — what am I supposed to do?"*

B. *He said to him, "Well,* take it from your mother but not from your father, *since he, too, is obligated to study the Torah, it may be an insult to him."*

II.16 A. *R. Tarfon's mother — whenever she wanted to get into bed, he would bend down and let her climb up on his back, and when she wanted to get out, she would step down on him. He went and praised himself in the schoolhouse.* They said to him, "So you still haven't got to half the honor that is owing: Has she thrown down a money bag in your presence into the sea, without your answering back to her?"

II.17 A.   *R. Joseph – when he heard the sound of his mother's steps, he said, "Let me arise before the Presence of God, who approaches."*

II.18   A.   Said R. Yohanan, "Happy is he who never knew his parents [since it is so hard properly to honor them]."

II.19 A.   R. Yohanan – when his mother was carrying him, his father died, and when his mother bore him, she died.

B.   The same is so of Abbayye.

C.   *But how can that be so, when he was always saying, "Mother told me"?*

D.   *That was his stepmother.*

II.20 A.   *R. Assi had an aged mother. She said to him, "I want some jewelry."* So he made it for her.

B.   *"I want a man."*

C.   *"I'll go looking for someone for you."*

D.   *"I want a man as handsome as you."*

E.   *At that he left her and went to the Land of Israel. He heard that she was coming after him. He came to R. Yohanan and asked him,* "What is the law on my leaving the Land and going abroad?"

F.   He said to him, "It is forbidden."

G.   "What is the law as to going to greet my mother?"

H.   He said to him, "I don't know."

I.   *He waited a bit and then went and came back.* He said to him, "Assi, you obviously want to go. May the Omnipresent bring you back here in peace."

J.   *Assi came before R. Eleazar. He said to him, "God forbid! Maybe he was mad?"*

K.   *"What did he say to you?"*

L.   "May the Omnipresent bring you back here in peace."

M.   *He said to him, "Well, if he had been angry, he wouldn't have given you a blessing."*

N.   *In the meanwhile he heard that it was her coffin that was coming. He said, "If I had known that, I wouldn't have gone out."*

LOSING ONE'S TEMPER AND TAKING A VOW

B AVLI 3:1 22A

I.14 A.   Said R. Samuel bar Nahman said R. Yohanan, "Whoever loses his temper – all the torments of Hell rule over him: 'Therefore remove anger from your heart, thus will you put away evil from your flesh' (Qoh. 11:10), and the meaning of 'evil' is only Hell: 'The Lord has made all things for himself, yes, even the wicked for the day of evil' (Prov. 16:4). Moreover, he will get a belly ache: 'But the Lord shall give you there a trembling heart and failing of eyes and sorrow of mind' (Deut. 28:65). And what causes weak eyes and depression? Stomach aches."

I.15 A. *Ulla went up to the Land of Israel, accompanied by two men*
         from Khuzistan. One of them went and killed the other. He said
         to Ulla, "So didn't I do the right thing?"

   B.   *He said to him, "Yessirree! And now cut his throat right across."*

   C.   *When he came before R. Yohanan, he said to him, "Maybe – God*
         forbid – I have encouraged sinners?"

   D.   He said to him, "You saved your life."

   E.   *R. Yohanan expressed surprise:* "It is written, 'There the Lord
         will give them a temperamental heart' (Deut. 28:65) – this speaks
         of Babylonia – so how could such a thing have happened in the
         Land of Israel, where people are patient with one another?]"

   F.   *Ulla said to him, "At that moment* [22B] *we had not yet crossed*
         the Jordan."

I.16 A. **Said Rabbah bar R. Huna, "Whoever loses his temper – even**
         the Presence of God is not important to him: 'The wicked,
         through the pride of his countenance, will not seek God; God is
         not in all his thoughts' (Ps. 10:4)."

I.17 A. **R. Jeremiah of Difti said, "[Whoever loses his temper] – he**
         forgets what he has learned and increases foolishness: 'For
         anger rests in the heart of fools' (Qoh. 7:9), and 'But the fool
         lays open his folly' (Prov. 13:16)."

   B.   R. Nahman bar Isaac said, "One may be sure that his sins outnumber
         his merits: 'And a furious man abounds in transgressions' (Prov.
         29:22)."

I.18 A. **Said R. Ada b. R. Hanina, "If the Israelites had not sinned, to**
         them would have been given only the Five Books of the Torah
         and the book of Joshua alone, which involves the division of
         the Land of Israel. *How come?* **'For much wisdom proceeds**
         from much anger' (Qoh. 1:18)." [Freedman: The anger of God
         caused him to send prophets with their wise teachings.]

MARRYING A WOMAN OF BAD NAME OR HER DAUGHTER

BAVLI SOTAH 4:4 26B-27A

4. A. Said Samuel, "A man should marry [27A] a woman of bad name
        rather than a daughter of a woman of bad name, because the former
        comes from suitable stock, while the latter comes from unsuitable
        stock."

   B.   And R. Yohanan said, "A man should marry the daughter of a
        woman of bad name, rather than a woman of bad name, because
        the former enjoys the presupposition that she is a suitable person,
        while the latter does not enjoy the supposition that she is a suitable
        person."

   C.   *They objected, "Should a man marry a woman of bad name at*
        all?!"

D. *Said Raba, "But do you think that the advice at hand is that, to begin with, one should make such a marriage? Rather, if one has married [such a woman, he has the choice at hand]."*

E. *So too it has been taught on Tannaite authority:* "...the daughter of a woman of bad name."

F. *And the decided law is that* a man should marry the daughter of a woman of bad name, but he should not marry a woman of bad name.

G. *For R. Tahalipa of the West taught before R. Abbahu,* "When the mother is a whore, her children are nonetheless suitable [for Israelite marriage. Why so?] Most acts of sexual relationships are attributed to the husband, [and the husband is suitable, as an Israelite, to produce a valid offspring with the woman at hand. We assume that she has had sexual relations with an Israelite husband. As an unmarried woman, there is no marital obstacle to impede her producing, with an Israelite, a valid offspring.]

H. *R. Amram asked, "But if the woman is unusually dissolute, what is the law?*

I. *"In the view of the one who says that a woman becomes pregnant only right before her period, this is no problem, for a husband will not know and will not guard her, [so the children will be invalid].*

J. *"But in the view of him who says that the woman becomes pregnant only after she has immersed following her period, it is a question indeed.*

K. *"What is the rule? Since the husband knows [that the woman is fertile,] he will watch her very carefully?*

L. *"Or since the woman is unusually dissolute, that is not the case [so the children cannot be regarded as valid]?"*

M. *The question stands over.*

MEAL AS A RELIGIOUS DUTY

BAVLI PESAHIM 3:7-8 / 49A-B

3. A. R. Simeon says, "Any meal that is not in fulfillment of a religious duty — a disciple of a sage has no right to derive benefit from it."

B. *Like what, for instance?*

C. Said R. Yohanan, "For instance, the betrothal feast for the daughter of a priest marrying an Israelite, or the daughter of a disciple of sage marrying an unlettered man."

D. For said R. Yohanan, "When priest's daughter marries an Israelite, the match will never work."

E. *In what way?*

F. Said R. Hisda, "Either she will be widowed, or she will be divorced, or she won't have children."

G. *In a Tannaite formulation it is stated:* either he will bury her or she will bury him or she will bring him down to poverty.

H. *But is that so? Lo,* said R. Yohanan, He who wants to get rich will cleave to the seed of Aaron, for all the more will the Torah and the priesthood enrich them"*!*

I. *No, problem, in the one case it's to a disciple of a sage [who is a priest], in the other, to an unlettered man [who is a priest].*

4. A. *R. Joshua married a priest-woman. He got sick. He said, "It doesn't please Aaron that I should cleave to his seed and that he should have a son in law like me."*

B. *R. Idi bar Abin married a priest-woman. He had two sons who were ordained, R. Sheshet b. R. Idi and R. Joshua b. R. Idi.*

C. *Said R. Pappa, "If I hadn't married a priest's daughter, I wouldn't have gotten rich."*

D. *Said R. Kahana, "If I hadn't married a priest's daughter, I would not have gone into exile [from Babylonia to the Land of Israel]."*

E. They said to him, "Lo, you went into exile to a place of the Torah."

F. *"I wasn't exiled in the way people are exiled in general [but I had to run away]."*

5. A. Said R. Isaac, "Whoever derives benefit from an optional banquet in the end will go into exile: 'And you that eat lambs out of the flock and calves out of the midst of the stall' 'therefore now shall they go captive at the head of those who go captive' (Amos 6:4, 7)."

MARTYRDOM: GIVING ONE'S LIFE FOR THE SANCTIFICATION OF THE DIVINE NAME

BAVLI BERAKHOT 3:102 20A-B

V.3 A. *Said R. Papa to Abbayye, "What makes the difference that the former authorities have miracles done for them, while miracles are not done for us?*

B. *"If it is because of the issue of learning Tannaite traditions, in the time of R. Judah, all they learned to repeat was the matter of Damages, while, for our part, we repeat all six divisions [of the Mishnah, and their associated Tannaite traditions].*

C. *"And when R. Judah would come to the passage in tractate Uqsin,* **'A woman who presses vegetables in a pot'** *(M. Uqs. 2:1), or, some say,* **'Olives pressed with their leaves are clean'** *(M. Uqs. 2:1), he would say, 'Here I see the issues raised by Rab and Samuel for reflection.' But when we repeat tractate Uqsin, we have thirteen sessions [to devote to the matter].*

D. *"Yet when R. Judah would take off one sandal [in preparation for a fast for rain], it would rain right away, while we torture ourselves and cry out, and no one [in heaven] pays attention to us."*

E. *[Abbayye] said to [Papa], "The former authorities would give their lives for the sanctification of the Divine Name, while we do not give our lives for the sanctification of the Divine Name."*

V.4 A. *There was, for example, the case of R. Ada bar Ahba. He saw a Samaritan woman who was wearing a red cloak. Thinking that*

    she was an Israelite woman, he went and tore it off her. It turned
    out that she was a Samaritan, and he had to pay a fine of four
    hundred zuz.

  B.   *He said to her, "What is your name?"*

  C.   *She said to him, "Matun."*

  D.   *He said to her, "Matun? Matun [the letters of which add up to*
       four hundred in numerical value] is worth four hundred zuz."

V.5 A.   *R. Giddal had the habit of going and sitting at the gates of the*
       ritual bath. He would say to [the women], "This is how to immerse
       [for purposes of cleanness], that is how to bathe."

  B.   Rabbis said to him, "Does not the Master fear that his evil impulse
       will be aroused?"

  C.   He said to them, "To me they look like so many white geese."

V.6 A.   *R. Yohanan had the habit of going and sitting at the gates of the*
       ritual bath. He explained, "When the Israelite women go and
       come up from the immersion [thus preparing for sexual relations
       after their period of menstruation], they gaze at me, so they will
       have seed which is as beautiful as I am."

  B.   *Rabbis said to him, "Does not the Master fear on account of the*
       evil eye [of envy]?"

  C.   *He said to them, "I come from the seed of Joseph, over which the*
       evil eye does not rule.

  D.   "For it is written, 'Joseph is a fruitful vine, a fruitful vine above
       the eye' (Gen. 49:22).'

  E.   "And R. Abbahu said, 'Do not read what is written, but rather,
       'superior to the evil eye.'"

  F.   *R. Yosé b. R. Hanina said, "Proof comes from here:* 'And let them
       multiply like fishes in the midst of the earth' (Gen. 48:16). Just as
       the fish of the sea are covered by water so that the evil eye cannot
       get at them, so the evil eye cannot get at the seed of Joseph.'

  G   *"And if you wish, I shall say,* 'Over an eye [namely, Joseph's,]
       which did not want to feast upon what did not belong to him the
       evil eye has no power."

MOURNER FORBIDDEN TO WORK

BAVLI MOED 204QATAN 3:5-6/19B

21. A.   *Our rabbis have taught on Tannaite authority:*

  B.   These are the things that are forbidden to a mourner: he is forbidden
       to perform work, bathe, anoint himself, have sexual relations, wear
       sandals; he is forbidden to recite Scripture, Prophets, or Writings;
       to repeat the Mishnah, Midrash, laws, Talmud or lore. If the
       community needs him, however, he does not have to abstain [but
       may repeat the required formulas].

  C.   And there was the case in which the son of R. Yosé died in
       Sepphoris, and he entered the house of study and gave an exposition
       throughout the entire day.

D.   *A bereavement happened to Rabbah bar bar Hannah. He thought of not going out to the public gathering. Said to him R. Hanina, "* If the community needs him, however, he does not have to abstain."

E.   *He considered appointing someone to repeat in a loud voice what he was saying. Said to him Rab, "It has been taught on Tannaite authority:* but that is on condition that he not appoint someone to repeat in a loud voice what he was saying."

F.   So what is one to do?

G.   *He should act along the lines of the following, which has been taught on Tannaite authority:* There was the case in which the son of R. Judah bar Ilai died, and he went into the house of study, and R. Hananiah b. Aqabayya went in and sat beside him, and he spoke in whispers to R. Hananiah b. Aqabayya, and R. Hananiah b. Aqabayya to the one appointed to repeat in a loud voice what he was saying, who repeated to the public in a loud voice what he was saying.

22. A.   *Our rabbis have taught on Tannaite authority:*

B.   "A mourner is forbidden to put on his prayer boxes containing verses of Scripture for the first three days of his bereavement. From the third and onward, and the third is included, it is permitted for him to put them on. And if new people came to pay their respects, he does not remove them," the words of R. Eliezer.

C.   R. Joshua says, "A mourner is forbidden to put on his prayer boxes containing verses of Scripture for the first two days of his bereavement. From the second and onward, and the second is included, it is permitted for him to put them on. And if new people came to pay their respects, he does remove them."

D.   *Said R. Mattenah, "What is the scriptural basis for the position of R. Eliezer? It is written,* 'And the days of weeping in the mourning for Moses were ended' (Dt. 34:8) [There are three key words, days, weeping, mourning, hence three days]."

E.   *Said R. Ina, "What is the scriptural basis for the position of R. Joshua? It is written,* 'And I will turn your feasts into mourning...and I will make it as the mourning for an only son and the end therefore as a bitter day' (Amos 8:10) [so the essential period of mourning is one bitter day]."

F.   *And does not R. Joshua have to take account of the verse,* "And the days of weeping in the mourning for Moses were ended" (Dt. 34:8)?

G.   *He will say to you, "Moses was exceptional, because the mourning for him was enormous."*

H.   *And does not R. Eliezer have to take account of the verse,* 'And I will turn your feasts into mourning...and I will make it as the mourning for an only son and the end therefore as a bitter day' (Amos 8:10)?

I.   *The principal moment is bitterness is one day.*

J.   Said Ulla, "The decided law accords with the view of R. Eliezer as to removing the prayer boxes containing phylacteries, and the decided law accords with the view of R. Joshua as to putting them on."

K.   *The question was raised:* "As to the second day, from the perspective of Ulla, would he have to take them off, or not have to take them off, when new people come in?"

L.   *Come and take note:* said Ulla, "He removes them and puts them back on, even a hundred times."

M.   *So too it has been taught on Tannaite authority:*

N.   Judah b. Tema says, "He removes and puts on his prayer boxes containing verses of Scripture, even a hundred times."

O.   Raba said, "Once he has put them on, he does not again take them off.:"

P.   *Yeah, but Raba is the one who said, "The decided law accords with our Tannaite authority, who said, 'The minimum period for observing mourning is three days"!*

Q.   **[21B]** *The case of a religious duty is exceptional.*

23. A.   *Our rabbis have taught on Tannaite authority:*

B.   During the first three days of bereavement, a mourner is forbidden to do work, even a poor person who is supported from public funds. Afterward he may work discreetly, at home, and a woman may work her spindle at home.

24. A.   *Our rabbis have taught on Tannaite authority:*

B.   During the first three days of bereavement, a mourner does not go to a house of mourning. Thereafter, he may go, but he may not take a seat among the comforters, but only among the mourners.

25. A.   *Our rabbis have taught on Tannaite authority:*

B.   During the first three days of bereavement, a mourner is forbidden to give a greeting. From the third to the seventh day he may reply, but may not ask after another. From that point he both asks and responds in his normal way.

26. A.   [Supply: *Reverting to the body of the foregoing:*] During the first three days of bereavement, a mourner is forbidden to give a greeting:

B.   *But has it not been taught on Tannaite authority:*

C.   There was the case when the sons of R. Aqiba died. All the Israelites came in and made a great lamentation for them. When they were to leave, [Aqiba chose to greet the mourners, doing so in the following manner:] R. Aqiba stood on a big bench and spoke to them as follows: "Our brothers, house of Israel, listen! Even though these two sons of mine were yet bridegrooms [and in the fullness of life], I am comforted because of the honor that you have paid. But if it was on account of Aqiba that you came, well, then, how many Aqibas are there out in the market! But this is what you have said [by coming here to comfort me]: 'The Torah of God is in his heart, his footsteps will not falter' (Ps. 37:31). All the more so should your reward be doubled [and this is your greeting:] 'Go

home to peace.'" [This he said even on the first days of the
bereavement.]

D.   *Paying respect to the public represents an exceptional case.*

27. A.   [Supply: *Reverting to the body of the foregoing:*] From the third
to the seventh day he may reply, but may not ask after another.
From that point he both asks and responds in his normal way:

B.   *They contrasted the foregoing with the following:* He who comes
across a fellow mourner within thirty days of his bereavement offers
him words of consolation but does not give him a greeting; after
that span of time, he gives him a greeting, but does not offer him
words of consolation. If his wife died and he married another, he
is not allowed to call upon him at home to offer him words of
consolation, but if he meets him in the street, there he offers words
of consolation, but in a low voice and downcast demeanor. [So
within thirty days one may not greet a mourner, on contrast to the
claim that the mourner may exchange greetings after the seven
days have passed.]

C.   Said R Idi bar Abin, "The mourner asks about others [during the
mourning period] because others are in good shape, but others do
not ask about him, because he is not in good shape."

D.   *But since it states,* From the third to the seventh day he may reply...,
does it not follow that people may greet him?

E.   *That would be a case where they are not aware of his situation.*

F.   *Well, if that is so, then in the earlier period too the same rule
applies.*

G.   *In the earlier period, he would have to tell them about his situation
and not answer further, while here, he does not have to tell them
about it at all.*

H.   *In contrast to the passage already cited* [at B] *the following was
introduced:* He who comes across a fellow mourner within twelve
months of his bereavement offers him words of consolation but
does not give him a greeting; after that span of time, he gives him
a greeting, but does not offer him words of consolation. But he
may refer to the matter tangentially.

I.   Said R. Meir, "He who comes across a fellow mourner within
twelve months of his bereavement and who then offers words of
consolation — to what is he to be compared? To a man who had a
broken leg, which got better, and a physician met him and said to
him, 'So come to me and let me break it and set it again, to prove
to you what a first-rate doctor I am!'"

J.   *There is no contradiction, since the latter speaks of the death of a
father or mother, and the former, the death of other near of kin.*

K.   *Well in that case [to which the former speaks], why not offer
consolation in an indirect manner?*

L.   *Well, he can do just that, and the sense is this:* After thirty days he
may not offer words of consolation, meaning, not in the usual way,
but he may refer to the loss in an indirect way.

28. A.   *Our rabbis have taught on Tannaite authority:*

B.   A mourner who reaches home during the first three days of bereavement, if he comes from nearby, counts along with those who are already in place. If he came from some distant place, he counts the days on his own. From that time onward, even if he came from some nearby place, he counts on his own.

C.   R. Simeon says, "Even if he came on the seventh day, if it is from a nearby place, he counts along with those who are there in place."

29. A.   The master has said: "A mourner who reaches home during the first three days of bereavement, if he comes from nearby, counts along with those who are already in place."

B.   Said R. Hiyya bar Abba said R. Yohanan, "But that is the case only if the principal of the household there at home."

C.   *The question was raised:* **[22A]** "If the principal of the household went to the place of burial, what is the law?"

D.   *Come and take note of the following, for* said R. Hiyya bar Abba said R. Yohanan, "Even if the principal of the household went to the place of burial, he counts with them."

E.   "…he counts with them"? *But has it not been taught on Tannaite authority, He counts on his own?*

F.   *There is no contradiction. The one speaks of a case in which he came home within three days, the latter in which he did not come home within three days. That is in line with what Rab instructed the sons of Hazzalponi, "Those who come home within three days count with you, and those who do not come home within three days count on their own."*

G.   *Said Raba to the people of Mahoza, "You do not follow the bier to interment begin counting the days of mourning as soon as you turn back toward the city gates."*

30. A.   R. Simeon says, "Even if he came on the seventh day, if it is from a nearby place, he counts along with those who are there in place:"

B.   Said R. Hiyya bar Gameda said R. Yosé b. Saul said Rabbi, "But that is the case only if he came home and found comforters still present."

C.   *R. Anan raised this question:* "If the comforters were just stirring to get up and leave, but had not yet left, what is the law?"

D.   *That question stands.*

31. A.   *The colleague of R. Abba bar Hiyya learned as a tradition from R. Abba, and who was it? It was R. Zira, and some say it was learned by the colleague of R. Zira from R. Zira, and who was it? It was R. Abba b. R. Hiyya bar Abba,* said R. Yohanan, "The decided law accords with the position of R. Simeon b. Gamaliel when it comes to the law of whether or not a beast is defective and so unfit for Israelites to it, and the decided law accords with R. Simeon on the matter of mourning."

B.   *As to the matter of mourning, it is the one we have just cited.*

C. *As to the decided law that accords with the position of R. Simeon b. Gamaliel when it comes to the law of whether or not a beast is defective and so unfit for Israelites to it, it is in line with what it has been taught on Tannaite authority:* "If the intestines had a hole but mucilage blocks the hole, the beast is valid for Israelite conception," the words of Rabban Simeon b. Gamaliel.

D. *What is mucilage? Said R. Kahana, "It is viscous material in the intestines that comes away under pressure."*

E. *Someone said, "May I have the privilege of going up and learning the statement from the mouth of the master himself."*

F. *When he went up, he čame upon R. Abba b. R. Hiyya bar Abba, and he said to him, "Did you, sir, say that the law accords with the opinion of R. Simeon b. Gamaliel on matters having to do with defects that lead to the rejection of the beast for Israelite consumption?"*

G. *He said to him, "I said that that is not the decided law."*

H. *"And what about the matter of mourning, is the law to follow R. Simeon?"*

I. *He said, "There are diverse opinions on that matter, as has been stated: 'R. Hisda said, "The view of R. Simeon is the decided law," and R. Yohanan said the same, but R. Nahman said, "It is not the decided law."'*

J. And the law at hand is not decided in accord with R. Simeon b. Gamaliel's view as to questions involving defects in animals.

K. And as to the matter of mourning, the decided law does accord with R. Simeon, in line with what Samuel said, "In matters of mourning, the decided law follows the position of the more lenient authority."

32. A. [Supply:] *Our rabbis have taught on Tannaite authority:*

B. For all other deceased, one who hastens the bier to its grave — lo, such a one is praiseworthy, but as to doing so in the case of his father and his mother, lo, such a one is disgusting.

C. If it was the eve of the Sabbath or the eve of the festival, lo, this one too is praiseworthy, for he does what he does only on account of the honor owing to his father or to his mother.

D. As to the case of all other deceased, if he wants, he may keep the expenses down, and if he wants, he does not **[22B]** keep the expenses down, but in the case of his father and his mother, as a matter of fact, he should keep the expenses down.

E. As to the case of all other deceased, if he wants, he may bare his shoulder, and if he wants, he does not bare his shoulder,, but in the case of his father and his mother, as a matter of fact, he should bare his shoulder.

F. There was the case of a certain "great man of the age," whose father died, and who wanted to bare his shoulder, and another "great man of the age" who was with him also wanted to bare his shoulder, but on that account the former did not do so and did not bare his shoulder."

G.   Said Abbayye, "The great man of the age is Rabbi, the great man of the age who was with him was R. Jacob bar Aha."

H.   *There are those who say, "The great man of the age was R. Jacob bar Aha, the great man of the age who was with him was Rabbi."*

I.   *Now from the perspective of him who said, "the great man of the age who was with him was R. Jacob bar Aha," that explains why he refrained from baring the shoulder. But from the perspective of him who has said that it was R. Jacob bar Aha, why in the world would he have refrained from baring his shoulder? For, after all, Rabban Simeon b. Gamaliel [Rabbi's father] was the patriarch, and everybody is obligated to bear his shoulder on that account?*

J.   *So that's a problem.*

33. A.   For all other deceased, one may get a haircut after thirty days, but for one's father and one's mother, one does so only after his colleagues pressure him to do so.

B.,   For all other deceased, one may go to a banquet house after thirty days. But for one's father and one's mother, one observes an entire year of mourning.

C.   Said Rabbah bar bar Hanna, "And one may go to a celebration of collegiality."

D.   *An objection was raised:* One may go to a celebration of collegiality after thirty days.

E.   *So that's a problem.*

F.   *Amemar repeated the matter in this way: "* Said Rabbah bar bar Hanna, 'And to a celebration of collegiality one is permitted to go forthwith.' *But lo, it has been taught on Tannaite authority:* One may go to a celebration of collegiality after thirty days? *That's not a problem. The latter speaks to a party that can be postponed, the other, a party that is obligatory and cannot be postponed."*

34. A.   For all other deceased, one tears a handbreadth of one's garment, but for one's father or mother, he bares his chest.

B.   *Said R. Abbahu, "What verse of Scripture serves?* 'Then David grabbed his clothes and tore them' (2 Sam. 1:11), *and grabbing involves no less than a handbreadth."*

35. A.   For all other deceased, even if one is wearing ten garments, one tears only the uppermost one. But for one's father or one's mother, one makes a tear in all of them. And, whether man or woman, tearing one's undershirt is not an indispensable part of properly carrying out the act.

B.   R. Simeon b. Eleazar says, "A woman tears the undergarment and turns it front to back and then tears her outer garment."

36. A.   For all other deceased, if one wanted, he may divide the upper [Lazarus:] selvage-border of his garment, and if does not want, he does not divide it. But for his father or his mother, he must divide it.

B. R. Judah says, "Any act of tearing that does not involve the dividing of the upper selvage-border of the garment is only a random-tear [and bears no consequence for the rite of mourning]."

C. *Said R. Abbahu, "What verse of Scripture serves R. Judah's view?* 'And Elisha saw it and he cried, My father, my father, the chariots of Israel and the horsemen thereof! And he saw him no more, and he took hold of his clothing and tore it into two pieces' (2 Kgs. 2:12). Now since Scripture states, 'and he tore...,' do I not know that it is into two pieces? But the addition of that qualifying language bears the meaning that, at the tear, the garments appeared to be torn into two separate pieces."

37. A. For all other deceased, one may after seven days one bastes the tear together, and sews them together wholly after thirty days. But for one's father or one's mother, he bastes it together after thirty days and never sews it together.

B. But a woman bastes it together on the spot out of the honor owing to her.

38. A. *When Rabin came,* he said R. Yohanan [said], "For all other deceased, if one wanted, he makes the tear by hand, and if he wants, he makes it by a sharp object. But for his father or his mother, he must make it by hand."

B. And said R. Hiyya bar Abba said R. Yohanan, "For all other deceased, one tears in seclusion, but for the father or the mother, one tears outside."

C. Said R. Hisda, "And the same is so at the death of the patriarch."

D. *An objection was raised:* "'[The master, patriarch or principal of the court] are comparable to not his father or his mother but only to his brothers alone.' *Does this not pertain even to the patriarch?"*

E. *Not at all, the patriarch alone is exceptional.*

39. A. *The patriarch died. Said R. Hisda to R. Hanan bar Raba, "Turn over the mortar, stand on it, and show everybody how to tear their garments [in accord with the following law:*

B. "On the occasion of the death of a sage, one bares the right, for the principal of a court, on the left, and for the patriarch, on both sides."

40. A. *Our rabbis have taught on Tannaite authority:*

B. When a sage dies, the house of study that he conducted is dissolved.

C. When the principal of a court died, all houses of study in his town are dissolved, and they go into the synagogue and change their usual assigned places. The ones who ordinarily sit at the north take their seats at the south, and those who ordinarily sit at the south take places at the north.

D. When the patriarch dies, all of the houses of study are dissolved. Those who belong to the synagogue enter the synagogue [23A] and tear their garments, and seven persons recite the Torah-portion of the week, and then they go forth.

E.   R. Joshua b. Qorhah says, "It is not that they go out and just wander about the market place, but they sit in silence and say neither a tradition nor a tale in the house of mourning."

F.   They said about R. Hananiah b. Gamaliel that in the house of a mourner he would say a tradition or a tale.

41. A.   *Our rabbis have taught on Tannaite authority:*

B.   On the first Sabbath after bereavement a mourner does not go out of the door of his house. On the second he goes out, but he does not sit in his usual place. On the third he sits in his usual place but does not speak. On the fourth, lo, he is like anybody else.

C.   R. Judah says, "There was no requirement to state, 'On the first Sabbath after bereavement a mourner does not go out of the door of his house,' for lo, everybody comes into his house to bring him comfort. But it is on the second that a mourner does not go out of the door of his house; on the third he goes out, but he does not sit in his usual place. On the fourth he sits in his usual place but does not speak. On the fifth, lo, he is like anybody else."

42. A.   *Our rabbis have taught on Tannaite authority:*

B.   For the entire thirty days [the mourner may not] take a wife. If his wife died, he is forbidden to marry another until three festivals [a full year] have gone by.

C.   R. Judah says, "He is forbidden until the first and second festivals [in sequence after her death] have gone by, but prior to the third, he is permitted to remarry."

D.   But if he has no children, he is permitted to marry immediately, because of the consideration of the requirement of procreation.

E.   If she left him small children, he is permitted to remarry on the spot, on account of taking care of them.

F.   There was the case, in which the wife of Joseph the Priest died, and he said to her sister while standing in the graveyard, "Come and take care of your sister's children." But even so, he did not have sexual relations until considerable time had gone by.

G.   *What is the definition of " until considerable time had gone by"?*

H.   Said R. Pappa, "After thirty days."

43. A.   *Our rabbis have taught on Tannaite authority:*

B.   The entire thirty days are marked by the prohibition of putting on ironed clothing, without distinction as to whether they are old or new clothes coming out of the press.

C.   Rabbi says, "They have prohibited only the wearing of new garments alone."

D.   R. Eleazar b. R. Simeon says, "They prohibited only new clothes of white linen."

44. A.   *Abbayye went out in a worn garment, following the ruling of Rabbi.*

B.   *Raba went out in a new roman red cloak, following the opinion of R. Eleazar b. R. Simeon.*

MOURNING FOR NEXT OF KIN

BAVLI MOED QATAN 3:5-6/19B

17. A. *Our rabbis have taught on Tannaite authority:*

B. For all of the nearest of kin that are listed in the passage pertaining to the priests [Lev. 21:1ff.] on account of burying whom the priest contracts corpse uncleanness, a mourner must observe mourning: wife, father or mother, brother or sister, son or daughter. To the list they added: his brother or sister from the same mother; his married sister, whether from the same mother or from the same father.

C. "And just as he observes mourning for these, so he observes mourning rites for their relatives in the second remove [grandfather, grandmother, grandchildren, brothers and sisters of parents]," the words of R. Aqiba.

D. R. Simeon b. Eleazar says, "Mourning is observed only for one's son's child and father's father."

E. Sages say, "For whomever one mourns, with that one one also joins in mourning." [Lazarus: one mourns with his father on the death of his father's father, the father mourns with the son who loses a child.]

F. *Then is not the sages' opinion pretty much the same as R. Simeon b. Eleazar's?*

G. *No, there is a concrete difference between them, which is, whether we impose the obligation of mourning only when he is living in the same house. That is in line with what Rab said to his son, Hiyya, and as R. Huna said to his son, Rabbah, "When you are in her presence, you have to observe the rites of mourning, but when not, you do not."*

18. A. *Mar Uqba's father-in-law's son died. He considered sitting in mourning for him for seven days and through the thirty. When R. Huna went to see him, he found him in mourning. He said to him, "Do you really want to eat a mourner's meal? When sages made their ruling concerning mourning out of deference to his wife, it was only in the case of his father-in-law or mother-in-law, as it has been taught on Tannaite authority:* he who has suffered a bereavement by reason of the death of his father-in-law or mother-in-law, the husband may not compel the wife, who is in mourning, to put on eye shadow or do her hear, and he should overturn his own bed and observe the rites of mourning with her, and when her father-in-law or mother-in-law dies, she should not put on eye shadow or do her hair, and she overturns her couch and observes mourning with him.' *There is a further Tannaite formulation:* 'Even though they said that he may not force his wife to put on eye shadow or do her hair, they further said she mixes his wine for him, makes his bed, washes his face, hands, and feet.' *Obviously there is a contradiction between these two statements. So we must infer that*

       one of them refers to the death of a father-in-law or mother-in-law, and the other to the death of any other near of kin."

B.   *That is decisive.*

C.   *So too it has been explicitly stated on Tannaite authority:*

D.   They spoke concerning the honor owing to his wife is concerned, only when the bereavement came about through the death of his father-in-law or mother-in-law alone.

19. A.   *The son of the son of Amemar died, and he tore his clothing. His son came, and he again tore his clothing in the presence of the son. He remembered that he did it while seated, so he stood up and tore it again while standing.*

B.   *Said R. Ashi to Amemar, "How on the basis of Scripture do we know that the tearing of the clothes should be done while standing? It is in line with this verse: 'Then Job rose and tore his cloak' (Job 1:20)."*

C.   [21A] *Then what about the following:* "And if he stand and say I do not want to take her" (Dt. 25:8), *will that be interpreted in the same way [so that if the levir wishes to decline to enter into levirate marriage, it must be done when he is standing]? But lo, it has been taught on Tannaite authority:* it may be done whether he is sitting or standing or lying?

D.   *He said to him, "There it is not written, 'Then he stood and said,' while in our case, it is written, 'Then Job rose and tore his cloak' (Job 1:20)."*

20. A.   Said R. Ammi bar Hama, "How on the basis of Scripture do we know that the tearing of the clothes should be done while standing? It is in line with this verse: 'Then Job rose and tore his cloak' (Job 1:20)."

B.   *But maybe he stood up for some other reason? For if you do not take that view,* "and he shaved his head" (Job 1:20) *would mean that that too has to be done standing!*

C.   *Rather the proof is from the following:* "Then the king stood up and tore his clothing" (2 Sam. 13:31).

D.   *But maybe he stood up for some other reason? For if you do not take that view,* "and he lay on the ground" (2 Sam. 13:31) *would mean that that too has to be done!*

E.   *But has it not been taught on Tannaite authority:* If a mourner sat on a bed, chair, or stall for urns, or even sleeps on the bare ground, he has not carried out his duty," and said R. Yohanan, "He has not in doing these actions carried out the obligation of turning the bed over"?

F.   He said to him, "It is as though he were on the ground."

MOURNING FOR SAGES

BAVLI MOED QATAN 3: /25B-26A

3. A. *When R. Huna's soul came to rest, they considered putting a scroll of the Torah on his bier. Said to them R. Hisda, "Something that in his lifetime he never considered proper are we now going to go and do to him? For said R. Tahalipa, 'I saw R. Huna, when he wanted to sit down on his couch, he saw a scroll of the Torah lying there, so he put an inverted jar on the ground and put the scroll of the Torah into it. So he took for granted that* it is forbidden to sit on a sofa on which a scroll of the Torah was lying.'"

   B. *His bier would not go through the doorway. They considered letting it down from the roof. Said R. Hisda, "I learned the following tradition from him himself: As to a deceased sage, the correct manner of paying respect to him is to take out his bier through the door."*

   C. *They then considered moving him into another [narrower] bier for the same purpose. Said R. Hisda, "I learned the following tradition from him himself: As to a deceased sage, the correct manner of paying respect to him is to make use of the initial bier into which his corpse has been placed.* For said R. Judah said Rab, 'How do we know on the basis of Scripture that as to a deceased sage, the correct manner of paying respect to him is to make use of the initial bier into which his corpse has been placed? As it is said, 'And they set the ark of God on a new cart and brought it out of the house of Abinadab that was on the hill' (2 Sam. 6:3)."

   D. *So they cut a hole in the door and brought out the bier that way.*

4. A. In connection with his eulogy, R. Abba commenced with these words: "Our master was worthy of having the Presence of God rest upon him, *but the fact that he lived in Babylonia explains why that did not happen."*

   B. Objected R. Nahman bar Hisda, and some say, R. Hanan bar Hisda, "'And the word of the Lord came expressly to Ezekiel the priest, son of Buzi, in the land of the Chaldeans, by the river Chebar' (Ez. 1:3)."

   C. *His father knocked him with his shoe, saying, "Didn't I tell you not to bother people? What is meant by,* 'came expressly'? It means that this had happened prior to his arrival in Babylonia."

5. A. *When the brought him up [to the Land of Israel for burial] they told R. Ammi and R. Assi that R. Huna had come. They said, "When we were over there, we could not lift up our heads against him. Now we have come here, so he has followed us."*

   B. They told them, "So it's his bier."

   C. *R. Ammi and R. Assi went out to receive him. R. Ila and R. Hanina did not go out. Some say, R. Ila went out, R. Hanina did not go out.*

D.   *What was the thinking of him who went out? It is in line with that which has been taught on Tannaite authority:* In the case of a bier that is passing from place to place, the bystanders form a row in respect to the deceased and recite in that regard the blessing of the mourners and the consolation mourners.

E.   *What was the thinking of him who did not go out? It is in line with that which has been taught on Tannaite authority:* In the case of a bier that is passing from place to place, the bystanders do not form a row in respect to the deceased and do not recite in that regard the blessing of the mourners and the consolation mourners.

F.   *So the two statements contradict one another!*

G.   There really is no contradiction, in the one case, the backbone of the corpse is still intact, in the other, it is not still in tact.

H.   *But while R. Huna's backbone was still intact, the one who did not come out did not actually know that fact.*

I.   *They said, "So where shall we lay R. Huna to rest? [Alongside R. Hiyya,] for* R. Huna brought Torah-teachings throughout Israel, and R. Hiyya did the same.

J.   *"Then who will bring his corpse into the burial niche?"*

K.   *Said to them R. Hana, "I will bring him in, for I conducted my studies before him when I was eighteen years old, and I never had a seminal emission, and I served as his attendant so know his deeds. For one day the leather thong of his prayer boxes containing verses of Scripture got twisted around, and he fasted on that account for forty days."*

L.   *He brought him in. Judah was laid out at the right of his father [Hiyya], on the left his twin brother, Hezekiah. Said Judah's corpse to Hezekiah's, "Get up, since it is not proper for R. Huna to be left standing."*

M.   *As he arose, a column of fire rose with him. R. Hagga saw and was overwhelmed with fright, so he set up the coffin and ran out. But the reason that he was unharmed was that he set up the bier of R. Huna in particular.*

6. A.   *When R. Hisda's soul came to rest, they considered putting a scroll of the Torah on his bier. Said to them R. Isaac, "Should we go and do something for him that he himself did not consider doing for his master?"*

B.   *They considered not sewing up the tear in their garments. Said to them R. Isaac bar Ammi, "As to the case of a sage, when they have turned their faces away from him at the rear of the bier, they may sew up the tear."*

7. A.   *When Rabbah b. R. Huna's soul came to rest as well as R. Hamnuna's, they took both corpses up there [to the land of Israel].* [25B] *When they got to a bridge, the camels stopped. Said to them a Tai-Arab, "What's going on?"*

B. *They said to him, "Well, our rabbis pay a good bit of respect to one another. So one has said, 'Let the master go first,' and the other said, 'Let the master go first.'"*

C. *He said, "It is reasonable that Rabbah b. R. Huna should go first."*

D. *So the camel that bore the corpse of Rabbah b. R. Huna went along first. The molars and teeth of the Tai-Arab fell out.*

8. A. *A certain youngster commenced the eulogy in this way:*

[Lazarus:] A scion of ancient stock from Babylon came
With records of prowess in combat and fame;
Twice numerous pelican and bittern from far
Came from the ravage and ruin in Shinear.
When God views his world with displeasure,
He seizes great souls in exacting measure,
Awaiting their coming as new brides with delight
And riding on Arabot in empyrean height,
He welcomes the souls of the pure and the right.

9. A. *When Rabina's soul came to rest, a certain professional eulogizer commenced in this way:*

[Lazarus:] You Palms, sway your heads and deplore
A saint, a noble palm, that is no more
Who days and nights in meditation spent;
For him, day and night, let us lament.

10. A. *Said R. Ashi to Bar Qipoq, "On that day what will you say?"*

B. *He said to him, "This is what I shall say:*

[Lazarus:] "If a flame among the cedars fall
"What will save the lichen on the wall?
"If Leviathan by hook be hauled to land,
"What hope have fishes of a shallow strand?
"If fish in rushing stream by hook be caught,
"What death may in marshy ponds be wrought!"

C. *Said to him Bar Abin, "God forbid that there should be talk of 'hooks;' or 'flames' in regard to the righteous!"*

D. *"So what will you say?"*

E. *"This is what I would say:*

[Lazarus:] "Weep, you more the mourners,
"Nor for what is lost; He found him rest;
"it is we who are left distressed."

F. *R. Ashi was offended by them, and their feet were turned. On that day they did not come to eulogize him, and that is in line with what R. Ashi said, "On my account [when I die], Bar Qipoq is not to remove his shoulder nor Bar Abin is not to bare his.".*

G. *Raba once came to Daglet [Takrit]. He said to Bar Abin, "Get up and say an appropriate word."*

H. *He arose and said the following:*

[Lazarus:] "When more than a third wades in water deep
"Remember the covenant and mercy keep.

"We strayed from you as a wayward wife;
"Leave us not; as at Marah, save our life."

11. A.　*R. Hanin was the son-in-law of the patriarch. He had no children.*
He prayed for mercy and he had. On the day that the child was
born, he died, and the eulogizer commenced with these words:
[Lazarus:] "Joy is turned to sorrow, and
"Gladness linked with sadness.
"When the time of joy came nigh,
"The father heaved a dying sigh;
"At the birth of his Gracious-little-son,
"The gracious-sire's life was done."

B.　*They called the son Hanan in memory of his father.*

12. A.　*When R. Pedat's soul came to rest, R. Isaac b. Eleazar commenced*
with these words: "This day is as hard for Israel as the day on
which the sun set at noon, as it is written, 'And it shall come to
pass in that day...that I will cause the sun to set at noon and darken
the earth on a clear day and turn hour feasts into mourning and
your songs into lamentation...as the mourning for an only child'
(Amos 8:9-10)."

B.　"And said R. Yohanan, 'This refers to the day on which King Josiah
died.'"

13. A.　*When R. Yohanan's soul came to rest, R. Ammi sat in mourning*
for the seven and thirty day period. Said R. Abba b. R. Hiyya bar
Abba, "What R. Ammi did, he did on his own account. For this is
what R. Hiyya bar Abba said R. Yohanan said, 'Even if it is his
master who taught him wisdom, he sits in mourning on his account
for only one day.'"

14. A.　*When R. Zira's soul came to rest, the professional eulogizer*
commenced with this language:
[Lazarus:] "The land of Shinear was his home of birth,
"The land of Glory reared her darling to fame;
"'Woe is me,' says Rakath in lament,
"'For she has lost her choicest ornament.'"

15. A.　*When R. Abbahu's soul came to rest, the pillars of Caesarea wept.*

B.　*When R. Yosé came to rest, the roof gutters at Sepphoris ran with*
blood.

C.　*When R. Jacob died, the stars came out in daylight.*

D.　*When R. Assi died, the cedars were uprooted. When R. Samuel bar*
Isaac died, every tree was uprooted.

E.　*When R. Hiyya died, fiery stones came down from the sky.*

F.　*When R. Menahem b. Simai died, all the images were blotted out*
and were used as rollers.

G.　*When R. Tanhum b. R. Hiyya died, all the statues of people were*
ripped out of position.

H.　*When R. Isaac b. R. Eliashib died, seventy houses were broken*
into by thieves in Tiberias.

I.　*When R. Hamnuna died, hail stones came down from heaven.*

J. *When Rabbah and R. Joseph died, the rocks of the Euphrates kissed each other [in an earthquake].*

K. *When Abbayye and Raba died, the rocks of the Tigris kissed each other.*

L. *When R. Mesharshayya died, palms grew thorns.*

The composite of rather nicely crafted compositions on the topic of eulogies for sages has drawn to a close, and we take up the theme of the Mishnah once more, now as it is worked out in other Tannaite formulations.

16. A. *Our rabbis have taught on Tannaite authority:*

B. [26A] These tears on the garments are not to be sewn up again: he who makes a tear for his father or his mother, his master who taught him wisdom, a patriarch, a principal of the court, for having bad news, for having heard blasphemy, when a scroll of the Torah has been burned, for seeing the ruined cities of Judea, the holy house, or Jerusalem. One makes a tear first for the Temple and then enlarges it for Jerusalem.

The Tannaite statement is now given its own talmud, in the form of amplification and proof-texts.

17. A. "he who makes a tear for his father or his mother, his master who taught him wisdom:" how on the basis of Scripture do we know this fact?

B. As it is written, "And Elisha saw it and cried, My father, my father, the chariots of Israel and the horsemen thereof" (2 Kings 2:12) —

C. "My father, my father:" this means to tear one's garment on the death of a father or mother.

D. "the chariots of Israel and the horsemen thereof:" this means that one tears one's garment on the death of his master who taught him wisdom

E. *And what is the sense?*

F. *It is in line with the Aramaic version given by R. Joseph, "My master, my master, who protected Israel with his prayer better than chariots and horsemen could."*

18. A. And how on the basis of Scripture do we know that these tears are not to be sewn up again?

B. "And he took hold of his own clothes and tore them into two pieces" (2 Kgs. 2:12) — having said "and tore them," do I not know that it was "into two pieces"? But it teaches that they remain torn into two parts for all time."

C. Said R. Simeon b. Laqish to R. Yohanan, "Elijah yet lives [so how can a rite performed at his disappearance prove exemplary]?"

D. *He said to him, "Since it is written, 'and he saw him no more,' he was as dead to Elisha."*

19. A. "A patriarch, a principal of the court, for having bad news:" how on the basis of Scripture do we know this fact?

B. As it is written, "Then David took hold of his clothes and tore them, and so all the men who were with him, and they wailed and wept and fasted until evening, for Saul and for Jonathan his son and for the people of the Lord and for the house of Israel, because they had fallen by the sword" (2 Sam. 1:11-12).

B. "Saul" — this refers to the patriarch.

C. "and for Jonathan his son" — this refers to the principal of the court.

D. "and for the people of the Lord and for the house of Israel" — this refers to the bad news.

E. *Said Rab bar Sheba to R. Kahana, "But might I not suppose that this was not done until they had heard that all those things had happened?"*

F. He said to him, "The repeated use of the word 'for' serves to itemize each entry from the others."

G. *But do we have to tear our clothes for hearing bad news? And lo, they said to Samuel, "King Shapur has killed thirteen thousand Jews in Caesarea Mazaca," and he did not tear his clothes!*

H. They said it is only when the majority of the community is involved and in accord with the exemplary case [of Saul and Jonathan].

I. *Anyhow, did King Shapur ever kill Jews? And lo, King Shapur said to Samuel, "May a terrible thing happen to me, if I have ever killed a Jew!"*

J. *In that case, they brought it on themselves, for said R. Ammi, "From the noise of harp strings in Caesarea Mazaca the wall of Laodicea burst."*

20. A. "for having heard blasphemy:" how on the basis of Scripture do we know this fact?

B. As it is written, "Then came Eliakim son of Hilkiah who was in charge of the household and Shebna the scribe and Joah son of Asaph recorder to Hezekiah, with their clothes torn, and told him the blasphemous words of Rabshakeh" (2 Kgs. 18:37).

21. A. *Our rabbis have taught on Tannaite authority:*

B. All the same are the one who actually hears [the blasphemy] and the one who hears it from the one who heard it. Both are liable to tear their garments.

C. But the witnesses are not liable to tear their garments, for they already did so at the moment when they heard the original blasphemy.

D. But if they did so at the moment when they heard the original blasphemy, *what difference does that make? Lo, they are now hearing it again!*

E. *Do not let that argument enter your mind, for it is written,* "And it came to pass, when King Hezekiah heard it, that *he* tore his clothes? (2 Kgs. 18:37).

F.   King Hezekiah tore his clothes, but they did not tear their clothes.

22. A.   "are not to be sewn up again:" how do we know this fact?

B.   It derives from the analogy to be drawn between the act of tearing done by King Hezekiah and acts of tearing done elsewhere [2 Kgs. 2:12].

23. A.   "when a scroll of the Torah has been burned:" how on the basis of Scripture do we know this fact?

B.   As it is written, "And it came to pass that when Jehudi had read three or four columns that he cut it with a pen knife and cast it into the fire that was in the brazier" (Jer. 36:23f.).

C.   *What is the point of saying* "three or four columns"?

D.   *They said to Jehoiakim that Jeremiah had written the book of Lamentations. He said to them, "What is written in it?"*

E.   "How does the city sit solitary" (Lam. 1:1).

F.   *He said to them, "I am king!"*

G.   "She sweeps sore in the night" (Lam. 1:2).

H.   *He said to them, "I am king!"*

I.   "Judah has gone into exile before of affliction" (Lam. 1:3).

J.   *He said to them, "I am king!"*

K.   "The ways of Zion mourn" (Lam. 1:4).

L.   *He said to them, "I am king!"*

M.   "Her adversaries are become the head" (Lam. 1:5).

N.   *"Who said that!"*

O.   "For the Lord has afflicted her for the multitude of her transgressions" (Lam. 1:5).

P.   Forthwith he cut out all the instances in which the name of god is written therein and he burned the rest in fire, so it is written, "Yet they were not afraid nor tore their garments, neither the king nor any of his servants who heard all these words" (Jer. 36:24), *implying that they ought to have done so.*

Q.   *Said R. Pappa to Abbayye, "But maybe they did so because of the bad news?"*

R.   *He said to him, "But had any bad news actually come to them as yet?"*

24. A.   Said R. Helbo said R. Huna, "He who sees a scroll of the Torah that is torn is obligated to make two tears, one for the harm done to the parchment, the other for the harm done to the writing:

B.   "'Then the word of the Lord came to Jeremiah after the king had burned the roll and the words that Baruch had written at the dictation of Jeremiah' (Jer. 36:27).— 'the words,' refer to the parchment, 'and the words,' to the writing on the parchment."

25. A.   *R. Abba and R. Huna bar Hiyya were in session. R. Abba got up to relieve himself He took off his prayer-box containing verses of Scripture and put it on a pillow, and a young ostrich came along and tried to swallow it. He said, "If it had happened, I would have had to make two tears."*

B. *He said to him, "How do you know that? The same thing happened
    to me, and I asked R. Mattenah and he had nothing to say, so I
    came to R. Judah, and he said to me, 'This is what Samuel said,*
    "The rabbis said that one should make a tear only when the scroll
    is destroyed by force and as in the limits of the details of the
    exemplary case."""

26. A. "for seeing the ruined cities of Judea, the holy house, or Jerusalem:"
        how on the basis of Scripture do we know this fact?

    B. As it is written, "And it came to pass the second day after he had
        slain Gedaliah and no man knew it that there came certain men
        from Shechem, from Shiloh, and from Samaria, even fourscore
        men, having their bears shaven and their clothing torn and having
        cut themselves, with meal offerings and frankincense in their hand,
        to bring them in the house of the Lord" (Jer. 41:4-5).

    C. Said R. Helbo said Ulla Biraah said R. Eleazar, "He who sees the
        ruined cities of Judah recites this verse: 'Your holy cities have
        become wilderness' (Is. 54:9), and he tears his clothing. When he
        sees Jerusalem in its ruin, he says, 'Our holy and our beautiful
        house, where our fathers praised you, is burned with fire and all
        our pleasant things are laid waste' (Is. 54:10), and he tears his
        clothing."

27. A. "One makes a tear first for the Temple and then enlarges it for
        Jerusalem:"

    B. *An objection was raised on the basis of the following:* All the
        same are hearing and seeing, once one has reached Mount Scopus,
        he tears his garment, and he tears his garment for the sanctuary on
        its own, and for Jerusalem on its own.

    C. *There is no contradiction, the one speaks of a case in which he
        hits the site of the sanctuary first, the other, when he hits Jerusalem
        first and then the sanctuary.*

MOURNING FOR THIRTY DAYS

BAVLI MOED QATAN 3:5-6/2'1A-B

I.5.A. *How on the basis of Scripture do we know that the span of thirty
        days is required for mourning?*

    B. *It derives from a verbal analogy based on the presence of the word
        "disheveled" that occurs with regard to mourning [at Lev. 10:6]
        and with regard to the Nazirite [at Num. 6:5].*

    C. Here: "Let not the hair of your heads become disheveled" (Lev.
        10:6) and there: "He shall let the locks of the hair of his head
        become disheveled" (Num. 6:5). Just as in the latter case, the
        period of observance is thirty days, so in the former it is thirty
        days.

    D. *And how do we derive that span of time in the latter case?*

    E. Said R. Mattena, "Where there is a Nazirite vow without a specified
        limit, it is for thirty days."

F. *What is the Scriptural basis?*

G. *The word "shall be holy" is used there, and the numerical value of the letters for "shall be" is thirty.*

I.13.A. *Our rabbis have taught on Tannaite authority:*

B. "If one has received news of a bereavement from nearby, the mourning lasts for seven days and then the usual thirty. If it is from a distant place, it lasts only for one day.

C. "What defines 'nearby' and what defines 'a distant place'?

D. "'Nearby' is news that comes within thirty days of the event, and 'from far' away is news that comes after thirty days of the event," the words of R. Aqiba.

E. And sages say, "All the same is what is required in both cases: if the news comes from nearby or from a distant place, the mourning is for seven days and up to the usual thirty days."

F. Said Rabbah bar bar Hannah said R. Yohanan, "In any case in which you find that the individual gives a lenient ruling and the majority gives a strict ruling, the decided law accords with the majority, except for this case, in which, even though R. Aqiba is an individual who gives a lenient ruling, and sages are the ones who give the strict ruling, the decided law accords with R. Aqiba, for, said Samuel, 'In matters of bereavement, the law is in accord with the opinion of the one who gives the lenient ruling.'"

14. A. *R. Hanina got from Khuzistan news about his father's death, so he consulted R. Hisda, who said to him, "If it is from a distant place, it lasts only for one day."*

B. *R. Nathan bar Ammi got from Khuzistan news of the death of his mother, so he consulted Raba, who said to him, "Lo, they have said, 'If it is from a distant place, it lasts only for one day.'"*

C. *An objection was raised:* Under what conditions does this rule apply? In the case of the five close relatives [for whom mourning is required [brother, sister, wife, son, daughter], but as to one's mother or father, the mourning covers the seven and the thirty days."

D. *He said to him, "That is the ruling of a minority, and we do not concur, on account of a case."*

E. *For it has been taught on Tannaite authority:* There was the case in which the father of R. Sadoq died in Ginzaq, and they told him only after three years had passed, and he came and inquired from Elisha b. Abbuyah and elders with him, who said, "Observe the seven and thirty days."

F. And when the died of R. Ahayyah died in the Exile, he sat in mourning for him for the seven and thirty day spell.

G. *Is that so? But lo, Rab son of the brother of R. Hiyya, the son of the sister of R. Hiyya, when he went up there, said to him, "How's Dad?"* **[20B]** *and he said to him, "Mother's fine." 'How's* *mother?" "Father's fine."* So R. Hiyya said to his attendant, "Remove my shoes and carry my things after me to the baths." *And from that story we inferred three rules.*

H. *We inferred that a mourner is forbidden to wear shoes.*

I. *We learned that news that come only from a distance require only a single day of mourning.*

J. *And we learned that part of the day counts as a whole day of mourning.*

K. *So R. Hiyya represents a private party, and R. Ahayyah represents another private party [and there is no majority opinion in hand].*

15. A. Said R. Yosé bar Abin, "If one got news from near at hand on a festival, but by the time of the end of the festival, it turns out to be classified as news from far off, the festival counts in the mourning period, so he observes only one day of formal mourning."

B. *R. Adda of Caesarea repeated before R. Yohanan as a Tannaite statement,* "If on the Sabbath day one hears news, that qualifies as news from near at hand, but by the end of the Sabbath it turns out to be classified as news from far off, he observes only one day of formal mourning."

16. A. Does he tear his clothing or does he not tear his clothing?

B. R. Mani said, "He does not tear his clothing."

C. R. Hanina said, "He does tear his clothing."

D. *Said R. Mani to R. Hanina, "Now in accord with my position, which is that he does not tear his clothing, that explains also why there is no seven day period of mourning, but within your view, that he does tear his garment, tell me, can there be a case in which one tears one's clothing but does not observe the seven days of mourning?"*

E. *Well is there no such case at all? But did not Idi father of R. Zira, or some say, brother of R. Zira, recite as a Tannaite rule in the presence of R. Zira,* "He who has only a single garment to tear at the time, but who got one during the seven days of mourning should tear it at that time. If he got it only after the seven does, he does not tear it"?

F. *R. Zira replied in response to this, "Under what circumstances? If this was in respect to the five nearest of kin, for whom there is a religious duty to mourn, but in regard to one's father or mother, one always tears one's garment, and what you cited speaks of the honor that is owing to one's father or mother [even though one does not observe the seven days, in respect to the parents, he tears his clothing, but this really is not an obligation]."*

MOURNING RITES: SOURCES IN SCRIPTURE

BAVLI MOED QATAN 3:1 14B I:4, 8FF.

I:4. A. A mourner does not observe the rules of mourning on the festival, as it is said, "And you shall rejoice in your feast" (Dt. 16:14).

B. *If the period of bereavement commenced prior to the festival, then the affirmative action that pertains to the community at large comes along and overrides the affirmation action required of an individual. And if it is a bereavement that has begun now, on the festival, the affirmative action required of an individual does not come along and override the affirmative action that pertains to the community at large.*

8. A. A mourner has to cover his head, *since the All-Merciful said to Ezekiel,* "And do not cover your upper lip," *it follows that everybody else [but Ezekiel] is required to do so [as a mark of mourning].*

B. *What is the rule concerning those who have been excommunicated or those who are unclean by reason of the skin ailment in respect to their having to cover the head?*

C. Said R. Joseph, *"Come and take note:* And they cover themselves and sit like those who are excommunicated or like mourners, until from Heaven they are shown mercy."

D. *Said to him Abbayye, "But perhaps the case of one who is excommunicated on account of Heaven is exceptional, because such a one is subject to a more stringent rule?"*

E. What is the rule as to a person afflicted by the skin ailment's having to cover his head?

F. *Come and take note:* "And he shall cover his upper lip" (Lev. 13:45) — from which it follows that he is obligated also to cover his head.

G. *That is decisive.*

9. A. A mourner is forbidden to put on *Tefillin* [prayer boxes containing verses of Scripture], *since the All-Merciful said to Ezekiel,* "And bind your head tire upon you" (Ez. 24:17), *it follows that everybody else is required to do so.*

B. What is the rule concerning those who are excommunicated, in respect to putting on prayer boxes containing verses of Scripture?

C. *That question stands.*

D. What is the rule concerning those who are afflicted with the skin ailment in respect to putting on prayer boxes containing verses of Scripture?

E. "[And] the leper" (Lev. 13:45) — even though he is a high priest.

F. Since it is said, "His [the high priest's] head he will not dishevel, and his clothing he will not tear" (Lev. 21:10), might one say, Even if he is smitten with plague [he should not do so]? How then shall I carry out, "His clothing will be torn and his head will be disheveled" (Lev. 13:45)?

G. Does this apply to any person outside of the high priest?

H. Scripture says, "Who has the disease" (Lev. 13:45) — even though he is a high priest.

I. "His clothing will be torn" (Lev. 13:45) — they will be cut up.

J. "'And his hair will be disheveled' (Lev. 13:45) — the only meaning of 'disheveled' is, to be made loose," the words of R. Eliezer.

K. R. Aqiba says, "'Being' is stated with reference to his head, and 'being' is mentioned with reference to the clothing. Just as 'being' stated with reference to clothing refers to things which are outside of his body, so 'being' which is referred to in respect to the head means things which are outside his body" [CXLIII:I.3-4].

E. *Does this not, then, refer to prayer boxes containing verses of Scripture?*

F. *Said R. Pappa, "No, it refers to not putting on a cap or kerchief."*

10. A. A mourner is forbidden to give a greeting, *since the All-Merciful said to Ezekiel,* "And sigh in silence," (Ez. 24:17).

B. *What is the rule concerning those who have been excommunicated in respect to giving people a greeting?*

C. Said R. Joseph, *"Come and take note:* And as to greeting one another, they are in the status of person who are excommunicated by the Omnipresent."

D. *Said to him Abbayye, "But perhaps the case of one who is excommunicated on account of Heaven is exceptional, because such a one is subject to a more stringent rule?"*

E. *What is the rule concerning those who are unclean by reason of the skin ailment in respect to giving a greeting?*

F. *Come and take note:* "And he shall cover his upper lip" (Lev. 13:45) — meaning that his lips should be sealed together, so that he is to be in the status of a person who has been excommunicated or of a mourner and be forbidden to give a greeting.

G. *That is decisive proof.*

H. *So why not solve from this matter the question raised earlier concerning the one who has been excommunicated?*

I. *Said R. Aha bar Phineas in the name of R. Joseph, "Does it really say, 'he is forbidden'? It only says, he is to be in the status of a person who has been excommunicated or of a mourner, so far as other things is concerned, and he also is forbidden to give a greeting."*

11. A. A mourner is forbidden to study Torah, *since the All-Merciful said to Ezekiel,* "Sigh in silence" (Ez. 24:17).

B. *What is the rule concerning those who have been excommunicated in respect to study of the Torah?*

C. *Come and take note:* As to a person who is excommunicated, he may repeat Mishnah-teachings, and others may repeat Mishnah-teachings to him, he may be hired and others may be hired by him. As to a person who has been declared anathema, he may not repeat Mishnah-teachings, and others may not repeat Mishnah-teachings to him, he may not be hired and others may not be hired by him. A mourner repeats Mishnah-teachings to himself, so that he may not interrupt his study. He makes himself a small stall to support himself.

D. *And said Rab, "He may sell water at the pass at Arabot."*

E. *That proves the matter.*

F. *What is the rule concerning those who are afflicted with the skin ailment in respect to study of the Torah?*

G. *Come and take note of the following:* "And you shall make them known to your children and your children's children" (Deut. 4:9), and immediately afterward, "The day on which you stood before the Lord your God in Horeb" (Deut. 4:10). Just as in the latter case there are fear, trembling, dread and awe, so in this case [study of Torah] there must be fear, trembling, dread and awe. On the basis of the exegesis at hand they have said, "Those who have suffered a flux, those who are afflicted with the skin disease [of Lev. 13-14], those who have had sexual relations with menstruating women are permitted to recite the Torah, prophets, and writings, to repeat teachings of the Mishnah and the Gemara and the laws and lore, but those who have had a seminal emission are forbidden to do so.

H. *That proves the matter.*

12. A. A mourner is forbidden to wash his clothes, for it is written, "And Joab sent to Tekoa and called from there a wise woman and said to her, I pray you, pretend to be a mourning and put on mourning clothes, I ask, and do not anoint yourself with oil, but be as a woman who has for a long time mourned for the dead" (2 Sam. 14:2).

B. *What is the rule concerning those who have been excommunicated or those who are unclean by reason of the skin ailment in respect to their washing their clothes?*

C. *Come and take note:* Excommunicated persons and those suffering from the skin ailment may not have a hair cut or wash their clothes.

D. *That proves the matter.*

13. A. A mourner is required to tear his clothes, *for the All-Merciful has said to the sons of Aaron,* "Nor tear your clothes" (Lev. 10:6). On that basis it must follow that everybody else has to do so.

B. *What is the rule concerning those who have been excommunicated in respect to their tearing their clothes?*

C. *The question stands.*

D. As to a person afflicted with the skin ailment, what is the rule on whether or not he has to tear his clothes?

E. "His clothes shall be disheveled" (Lev. 13:45), meaning, they shall be torn.

F. *That proves the matter.*

14. A. The mourner is required to turn over his bed.

B. *That is in line with what Bar Qappara repeated as a Tannaite statement:* [15B] "I have set the likeness of my image on them and through their sins I have upset it, so let your beds be turned over on that account."

C. *What is the rule concerning those who have been excommunicated and those afflicted with the skin ailment as to turning over the bed?*

D. *The question stands.*

15. A. A mourner is forbidden to do work, since it is written, "And I shall turn your feasts into mourning" (Amos 8:10) — just as on a festival it is forbidden to do work, so a mourner is forbidden to do work.

B. What is the rule as to an excommunicated person's doing work?

C. Said R. Joseph, *"Come and take note:* When sages said that it is forbidden for those who are fasting to do work, they said that this was the case only in daytime, but at night it is permitted, and the same applies also to one who has been excommunicated and to a mourner. *Does this not, then, refer to all restrictions?"*

D. *Not, it refers to other items on the list but not to doing work.*

E. *Come and take note:* As to a person who is excommunicated, he may repeat Mishnah-teachings, and others may repeat Mishnah-teachings to him, he may be hired and others may be hired by him.

F. *That proves the matter.*

G. What about a person afflicted with the skin ailment?

H. *The question stands.*

16. A. A mourner is forbidden to wash, since it is said, "And do not anoint yourself with oil" (2 Sam. 14:2), and anointing covers bathing as well.

B. What is the law on the excommunicated person's washing?

C. Said R. Joseph, *"Come and take note:* When they said that it is forbidden to wash, that referred to the entire body, but as to one's face, hands, and feet, it is permitted, and so you find in the case of the person who has been excommunicated and the mourner. *Does this not, then, refer to all restrictions?"*

D. *Not, it refers to other items on the list but not to washing.*

E. What about a person afflicted with the skin ailment?

F. *The question stands.*

17. A. A mourner is forbidden to put on sandals, *since the All-Merciful said to Ezekiel,* "And put your shoes on your feet" (Ez. 24:17), the implication is that for everybody else it is forbidden to do so."

B. What is the law on the excommunicated person?

C. Said R. Joseph, *"Come and take note:* When they said that it is forbidden to put on sandals, that doing so in town, but on a journey, it is permitted. How so? If he set out on a journey, he puts on sandals, but on coming into town, he removes them, and so you find in the case of on who was excommunicated. *Does this not, then, refer to all restrictions?"*

D. *Not, it refers to other items on the list but not to washing.*

E. What about a person afflicted with the skin ailment?

F. *That question stands.*

18. A. A mourner is forbidden to have sexual relations, as it is written, "And David comforted Bath Sheba his wife and went in unto her" (2 Sam. 12:24), *bearing the implication that before then it was forbidden.*

B. What is the law on the excommunicated person?

C. Said R. Joseph, *"Come and take note:* All those years that the Israelites were in the wilderness, they were regarded as excommunicated, but nonetheless they had sexual relations."

D. *Said to him Abbayye, "But perhaps the case of the one who is excommunicated unto Heaven is exceptional, being less serious?"*

E. *Less serious! You just said it was more serious!*

F. *He was confused on the matter. If you take this route, he can answer you and if you take the other, he can answer you.*

G. What about a person afflicted with the skin ailment in respect to having sexual relations?

H. *Come and take note of that which has been taught on Tannaite authority:*

I. "And he will dwell outside his tent" (Lev. 14:8) —

J. he is to be like one who has been excommunicated.

K. And he is prohibited from having sexual relations

L. **"His tent" (Lev. 14:8) — his tent means only his wife, as it is said, "Return to your tents" (II Kings 15:1) [Sifra CL:I.9-10].**

M. *That proves it.*

N. *Then why not use that case to settle the question regarding the one who has been excommunicated?*

O. Said R. Huna b. R. Phineas in the name of R. Joseph, "Now does the passage state that he should be forbidden like one who was excommunicated? What it says is only, 'like one who has been excommunicated and like a mourner in regard to other matters, and he also is forbidden to have sexual relations."

19. A. *A mourner does not have to send his sacrifices to the Temple, for it has been taught on Tannaite authority:*

B. R. Simeon says, "['And you shall sacrifice peace offerings and eat there and you shall rejoice before the Lord your God' (Dt. 27:7):] The meaning of 'peace offerings' [since the word for peace bears the meaning of whole and complete as well] is that the one may present such an offering only when he is whole, but not when he is in the status of bereavement."

C. What is the law concerning a person who has been excommunicated as to sending his offerings?

D. Said R. Joseph, *"Come and take note:* All those years that the Israelites were in the wilderness, they were regarded as excommunicated, but nonetheless they sent their offerings."

E. *Said to him Abbayye, "But perhaps the case of the one who is excommunicated unto Heaven is exceptional, being less serious?"*

F. *Less serious! You just said it was more serious!*

G. *He was confused on the matter. If you take this route, he can answer you and if you take the other, he can answer you.*

H. What about a person afflicted with the skin ailment in respect to sending his offerings?

I. *Come and take note of that which has been taught on Tannaite authority:*

J. "'And after a defiled priest has been rendered clean' — after he has come away from his deceased relatives, 'they shall count seven days for him' — he counts those seven days, 'and in the day that he goes into the sanctuary, into the inner court, to minister in the sanctuary, he shall offer his sin offering' (Ez. 44:26) — [16A] this refers to that which is his own, a tenth part of an ephah of fine flour," the words of R. Judah.

K. R. Simeon says, "'and in the day that he goes into the sanctuary, into the inner court, to minister in the sanctuary, he shall offer his sin offering' (Ez. 44:26) — only when he is fit to go into the Temple is he fit to offer his own offering, but when he is not fit to go into the sanctuary, he is not fit to present his own offering [and none of these then may send offerings to the Temple]."

OLD AGE

BAVLI SHABBAT 23:6 152A

I.15 A. **"In the day when the keeper of the house shall tremble, and the strong men shall bow themselves" (Qoh. 12:2) —**

B. "In the day when the keeper of the house shall tremble": This refers to the sides and the ribs.

C. "And the strong men shall bow themselves": This refers to the legs.

D. "And the grinders cease" — the teeth;

E. "And those that look out of the windows darkened" — the eyes.

I.16A. **Said Caesar to R. Joshua b. Hananiah, "How come you didn't come to the celebration?"**

B. *"The mountain is snow, surrounded by ice, the dog doesn't bark, the grinders don't grind."*

C. *The household of Rab said, "What I didn't lose I'm looking for."*

I.17A. **It has been taught on Tannaite authority: R. Yosé bar Qisma says, "Better are two than three, woe is for the one thing that goes and doesn't come back."**

B. *So what's that?*

C. *Said R. Hisda, "It's youth."*

I.18A. *When R. Dimi came, he said, "Youth is a crown of roses, age, a crown of willow-rods."*

I.19A. *It has been taught on Tannaite authority in the name of R. Meir, "Chew well with your teeth and you will find it in your steps: 'For then we had plenty of food and were well and saw no evil' (Jer. 44:17)."*

I.20 A. *Said Samuel to R. Judah, "Sharp wit! Open your mouth and let your food come in. Until age forty food is better, then, drink is better."*

I.21 A. *Said a eunuch to R. Joshua b. Qorhah [that is, the bald], "How far is it from here to Baldtown?"*

B. *"As far as from here to Eunuch-city."*

C.   *Said a Sadducee to him, "A bald buck is forth four denars."*

D.   *"A castrated goat is worth eight."*

E.   *He saw he wasn't wearing shoes and remarked, "He who rides on a horse is king, on an ass, a free man, who walks with shoes on his feet is human; who has none of these — one who is dead and buried is better off."*

F.   *He said to him, "Eunuch, eunuch, you said three things to me, now hear three things from me: The glory of a face is its beard, the joy of the heart is a wife, 'the heritage of the Lord is children' (Ps. 127:3); blessed be the Omnipresent, who denied you all of these things!"*

G.   *"He said to him, "Baldy, contentious baldy!"*

H.   *"You're a castrated buck and you want to pick a fight?"*

I.22 A.   **Said Rabbi to R. Simeon b. Halafta, "How come we didn't receive you on the festival in the way in which my ancestors would receive yours?"**

B.   He said to him, "You know, the rocks have gotten tall, what is near has gotten distant, two have become three, and the peacemaker of the household [sexual relations] has ceased."

I.23 A.   **"And the doors shall be shut in the streets" (Qoh. 12:4) — this refers to the holes of a man.**

B.   "And the sound of the grinding is low" — because the stomach doesn't digest things.

C.   "And one gets up at the sound of a bird" — even a bird will wake him from sleep.

D.   "And all the daughters of the music shall be brought low" — even the voices of male and female singers sound like a whisper.

I.24 A.   **And so said Barzillai the Gileadite say to David, "I am today four score years old, can I discern between good and bad?" (2 Sam. 19:35) — this shows that opinions of old men change.**

B.   "Can your servant taste what I eat or drink" — this shows that the lips of the old grow slack.

C.   "Can I hear any more the voice of men and women singers?" — this shows that the ears of the old are heavy.

I.25 A.   *Said Rab, "Barzillai the Gileadite was a liar, for there was a servant in Rab's house who was ninety-two years old, and he could taste food."*

B.   *Raba said, "Barzillai the Gileadite was lewd, and whoever is lewd — old age catches up with him."*

I.26 A.   *It has been taught on Tannaite authority:*

B.   R. Ishmael b. R. Yosé says, "Disciples of sages, as they grow old, get more wisdom: 'With aged men is wisdom and in length of days understanding' (Job 12:12). But when the ignorant get older, they get stupider: 'He removes the speech of the reliable and takes away the understanding of elders' (Job 12:20)."

I.27 A.   **"Yes, they shall be afraid of that which is high" (Qoh. 12:5) — even a little hill looks like a high mountain.**

B. "And terrors shall be in the way" — when he walks on the road, his heart is filled with fear.

C. "And the almond tree shall blossom" — that is the coccyx [Freedman: the lowest end of the vertebrae protrudes in old age].

D. "And the grasshopper shall be a burden" — the rump.

E. "And desire shall fail" — the passions.

I.28 A. *R. Kahana was reciting this passage before Rab. When he reached this verse, Rab sighed.*

B. *That shows that Rab's sexual desire had come to an end.*

C. *Said R. Kahana, "What is the meaning of the verse of Scripture, 'For he decreed and it was' (Ps. 33:9)? This refers to a woman. 'He commanded, and it stood' — this refers to children."*

I.29 A. *A Tannaite statement:* **Though a woman is a pot full of shit and her mouth is full of blood, everybody pursues her.**

I.30 A. **"Because man goes to his long home" (Qoh. 12:5) —**

B. Said R. Isaac, "This teaches that to every righteous person is given a dwelling appropriate to his standing. The matter may be compared to the case of a king who came into town together with his staff. All go into the same gate, but each spends the night in a lodging fitting to the honor that is owing to him."

I.31 A. *And said R. Isaac, "What is the meaning of the verse, 'For youth and the prime of life are vanity' (Qoh. 11:10)? What a man does in his youth blacken his face in old age."*

I.32 A. **And said R. Isaac, "The worm causes pain for the corpse as much as does a needle in the flesh of a living person: 'But his flesh upon him who has pain' (Job 14:22)."**

I.33 A. Said R. Hisda, "A man's soul mourns for him for seven days: 'And his soul mourns for him' (Job 14:22), 'and he made a mourning for his father seven days' (Gen. 50:10)."

POVERTY

BAVLI GITTIN 6:1 50B-51A

IV.3 A. *There was a man who handed over his slave to a friend to teach him a thousand ways of making pap, but he taught him only eight hundred. He called him to court before Rabbi.* Said Rabbi, "Our fathers have said, 'We have forgotten prosperity' (Lam. 3:17) – but for our part, we never even saw it."

IV.4 A. *Rabbi made a wedding celebration for his son Simeon without inviting Bar Qappara, who wrote above the banquet hall, "Twenty-four thousand myriad of denarii have been spent on this celebration."*

B. [Bar Qappara] said, "If that is how things are for those who violate his will, all the more so will be the good fortune of those who do his will."

C. *He invited him.*

D. [Bar Qappara] said, "If that is how things are in this world for those who do his will, all the more so in the world to come!"

IV.5   A. *On the day on which Rabbi laughed [and didn't suffer pain], punishment came into the world. He said to Bar Qappara, "Don't make me laugh, and I'll give you forty measures of wheat."*

B. *He said to him, "But let the master see [51A] that whatever measure I want, I may take."*

C. *He took a big basket, turned it over [to hold the wheat], put it on his head, and came and said to him, "Fill me the forty measures of wheat that I demand from you."*

D. *Rabbi burst out laughing. He said to him, "Didn't I warn you not to make jokes?"*

E. *He said to him, "It's the wheat that I'm demanding that I have every right to take."*

IV.6   A. *Said Bar Qappara to the daughter of Rabbi, "Tomorrow I'm going to drink wine while your father dances and your mother croaks."*

B. *Ben Eleasa, Rabbi's son-in-law, was rich and eminent. He was invited to the wedding of R. Simeon b. Rabbi. Bar Qappara said to Rabbi, "What is the meaning of [the sexual kink referred to in] the verse, 'abomination' (Lev. 20:13)?"*

C. *Everything Rabbi said to him he refuted, so he said to him, "So what's 'abomination' (Lev. 20:13)?"*

D. *He said to him, "Let your wife come and fill up a cup for me."*

E. *She came and filled a cup for him.*

F. *He said to Rabbi, "Get up and dance for me, and I'll tell it to you."*

G. *[He did so, and he said to him,] "This is what the All-Merciful said, 'the meaning of the word for abomination is found in the meaning of its syllables, which may be read to mean "you err in respect to her"'* [Freedman: by forsaking the permitted and indulging in the forbidden]."

H. *At the next cup, he said to him, "What is the meaning of 'disgrace' (Lev. 18:23) [bestiality]?"*

I. *He said to him, "It's pretty much like what I just told you."*

J. *He said to him, "Do something and I'll tell you."*

K. *He did something.*

L. *He said to him, "'It is a disgrace' means, 'is there perfume in [the animal]?' What makes sexual relations with this creature better than sexual relations with all others?"*

M. *He said to him, "And what is the meaning of, 'lewdness'?"*

N. *He said to him, "Do as you did before."*

O. *He did it.*

P. *He said to him, "The word means, 'who is she?'"* [Through fornication, the parentage is unknown, so a father may marry his daughter (Freedman).]

Q. *Ben Eleasa couldn't take all this, he got up and left, he and his wife.*

IV.7 **A. Who's Ben Eleasa?**

B. *It is in line with that which has been taught on Tannaite authority:*

C. Rabbi says, "It is not for nothing that the son of Eleasa spent so much money for a haircut, but so that he may show what sort of haircut a high priest got."

D. For it is written, "They shall only poll their heads."

IV.8 **A. It has been taught on Tannaite authority:**

B. This is in the Julian manner.

C. *So what was the Julian manner?*

D. *Said R. Judah, "A unique kind of haircut."*

E. *And what's that?*

F. Said Raba, "The end of one row of hair reached the roots of the other, and that was the manner of haircut that the high priest got."

Praying the Prayer, Reciting the Shema

Bavli Sotah 7:1 32B-33A

III.1 A. The recital of the Shema [M. 7:1A3]:

B. *How do we know it? Since it is written,* "Hear, O Israel" (Deut. 6:4) — in any language that you can hear [with comprehension].

2. A. *Our rabbis have taught on Tannaite authority:*

D. "The recitation of the Shema must be in accord with the way it is written [that is, only in Hebrew]," the words of Rabbi.

E. And sages say, "In any language."

F. *What is the scriptural basis for Rabbis' position?* Scripture has said, "And they shall be..." (Deut. 6:4), meaning they are to be just as they are [and that is, in Hebrew].

G. And sages? Scripture has said, "Hear...," meaning, in any language that you hear with understanding.

H. *And as to rabbis, lo, it indeed is written,* "And they shall be..."

I. That serves to teach the lesson that one should not read the Shema in reverse order [backward].

J. *And how does Rabbi derive the same lesson,* that one should not read the Shema in the wrong order [reversing the sequence of the component paragraphs]?

K. *They derive that fact from the use of the definite article with "things," [thus, "these things" and hence in this order and no other].*

L. *And as to rabbis, from the use of the definite article with the word "things" they derive no lesson whatsoever.*

M. *And confronting Rabbi is yet the question of the use of the word "hear."*

N. *He requires that usage to make the point that you should make audible to your ear what you are saying with your lips.*

O. *And rabbis [in this connection] take the position of him who has said,* "He who recites the Shema but does not make it audible to his ear nonetheless has carried out his obligation."

P. *May I then draw the conclusion that Rabbi takes the view* [33A] *that it is permitted to read the entire Torah in any language. For, if you think that it may be read only in the Holy Language, then what need do I have for the word, "And they shall be," which the All-Merciful has written?*

Q. *[From Rabbi's viewpoint], it was necessary [to specify that the words are to be read as they are] because it is written,* "Hear..."

R. *Then may I propose that rabbis take the view that* the entire Torah was stated only in Hebrew, *for if you take the view that it was in any language, why did the All-Merciful find it necessary to use the word* "hear"?

S. *It was necessary to make explicit reference to that word, for, after all, it is written,* "And they shall be..."

IV.1 A. The Prayer [M. 7:1A4]:

B. *[That is because] it is a prayer for mercy, and one may pray [for mercy in any language].*

C. *And may the Prayer indeed be said in any language?*

D. And did not Rab Judah say, "A person should never ask for what he needs in the Aramaic language, for R. Yohanan has said, 'Whoever asks for what he needs in Aramaic language [will be disappointed], for the ministering angels will pay no attention to him, for the ministering angels do not know the Aramaic language.'"

E. *There indeed is no contradiction. The one view [given first] speaks of the case of an individual, the other, the case of the community.*

F. And do the ministering angels not know Aramaic?

G. *And has it not been taught on Tannaite authority:* Yohanan, high priest, heard an echo from the house of the Holy of Holies, proclaiming in Aramaic, *"The young men who went to make war against Antioch have conquered."*

H. There was the further case of Simeon the Righteous, who heard an echo from the house of the Holy of Holies, proclaiming in Aramaic, *"The decree which the enemy planned to bring upon the Temple has been nullified, and [in Hebrew] Gasqalges has been killed and his decrees nullified."* They made a note of the exact hour, and it turned out to be [exactly the hour at which the event took place].

I. *Now [as noted], this was said in Aramaic.*

J. *If you wish, I may reply that the case of an echo is different, since it serves to make the matter well known [and hence it was better to use Aramaic, which is more widely understood].*

K. *And if you wish, I may propose that it was Gabriel.*

L. *For a master has said,* "Gabriel came and taught [Joseph] seventy languages." [So Gabriel does know Aramaic, but the other angels do not.]

V.1 A. Grace after Meals [M. 7:1A5]:

B. For it is written, "And you will eat and be satisfied and bless the Lord your God" (Deut. 8:10) —

C. in any language in which you say a blessing.

PROPER CONDUCT

BAVLI GITTIN 1:1-3 7A

I.30 A. **Mar Uqba sent word to R. Eleazar, "Some people are opposing me, and I have the power to hand them over to the government. What is the ruling?"**

B. He underlined and wrote the verse, "'I said, I will take heed to my ways, that I sin not with my tongue; I will keep a curb upon my mouth, while the wicked is before me' (Ps. 39:2). Even though the wicked is before me, I will keep a curb upon my mouth."

C. *He sent word to him, "But they're bothering me a lot, and I can't resist them."*

D. He sent back, "'Resign yourself to the Lord and wait patiently for him' (Ps. 37:7) – wait for the Lord, and he will throw them down prostrate before you. Go to the house of study morning and night, and soon they will meet their end."

E. The word had scarcely left the mouth of R. Eleazar, before Geniba was thrown into chains.

I.31 A. **They sent word to Mar Uqba, "How on the basis of Scripture do we know that it is forbidden to sing?"**

B. He underlined and wrote the verse, "'Do not rejoice, Israel, as do the peoples, for you have gone astray from your God' (Hos. 9:1)."

C. *Shouldn't he send him the following verse: "They shall not drink wine with music, strong drink shall be better to them who drink it" (Isa. 24:9)?*

D. *Had he sent that verse, one might have concluded that what is forbidden is the use of musical instruments, but not a cappella singing; from the other verse I derive that fact.*

I.32 A. **Said R. Huna bar Nathan to R. Ashi, "What is the meaning of the verse of Scripture, 'Kinah and Dimonah and Adabah' (Josh. 15:22)?"**

B. *He said to him, "The verse of Scripture is reckoning with towns in the Land of Israel."*

C. *He said to him, "So don't I myself know that the verse of Scripture is reckoning with towns in the Land of Israel? But R. Gebiha from Be Argiza derived a lesson from the letters that make up these place-names, specifically: 'Whoever has a basis for anger against his* neighbor but holds his peace – he who endures for all eternity will make his cause his own.'"

D. *He said to him, "What about [a message based on the letters of the place-names used in] this verse:* 'Ziklag and Madmanah and Sansanah' (Josh. 15:22)?"

E. *He said to him, "Well, if R. Gebiha from Be Argiza were here, he would find something interesting to say about that verse, too. Anyhow, R. Aha of Khuzistan said about it the following lesson [built out of the letters of those words]:* 'Whoever has a just cause for complaint on account of the other's disrupting his livelihood and holds his peace – he who dwells in the bush will make his cause his own.'"

I.33 A. *Said the exilarch to R. Huna, "How do we know that wearing garlands is forbidden?"*

B. *He said to him, "On the authority of rabbis, it is in accord with what we have learned in the Mishnah:* In the war against Vespasian they decreed against the wearing of wreaths by bridegrooms and against the wedding drum [M. Sot. 9:14A]."*

C. *In the meantime R. Huna got up to use the toilet. Said to him R. Hisda, 'There is a verse of Scripture to the same effect:* 'Thus says the Lord God, the miter shall be removed, and the crown taken off; this shall be no more the same: that which is low shall be exalted, and that which is high, brought low' (Ezek. 21:31). Now what has the miter to do with the crown? It is to teach the lesson that, when the miter is worn by the high priest in the Temple, common folk can wear the crown at weddings, but when the miter has been removed from the head of the high priest, then the crown must be removed from the head of common folk."

D. *Now R. Huna came back from the toilet, and found them yet in session on the matter. He said to them, "By God! It derives only from the authority of rabbis. But just as your name is Hisda, meaning, favor, so what you say is full of favor."*

I.34 A. *Rabina came across Mar bar R. Ashi, weaving a wreath for his daughter. He said to him, "Does not the master accord with the verse, 'Thus says the Lord God, the miter shall be removed, and the crown taken off; this shall be no more the same: that which is low shall be exalted, and that which is high, brought low' (Ezek. 21:31)?"*

B. *He said to him, "The analogy is drawn to the high priest, therefore the rule applies to men, not women."*

I.35 A. *What is the meaning of the passage, this shall be no more the same?*

B. *R. Avira expounded the passage, sometimes saying what he said in the name of R. Ammi, sometimes saying what he said in the name of R. Assi,* "When the Holy One, blessed be He, said to Israel, 'The miter shall be removed, and the crown taken off,' said the ministering angels before the Holy One, blessed be He, 'Lord of the world, is "this" appropriate for Israel, who at Mount Sinai proclaimed "we shall do" before even "we shall hear"?'

C.   "He said to them, 'Should not "this" be for Israel, who brought low that which is high, and exalted that which is low? And who set up a statue in the Temple?'"

I.36 A.   *R. Avira expounded the passage, sometimes saying what he said in the name of R. Ammi, sometimes saying what he said in the name of R. Assi, "What is the meaning of the verse of Scripture, 'Thus says the Lord, though they be in full strength and many, even so shall they be sheared off and he shall cross...' (Nah. 1:12)? If someone sees that his income is insufficient, then he should give charity from it, and all the more so if it is ample."*

I.37 A.   *What is the meaning of the phrase, even so shall they be sheared off and he shall cross?*

B.   *A Tannaite statement of the Household of R. Ishmael:*

C.   Whoever shears his property and gives to charity will be saved from the judgment of Gehenna. The matter is comparable to two sheep crossing a river, one shorn, the other not; the shorn one crosses, the other sinks.

I.38 A.   [7B] **"Though I have afflicted you" (Nah. 1:12):**

B.   Said Mar Zutra, "Even a poor person who derives support from charity should give charity."

I.39 A.   **"I will afflict you no more" (Nah. 1:12):**

B.   R. Joseph stated a Tannaite statement: "They don't ever again show him the marks of poverty."

SEXUAL OBLIGATIONS OF A HUSBAND TO A WIFE

BAVLI KETUBOT 5:6 63A

VI.2 A.   ["The sexual duty of which the Torah speaks (Ex. 21:10): (1) those without work [of independent means] – every day; (2) workers – twice a week; (3) ass drivers – once a week; (4) camel drivers – once in thirty days; (5) sailors – once in six months," the words of R. Eliezer:] **As to the sexual duty of disciples of sages, when is it?**

B.   Said R. Judah said Samuel, "Once a week, on Friday night."

VI.3 A.   **"Who brings forth its fruit in its season" (Ps. 1:3) – said R. Judah, and some say R. Huna, and some say R. Nahman, "This refers to one who has sexual relations every Friday night."**

VI.4 A.   *Judah, son of R. Hiyya, son-in-law of R. Yannai, would go and remain at the session of the household of the master, but every Friday he would come home, and when he would come home, people saw a pillar of light moving before him. But once, he was so distracted by his subject that he didn't go home. Since that sign was not seen, said R. Yannai to them, "Turn over his bed, for if Judah were alive, he would not neglect his duty." It was like* "an error that comes from the king" (Qoh. 10:5), *and he died.*

VI.5 A. *Rabbi was involved in the marriage preparations for his son into the household of R. Hiyya. When the time came to write the marriage contract, the bride dropped dead. Said Rabbi, "God forbid, is there some reason that the union was invalid?"*

B. *They went into session and examined the genealogy of Rabbi [and found:] "Rabbi comes from Shephatiah [2 Sam. 3:4, son of David], son of Abital, and R. Hiyya is from the family of Shimei, brother of David."* [Slotki: As the latter was not a descendant of the anointed king's family, it was not proper for his daughter to be united in marriage with one who was.]

C. *He went on to take up the marriage preparations for his son into the household of R. Yosé b. Zimra. They contracted that the son would spend twelve years at the schoolhouse. They brought the girl by him. He said to them, "Let it be six years."*

D. *They brought the girl past him again. He said, "I'd rather marry her now [no waiting], then I'll go." He was embarrassed before his father.*

E. *He said to him, "My son, you have the very mind of the one who created you, for it is written first, 'You bring them in and plant them' (Ex. 15:17), and then, 'and let them make me a sanctuary that I may dwell among them' (Ex. 15:17)."*

F. *He went and remained at the session for two years in the schoolhouse, but by the time he came home, his wife went sterile. Said Rabbi, "What should we do? Should he divorce her?* People will say, 'This poor woman waited for him for nothing.' *Should he marry someone else?* People will say, 'This one is his wife, that one is his whore.' *So he prayed for mercy for her, and she was healed."*

VI.6 A. **R. Hananiah b. Hakhinai was going to the schoolhouse at the end of R. Simeon b. Yohai's wedding celebration. The other said to him, "Wait for me, so I can come with you." He didn't wait for him. He went off and remained at the session for twelve years in the schoolhouse. By the time he got home, the streets of the town had changed, and he didn't know how to get to his house. He went and sat down at the river bank, and there he heard a girl being spoken to in this language: "Daughter of Hakhinai, daughter of Hakhinai, fill up your jug and let's go."**

B. *He thought, "It must follow that this girl is ours."*

C. *He followed her. His wife was sitting and sifting flour. She looked up and saw him, her heart was overwhelmed and she died.* He said before him, "Lord of the world, is this to be the reward of this poor woman?" *So he prayed for mercy for her, and she lived.*

VI.7 A. **R. Hama bar Bisa went to the session for twelve years at the house of study. When he came home, he said, "I'm not going to act like Ben Hakhinai." He went into the session and sent word**

to his wife. His son [born after he left town], R. Oshayya, came
along and went into session before him. He asked him a question
on a tradition. He saw he was a sharp wit in his traditions. He
became depressed. He said, "If I had been here, I could have
produced children like this one."

B.   *He went home. His son came in. He rose before him, thinking he*
     wanted to ask him some more questions. Said to him his wife, "Is
     there a father who rises before his son?"

C.   *R. Ammi bar Hama recited in his regard:* "'And a threefold cord is
     not quickly broken' (Qoh. 4:12) – this refers to R. Oshayya son of
     R. Hama son of Bisa."

VI.8 A.   **R. Aqiba was the shepherd of Ben Kalba Sabua. His daughter**
          saw that he was chaste and noble. She said to him, "If we become
          betrothed to you, will you go to the schoolhouse?"

B.   *He said to her, "Yes."*

C.   *She became betrothed to him secretly and sent him off.*

D.   *Her father heard and drove her out of his house and forbade her*
     by vow from enjoying his property.

E.   **He went and remained at the session for twelve years at the**
     schoolhouse. When he came back, he brought with him twelve
     thousand disciples. He heard a sage say to her, "How long [63A]
     are you going to lead the life of a life-long widow?"

F.   *She said to him, "If he should pay attention to me, he will spend*
     another twelve years in study."

G.   *He said, "So what I'm doing is with permission." He went back*
     and stayed in session another twelve years at the schoolhouse.

H.   *When he came back, he brought with him twenty-four thousand*
     disciples. His wife heard and went out to meet him. Her neighbors
     said to her, "Borrow some nice clothes and put them on."

I.   *She said to them,* "'A righteous man will recognize the soul of his
     cattle' (Prov. 12:10)."

J.   *When she came to him, she fell on her face and kissed his feet. His*
     attendants were going to push her away. He said to them, "Leave
     her alone! What is mine and what is yours is hers*."*

K.   *Her father heard that an eminent authority had come to town. He*
     said, "I shall go to him. Maybe he'll release me from my vow."
     He came to him. He said to him, "Did you take your vow with an
     eminent authority in mind [as your son-in-law]?"

L.   He said to him, "Even if he had known a single chapter, even if he
     had known a single law [I would never have taken that vow]!"

M.   *He said to him, "I am the man."*

N.   *He fell on his face and kissed his feet and gave him half of his*
     property.

O.   *The daughter of R. Aqiba did the same with Ben Azzai, and that is*
     in line with what people say: "A ewe copies a ewe, a daughter's
     acts are like the mother's."

VI.9 A.   **R. Joseph b. Raba was sent by his father to the schoolhouse before R. Joseph. They contracted that he could stay for six years. When he had been there three years, at the approach of the Day of Atonement, he said, "I'll go and see the men of my household."**

B.   *His father heard about it. He took a tool and went to meet him, saying to him, "What you remember is your whore."*

C.   *There are those who say: "He said to him, 'You remember your dove.'"*

D.   They quarreled, and this master did not eat a final meal prior to the fast, nor did that one.

SEXUAL RELATIONS

BAVLI NIDDAH 2:4 16B

3. A.   Said R. Yohanan, "It is forbidden to have sexual relations by day. What verse of Scripture shows that that is the fact? 'Let the day perish on which I was born, and the night on which it was said, 'a male child has been brought forth' (Job 3:3). Thus the Torah has said that for conception the night has been designated as appropriate, but not the day."

B.   *R. Simeon b. Laqish said, "Proof is from this verse: 'He who despises his ways shall die' (Prov. 19:16)."*

C.   *And how does R. Simeon b. Laqish interpret the verse adduced in evidence by R. Yohanan?*

D.   *He requires it to make the point that R. Hanina bar Pappa made in his interpretation. For R. Hanina bar Pappa interpreted as follows:* "The angel who is appointed in charge of conception is called 'night,' and he takes a drop of semen and sets it before the Holy One, blessed be he, and says to him, 'Lord of the ages, as to this drop of semen, what will be its fate? Will it produce a strong man or a weak man, a sage or a fool? a rich man or a poor man?'"

E.   *But it does not ask whether it will be a wicked man or a righteous man!*

F.   *That is in accord with what R. Hanina said. For* R. Hanina said, "Everything is in the hands of Heaven except for the fear of Heaven, as it is said, 'And now Israel, what does the Lord your God require of you but to fear' (Dt. 10:12)."

G.   And R. Yohanan?

H.   *If matters were as the other has read them, Scripture should have said, 'a male child is brought forth.' Why does it say, 'there has been brought forth a male child'?* It is to prove that for conception the night has been designated as appropriate, but not the day."

I.   *And how does R. Yohanan interpret the verse that has been adduced in evidence by R. Simeon b. Laqish?*

J.   *He requires it to make the point that is written in the book of Ben Sira:*

K.   Three types I hate, and four I do not love: an official who frequents wine-shops, and some say, an official who is a common gossip; a person who calls a session in the high part of town, one who holds his penis when he urinates, and one who appears in his fellow's home without warning.

L.   Said R. Yohanan, "Even one who appears in his own home without warning."

4. A.   Said R. Simeon b. Yohai, "There are four sorts that the Holy One, blessed be he, hates, and I don't love them either: one who appears in his own home without warning, and, it goes without saying, his fellow's home; one who holds his penis when he urinates; [17A] one who urinates naked before his bed; and one who has sexual relations in the presence of any living creature whatsoever."

B.   Said R. Judah to Samuel, "Even before mice?"

C.   *He said to him, "Sharpie! No, of course not.* But it is like the household of so-and-so, who have sexual relations in front of their boy-slaves and girl-slaves. *And what verse of Scripture can they have in mind?* 'Stay here with the ass' (Gen. 22:5), meaning, a people that is in the classification of asses."

D.   Rabbah b. R. Huna would drive away wasps from his [Slotki:] curtained bed.

E.   Raba would chase away even mosquitoes.

5. A.   Said R. Simeon b. Yohai, "There are five things that impose liability to the death penalty upon those who do them, and their blood is on their own head: eating peeled garlic, a peeled onion, or a peeled egg, drinking diluted liquids that were left standing over night, spending a night in a graveyard, clipping one's nails and tossing them out into the public domain, and having sexual relations immediately after blood-letting."

B.   "eating peeled garlic:" *that is so even though they are put into a basket, tied up, and sealed,* for an evil spirit dwells upon them.

C.   *But that rule applies only where their roots or peel did not remain with them; but if the roots or peel remained with them, we have no objection.*

D.   "drinking diluted liquids that were left standing over night:"

E.   Said R. Judah said Samuel, "That rule applies if they were left standing in a metal utensil."

F.   Said R. Pappa, "Utensils made of alum crystals are in the same category as those made of metal."

G.   And so said R. Yohanan, "That rule applies if they were left standing in a metal utensil. Utensils made of alum crystals are in the same category as those made of metal."

H.   "spending a night in a graveyard:"

I.   that is done so that a spirit of uncleanness may come to rest on him.

J.   *Sometimes it endangers him.*

K.   "clipping one's nails and tossing them out into the public domain:"

L. This is because a pregnant woman may pass over them and miscarry.

M. *But this rule has been stated only in a case in which one removes the nails with a pair of scissors.*

N. *And this rule has been stated only in a case in which one clips the nails of both his hands and his feet.*

O. *And this rule has been stated only in a case in which one did not cut anything after cutting them, but if something was cut immediately after one cut the nails, there is no objection. But that is not the entire story. In all these matters one has to take precautions.*

P. *Our rabbis have taught on Tannaite authority:*

Q. Three statements were made with reference to the disposal of fingernails: one who burns them is pious, who buries them is righteous, who simply tosses them away is wicked.

R. "and having sexual relations immediately after blood-letting:"

S. For a master has said, "He who has a blood-letting and then has sexual relations will have neurasthenic children; if it took place after both the husband and the wife have had a blood-letting, they will have children suffering with *raatan.*"

T. *Said Rab, "But that statement pertains only to a case in which one has eaten nothing, but if one has eaten something, then there is no objection."*

6. A. Said R. Hisda, "It is forbidden for someone to have sexual relations by day, as it is said, 'You will love your neighbor as yourself' (Lev. 19:18)."

B. *What is the implication of that proof-text?*

C. Said Abbayye, "The husband may discern in the wife some repulsive trait, and she will be revolting to him."

7. A. Said R. Huna, "Israelites are holy and do not have sexual relations by day."

B. Said Raba "But if it was a darkened room, it is permitted, and a disciple may create a dark space with his cloak and have sexual relations."

C. *But we have learned in the Mishnah:* **Or she should have intercourse in the light of a lamp.**

D. *Then say as follows:* she should conduct an examination in the light of the lamp.

E. *Come and take note:*

F. Even though they have said, "He who has sexual relations to the light of a candle, lo, this one is vile,"

G. *Say it as follows:* he who examines the condition of his bed in the light of a lamp — lo, this one is vile.

H. *Come and take note:*

I. And the members of the household of King Monobases would do three things, on which account they are remembered for praise: they would have sexual relations by day; and they would inspect their beds with cotton; and they would impose the rules of uncleanness and cleanness in connection with snow.

J. *Now it is stated, therefore,* they would have sexual relations by day!

K. *State it in these terms:* they would examine their beds by day. *And that stands to reason, for if you think that they had sexual relations by day, would they be remembered for praise?*

L. *Well, as a matter of fact, they would, for since by night sleepiness overtakes the couple, she would be repulsive to him.*

M. "they would inspect their beds with cotton:"

N. *This supports the position of Samuel, for* Samuel has said, "The bed is to be inspected only with cotton tufts or with clean, soft wool."

O. *Said Rab, "That explains what I heard on the eves of the Sabbaths when I was there: 'Does anybody need cotton tufts for his "bread,"' and I did not know what they were talking about."*

P. *Said Raba, "Old flax garments are the best for making examinations."*

Q. *Is that so? And lo, the Tannaite authority of the household of Manasseh [said],* "People are not to inspect the bed with a red rag or a black one or with flax, but only with cotton tufts or with clean, soft wool"?

R. *That forms no contradiction, the one speaks of flax, the other, flax garments.*

S. *And if you prefer, I shall say, both speak of flax garments, but the latter refers to new ones, the former, old ones.*

T. "and they would impose the rules of uncleanness and cleanness in connection with snow:"

U. *There we have learned in the Mishnah:* **Snow is neither food nor liquid. If one gave thought to it for use as food, his intention is null [Bavli: it does not impart uncleanness as food]. [Tosefta:] If one thought of it as liquid, it receives or imparts uncleanness as liquid. If part of it is made unclean, the liquid is made unclean. If part of it is made unclean, the whole of it is not made unclean. If part of it is clean, the whole of it is clean** [T. Toh. 2:5L-O].

V. *Now there is an internal contradiction, for you have said,* **If part of it is made unclean, the liquid is made unclean** *and then you have proceeded to say,* **If part of it is clean, the whole of it is clean***! The latter then bears the implication that the whole of it has been made unclean!*

W. Said Abbayye, "It would be a case in which [the snow] had been carried through the air-space of an oven [containing a dead creeping thing], for the Torah has given testimony concerning a clay utensil, that **[17B]** even if it was full of mustard seed [everything in it is unclean]." [Slotki: Even though only those seeds that are actually around the sides of the oven can come into direct contact with the oven, the entire contents are unclean, which proves that in the case of an earthenware oven, uncleanness is imparted to everything in it even though they did not come into direct contact with it].

VISITING THE SICK

BAVLI NEDARIM 4:4A-C

A. He who is prohibited by vow from enjoying benefit from him – he [the fellow] goes in to visit him when he is sick,

B. remaining standing but not sitting down.

C. And he heals him himself but not what belongs to him.

I.1 A. [39A] [Remaining standing but not sitting down:] *With what situation do we deal? If it is a case in which the property of the visitor is forbidden to the one who is sick, then he may even sit down. And if it is a case in which the property of the sick man is forbidden to the visitor, then he may not even stand up!*

B. Said Samuel, "In point of fact, it is a case in which the property of the visitor is forbidden to the sick man, and it is a place in which people collect a fee for sitting down with a sick person, but not for standing by him."

C. *Yeah, so how do you know for sure?*

D. *This is how the Tannaite framer states matters: Even in a case in which one is paid a fee for visiting, he may be paid only for sitting but not for standing. But if you prefer, I shall explain in accord with* R. Simeon b. Eliaqim: "It is a precautionary decree, lest he tarry even while standing." *Here, too,* it is a precautionary decree lest he stay for a long time while sitting.

E. Ulla said, "In point of fact, it is a case in which the property of the sick man is forbidden to the visitor. *But it is a case in which he did not take a vow if the vow would affect his health."*

F. *Yeah, well, then, why can't he sit too?*

G. *In this case, he can accomplish his goal through standing.*

H. *An objection was raised:* He [the fellow] goes in to visit him when he is sick. **If his son got sick, in the marketplace he may inquire as to his health.** *Now, from the perspective of Ulla, who has said,* **"In point of fact, it is a case in which the property of the sick man is forbidden to the visitor,"** *then this is readily explained as a case in which he did not take a vow if the vow would affect his health. But from the perspective of Samuel, who explained the rule to refer to a case in which* **the property of the visitor is forbidden to the sick man,** *then what's the difference between the man himself and his son?*

I. *He will say to you, "Our Mishnah passage refers to a case in which* the property of the visitor is forbidden for use by the sick person. *The external rule refers to a case in which* the property of the sick person is forbidden for the use of the visitor."

J. *Yeah, so how do you know for sure?*

K.   ***Said Raba, "For Samuel** [39B] **our Mishnah passage presents this problem: How come they formulate the rule as** remaining standing but not sitting down? **So the rule, to make that distinction sensible, must refer to a case in which the sick person is forbidden to receive a benefit from the visitor."***

I.2 **A.**   **Said R. Simeon b. Laqish, "Whence in Scripture do we find an allusion to the duty of visiting the sick? 'If these men die the common death of all men, or if they be visited after the visitation of all men' (Num. 16:29)."**

B.   *So what's the pertinent implication?*

C.   Said Raba, "If these men die like all men, who fall sick and have people come to visit them, what will people say? 'The Lord has not sent me' for this task." [So they must die in some other than the proper way.]

I.3 **A.**   **Raba interpreted a verse of Scripture, "What is the meaning of what is written, 'But if the Lord make a new thing and the earth open her mouth' (Num. 16:30)?**

B.   "Said Moses before the Holy One, blessed be He, 'If Gehenna has been created, well and good, and if not, let the Lord now create it.'"

C.   *Is this so? But has it not been taught on Tannaite authority:* Seven things were created before the world was made, and these are they: Torah, repentance, the Garden of Eden, Gehenna, the throne of glory, the house of the sanctuary, and the name of the Messiah.

D.   Torah: "The Lord possessed me in the beginning of his way, before his works of old" (Prov. 8:22).

E.   Repentance: "Before the mountains were brought forth, or ever you had formed the earth and the world...you turn man to destruction and say, Repent, you sons of men" (Ps. 90:23).

F.   The Garden of Eden: "And the Lord God planted a garden in Eden from aforetime" (Gen. 2:8).

G.   Gehenna: "For Tophet is ordained of old" (Isa. 30:33).

H.   The throne of glory: "Your throne is established from of old" (Ps. 93:2).

I.   The house of the sanctuary: A glorious high throne from the beginning is the place of our sanctuary" (Jer. 17:12).

J.   And the name of the Messiah: "His name shall endure for ever and has existed before the sun" (Ps. 72:17).

K.   *Rather, this is what he said: "If a mouth has already been created for Gehenna, well and good, but if not, then let the Lord make one."*

L.   *But isn't it written,* 'There shall be no new thing under the sun" (Qoh. 1:9)?

M.   *Rather, this is what he said: "If the mouth of Gehenna is not near here, then bring it near."*

I.4 **A.**   ***Raba – and some say, R. Isaac – expounded, "What is the meaning of the verse,* 'The sun and the moon stood still in their*** *zebul*, at the light of your arrows they went' (Hab. 3:1)? [Freedman, p. 757, n. 1: There are seven heavens, of which *zebul* is one.] *What were they doing in zebul, seeing that they are set in the firmament, a lower heaven?*

B. "This teaches that the sun and the moon went up to the firmament called *Zebul.* They said before the Holy One, blessed be He, 'Lord of the world, if you do justice with the son of Amram, we shall go forth, and if not, we shall not go forth.'

C. "At that moment he shot arrows at them and said to them, 'people bow down to you and yet you give light. On account of the honor owing to me you never objected, but on account of the honor owing to a mortal man, you make a protest!' So spears and arrows are shot at them every day before they agree to shine: 'And at the light of your arrows they go forth' (Hab. 3:11)."

REVERSION TO THE TOPIC OF VISITING THE SICK

I.5 A. *It has been taught on Tannaite authority:* **As to visiting the sick, there is no fixed limit.**

B. *What is the meaning of* there is no fixed limit?

C. *R. Joseph considered saying,* "There is no fixed limit, in that the reward for doing it is unlimited."

D. **Said to him Abbayye, "So is there a fixed limit to the reward that is given for doing any of the religious duties?** *And lo, we have learned in the Mishnah:* Be meticulous in a small religious duty as in a large one, for you do not know what sort of reward is coming for any of the various religious duties [M. Abot 2:1]."

E. Rather said Abbayye, "Even an eminent authority must come to a minor one."

F. Raba said, "Even a hundred times a day."

I.6 A. **Said R. Aha bar Hanina, "Whoever visits the sick takes away a sixtieth of his illness."**

B. *They said to him, "If so, then let sixty people visit him and bring him back to health."*

C. *He said to him, "The sixtieth is as the tenth of which they speak in the household of Rabbi, and that depends on the visitor's being subject to the same astrological sign anyhow."*

D. *For it has been taught on Tannaite authority:* Rabbi says, "The daughter is supported from the property of the brothers; she takes a tenth of the estate."

E. They said to Rabbi, "In line with what you say, one who has ten daughters and a son – the son has no portion whatever in the face of the daughters' claim on the estate!"

F. He said to them, "This is how I rule: The first takes a tenth of the estate, the second, a tenth of what's left, the third, a tenth of what's left, and then they go back and divided equally what all had received."

I.7 A. *R. Helbo fell sick. R. Kahana went and announced,* [40A] *"R. Helbo is sick." Nobody came to see him.*

B. *He said to them,* "Wasn't there the incident involving a disciple among the disciples of R. Aqiba who fell ill, and sages didn't come to visit him. R. Aqiba came to visit him. Because they swept and cleaned the house before him, the other got better."

C. "He said to him, 'My lord, you have brought me back to life.'

D. "R. Aqiba went out and expounded, 'Whoever doesn't visit the sick is as though he shed blood.'"

I.8 A. *When R. Dimi came,* he said, "Anyone who visits the sick makes him live, and anyone who does not visit the sick makes him die."

B. So what makes this happen? Should I say, Anyone who visits the sick seeks mercy for him that he may live, and anyone who does not visit the sick seeks mercy for him that he may die, *well, then, could it enter your mind that he would want him to die? Rather,* anyone who does not visit the sick does not seek mercy for him, neither so that he will live nor that he will die.

I.9 A. *When Raba got sick, on the first day he would tell them not to tell anyone. From that point he would tell his servant, "Go out and tell people in the market, 'Raba is sick. Whoever loves him should pray for mercy for him. And whoever hates him should rejoice over him.'*

B. *"For it is written,* 'Rejoice not when your enemy falls, and let not your heart be glad when he stumbles, lest the Lord see it and it displease him, and he turn away his wrath from him' (Prov. 24:17), *and he who loves me will pray for me."*

I.10 A. Said Rab, "He who visits the sick is saved from judgment to Gehenna: 'Blessed is he who considers the poor, the Lord will deliver him in the day of evil' (Ps. 41:2). 'The poor' refers to the ill: 'He will cut me off from pining sickness' (Isa. 38:12), or 'Why are you so poorly, you son of the king' (2 Sam. 13:4). 'Evil' refers only to Gehenna: 'The Lord has made all things for himself, yes, even the wicked for the day of evil' (Prov. 16:4)."

B. So if he does visit the sick, what is his reward?

C. *What is his reward? It is just what you said:* He is saved from judgment to Gehenna!

D. Rather, what is his reward in this world?

E. "The Lord will preserve him and keep him alive and he shall be blessed upon the earth and you will not deliver him to the will of his enemies" (Ps. 41:3):

F. "The Lord will preserve him": From the impulse to do evil.

G. "And keep him alive": From suffering.

H. "And he shall be blessed upon the earth": All will take pride in him.

I. "And you will not deliver him to the will of his enemies": He will have friends like Naaman's, who cured his skin ailment, and not like Rehoboam's, who divided his kingdom.

I.11 A. *It has been taught on Tannaite authority:*

B. R. Simeon. b. Eleazar says, "If children tell you, 'build,' and old folk tell you, 'destroy,' obey the aged and don't obey the children, for the building of children is destruction, but the destruction of the aged is building, and proof of that is Rehoboam son of Solomon" [T. A.Z. 1:19].

I.12 **A.** *Said R. Shisa b. R. Idi, "Someone should not visit the sick either during the first three hours of the day or during the last three hours of the day, so as not to forget to pray for him.*

B. *"During the first three hours of the day, the illness lets up, during the last three hours of the day it heats up."*

I.13 **A.** Said Rabin said Rab, "How on the basis of Scripture do we know that the Holy One, blessed be He, nourishes the sick? 'The Lord will strengthen him upon the bed of languishing' (Ps. 41:4)."

B. Further said Rabin said Rab, "How on the basis of Scripture do we know that the Presence of God hovers above the bed of the sick? 'The Lord sets himself upon the bed of languishing' (Ps. 41:4)."

C. *So, too, it has been taught on Tannaite authority:*

D. He who goes in to visit the sick should not sit on the bed or on the stool or chair but must cloak himself and sit on the ground, for that the Presence of God hovers above the bed of the sick, as it is said, "The Lord sets himself upon the bed of languishing" (Ps. 41:4)."

I.14 **A.** *Also said Rabin said Rab, "The rise of the Euphrates indicates that there was abundant rain in the West."*

B. *He differs from Samuel, for said Samuel, "A river increases in volume from the springs in its bed."*

C. *There is then a contradiction between two statements of Samuel, for* said Samuel, "Running water does not effect cultic cleanness, [40B] except in the case of the Euphrates in Tishré."

D. *Samuel's father made for his daughters immersion pools in Nisan* [Slotki: Bekhorot 55a: When the flowing river, swollen by rainwater, could not be used for the purpose, since immersion may not be performed in rainwater that is not collected and stationary], *and he made mats for them in the days of Tishré [so as to protect their feet from the river mud].*

I.15 **A.** Said R. Ammi said Rab, "What is the meaning of the verse of Scripture, 'Therefore you son of man, prepare for yourself stuff for removing' (Ezek. 12:3)? this refers to a lamp, plate, [41A] and rug."

I.16 **A.** "And you shall serve your enemies in want of all things" (Deut. 28:48):

B. Said R. Ammi said Rab, "That is, without lamp or table."

C. R. Hisda said, "Without a wife."

D. R. Sheshet said, "Without a servant."

E. R. Nahman said, "Without knowledge."

F. *A Tannaite statement:* Without salt and without fat.

G.   Said Abbayye, "We have in hand the statement: 'Poverty refers
     only to the absence of knowledge.'"

H.   *In the West they say, "One who has this has it all, one who doesn't
     have this, so what's he got? One who's gotten this – so what doesn't
     he have? One who's not gotten this, so what's he got?"*

I.17 A.   **R. Alexandri in the name of R. Hiyya bar Abba, "A sick person
          does not recover from his ailment before all of his sins are
          forgiven: 'Who forgives all your sins, who heals all your
          diseases' (Ps. 103:3)."**

B.   R. Hamnuna said, "He goes back to the days of his youth: 'His
     flesh shall be fresher than a child's, he shall return to the days of
     his youth' (Job 33:25)."

I.18 A.   **"You have turned his bed in his sickness" (Ps. 41:4):**

B.   *Said R. Joseph, "That is to say that he forgets what he has learned."*

C.   *R. Joseph fell sick. What he knew was taken from him. Abbayye
     brought it back to him.*

D.   *That is in line with what we say in so many passages, "Said R.
     Joseph, 'I have not heard a thing about this.' Said to him Abbayye,
     'You yourself have said it to us, and it is on the basis of the following
     Tannaite statement that you said it....'"*

I.19 A.   **While Rabbi repeated his [traditions of] decided law thirteen
          times, he taught it to R. Hiyya only seven of them. Then he got
          sick. R. Hiyya restored to him the seven versions that he had
          taught him, but the other six perished.**

B.   *There was a certain laundryman who had overheard Rabbi when
     he was repeating the traditions. R. Hiyya went and learned the
     traditions before the laundryman, and then he went and repeated
     them before Rabbi. When Rabbi saw that laundryman,* Rabbi said
     to him, "You have made me and Hiyya!"

C.   *There are those who say that this is what he said to him,* "You
     have made Hiyya and Hiyya made me."

I.20 A.   **R. Alexandri also said in the name of R. Hiyya bar Abba,
          "Greater is the miracle that is done for a sick person than the
          miracle that was done for Hananiah, Mishael, and Azariah.
          That of Hananiah, Mishael, and Azariah was fire made by man,
          which anybody can put out, but that of a sick person is fire
          made by Heaven, and who can put that out?"**

I.21 A.   **R. Alexandri also said in the name of R. Hiyya bar Abba, and
          some say, said R. Joshua b. Levi, "When the end time of a person
          has come, everything conquers him: 'And it will be that
          whosoever finds me will slay me' (Gen. 4:14)."**

B.   *Rab said, "That derives from this verse of Scripture:* 'They stand
     forth this day to receive your judgments, for all are your servants'
     (Ps. 119:91)."

I.22 A.   **They said to Rabbah bar Shila that a tall man died. He was
          riding a small mule, and when he came to a bridge, the mule
          shied and threw the man, and he was killed. To him Rabbah**

applied this verse: "They stand forth this day to receive your
judgments, for all are your servants" (Ps. 119:91).

I.23 A. *Samuel saw a scorpion carried across a river by a frog. Then it
stung someone who died. He cited this verse:* **"They stand forth
this day to receive your judgments, for all are your servants"
(Ps. 119:91).**

I.24 A. Samuel said, "They pay a visit only upon a sick person who is
suffering a fever."

B. *To exclude what class of sick people?*

C. *To exclude that to which the following, taught on Tannaite authority,
makes reference:*

D. R. Yosé b. Parta says in the name of R. Eliezer, "They do not pay
a sick call either on those suffering intestinal illness or on those
suffering eye disease or headaches."

E. *There is no problem understanding why one should not visit those
suffering intestinal illness: It is because of the embarrassment of
the sick person. But what about those suffering eye disease or
headaches?*

F. *It is on account of the reason given by R. Judah, for said R. Judah,
"Talking is bad for the eyes and for headaches."*

I.25 A. *Said Raba, "If fever were not the messenger of the angel of death,
it would be healthy once every thirty days* [41B] *as thorns that
surround a palm tree, and as an antidote to snake venom to the
body."*

B. R. Nahman bar Isaac said, "Give me neither it nor its antidote!"

I.26 A. Said Rabbah b. Jonathan said R. Yehiel, **"*Arsan* is good for the
healing of the sick."**

B. *So what's arsan?*

C. *Said R. Jonathan, "[Freedman:] It is old peeled barley that sticks
to the sieve."*

D. *Said Abbayye, "It has to be boiled like the meat of an ox."*

E. *R. Joseph said, "It is fine barley flour that sticks to the sieve."*

F. *Said Abbayye, "It has to be boiled like the meat of an ox."*

I.27 A. **Said R. Yohanan, "One ill with dysentery is not to be visited,
and his name is not to be mentioned."**

B. *How come?*

C. Said R. Eleazar, "Because it is like a gushing spring."

D. And said R. Eleazar, "Why does it bear the name that it has?
Because it is like a gushing spring."

THE WIDOW AFTER HUSBAND'S DEATH. THE DEATH OF RABBI

BAVLI KETUBOT 12:3 103A-B

A. A widow who said, "I don't want to move from my husband's
house" –

B. the heirs cannot say to her, "Go to your father's house and we'll
take care of you [there]."

C.   But they provide for her in her husband's house,

D.   giving her a dwelling in accord with her station in life.

E.   [If] she said, "I don't want to move from my father's house,"

F.   the heirs can say to her, "If you are with us, you will have support. But you are not with us, you will not have support."

G.   If she claimed that it is because she is a girl and they are boys, they do provide for her while she is in her father's house.

I.1 **A.**   ***Our rabbis have taught on Tannaite authority:***

B.   She may make use of the old home just as she used it when her husband was alive, so, too, the boy slaves and girl slaves just as she did when her husband was alive, so, too, the pillows and blankets, silver and gold utensils, just as she did when her husband was alive, for thus does he write for her in her marriage contract, "You will dwell in my house and enjoy support from my property so long as you spend your widowhood in my house" [T. Ket. 11:5].

C.   *R. Joseph stated a Tannaite rule:* "In my house – not in my hovel."

I.2 **A.**   **Said R. Nahman, "If the heirs of an estate sold off the house set aside for the widow, they have done nothing whatsoever"**

B.   *Then how is that matter distinguished from what R. Assi said in the name of R. Yohanan, for* said R. Assi said R. Yohanan, "Heirs of an estate who went ahead [before the females claimed what was theirs for support] and sold property from a small estate – what they have sold is validly sold"?

C.   *There the property was not mortgaged to the female heirs while the husband was yet alive, but here the property was mortgaged to the marriage settlement while the husband was still alive."*

I.3 **A.**   *Said Abbayye, "We hold as a tradition: If the dwelling set aside for the widow fell down, the heirs are not obligated to build it up again."*

B.   *So, too, it has been taught on Tannaite authority:* If the dwelling set aside for the widow fell down, the heirs are not obligated to build it up again, and not only so, but even if she says, "Let me be, and I'll build it up again out of my own resources," they pay no attention to her.

I.4 **A.**   *Asked Abbayye, "If she repaired it, what is the law?"*

B.   *The question stands.*

II.1 **A.**   [If] she said, "I don't want to move from my father's house," the heirs can say to her, "If you are with us, you will have support. But you are not with us, you will not have support":

B.   *But let them support her while she is living there [in her father's household]? [Since that is not the case,] it supports what R. Huna said, for* said R. Huna, "The blessing bestowed on a household is in accord with its size [the more people in a household, the cheaper the per unit cost of maintenance]."

C.   *Well, then, why can't they give her in accord with the blessing of the household [that is, a smaller allowance, in accord with what it would have cost to keep her at the household of the heirs]?*

D. *They can.*

II.2 A. Said R. Huna, "The sayings of sages are a source of blessing, the sayings of sages are a source of wealth, and the sayings of sages are a source of healing."

B. "The sayings of sages are a source of blessing": as we just said.

C. "The sayings of sages are a source of wealth": *For we have learned in the Mishnah,* He who sells produce to his fellow – [if the buyer] drew it but did not measure it, he has acquired possession of it. [If] he measured it but did not draw it [to himself], he has not acquired possession. If he was smart, he will rent the place [in which the produce is located] [M. B.B. 5:7A-D].

D. "The sayings of sages are a source of healing": *For we have learned in the Mishnah,* A person should not chew grains of wheat to put on his sore on Passover, because they ferment [M. Pes. 2:7E].

II.3 A. *Our rabbis have taught on Tannaite authority:*

B. At the time that Rabbi was dying, he said, "I need my children."

C. His children came in to him. He said to them, "Take good care of the honor owing to your mother. Let a light be kindled in its proper place, a table set in its proper place, a bed laid in its proper place.

D. "Joseph Hofni, Simeon Efrati – they are the ones who served me when I was alive, and they will take care of me when I have died."

II.4 A. "Let a light be kindled in its proper place":

B. *[Why did he have to give instructions to that effect?] The obligation derives from the Torah:* "Honor your father and your mother" (Ex. 20:12).

C. *She was a stepmother.*

D. *Honoring the stepmother also is a requirement of the Torah, for it has been taught on Tannaite authority:* "Honor your father and your mother," "your father" encompasses "your stepmother," and "your mother" encompasses "your stepfather," and the redundant "and" encompasses "your elder brother."

E. *That applies when they are alive, but not after death.*

II.5 A. "Let a light be kindled in its proper place, a table set in its proper place, a bed laid in its proper place":

B. *How come?*

C. *[After he died,] every Friday evening at twilight he would come to his house. On a certain Friday at twilight, a neighbor came to the door, talking in a loud voice; his slave girl whispered, "Shush, Rabbi is in session." When he heard that, he never again came,* so as not to cast a bad light on the earlier righteous men [who did not have the privilege of coming back after death].

II.6 A. "Joseph Hofni, Simeon Efrati – they are the ones who served me when I was alive, and they will take care of me when I have died":

B. *They thought he meant, "In this world." But when people saw that their biers preceded his [their having died at the same time], they concluded that he was referring to the other world, and the reason that he said what he did was so that people might not suppose they had done some offense and that only the merit owing to Rabbi protected them up to then.*

II.7 **A.** **He further said to them, "I need the sages of Israel."**

B. The sages of Israel came to him. He said to them, "Do not hold eulogies for me in the various towns [but only before large audiences in cities].

C. [103B] **"And call the session back after thirty days [beyond my death]. Simeon, my son, is to be the sage; Gamaliel, my son, is to be patriarch; Hanina bar Hama is to preside."**

II.8 **A.** **"Do not hold eulogies for me in the various towns [but only before large audiences in cities]":**

B. *They drew the conclusion that this was because of the trouble involved. But when they saw that they held eulogies in the big towns and everybody came, they concluded that it is to be inferred that it was on account of the honor.*

II.9 **A.** **"And call the session back after thirty days [beyond my death]":**

B. *"I'm not better than our lord, Moses, of whom it is written, 'And the children of Israel mourned for Moses in the plains of Moab thirty days' (Deut. 34:8)."*

II.10 **A.** *Thirty days they mourned him day and night; from that point on, they mourned by day and studied by night or mourned by night and studied by day, until twelve months of mourning had gone by.*

II.11 **A.** *On the day on which Rabbi died, an echo came forth and said, "Whoever was at the death of Rabbi is destined for the life of the world to come." There was a certain fuller, who would come to Rabbi every day. He didn't come that day. When he heard this, he went up to the roof, fell to earth, and died. An echo came forth and said, "That fuller, too, is destined for the life of the world to come."*

II.12 **A.** **"Simeon, my son, is to be the sage":**

B. *What was the sense of this statement?*

C. *This is the sense of this statement:* "Even though Simeon, my son, is to be the sage, nonetheless, Gamaliel, my son, is to be patriarch."

D. *Said Levi, "Was it necessary to make explicit [the fact that Gamaliel, the elder, was to inherit the patriarchate]?"*

E. *Said R. Simeon bar Rabbi, "It was necessary for you and for your gimpy question."*

F. *What bothered Levi? A verse of Scripture to the same effect:* "But the kingdom he gave to Jehoram, because he was firstborn" (2 Chr. 21:3).

G. That one [Jehoram] was correctly filling the place of his fathers, but Rabban Gamaliel did not properly fill the place of his fathers.

H. *So why did Rabbi do this anyhow?*

I. *Granting that* he was not properly filling the place of his fathers when it came to wisdom, as to fear of sin, he really did fill the place of his fathers.

II.13 A. **"Hanina bar Hama is to preside":**

B. *R. Hanina did not accept the position, because R. Efes was older than he by two and a half years.*

C. *R. Efes presided, and R. Hanina went into session outside, and Levi came and went into session with him. R. Efes died, and R. Hanina presided, and Levi had no one in session with him, so he came to Babylonia.*

II.14 A. *And that is in line with what they said to Rab, "An eminent authority has come to Nehardea, who is lame; and he expounded concerning a wreath that it is permitted to wear one [on the Sabbath]."*

B. *He said, "It is to be inferred that R. Efes has died, R. Hanina presides, and Levi had no one in session with him, so he has come to Babylonia."*

C. *So maybe R. Hanina has died, R. Efes remains the presiding officer, Levi had no one in session with him, so he has come to Babylonia?*

D. *If you prefer, I shall say, Levi would have accepted the suzerainty of R. Efes, and if you prefer, I shall say, since Rabbi said, "Hanina bar Hama is to preside," therefore it just isn't possible that he didn't take over, for concerning the righteous, it is written,* "You shall also decree something and it shall come about for you" (Job 22:28).

E. *But lo, wasn't there R. Hiyya?*

F. *He had already died [before Rabbi].*

G. But didn't R. Hiyya say, "I saw the burial place of Rabbi, and I shed tears on it"?

H. *Reverse the names of the saying just cited.*

I. But didn't R. Hiyya state, "On the day on which Rabbi died, sanctity came to an end"?

J. *Reverse the names of the saying just cited.*

K. *But hasn't it been taught on Tannaite authority:* When Rabbi died, R. Hiyya came in to him, and found him weeping. He said to him, "My lord, how come you're weeping? *And has it not been taught on Tannaite authority,* 'If someone died smiling, it is a good sign for him, if he died weeping, it is a bad sign for him, if he is facing upward, it is a good sign for him, if he is facing downward, it is a bad sign for him, if his face is toward people, it is a good sign for him, if his face is toward the wall, it is a bad sign for him, if his face is green, it is a bad sign for him, if his face is bright and red, it is a good sign for him, if it is on the Sabbath eve, it is a good sign for him, if it is at the end of the Sabbath, it is a bad sign for him, if it is on the eve of the Day of Atonement, it is a bad sign for him, if it is at the end of the Day of Atonement, it is a good sign for him, if it is on account of dysentery, it is a good sign for him, since most righteous men die of dysentery'? *And he said to him, "I am weeping because of the Torah and the commandments [from which I now take my leave]."*

L. *If you wish, I shall say, reverse the names of the saying just cited, and if you wish, I shall say, don't reverse the names of the saying just cited, but, since R. Hiyya was involved in doing religious deeds, Rabbi didn't want to bother him.*

II.15 A. **That [description of Hiyya] is in line with what follows:**

B. *When R. Hanina and R. Hiyya would argue, R. Hanina said to R. Hiyya, "Are you going to have a fight with me? God forbid, if the Torah were to be forgotten from Israel, I could restore it through my deep master of its logic."*

C. *Said R. Hiyya to R. Hanina, "Are you going to have a fight with me, who has arranged it so that the Torah will never be forgotten in Israel? What have I done? I went and sowed flax, made nets, trapped deer, the meat of the deer I gave to orphans, from the skins I made scrolls, on which I wrote the five books of Moses. I went to a town and taught the five books to five children, and the six divisions of the Mishnah to six others. Then I told them, 'Until I return, teach each other the Pentateuch and the Mishnah.' And that is how I prevented the Torah from being forgotten in Israel."*

D. *That is in line with what Rabbi said,* "How great are Hiyya's deeds!"

E. Said to him R. Ishmael b. R. Yosé, "Even greater than those of the master?"

F. *He said to him, "Indeed so."*

G. *"Even greater than those of father?"*

H. "God forbid, let not such a thing be in Israel."

II.16 A. **[Rabbi] said to them, "I need my younger son."**

B. **Entered R. Simeon. He handed over to him the divisions of wisdom.**

C. **[Rabbi] said to them, "I need my older son."**

D. **Entered Rabban Gamaliel. He handed over to him the divisions of the patriarchate.**

E. **He said to him, "My son, exercise your task as patriarch on the heights, pour bile on the disciples."**

F. *Oh, now, can that really be true? And is it not written,* "But he honors those who fear the Lord" (Ps. 15:4), *and a master said,* "This speaks of Jehoshaphat, king of Judah. When he would see a disciple of a sage, he would rise from his throne and embrace and kiss him and call him, 'My lord, my lord, my master, my master'"?

G. *That presents no contradiction, the former attitude is for private conduct, the latter for public conduct.*

II.17 A. **It has been taught on Tannaite authority:**

B. Rabbi was lying in Sepphoris, and a place was made ready for him in Beth Shearim.

C. *But has it not been taught on Tannaite authority:* "Justice, justice pursue" (Deut. 16:20) – follow Rabbi to Beth Shearim?

D. *Well, Rabbi really was in Beth Shearim, but when he got sick, they brought him to Sepphoris,* [104A] *which is higher up and which had healthier air.*

II.18 A. *On the day on which Rabbi died, rabbis decreed a fast and prayed for mercy, saying, "Whoever says that Rabbi is dead will be stabbed with a sword."*

B. The slave girl of Rabbi went up to the roof. She said, "Those in the upper world want Rabbi, and those in the lower world down here want Rabbi. May it be God's will that those of the lower world will overcome those in the upper world."

C. *But when she saw how many times he went to the privy, removing his prayer boxes containing verses of Scripture and putting them back on, and how pained he was,* she said, "May it be God's will that those of the upper world will overcome those in the lower world."

D. *Now since the rabbis did not fall silent but kept praying for mercy for him, she took a cruse and threw it from the roof to earth. They shut up for a moment from asking for mercy, and Rabbi's soul found its rest.*

II.19 A. *Rabbis said to Bar Qappara, "Go, see how he is." He went and found that his soul had found its rest. He tore his cloak and burned the tear backward. When he got back,* he opened with these words: "[Slotki:] The angels and the mortals have seized the holy ark. The angels have overcome the mortals and the holy ark has been captured."

B. *They said to him, "Has he died?"*

C. *He said to them, "You said it, I didn't."*

II.20 A. When Rabbi died, he raised his ten fingers heavenward and said, "Lord of the world, you know full well that with these ten fingers of mine, I have labored in the Torah, and I didn't take any selfish benefit from even my littlest finger. May it please you that there be peace where I am laid to rest."

B. An echo came forth and said, "'He shall enter into peace, they shall rest on their biers' (Isa. 57:2)."

C. *But shouldn't it be, in this setting, "On your bier"?*

D. *That supports R. Hiyya bar Gameda, for* said R. Hiyya bar Gameda said R. Yosé b. Saul, "When a righteous man takes his leave of the world, the serving angels say before the Holy One, blessed be He, 'Lord of the world, Mr. So-and-so, a righteous man, is coming.' He said to them, 'Let the righteous come [from where they are at rest] and go out and meet him and say to him, "He shall enter into peace," and then, "They shall rest on their biers."'"

II.21 A. Said R. Eleazar, "When a righteous person takes leave of this world, three bands of serving angels go forth to meet him. One says to him, 'Come to peace,' the next, "'He who walks in his uprightness"' (Isa. 57:2), the third, 'He shall enter into peace, they shall rest on their biers.'"

B.   "When a wicked man takes his leave from the world, three bands of serving angels go forth to meet him. One says to him, "'There is no peace, says the Lord, for the wicked" (Isa. 48:22),' the next, "'He shall lie down in sorrow" (Isa. 50:11),' and the third, "'Go down and be laid with the uncircumcised" (Ezek. 32:19).'"

WIVES AND MARRIAGE

BAVLI YEBAMOT 6:6 /63A-B

38. A.   *Rab was taking leave of R. Hiyya. He said to him, "May the All-Merciful shield you from something worse than death."*

B.   *"And is there anything that is worth than death?"*

C.   *He went out and found the verse:* "And I find more bitter than death the woman" (Qoh. 7:26).

39. A.   *Rab was tormented by his wife. When he said to her, "Make me lentils," she made him small peas, "Small peas," she made him lentils. When his son, Hiyya, matured., he passed on his father's orders in reverse [so he asked for peas if the father wanted lentils].*

B.   *He said to him, "Golly, your mother's coming up in the world."*

C.   *He said to him, "I'm the one who passed on your orders in reverse."*

D.   *He said to him, "That's what people say: 'Your own offspring will teach you right thinking.' But you shouldn't do that any more:* 'They have taught their tongue to speak lies, they wear themselves' (Jer. 9:4)."

40. A.   *R. Hiyya was tormented by his wife. Still, when he found something nice, he wrapped it in his scarf and brought it to her. Said to him Rab, "Yeah, but she's always pecking away at you!"*

B.   He said to him, "It's enough for us that they raise our children and save us **[63B]** from sin."

41. A.   *R. Judah was reciting to his son R. Isaac the verse,* "And I find more bitter than death the woman" (Qoh. 7:26).

B.   *He said to him, "Give me a for instance."*

C.   *He said to him, "For instance, your very own momma-san."*

D.   *But isn't it so that R. Judah repeated on Tannaite authority to his son, R. Isaac,* "A man finds true serenity only with his first wife, as it is said, 'Let your fountain be blessed and have joy of the wife of your youth' (Prov. 5:18)."

E.   He said to him, "Such as whom?"

F.   He said to him, "Such as your mother."

G.   She was easy to anger but easy to appease with a good word.

42. A.   *What is the definition of a bad wife?*

B.   Said Abbayye, "It is one who 'serves him a tray of food' when her 'mouth' is ready for him too."

C.   Raba said, "It is one who 'serves him a tray of food' and then turns her back on him."

43. A.   Said R. Hama bar Hanina, "When a man marries a wife, his sins are buried: 'Whoso finds a wife finds a great good and gets favor of the Lord' (Prov. 18:22)."

44. A.   In the West, when somebody got married, they should say to him, "Is it 'finds' or 'find'? 'Who finds a wife finds a great good' (Prov. 18:22), or 'and I find more bitter than death the woman' (Qoh. 7:26)."

45. A.   Said Raba, "As to a bad wife, it is a religious duty to divorce her: 'Cast out the scoffer and contention will go out, yes, strife and shame will cease' (Prov. 22:10)."

46. A.   Raba further stated, "A bad wife with a weighty marriage-settlement — put a co-wife at her side: *'By her partner, not by a thorn.'"*

    B.   Raba further stated, "A bad wife is as hard as a stormy day: 'A continual dropping in a very rainy day and a contentious woman are alike' (Prov. 27:15)."

47. A.   Raba further stated, "Come and see how good is a good wife and how bad is a bad wife. How good is a good wife: 'Who finds a wife finds a great good' (Prov. 18:22). If Scripture speaks of the woman herself, then how good is a good wife whom Scripture praises! If Scripture speaks of the Torah, then how good is a good wife, with whom the Torah is to be compared.

    B.   "and how bad is a bad wife: 'And I find more bitter than death the woman' (Qoh. 7:26): If Scripture speaks of the woman herself, then how dreadful is a bad wife whom Scripture condemns! If Scripture speaks of Gehenna, then how bad is a bad wife, with whom Gehenna is to be compared!"

48. A.   "Behold I will bring upon them evil, which they shall not be able to evade" (Jer. 11:11) — said R. Nahman said Rabbah bar Abbuha, "This refers to a bad wife with a weighty marriage settlement."

49. A.   "The Lord has delivered me into their hands against whom I am not able to stand: (Lam. 1:14) — said R. Hisda said Mar Uqba bar Hiyya, "This refers to a bad wife with a weighty marriage settlement."

    B.   In the West they say, "This refers to one who completely depends upon his own cash to buy food [owning no land to provide his meals]."

50. A.   "Your sons and daughters shall be given to another people" (Dt. 38:32) — said R. Hanan bar Raba said Rab, "This refers to the father's wife [stepmother to his children]."

51. A.   "I will provoke them with a vile nation" (Dt. 32:21) — said R. Hanan bar Raba said Rab, "This refers to a bad wife with a weighty marriage-settlement."

    B.   R. Eliezer says, "This refers to the *minim:* 'The fool has said in his heart, there is no God' (Ps. 14:1)."

    C.   *In a Tannaite formulation it is stated:* This refers to the people of Barbary and of Mauritania, who walk around naked in the streets.

There is nothing more abominable and disgusting before the Omnipresent than someone who walks around naked in the streets.

D. R. Yohanan said, "This refers to the Magi."

52. A. *They told R. Yohanan, "The Magi have come to Babylonia." He reeled and fell.*

B. *They said to him, "They take bribes."*

C. *He cheered up and took his seat again.*

53. A. They made decrees on three counts: they made a decree concerning meat [that parts of every animal that was slaughtered had to be offered on their altar]; this was on account of the neglect by Israelites of handing over to their own priesthood the gifts that were owing to the priests from all beasts that were slaughtered;

B. they made a decree against baths; this was on account of the neglect by Israelites of the religious requirement of immersion;

C. *they dug up the dead [not permitting burial];* this was because Jews took part in the celebration of their festivals: "Then shall the hand of the Lord be against you and against your fathers" (1 Sam. 12:15).

D. Said Rabbah bar Samuel, *"This refers to digging up corpses,* for a master has said, 'On account of the sins of the living are the dead exhumed.'"

54. A. Said Raba to Rabbah bar Mari, "It is written, 'They shall not be gathered nor be buried, they shall be for dung upon the face of the earth' (Jer. 8:2), and further, 'And death shall be preferable to life' (Jer. 8:32)!"

B. He said to him, "'Death shall be preferable' for the wicked, so that they may not live in this world but will sin and fall into Gehenna."

55. A. It is written in the book of Ben Sira:

B. "A good woman is a good gift, who will be put into the bosom of a God-fearing man. A bad woman is a plague for her husband. *What is his remedy?* Let him drive her from his house and be healed from what is plaguing him.

C. "A lovely wife — happy is her husband. The number of his days is doubled.

D. "Keep your eyes from a woman of charm, lest you be taken in her trap. Do not turn to her husband to drink wine with him, or strong drink, for through the looks of a beautiful woman many have been slain, and numerous are those who have been slain by her.

E. "Many are the blows with which a peddler is smitten [for dealing with women]. Those who make it a habit of committing fornication are like a spark that lights the ember. As a cage is full of birds, so are their houses full of deceit" (Jer. 5:27).

F. "Many are the wounds of a peddler, which lead him into temptation, like a spark that lights a coal.

G. "As a cage is full of birds, so whorehouses are full of deceit.

H. "'Do not worry about tomorrow's sorrow,' "For you do not know what a day may bring forth" (Prov. 27:1). Perhaps tomorrow you

will no longer exist and it will turn out that you will worry about a
world that is not yours.

I. "Keep large numbers of people away from your house, and do not
let just anybody into your house.

J. "Let many people ask how you are, but reveal your secret to one
out of a thousand."

56. A. Said R. Assi, "The son of David will come only after all of the
souls in the body: 'For the spirit that wraps itself is from me, and
the souls that I have made' (Is. 57:16)."

57. A. *It has been taught on Tannaite authority:*

B. R. Eliezer says, "Anybody who does not get busy with being fruitful
and multiplying is as though he shed blood: 'whoever sheds man's
blood by man shall his blood be shed' (Gen. 9:6) followed by,
'and you, be fruitful and multiply' (Gen. 9:7)."

C. R. Jacob says, "It is as though he diminished the divine form: 'For
in the image of God made he man' (Gen. 9:6) followed by 'and
you, be fruitful and multiply' (Gen. 9:7)."

D. Ben Azzai says, "It is as though he shed blood and diminished the
divine form: 'and you, be fruitful and multiply' (Gen. 9:7)."

E. They said to Ben Azzai, "There are some talk a good game and
play a good game, play a good game but don't talk a good game,
but you talk a good game and don't play at all."

F. He said to him, "What am I supposed to do? For my soul lusts
only after the Torah. So let the world be kept going by others."

58. A. *It has further been taught on Tannaite authority:*

B. R. Eliezer says, "Anybody who does not get busy with being fruitful
and multiplying is as though he shed blood: 'whoever sheds man's
blood by man shall his blood be shed' (Gen. 9:6) followed by,
'and you, be fruitful and multiply' (Gen. 9:7)."

C. R. Eleazar b. Azariah says, "It is as though he diminished the divine
form: 'For in the image of God made he man' (Gen. 9:6) followed
by 'and you, be fruitful and multiply' (Gen. 9:7)."

D. Ben Azzai says, "It is as though he shed blood and diminished the
divine form: 'and you, be fruitful and multiply' (Gen. 9:7)."

E. They said to Ben Azzai, "There are some talk a good game and
play a good game, play a good game but don't talk a good game,
but you talk a good game and don't play at all."

F. He said to him, "What am I supposed to do? For my soul lusts
only after the Torah. So let the world be kept going by others."

59. A. *Our rabbis have taught on Tannaite authority:*

B. "And when it rested, he said, Return O Lord to the tens of
thousands and thousands of Israel" (Num. 10:36) — **[64A]** this
teaches you that the Presence of God comes to rest on Israel only
if there are two thousand and two tens of thousands. If they lacked
one, and someone did not engaging in being fruitful and
multiplying, will that one not turn out to cause the Presence of
God to remove from Israel?

C.   Abba Hanan said in the name of R. Eliezer, "He is liable to the
     death penalty: 'and they [Nadab and Abihu] had no children' (Num.
     3:4). So if they had children, they would not have died."

D.   Others say, "He causes the Presence of God to remove from Israel:
     'to be a God to you and to your children after you' (Gen. 17:7) —
     where there is 'children after you' the Presence of God comes to
     rest, but where there is no 'children after you,' among whom will
     it come to rest? Among trees or stones?"

WOMEN EXEMPT FROM COMMANDMENTS

BAVLI QIDDUSHIN 1:7 34A-B

III.1 A.   For every positive commandment dependent upon the time [of
           year], men are liable, and women are exempt:

B.   *Our rabbis have taught on Tannaite authority:*

C.   What is the definition of a positive commandment dependent upon
     the time [of day or year]? Building a tabernacle at the festival of
     Tabernacles, carrying the palm branch on that festival, sounding
     the ram's horn, wearing shoe fringes, **[34A]** putting on Tefillin.
     And what is the definition of a positive commandment not
     dependent upon time? The fixing of an amulet to the doorpost, the
     erection of a parapet (Deut. 22:8), returning lost property, sending
     forth the dam from the nest [T. Qid. 1:10A-C].

III.2 A.   *Is this an encompassing generalization here?* **But what about
           unleavened bread, rejoicing on the festivals, and assembly on
           the Festival of Sukkot in the Seventh Year (Deut. 31:12) [which
           include women, but which] depend on a particular time, and
           for which women are obligated!** *And furthermore:* **What about
           study of the Torah, procreation, and the redemption of the
           firstborn, which are not religious duties that depend on a
           particular time, and yet women are exempt from these?**

B.   Said R. Yohanan, **"We may not establish analogies resting on
     encompassing principles, and that is so even though exceptions
     are explicitly stated,** *for we have learned in the Mishnah:* With
     any [food] do they prepare an erub and a shittuf [partnership meal],
     except for water and salt [M. Er. 3:1A]. *Now aren't there any
     other exceptions? Lo, there is the matter of mushrooms and
     truffles. So it must follow,* **We may not establish analogies resting
     on encompassing principles, and that is so even though
     exceptions are explicitly stated."**

III.3 A.   For every positive commandment dependent upon the time [of
           year], men are liable, and women are exempt:

B.   *How do we know this rule?*

C.   We derive an analogy from the matter of Tefillin: Just as women
     are exempt from the requirement to put on Tefillin, so they are
     exempt from every positive commandment dependent upon the
     time of day or year.

D. And the rule in respect to Tefillin itself derives from the matter of study of the Torah: Just as in the case of study of the Torah, women are exempt, so in the case of Tefillin, women are exempt.

E. *But why not draw an analogy to the mezuzah from Tefillin [exempting a woman there as well]?*

F. Tefillin are treated as comparable to study of the Torah in both the first and the second sections [Deut. 6:4-9, Deut. 11:13-21], but they are not comparable to the mezuzah in the second section.

G. *But why not draw an analogy to the mezuzah from study of the Torah [exempting a woman there as well]?*

H. *Don't let it enter your mind, for it is written, "That your days may be long"* (Deut. 11:21) – *so do men need a long life but not women?*

III.4 A. **What about the building of the tabernacle, which is a positive commandment dependent upon the time of year?**

B. Scripture says, "You shall dwell in booths for seven days" (Lev. 23:42). *Now the reason for women's being exempt from this obligation is that Scripture referred to "the homeborn"* [males, not females], *but otherwise, women would be liable!*

C. *Said Abbayye, "It is necessary to make that exclusion explicit. I might have thought, since it is written,* 'You shall dwell in booths for seven days,' 'you should dwell' is comparable to 'you should live in a house,' and just as normal living in a house involves a husband and wife together, so the sukkah must be inhabited by husband and wife together."

D. *And Raba said,* [34B] *"It is necessary to make that exclusion explicit. I might have thought,* **we should establish a verbal analogy involving the fifteenth of the month from another holiday in which there is the requirement that it be on the fifteenth of the month. Just as in that other holiday, that is, Passover, women are subject to the obligation, so here too, women are subject to the obligation.** *So it was necessary."*

III.5 A. **But what about the pilgrimage, which is a positive commandment dependent upon the time of year?**

B. *Now the reason that a woman is exempt is that* Scripture said, "Three times in the year all your males shall appear" (Ex. 23:17) – excluding women. *But if it were not for that fact, women would be liable!*

C. *It is necessary to make that exclusion explicit, for otherwise I would have thought that we derive the rule governing the appearance on the festival from the rule governing assembling once in seven years, which a woman is obligated to do.*

D. *Well, then, instead of deriving an exemption from Tefillin, why not deduce that she is obligated based on the requirement of participation in the rejoicing of a festival [which a woman is obligated to do by Deut. 16:14]?*

E. Said Abbayye, "As to a woman, the obligation is on her husband to provide for her rejoicing."

F.   *So what are you going to say of a widow?*

G.   It would speak of the one with whom she is living.

H.   *Why not derive the obligation of a woman from the religious duty of assembling every seven years on Tabernacles?*

I.   The reason is that the obligation to eat unleavened bread on Passover and the obligation of assembling are two verses of Scripture that go over the same matter, and where you have a case in which two verses of Scripture go over the same matter, they do not establish an analogy for other cases [but the rule is limited to those explicit cases].

J.   *If that's so, then Tefillin and the pilgrimage also are two verses that go over the same matter and these two cannot serve to establish an analogy governing other matters!*

K.   *Both matters are required. For if the All-Merciful had made reference to Tefillin but not made reference to the pilgrimage, I might have thought we should establish an analogy between the meaning of the pilgrimage and the requirement of assembling every seven years. If the All-Merciful had made reference to pilgrimage but not Tefillin, I might have supposed: Let the matter of Tefillin be treated as comparable to the mezuzah. So both are required.*

L.   *If so, then why shouldn't we say that it was necessary for Scripture to make reference to both the requirement of eating unleavened bread and also to gathering once in seven years. [Then these two are not items that go over the same matter, as we originally alleged.]*

M.   *Well, then, what are they required to show us? For if the All-Merciful had made reference to assembling every seven years, but not to the requirement of eating unleavened bread on Passover, it would make the latter unnecessary, for I would maintain, deduce the rule governing a holiday on the fifteenth from the feast of Tabernacles on the fifteenth. But if the All-Merciful had written unleavened bread, with the reference to assembling needless, I would have reasoned: If it is required for children, all the more so, women. So it really is a case of two* verses that go over the same matter, and they cannot serve to establish a generative analogy.

N.   *Well, now, that poses no problems from the perspective of him who maintains that* they cannot serve to establish a generative analogy. *But from the perspective of him who has said* they can serve to establish a generative analogy, *what is to be said? And furthermore, as to the fact that* for every positive commandment not dependent upon the time, women are liable – *how do we know that fact?*

O.   *We derive that fact from the matter of fear of parents:* Because women as much as men are required to fear their parents (Lev. 19:3): Just as fearing parents is required for women, so for every positive commandment not dependent upon time women are liable.

P. *But why not draw your generative analogy from the matter of study of Torah?*

Q. Because the study of Torah and the requirement of procreation are two verses of Scripture that go over the same matter, and wherever there are two verses of Scripture that cover the same matter, they cannot serve to establish a generative analogy.

R. [35A] **Well, from the perspective of R. Yohanan b. Beroqa, who has said, "The religious duty applies to them both: 'And God blessed them...be fruitful and multiply,' (Gen. 1:28)"** *what is to be said?*

S. *Well, the reason is that* study of the Torah and redeeming the firstborn are two verses of Scripture that go over the same matter, and wherever there are two verses of Scripture that cover the same matter, they cannot serve to establish a generative analogy.

T. *And then, also, from the perspective of R. Yohanan b. Beroqa,* the commandment concerning procreation and the commandment concerning fear of parents are two verses of Scripture that go over the same matter, and wherever there are two verses of Scripture that cover the same matter, they cannot serve to establish a generative analogy.

U. *In point of fact, those two matters both had to be spelled out [and do not therefore fall into the classification of two verses of Scripture that go over the same matter]. For if the All-Merciful had made reference to fear of parents but not to procreation, I might have supposed that when Scripture referred to* "and conquer it" (Gen. 1:28), Scripture spoke of man, whose nature it is to conquer, and not to woman, whose nature it is not to conquer, *so she would be omitted. And if Scripture had spoken of procreation but not of fear of parents, I might have thought that a man, who has the capacity to carry out such a requirement, would be covered by that requirement, but a woman, who has not got the means to carry out that commandment, since she has not got the means to do it, would be exempt from that requirement in any way at all. So it was necessary.*

V. *Well, now, that poses no problems from the perspective of him who maintains that* two verses of Scripture that go over the same matter cannot serve to establish a generative analogy. *But from the perspective of him who has said,* they can serve to establish a generative analogy, *what is to be said?*

W. *Said Raba, "The Papunian knows the reason for this item, and who might that be? It is R. Aha bar Jacob:* 'Said Scripture, "And it shall be a sign for you upon your hand and for a memorial between your eyes, that the Torah of the Lord may be in your mouth" (Ex. 13:9) – Thus the whole of the Torah is treated as analogous to Tefillin. Just as the rules governing Tefillin are an affirmative action dependent on a particular time, from which women are exempt, so are women exempt from all affirmative actions dependent upon a particular time. And, since women are exempt from all affirmative actions dependent on a particular time, it must follow that they also are subject to all of those affirmative actions that are not limited to a particular time.'"

X.   *Well, now that poses no problem to those who maintain that* Tefillin *are an affirmative action that depends on a particular time, but from the perspective of him who maintains that* wearing Tefillin is an affirmative action that does not depend upon a particular time, *what is to be said?*

Y.   *Whom have you heard who takes the view that* wearing Tefillin is an affirmative action that does not depend upon a particular time?

Z.   *It is R. Meir, and R. Meir takes the position that* there are two verses that go over the same matter and these do not generate an analogy serving other cases.

AA. And from the perspective of R. Judah, who has said, "Two verses that go over the same matter do establish a generative analogy for other cases, and, further, that wearing Tefillin is an affirmative action that does not depend upon a particular time," *what is to be said?*

BB. Since eating unleavened bread, rejoicing on the festivals, and assembling every seven years on Tabernacles represent three verses that go over the same matter [namely, positive duties, dependent on a particular time, but binding on women (Freedman)], as such, they do not generate an analogy governing any other case.

IV.1 **A.**   And for every positive commandment not dependent upon the time, men and women are equally liable. For every negative commandment, whether dependent upon the time or not dependent upon the time, men and women are equally liable:

B.   *What is the scriptural basis for this rule?*

C.   R. Judah said Rab said, *and so, too, did the Tannaite authority of the household of R. Ishmael state:* "'When a man or a woman shall commit any sin that men commit' (Num. 5:6) – in this way Scripture has treated women as equal to men in regard to all penalties that are in the Torah."

D.   *The household of R. Eleazar repeated as its Tannaite formulation:* "'Now these are the ordinances that you shall set before them' (Ex. 21:1) – in this language, Scripture has treated the woman as comparable to the man for the purpose of all the laws that are imposed by the Torah."

E.   *The household of Hezekiah and R. Yosé the Galilean presented as a Tannaite formulation,* "Said Scripture, 'It has killed a man or a woman' (Ex. 21:1) – in this language, Scripture has treated the woman as comparable to the man for the purpose of all the forms of the death penalty that are specified in the Torah.

F.   *And all three proofs are required to make the point. For had we heard only the initial one, we might have thought that it is in that area in particular that the All-Merciful has taken pity on a woman, so that she will have a means of atonement, but so far as civil laws in general, a man, who is engaged in business transactions, would be subject to the law, but I might have thought that a woman is not.*

G. *And had we been given the rule concerning the civil law, I might have thought that that is so that a woman should have a way of making a living, but as to atonement, since a man is responsible to carry out the religious duties, he would be given the means of making atonement for sin, but a woman, who is not responsible for keeping [all] religious duties, is not under the law.*

H. **And had we been given these two, the one because of making atonement, the other because of making a living, but as to the matter of manslaughter, a man, who is subject to the religious duty of paying a ransom in the case of manslaughter, [35B] would be subject to the law, but a woman would not.**

I. *And had we been given the matter of ransom, it might have been thought because in that matter, it is because a soul has perished, but as to these other matters, in which there is no issue of a soul's having perished, I might have thought that that was not the case. So all of them are required.*

V.1 A. ...Except for not marring the corners of the beard, not rounding the corners of the head (Lev. 19:27), and not becoming unclean because of the dead (Lev. 21:1):

B. *There is no problem understanding the exception of defiling oneself to bury a corpse, since it is explicitly written that this applies only to males:* "Speak to the priests, the sons of Aaron: No one shall defile himself for the dead among his people" (Lev. 21:1) – the sons of Aaron, not the daughters of Aaron. *But how on the basis of Scripture do we know that the same pertains to not marring the corners of the beard, not rounding the corners of the head?*

C. "You shall not round the corner of your heads nor mar the corners of your beard" (Lev. 19:27) – anyone who is subject to the prohibition of marring the corners of the beard is covered by the prohibition of rounding, *but women, who obviously are not subject to the prohibition of marring the corners of the beard, also are not subject to the prohibition of rounding.*

D. *So how do we know that women are not subject to the prohibition against marring the beard?*

E. *Well, friend, if you want, I'll just say it's a matter of common sense, since they don't have beards. Or, if you need it, I'll cite a verse of Scripture:* "You shall not rend the corner of your heads, nor shall you mar the corner of your beard" (Lev. 19:27) – since Scripture has varied its usage, moving from the you plural to the you singular, [clearly the latter does not apply to both genders]. *Otherwise, the All-Merciful should speak of* "the corner of your beards." Why "your beard"? *It means,* "your beard, but not your wife's beard."

F. *So is the woman's beard not covered? But hasn't it been taught on Tannaite authority:* A woman or a eunuch's beard that produced hair – lo, they are classified as an ordinary beard for all purposes affecting them? *Doesn't this mean, in respect to marring the beard?*

G. Said Abbayye, *"Well, now, you can't say that it is in regard to marring, for we derive the verbal analogy out of the rule governing the 'corner' of that of the sons of Aaron:* Just as there women are exempt from the commandment, so here, too."

H. *Yes, but if we take for granted that the language, "sons of Aaron," is stated with regard to everything covered in this section* [Israelites in general: "Nor shall you mar the corner of your beard," priests in particular: "Neither shall they shave off the corner of their beard," with "sons of Aaron" governing the whole section], *then let Scripture fall silent, and we should produce the same result by an argument a fortiori. For this is what I might propose:* If in the case of priests, for whom Scripture has provided an abundance of religious duty, yield the argument, "sons of Aaron" and not daughters of Aaron, then a fortiori the same rule should apply to ordinary Israelites!

I. *But if it were not for the verbal analogy, I might have said that* the matter is interrupted [so that "sons of Aaron" does not refer to "they shall not shave"]. *So here too, why not say that* the matter is interrupted, *and, so far as the argument resting on the verbal analogy, it is required for another purpose altogether, namely, for that which has been taught on Tannaite authority:*

J. "Neither shall the priests shave off the corner of their beard" (Lev. 21:5):

K. Might one suppose that he is liable even if he shaved it off with scissors?

L. Scripture says, "Neither shall you mar..." (Lev. 19:27).

M. Might one suppose if one removed it with tweezers or pincers he is liable?

N. Scripture says, "Neither shall you mar" – which involves destruction.

O. How so? It must be a kind of shaving that involves destruction, and that is with a razor.

P. *If it were the case that the verbal analogy covers only shaving and marring but not those to whom these acts apply, Scripture should have said, "You shall not round the corner of your heads nor should you mar that of your beard." Why say, "the corner of your beard"? It is to yield both points.*

Q. *Well, then, what about that which has been taught on Tannaite authority:* A woman or a eunuch's beard that produced hair – lo, they are classified as an ordinary beard for all purposes affecting them? *What purpose does this law serve?*

R. Said Mar Zutra, "It pertains to the uncleanness brought on by the skin ailment" (Lev. 13:1-17, 29-37.) [Freedman: If a woman or eunuch grows a beard, though normally their chins are free of hair, the test of the skin ailment are the symptoms of hair, not those of skin.]

S. *But the symptoms of uncleanness brought on by the skin ailment so far as these affect skin or hair are explicitly stated by Scripture:* "If a man or a woman have a mark of the skin ailment on head or beard (Lev. 13:29)."

T. Rather, said Mar Zutra, "These serve to indicate the marks of purification from the skin ailment." [Freedman: When a woman becomes clean from the marks of skin ailment of the beard, she must undergo the same ritual as a man.]

U. *Well, that, too, is a pretty obvious point since she can become unclean, she obviously can be made clean!*

V. *It was necessary to make the point nonetheless, for without this statement, I might have assumed that it covers distinct subjects, that is,* "If a man or a woman has a mark of the skin ailment on the head," *while when reference is made to* "or the beard," *it would revert to the man alone; so we are informed to the contrary.*

V.2 A. *Isi taught as a Tannaite statement:* **"So, too, are women exempt from the prohibition of baldness" (Lev. 21:5).**

B. *What is the scriptural basis for Isi's view?*

C. *This is how he expounds the matter:* "'You are sons of the Lord your God, you shall not cut yourselves nor make any baldness between your eyes for the dead, for you are a holy people to the Lord your God' (Deut. 14:1) – sons, but not daughters, in the matter of baldness.

D. "You maintain that it is in respect to baldness. But maybe it is in respect to cutting yourselves?

E. "When Scripture says, 'for you are a holy people to the Lord your God,' cutting is covered. So how do I interpret the sense of 'sons,' but not daughters? It is in respect to baldness.

F. "Well, why do you prefer to extend the law to cutting and to exclude from the law the matter of baldness?

G. "I extend the law to cutting, which is possible both where there is hair and where there is none, but I exclude the matter of baldness, which pertains only instead of hair."

H. *But why not say:* "sons and not daughters" in regard to both baldness and cutting, and the phrase, "for you are a holy people to the Lord your God," pertains to an incision [Lev. 21:5: Priests are not to make any incision]?

I. *Isi takes the view that* **incisions and cuttings [36A] are the same thing.**

J. *Said Abbayye, "This is the scriptural basis for the position of Isi: He derives a verbal analogy from the appearance in both contexts of the phrase, 'sons of Aaron,' in regard to baldness [both at Deut. 14:1-2, for Israelites, and Lev. 21:5, for priests]. Just as in the one case, women are exempt, so in the other, women are exempt."*

K. *But if we assume that Scripture refers to the entire matter in making reference to* "the sons of Aaron," *then let Scripture just fall silent, and the exemption of women I would derive from an argument a fortiori, as follows:* If in the case of priests, for whom Scripture has provided an abundance of religious duty, yield the argument, "sons of Aaron" and not daughters of Aaron, then a fortiori the same rule should apply to ordinary Israelites!

L. *But if it were not for the verbal analogy, I might have said that* the matter is interrupted [so that "sons of Aaron" does not refer to "they shall not shave"]. *So here too, why not say that* the matter is interrupted, *and, so far as the argument resting on the verbal analogy, it is required for another purpose altogether, namely, for that which has been taught on Tannaite authority:*

M. "They shall not make tonsures [upon their heads, nor shave off the edges of their beards, nor make any cuttings in their flesh]":

N. Might one suppose that for making four or five tonsures, one should be liable only on one count?

O. Scripture refers to "tonsure" in the singular, so imposing liability for each cut.

P. "Upon their heads":

Q. What is the point of Scripture here?

R. Since it is said, "[You are the sons of the Lord your God: You shall not cut yourselves nor make any baldness on your foreheads for the dead" (Deut. 14:1),

S. one might have thought that liability is incurred only for a cut on the forehead.

T. How do we know that the prohibition extends to the entire head?

U. Scripture says, "upon their heads,"

V. to encompass the entire head.

W. Might one suppose that in the case of priests, for whom Scripture has specified numerous supererogatory commandments, liability extends to each cut and also to the entire head,

X. while for ordinary Israelites, for whom Scripture has not specified supererogatory commandments, liability should be incurred only on one count for however many cuts and only for a cut on the forehead?

Y. Scripture refers to "tonsure" in several passages [here and at Deut. 14:1, here speaking of the priests, there speaking of Israelites as well], so establishing grounds for the following analogy:

Z. Just as in the case of "cutting" stated with reference to priests, liability is incurred for each cut and is incurred for a cut on any part of the head as much as on the forehead, so for "cut" spoken of in connection with an Israelite, liability is incurred for each cut and is incurred for a cut on any part of the head as much as on the forehead.

AA. And just as "cutting" stated with reference to an Israelite imposes liability only if it is made for a deceased, so "cutting" stated with reference to priests imposes liability only if it is made for a deceased [Sifra CCXII:I.1-3].

BB. [Abbayye responds:] *"If so, Scripture should write "baldness" [in abbreviated form. Why say "baldness" in a fully spelled out form]? It is to yield both points."*

CC. *Said Raba, "This is the scriptural basis for the position of Isi: He derives how the consideration of the phrase* 'between your eyes' applies from the case of Tefillin. Just as in the latter case, women are exempt, so here, too, they are exempt."

DD. *And how come Raba doesn't state matters as does Abbayye?*

EE. *Because he doesn't see any point in the variation of spellings of the word for baldness.*

FF. *And how come Abbayye doesn't state matters as does Raba?*

GG. *He will say to you, "The matter of Tefillin themselves derives from this very passage, namely:* Just as in that context 'between the eyes' means, a place where a bald spot can be made, which is the upper part of the head, so here too, the place at which Tefillin are located is the upper part of the head."

HH. *Now in regard to both Abbayye and Raba, how do they deal with the phrase, "you are sons" [since they make the same point on the basis of other language altogether]?*

II. *They require it in line with that which has been taught on Tannaite authority:*

JJ. "You are children of the Lord your God. You shall not gash yourselves or shave the front of your heads because of the dead. For you are a people consecrated to the Lord your God: The Lord your God chose you from among all other peoples on earth to be his treasured people" (Deut. 14:1-2):

KK. R. Judah says, "If you conduct yourselves in the way good children do, then you are children, and if not, you are not children [of the Lord your God]."

LL. R. Meir says, "One way or another, 'You are children of the Lord your God.'"

MM. And so Scripture says, "Yet the number of the children of Israel shall be as the sand of the sea...it shall be said to them, 'You are the children of the living God'" (Hos. 2:1) [B.'s version: "They are sottish children" (Jer. 4:22); "They are children in whom is no faith" (Deut. 32:20), "A seed of evil doers, sons that deal corruptly" (Isa. 1:4), then Hos. 2:1] [Sifré Deut. XCVI:IV.1].

NN. *Why all these further verses?*

OO. *If you should reply, then only when they are foolish are they classified as sons, but not when they lack faith, come and take note:* "They are children in whom is no faith" (Deut. 32:20).

PP. *If you should reply, then only when they have no faith they are classified as sons, but when they serve idols they are not classified as sons, then come and hear:* "A seed of evil doers, sons that deal corruptly" (Isa. 1:4).

QQ. *And should you say, well, they're called sons that act corruptly,*
but not good sons, then come and hear: "Yet the number of the
children of Israel shall be as the sand of the sea...it shall be said to
them, 'You are the children of the living God'" (Hos. 2:1).

STUDIES IN JUDAISM
TITLES IN THE SERIES
PUBLISHED BY UNIVERSITY PRESS OF AMERICA

Judith Z. Abrams
The Babylonian Talmud: A Topical Guide, 2002.

Roger David Aus
Matthew 1-2 and the Virginal Conception: In Light of Palestinian and Hellenistic Judaic Traditions on the Birth of Israel's First Redeemer, Moses, 2004.

My Name Is "Legion": Palestinian Judaic Traditions in Mark 5:1-20 and Other Gospel Texts, 2003.

Alan L. Berger, Harry James Cargas, and Susan E. Nowak
The Continuing Agony: From the Carmelite Convent to the Crosses at Auschwitz, 2004.

S. Daniel Breslauer
Creating a Judaism without Religion: A Postmodern Jewish Possibility, 2001.

Bruce Chilton
Targumic Approaches to the Gospels: Essays in the Mutual Definition of Judaism and Christianity, 1986.

David Ellenson
Tradition in Transition: Orthodoxy, Halakhah, and the Boundaries of Modern Jewish Identity, 1989.

Roberta Rosenberg Farber and Simcha Fishbane
Jewish Studies in Violence: A Collection of Essays, 2007.

Paul V. M. Flesher
New Perspectives on Ancient Judaism, Volume 5: Society and Literature in Analysis, 1990.

Marvin Fox
Collected Essays on Philosophy and on Judaism, Volume One: Greek Philosophy, Maimonides, 2003.

Collected Essays on Philosophy and on Judaism, Volume Two: Some Philosophers, 2003.

Collected Essays on Philosophy and on Judaism, Volume Three: Ethics, Reflections, 2003.

Zev Garber
Methodology in the Academic Teaching of Judaism, 1986.

Zev Garber, Alan L. Berger, and Richard Libowitz
Methodology in the Academic Teaching of the Holocaust ,1988.

Abraham Gross
Spirituality and Law: Courting Martyrdom in Christianity and Judaism,
2005.

Harold S. Himmelfarb and Sergio DellaPergola
Jewish Education Worldwide: Cross-Cultural Perspectives, 1989.

William Kluback
The Idea of Humanity: Hermann Cohen's Legacy to Philosophy and Theology,
1987.

Samuel Morell
Studies in the Judicial Methodology of Rabbi David ibn Abi Zimra, 2004.

Jacob Neusner
Amos in Talmud and Midrash, 2006.

Ancient Israel, Judaism, and Christianity in Contemporary Perspective, 2006.

The Aggadic Role in Halakhic Discourses: Volume I, 2001.

The Aggadic Role in Halakhic Discourses: Volume II, 2001.

The Aggadic Role in Halakhic Discourses: Volume III, 2001.

Analysis and Argumentation in Rabbinic Judaism, 2003.

Analytical Templates of the Bavli, 2006.

*Ancient Judaism and Modern Category-Formation: "Judaism," "Midrash,"
"Messianism," and Canon in the Past Quarter Century*, 1986.

Bologna Addresses and Other Recent Papers, 2007.

*Building Blocks of Rabbinic Tradition: The Documentary Approach to the Study
of Formative Judaism*, 2007.

Canon and Connection: Intertextuality in Judaism, 1987.

Chapters in the Formative History of Judaism, 2006.

Dual Discourse, Single Judaism, 2001.

The Emergence of Judaism: Jewish Religion in Response to the Critical Issues of the First Six Centuries, 2000.
Ezekiel in Talmud and Midrash, 2007.

First Principles of Systemic Analysis: The Case of Judaism within the History of Religion, 1988.

Habakkuk, Jonah, Nahum, and Obadiah in Talmud and Midrash: A Source Book, 2007.

The Halakhah and the Aggadah, 2001.

Halakhic Hermeneutics, 2003.

Halakhic Theology: A Sourcebook, 2006.

The Hermeneutics of Rabbinic Category Formations, 2001.

Hosea in Talmud and Midrash, 2006.

How Important Was the Destruction of the Second Temple in the Formation of Rabbinic Judaism? 2006.

How Not to Study Judaism, Examples and Counter-Examples, Volume One: Parables, Rabbinic Narratives, Rabbis' Biographies, Rabbis' Disputes, 2004.

How Not to Study Judaism, Examples and Counter-Examples, Volume Two: Ethnicity and Identity Versus Culture and Religion, How Not to Write a Book on Judaism, Point and Counterpoint, 2004.

How the Halakhah Unfolds: Moed Qatan in the Mishnah, Tosefta, Yerushalmi, and Bavli, 2006.   .

How the Halakhah Unfolds, Volume II, Part A: Nazir in the Mishnah, Tosefta, Yerushalmi, and Bavli, 2007.

How the Halakhah Unfolds, Volume II, Part B: Nazir in the Mishnah, Tosefta, Yerushalmi, and Bavli, 2007.

How the Halakhah Unfolds, Volume III, Part A: Abodah Zarah in the Mishnah, Tosefta, Yerushalmi, and Bavli, 2007.

How the Halakhah Unfolds, Volume III, Part B: Abodah Zarah in the Mishnah, Tosefta, Yerushalmi, and Bavli, 2007.

The Implicit Norms of Rabbinic Judaism, 2006.

Intellectual Templates of the Law of Judaism, 2006.

Isaiah in Talmud and Midrash: A Source Book, Part A, 2007.

Isaiah in Talmud and Midrash: A Source Book, Part B, 2007.

Is Scripture the Origin of the Halakhah? 2005

Israel and Iran in Talmudic Times: A Political History, 1986.

Israel's Politics in Sasanian Iran: Self-Government in Talmudic Times, 1986.

Jeremiah in Talmud and Midrash: A Source Book, 2006.

Judaism in Monologue and Dialogue, 2005.

Major Trends in Formative Judaism, Fourth Series, 2002.

Major Trends in Formative Judaism, Fifth Series, 2002.

Messiah in Context: Israel's History and Destiny in Formative Judaism, 1988.

Micah and Joel in Talmud and Midrash, 2006.

The Native Category – Formations of the Aggadah: The Later Midrash-Compilations – Volume I, 2000.

The Native Category – Formations of the Aggadah: The Earlier Midrash-Compilations – Volume II, 2000.

Paradigms in Passage: Patterns of Change in the Contemporary Study of Judaism, 1988.

Parsing the Torah, 2005.

Praxis and Parable: The Divergent Discourses of Rabbinic Judaism, 2006.

Rabbi Jeremiah, 2006.

Rabbinic Theology and Israelite Prophecy: Primacy of the Torah, Narrative of the World to Come, Doctrine of Repentance and Atonement, and the Systematization of Theology in the Rabbis' Reading of the Prophets, 2007.

The Rabbinic Utopia, 2007.

The Rabbis, the Law, and the Prophets. 2007.

Reading Scripture with the Rabbis: The Five Books of Moses, 2006.

The Religious Study of Judaism: Description, Analysis, Interpretation, Volume 1, 1986.

The Religious Study of Judaism: Description, Analysis, Interpretation, Volume 2, 1986.
The Religious Study of Judaism: Context, Text, Circumstance, Volume 3, 1987.

The Religious Study of Judaism: Description, Analysis, Interpretation, Volume 4, 1988.

Struggle for the Jewish Mind: Debates and Disputes on Judaism Then and Now, 1988.

The Talmud Law, Theology, Narrative: A Sourcebook, 2005.

Talmud Torah: Ways to God's Presence through Learning: An Exercise in Practical Theology, 2002.

Texts Without Boundaries: Protocols of Non-Documentary Writing in the Rabbinic Canon: Volume I: The Mishnah, Tractate Abot, and the Tosefta, 2002.

Texts Without Boundaries: Protocols of Non-Documentary Writing in the Rabbinic Canon: Volume II: Sifra and Sifre to Numbers, 2002.

Texts Without Boundaries: Protocols of Non-Documentary Writing in the Rabbinic Canon: Volume III: Sifre to Deuteronomy and Mekhilta Attributed to Rabbi Ishmael, 2002.

Texts Without Boundaries: Protocols of Non-Documentary Writing in the Rabbinic Canon: Volume IV: Leviticus Rabbah, 2002.

A Theological Commentary to the Midrash – Volume I: Pesiqta deRab Kahana, 2001.

A Theological Commentary to the Midrash – Volume II: Genesis Raba, 2001.

A Theological Commentary to the Midrash – Volume III: Song of Songs Rabbah, 2001.

A Theological Commentary to the Midrash – Volume IV: Leviticus Rabbah, 2001.

A Theological Commentary to the Midrash – Volume V: Lamentations Rabbati, 2001.

A Theological Commentary to the Midrash – Volume VI: Ruth Rabbah and Esther Rabbah, 2001.

A Theological Commentary to the Midrash – Volume VII: Sifra, 2001.

A Theological Commentary to the Midrash – Volume VIII: Sifre to Numbers and Sifre to Deuteronomy, 2001.

A Theological Commentary to the Midrash – Volume IX: Mekhilta Attributed to Rabbi Ishmael, 2001.

Theological Dictionary of Rabbinic Judaism: Part One: Principal Theological Categories, 2005.

Theological Dictionary of Rabbinic Judaism: Part Two: Making Connections and Building Constructions, 2005.

Theological Dictionary of Rabbinic Judaism: Part Three: Models of Analysis, Explanation, and Anticipation, 2005.

The Theological Foundations of Rabbinic Midrash, 2006.

Theology of Normative Judaism: A Source Book, 2005.

Theology in Action: How the Rabbis of the Talmud Present Theology (Aggadah) in the Medium of the Law (Halakhah). An Anthology, 2006.

The Torah and the Halakhah: The Four Relationships, 2003.

The Treasury of Judaism: A New Collection and Translation of Essential Texts (Volume One: The Calendar), 2008.

The Treasury of Judaism: A New Collection and Translation of Essential Texts (Volume Two: The Life Cycle), 2008.

The Treasury of Judaism: A New Collection and Translation of Essential Texts (Volume Three: Theology), 2008.

The Unity of Rabbinic Discourse: Volume I: Aggadah in the Halakhah, 2001.

The Unity of Rabbinic Discourse: Volume II: Halakhah in the Aggadah, 2001.

The Unity of Rabbinic Discourse: Volume III: Halakhah and Aggadah in Concert, 2001.

The Vitality of Rabbinic Imagination: The Mishnah Against the Bible and Qumran, 2005.

Who, Where and What is "Israel?": Zionist Perspectives on Israeli and American Judaism, 1989.

The Wonder-Working Lawyers of Talmudic Babylonia: The Theory and Practice of Judaism in its Formative Age, 1987.

Zephaniah, Haggai, Zechariah, and Malachi in Talmud and Midrash: A Source Book, 2007.

Jacob Neusner and Renest S. Frerichs

New Perspectives on Ancient Judaism, Volume 2: Judaic and Christian Interpretation of Texts: Contents and Contexts, 1987.

New Perspectives on Ancient Judaism, Volume 3: Judaic and Christian Interpretation of Texts: Contents and Contexts, 1987

Jacob Neusner and James F. Strange

Religious Texts and Material Contexts, 2001.

David Novak and Norbert M. Samuelson

Creation and the End of Days: Judaism and Scientific Cosmology, 1986.

Proceedings of the Academy for Jewish Philosophy, 1990.

Risto Nurmela

The Mouth of the Lord Has Spoken: Inner-Biblical Allusions in Second and Third Isaiah, 2006.

Aaron D. Panken

The Rhetoric of Innovation: Self-Conscious Legal Change in Rabbinic Literature, 2005.

Norbert M. Samuelson
Studies in Jewish Philosophy: Collected Essays of the Academy for Jewish Philosophy, 1980-1985, 1987.

Benjamin Edidin Scolnic
Alcimus, Enemy of the Maccabees, 2004.

If the Egyptians Drowned in the Red Sea, Where Are the Pharoah's Chariots?: Exploring the Historical Dimension of the Bible, 2005.

Thy Brother's Blood: The Maccabees and Dynastic Morality in the Hellenistic World, 2008.

Rivka Ulmer
Pesiqta Rabbati: A Synoptic Edition of Pesiqta Rabbati Based Upon All Extant Manuscripts and the Editio Preceps, Volume III, 2002.

Manfred Vogel
A Quest for a Theology of Judaism: The Divine, the Human and the Ethical Dimensions in the Structure-of-Faith of Judaism Essays in Constructive Theology, 1987.

Anita Weiner
Renewal: Reconnecting Soviet Jewry to the Soviet People: A Decade of American Jewish Joint Distribution Committee (AJJDC) Activities in the Former Soviet Union 1988-1998, 2003.

Eugene Weiner and Anita Weiner
Israel-A Precarious Sanctuary: War, Death and the Jewish People, 1989.

The Martyr's Conviction: A Sociological Analysis, 2002.

Leslie S. Wilson
The Serpent Symbol in the Ancient Near East: Nahash and Asherah: Death, Life, and Healing, 2001.